The Dynamics of Language Learning

The Dynamics of Language Learning

Research in Reading and English

Edited by
James R. Squire

National Conference on Research in English

 Clearinghouse on Reading and Communication Skills

Consultant Readers: Donna E. Alvermann, Patricia L. Anders, Richard Beach, David Bloome, Rita S. Brause, Bertram C. Bruce, Jerome C. Harste, Michael Kamil, Charles Peters, Gay Su Pinnell, Alan C. Purves, William L. Smith, M. Trika Smith-Burke, Robert Tierney, Beth Warren, Karen K. Wixson

Staff Editors: Tim Bryant et al.

Book Design: Tom Kovacs for TGK Design

NCTE Stock Number 12765

Published 1987 by the ERIC Clearinghouse on Reading and Communication Skills, 1111 Kenyon Road, Urbana, Illinois 61801, and the National Conference on Research in English. Printed in the United States of America.

Office of Educational
Research and Improvement
U.S. Department of Education

This publication was prepared with funding from the Office of Educational Research and Improvement, U.S. Department of Education, under contract no. 400-86-0045. Contractors undertaking such projects under government sponsorship are encouraged to express freely their judgment in professional and technical matters. Prior to publication, the manuscript was submitted to the National Conference on Research in English for critical review and determination of professional competence. This publication has met such standards. Points of view or opinions, however, do not necessarily represent the official view or opinions of either the National Conference on Research in English or the Office of Educational Research and Improvement.

Library of Congress Cataloging-in-Publication Data

The dynamics of language learning.

"Papers . . . prepared for the invitational Mid-Decade Seminar called by the National Conference on Research in English in 1985"—Pref.
  Bibliography: p.
  Includes index.
  1. Language arts (Elementary)—United States—Congresses. 2. Reading (Elementary)—United States—Congresses. 3. English language—Study and teaching—United States—Congresses. I. Squire, James R.
II. National Conference on Research in English.
LB1575.8.D96 1987   372.6   87-8827
ISBN 0-8141-1276-5

Contents

Foreword

The Educational Resources Information Center (ERIC) is a national information system operated by the Office of Educational Research and Improvement (OERI) of the U.S. Department of Education. It provides ready access to descriptions of exemplary programs, research and development efforts, and related information useful in developing effective educational programs.

Through its network of specialized centers or clearinghouses, each of which is responsible for a particular educational area, ERIC acquires, evaluates, abstracts, and indexes current significant information and lists this information in its reference publications.

ERIC/RCS, the ERIC Clearinghouse on Reading and Communication Skills, disseminates educational information related to research, instruction, and professional preparation at all levels and in all institutions. The scope of interest of the clearinghouse includes relevant research reports, literature reviews, curriculum guides and descriptions, conference papers, project or program reviews, and other print materials related to reading, English, educational journalism, and speech communication.

The ERIC system has already made available—through the ERIC Document Reproduction Service—much informative data. However, if the findings of specific educational research are to be intelligible to teachers and applicable to teaching, considerable amounts of data must be reevaluated, focused, and translated into a different context. Rather than resting at the point of making research reports readily accessible, OERI has directed the clearinghouses to work with professional organizations in developing information analysis papers in specific areas within the scope of the clearinghouses.

ERIC is pleased to cooperate with the National Conference on Research in English in making *The Dynamics of Language Learning: Research in Reading and English* available.

Charles Suhor
Director, ERIC/RCS

Preface

These papers on the dynamics of language learning were prepared for the invitational Mid-Decade Seminar called by the National Conference on Research in English in 1985 to explore the future direction of research in English and reading. For three days, thirty researchers—some new to the field, some well-established—examined learning, teaching, and the complex interplay of skills, processes, and classroom conditions that influences the development of children's competence in reading, writing, and the related language arts.

This volume presents the papers commissioned in advance of the seminar to stimulate thought and reflection, along with commentary on these papers by members of the assembled seminar of researchers. An analysis of the deliberations by the convener of the conference concludes the presentation. The gist of seminar discussions has been compiled separately and is available through the ERIC system.*

For the purpose of reviewing the current state of research and its future direction, the seminar was organized along the lines of six topics, each of which stressed interrelationships among the language arts. Two individuals were invited to prepare papers on each topic; two others, to respond to the papers. An effort was made to secure contrasting, complementary analysis on each topic from individuals associated with various research traditions: experimental, ethnographic, elementary school, secondary school, linguistic, literary, reading, writing, oral language.

Limited only by topic, the researchers were permitted freedom to develop the ideas as they wished. Some attempted a comprehensive review of all extant studies. Others chose to generalize from their present research experience. Many developed ideas along particularly promising areas. The result offers a perspective on the current state of knowledge with respect to the learning and teaching of language and literacy.

As general editor and chair for the conference, I am grateful not only for the high degree of involvement of all participants but for the strong support for these deliberations from the Executive Committee of NCRE, the Trustees of the Research Foundation of NCTE, and my colleagues at

---

* Squire, J. R., ed. (1985). *Discussions at the Mid-Decade Seminar on the Teaching of Reading and English.* ED 274 967. (See note on ERIC documents on the next page.)

xi

Silver Burdett & Ginn. Robert Gundlach contributed substantially to the conference by overseeing facilities.

I appreciate further the assistance in editing received from readers of the manuscript and from the staff of the ERIC/RCS Clearinghouse, as well as the assistance in manuscript typing from Sandra Smith.

James R. Squire
February 1987

Note on bibliographies: Most papers and commentaries in this text are followed by a list of references. In those lists, documents indexed in *Resources in Education (RIE)* are denoted by a 6-digit ED (ERIC Document) number. The majority of ERIC documents are reproduced on microfiche and may be viewed at ERIC collections in libraries and other institutions or can be ordered from the ERIC Document Reproduction Service (EDRS) in either paper copy or microfiche. For ordering information and price schedules, write or call EDRS, 3900 Wheeler Avenue, Alexandria, VA 22304. 1-800-227-3742.

Seminar Participants

Arthur N. Applebee, Associate Professor, School of Education, Stanford University

Rita S. Brause, Professor of Education, Fordham University at Lincoln Center

Bertram C. Bruce, Division Scientist, BBN Laboratories, Cambridge, Massachusetts

Robert C. Calfee, Professor, School of Education, Stanford University

Johanna DeStefano, Professor of Education, Ohio State University

David K. Dickinson, Assistant Professor, Eliot-Pearson Department of Child Study, Tufts University

David Dillon, Associate Professor, Elementary Education, University of Alberta

Dolores Durkin, Professor of Education, University of Illinois at Urbana-Champaign

Robert Dykstra, Professor of Education, University of Minnesota

Edmund J. Farrell, Professor of English Education, University of Texas at Austin

Bryant Fillion, Professor of Education, Fordham University at Lincoln Center

James Flood, Professor of Education, San Diego State University

Lawrence T. Frase, Technical Staff, AT&T Bell Laboratories, Summit, New Jersey

John T. Guthrie, Director, Center of Educational Research and Development, The University of Maryland

Robert Gundlach, Director of Writing Program, Northwestern University (Chair of Arrangements)

Jane Hansen, Associate Professor of Education, University of New Hampshire

Jerome C. Harste, Professor, Language Education, Indiana University

Roselmina Indrisano, Professor of Education, Boston University

Julie M. Jensen, Professor of Curriculum and Instruction, University of Texas at Austin

Peter Johnston, Assistant Professor, Reading Department, State University of New York at Albany

Stephen B. Kucer, Assistant Professor of Education, University of Southern California

Judith A. Langer, Associate Professor, School of Education, Stanford University

Geraldine E. LaRocque, Professor of English and University Liaison for Teacher Education, University of Northern Iowa

Diane Lapp, Professor of Education, San Diego State University (contributing author)

Miles Myers, Administrative Director, National Writing Program, University of California at Berkeley

P. David Pearson, Professor of Education, University of Illinois at Urbana-Champaign

Alan C. Purves, Professor of Education and Director of the Center for the Study of Literacy, State University of New York at Albany

Diane Lemonnier Schallert, Associate Professor of Education, University of Texas at Austin

M. Trika Smith-Burke, Professor of Educational Psychology, New York University

James R. Squire, Sr. Vice President (ret.), Silver Burdett & Ginn (Director of the Seminar)

Robert J. Tierney, Associate Professor of Education, Ohio State University

Merlin C. Wittrock, Professor of Education, University of California at Los Angeles

Introduction

The National Conference on Research in English came into being because of a common belief among its founders that the National Council of Teachers of English was not sufficiently interested in, nor committed to, research. Two of NCRE's early leaders were William S. Gray and Harry Greene, each of whom later became president of AERA. NCRE, then, began more than fifty years ago as an organization committed to research in English. We continue that commitment today, and it is fitting that this seminar, bringing together today's premier researchers in reading and English, has been organized by Jim Squire under the primary sponsorship of NCRE. The names have changed—Harry Greene, Emmett Betts, C. C. Certain, E. W. Dolch, Mildred Dawson, Maude McBroom, William S. Gray, and their colleagues have been replaced by a new set of contributors—but the beat goes on. This seminar strikes me as a throwback to the halcyon days of NCRE when small groups of scholars discussed at length with undisguised fervor research issues of the day. The deliberations constitute a most appropriate milestone in the early days of NCRE's second half-century of serving the profession.

Another carryover from the early days of NCRE is the tendency of its members to retain membership in such organizations as NCTE and AERA. Since the founding of IRA in 1956, moreover, many of us also have shared and continue to share membership with that organization. In this regard I should call attention to the contribution toward this seminar made by the NCTE Research Foundation. (Parenthetically, but not ungraciously, I would also like to acknowledge the support of this conference by Ginn and Company.)

There is considerable precedent for a seminar such as this as an NCRE event. Early meetings were give-and-take sessions at which researchers presented their research agendas, opening the way for frank and honest differing points of view. Early bulletins summarized and interpreted research in reading, composition, vocabulary, language, and grammar. The second annual bulletin, published in 1934, reported seventy-three problems needing to be studied in a systematic fashion (I wonder how many of these problems still beg for resolution). Much later, during the late 1950s and early 1960s, NCRE leadership was primarily responsible for the U.S. Office of Education's sponsorship of the First Grade Studies. Regardless of how one may feel about the studies themselves, it is difficult not to be impressed with the spirit of cooperation exhibited by the research leaders of that time (who were probably the mentors of contributors to this seminar, or the mentors' mentors). These researchers gave up considerable autonomy in order to work cooperatively toward advancing knowledge in the teaching of reading.

Partially as an outgrowth of the First Grade Studies, the next major research thrust of NCRE was its attempt to stimulate research on teacher effectiveness. Although this cooperative research program fell short of reaching the goals set by its proponents, it is interesting to conjecture the extent to which this effort served as a stimulus to the significant research in teaching effectiveness which has been carried out during the past fifteen years. NCRE has throughout its history been a leader in setting the research agenda for reading and English, and the present seminar certainly has the potential to continue this tradition.

The nagging concern of many of us who attend gatherings like this is that the educational implications resulting from our deliberations, regardless of the weight of research evidences supporting them, may never reach the classroom teacher, principal, or curriculum coordinator—let alone the children whom we expect to be the primary beneficiaries of our work. The proverbial gap between theory and practice appears to be as wide as ever. In what proportion of our nation's classrooms, for example, do children experience the satisfaction of composing as reflected in the work of Donald Graves and others? Despite fifty years of commitment to the NCRE goal of emphasizing the relationships among listening, speaking, reading, and writing, moreover, how many of the teacher education programs at our home institutions continue to offer separate methods courses in reading and the other language arts? How many American schoolchildren use separate unrelated textbooks and work-books for instruction in reading, language arts, and spelling? In how many classrooms do children have the opportunity to read a book of their own choosing? How much formal grammar practice continues to compete for valuable instructional time on the assumption that such practice will improve the composition skills of children? The message is obvious. Our deliberations here matter little unless we improve the way in which we influence classroom practice.

How can this be done? I wish I knew. Certainly our publications reach many teacher educators and some teachers. Publication of the present proceedings may help. The movement involving the teacher as researcher has also been positive, although necessarily limited in its impact. We also hope, of course, to influence the publishers of instructional materials.

We are all too familiar with the power of published materials in influencing classroom practices. But the ultimate policymakers determining what gets attention in the classroom are, in my judgment, (1) the test makers and (2) the test selectors. Consider the popularity of phonics drills, skills management systems, punctuation and spelling instruction, and the teaching of grammatical terminology. Doesn't their popularity primarily result from the ease with which student "progress" can be evaluated? And isn't much of the content of published instructional materials included because it can be easily tested? Can there be any doubt that the best way to implement curricular change in our schools is to change the testing program?

We all have our favorite examples of this phenomenon in action. Let me provide just two—a modern-day example and one from "ancient history":

1. The Minneapolis Public Schools recently adopted a benchmark testing program. Failure to meet minimal standards of performance, even in kindergarten, results in nonpromotion. You can well imagine the serious teaching to the test that goes on in Minneapolis classrooms today. There is nothing wrong with that, of course, if the tests really test the important things to be learned. How often does that happen?

2. I went to a one-room school through eighth grade. We had countywide examinations, the purpose of which I am not quite sure. What I do recall is that it was a real feather in a teacher's cap to have his or her eighth-grade pupils score at or near the top of this list. At any rate, the other eighth-grade students and I spent every afternoon of the last two months of the school year in the entryway asking each other questions from every standardized achievement test that the teachers could get their hands on. I have no doubt that every other entry to every other one-room school was similarly occupied by eighth graders hot in pursuit of the knowledge embedded in standardized tests.

These illustrations raise the kinds of issues that must be considered, and in the organization of this conference, Jim Squire has done a marvelous job of addressing these and other issues, pulling together a seminar focusing on a broad spectrum of similar issues spanning research in basic processes, classroom practice, materials, technology, and assessment.

Robert Dykstra
President, National Conference on Research in English, 1985

I Interrelating the Processes of Reading and Writing, Composing and Comprehending

Introduction

At no time in our recent history have researchers been so concerned and practitioners so interested in the connections between reading and writing. And the growth in research-based knowledge about the interrelationships has been increasing since cognitive psychologists rediscovered human learning twenty-five years ago. In the first paper James Flood and Diane Lapp review much of this current thinking and the studies that have given rise to it. Steven Kucer then probes beyond present conditions to formulate seven generalizations that appear applicable to any communication process. In his commentary, Alan Purves suggests that the relationship may be more at the activity level than in relation to basic process, and Julie Jensen relates the present seminar's search for answers to the continuing "troubled dream" of the researcher in English education.

Reading and Writing Relations: Assumptions and Directions

James Flood and Diane Lapp
San Diego State University

> Ever since I was first read to, then started reading to myself, there has never been a line read that I didn't *hear*. As my eyes followed the sentence, a voice was saying it silently to me. It isn't my mother's voice, or the voice of any person I can identify, certainly not my own. It is human, but inward, and it is inwardly that I listen to it. It is to me the voice of the story or the poem itself. The cadence, whatever it is that asks you to believe, the feeling that resides in the printed word, reaches me through the reader-voice. I have supposed, but never found out, that this is the case with all readers—to read as listeners—and with all writers, to write as listeners. It may be part of the desire to write. The sound of what falls on the page begins the process of testing it for truth, for me. Whether I am right to trust so far I don't know. By now I don't know whether I could do either one, reading or writing, without the other.

> —Eudora Welty, *One Writer's Beginnings*

Like Eudora Welty, most competent language users cannot engage in either activity, reading or writing, without the other or without the skills of listening and speaking. While the primary focus of this paper will be a description of the relations between reading and writing, both reading and writing will be discussed in relation to oral language skills, emphasizing the interrelationships among the language arts. Britton (1970) spoke directly to this point when he stated, "What is important in language study is the marriage of the process of composing in written language to that of reading, and the relating of both to the learner's spoken language resources" (p. 159).

In recent years, leading educators have acknowledged the intricate relations between reading and writing, describing the two activities in the following ways: as two sides of the same process (Squire 1983); as the dual governors of inner speech that change how we talk to ourselves, how we feel, and how we think (Moffett 1984); as similar dynamic processes of meaning construction (Tierney and Pearson 1984); as cyclical, mutually facilitative entities that support one another (Morris 1981); as generative cognitive processes that enable us to create meaning by building relations between texts and what we know, believe, and experience (Wittrock 1983); as similar language processes that produce and structure print (Farnan 1983); and as reciprocal acts of comprehending and composing (Moffett and Wagner 1983).

Composing and Comprehending

Many educators have espoused the view that reading and writing are both acts of composing and comprehending (e.g., Indrisano 1984, Squire 1983, Tierney and Pearson 1984). The complexity of the relations, however, has only begun to be explained. What we do know at this point is that comprehension is a composing process in the full sense of the term, just as composing is a comprehending process. Texts can be thought of as building blocks: letters, words, sentences, paragraphs, chapters, sections, and units. In preparing texts, writers arrange these elements into patterns designed to communicate messages. The reader gains understanding by using the text as a model for guiding construction of an image in the mind. Good writers are not totally explicit; as competent pattern-makers they bridge spaces for economy and aesthetics. Similarly, competent readers probably do not examine all of the building blocks; some blocks are recognized as chunks, while others are judged to be superfluous and are ignored.

In comprehending texts, competent readers use the knowledge that they have acquired from school and from home; skilled writers work from a similar knowledge base. To the extent that both readers and writers work from the same base, all is well. Readers can analyze textual information in a planned way, guided by their knowledge of the overall structure of the text and awareness of checkpoints that help them to remain on the right path.

Comprehension and composition are also *interactive* processes; they include both the analysis of text structure and the examination of preexisting memory structures (Purves 1979, Spivey 1983, Calfee and Curley 1984, Rumelhart 1984). Human memory is a repository for substantive knowledge; some of this knowledge is experiential (naturally occurring and not fully examined), and some is abstract (academic, vicarious, or rational). Most of what we remember is retained according to some organized scheme, prototype, network, hierarchy, or matrix. (This generalization is less true for those fleeting experiences that permit recognition but not reproduction). A distinctive element in the comprehension/construction unity is the mapping of segments of text onto preexisting substantive knowledge and the constructing of segments of text from preexisting knowledge. Although it is possible to carry out the formal structural analysis of a text and fail to relate the information to the structure of what is already known, and while it is possible to generate a text without fully relating it to preexisting knowledge structures, competent readers/writers understand the mutually supportive nature of the processes and use their understanding of this phenomenon to guide their reading and writing.

Similarities between Reading and Writing: What We Know

While it is obvious that reading and writing are dissimilar in myriad ways, especially in the overt behaviors of the reader and writer, it is equally apparent that these two language functions share certain linguistic and cognitive similarities. Many of the similarities that have been explained to date have been based on assumptions, best guesses, and data from studies that focused on reading or writing individually; few theories have been derived from studies that specifically examined the relations between reading and writing.

In synthesizing the research on reading/writing relations, Stotsky (1984) found that most studies were correlational and examined the influence of writing on the development of reading or vice versa. These studies consistently indicated that (*a*) "better writers tend to be better readers," (*b*) "better writers tend to read more than poorer writers," and (*c*) "better readers tend to produce more syntactically mature writing than poorer readers" (p. 16).

In examining studies specifically designed to improve writing by providing reading experiences instead of grammar study or additional writing practice, Stotsky found that reading experiences were more beneficial than either grammar study or extra writing practice. She also found that studies using literary models as examples of good writing proved effective in writing growth. As a result of her investigations, she concluded that "from both the correlational studies and the experimental studies, we find that reading experience seems to be a consistent correlate of, or influence on, writing ability" (pp. 16–17). Several limitations were noted in these studies: most were conducted with older students, and few researchers actually tested hypotheses about the ways in which reading and writing were linked. Rather, only through correlation did they demonstrate that reading and writing were consistently related to one another.

The findings from five key areas in which educators have examined reading and writing connections are summarized in Table 1.

Table 1

Research Studies in Reading/Writing Connections

The Role of the Learner	The Role of the Teacher	The Role of the Text	The Role of the School Curriculum	The Role of the Researcher
Reading and writing are:	*Assessment and teaching of reading and writing must:*	*For the reader/writer, texts:*	*Reading/writing should be viewed in a larger literacy context. Literacy:*	*Research in reading/writing:*
• Information processing, cognitive and linguistic phenomena in which successful readers and writers are able to monitor their own progress and change their own directions by means of their prior knowledge and their metacognitive and metalinguistic abilities.	• be comprehensive if it is to be instructional; provide directives and examples; provide experience with multiple formats; alleviate fear of failure; encourage an atmosphere of experimentation.	• can be considerate or inconsiderate. It is the responsibility of the writer to attempt to make texts considerate.	• requires context definition (Whose literacy? For what purpose?).	• extends beyond empirical studies and beyond a single time period.
• memory feats requiring organizing, accessing, and retrieving abilities.	• be process-oriented; engage students in experiences which provide monitored practice. Feedback must provide basis for sequential experience; activities must encourage students to take experimental risks.	• may contain somewhat fuzzy distinctions between form and content.	• begins at birth, in home, and in the child's environment.	• includes ethnographic studies in which literacy in context is investigated.
• perspective-taking activities that require an understanding of purpose and require appropriate affective states (motivation, attitude).	• include multiple measures and multiple interventions over time. Reader/writer must be made aware of continuous growth.	• should have a clear purpose created by the writer and discernible to the reader.	• extends beyond school, both during and after the school years.	• includes case studies and observations of students' learning to read and write.
• acts of composition and comprehension; both are mutually enhancing and both require: 1. planning 2. composing 3. revising 4. editing	• be tailored to individual child; successful experiences; end goal literacy. Specific competencies are realistic and known.	• have a life of their own, capable of several levels and types of interpretation depending upon purpose and match between reader and writer.	• is sometimes confused or eclipsed by literary skill education rather than literacy education.	• needs to be conducted in every classroom.
	• be evaluated continually. Product specifications must be clarified; time line must be realistic.		• develops in social contexts and has social functions.	• must be broad-based and comprehensive before results can be verified/certified.

Generalizations about Reading/Writing Relations

Three generalizations drawn from reading/writing studies will be the core of this paper. Before each of the generalizations is discussed, a caveat needs to be made. Like all generalizations, these are abstractions of commonalities. In actuality, every act of reading/writing is context-bound. Each is affected by many factors: students' individual differences (age, ability, culture, etc.); the text to be read or written; the reading/writing task; the purpose and perspective of the reader/writer; the situation and context in which reading and writing occur; and the type, nature, and extent of the instruction that was received by the individual student.

The three generalizations are:

1. Both reading and writing are related to and extend oral language abilities; the relations between oral language and written language are fundamental and reciprocal.

2. Both reading and writing are cognitive and metacognitive activities requiring analysis and synthesis; both require appropriate motivation and attitude.

3. Both reading and writing are developmental abilities, and the relations between them change over time.

Reading, Writing, and Oral Language

The interrelations between oral language and written language are as important to our understanding of how language works as are the relations between reading and writing. As Jensen (1984) notes, Loban's studies (1976) offer compelling evidence that all language processes are related and share common origins. While researchers are still not totally clear on the intricacies of the dependency relations, there has been a growing uneasiness with simplistic notions that written language is totally dependent upon oral language. As Flood and Menyuk (1983) explain, there are three ways in which the relation between oral language processing and development and written language processing and development has been traditionally viewed. These are (*a*) that written language processing is dependent upon oral language development, or (*b*) that both types of processing and development are dependent on the same superordinate cognitive abilities, or (*c*) that written language is initially dependent on oral language knowledge and then becomes independent in developmental stages that reflect changes in the level of acquisition of oral and written language knowledge.

The last position is the most explanatory, and evidence for it has been established in many language studies of young children. At the beginning of the reading/writing process, translation of written material into oral language categories and relations is required. This translation requires awareness of appropriate categories and relations. As structural oral language knowledge is established, the process becomes more automatic (or so rapid that it appears to be automatic). Such a possibility of automatic processing has also been suggested by LaBerge and Samuels (1974) in the acquisition stage of reading. As Vygotsky (1978) suggests, "Gradually the intermediate link, spoken language, disappears and written language is converted into a system of signs that directly symbolize the entities and relations between them" (p. 106).

This view is supported by research findings which indicate that the level of knowledge of particular linguistic structures affects the ease with which certain structures are read (Ryan 1980) and written (Flood, Menyuk, and Gordon 1981). Bowey (1980) also found that sentences containing structures that are known to be early acquisitions were read more quickly and with fewer errors by third-, fourth-, and fifth-grade children than sentences containing structures that are known to be later acquisitions. Variations in the structural complexity of well-learned structures did not affect oral reading performance in any way, whereas the relative complexity of less well-learned structures had a marked effect. Goldsmith (1977) found near-perfect performance by nine- to eleven-year-old children in listening to and reading simple types of relative clauses, which is an early acquisition.

These findings seem to indicate the following: (*a*) that children have great difficulty in reading sentences and passages which contain structures that they have not acquired (i.e., they cannot generate these sentences/ passages in writing), (*b*) that they have some difficulty in reading/writing sentences and passages containing structures that they are in the process of acquiring, and (*c*) that they read/write automatically those structures that are well-learned (once they're able to recognize or write the words that make up those structures).

Although many researchers have suggested that oral language knowledge in general and metalinguistic abilities in particular are critical to reading and writing success (Mattingly 1972, Flood and Menyuk 1981, Ryan 1980), the relation of these processes to one another beyond the morpho-phonemic level is only beginning to be thoroughly researched. Researchers are beginning to generate convincing data on the specific aspects of metalinguistic awareness that appear to be crucial to reading and writing success. (This research will be discussed in the section on reading and writing as developmental phenomena.)

Reading and Writing as Similar Cognitive Abilities

Reading and writing require similar cognitive processing; both develop and extend thinking skills. Squire (1983) emphasized this when he stated,

"Composing and comprehending seem basic reflections of the same cognitive process" (p. 582), and Jensen (1984) maintains that "both reading and writing processes require similar abilities, similar analysis and synthesis—comparing and contrasting, connecting and reevaluating—the same weighting and judging of ideas" (p. 4). Wittrock (1983) explained reading and writing as cognitive processes in his model of generative reading comprehension, suggesting that both good reading and effective writing involve generative cognitive processes; he also suggested that readers and writers create meaning by building relationships between the text and what they know and believe.

Vygotsky (1962) explained that language development and concept development are interrelated processes: both are manifestations of cognitive and linguistic development. Similarly, Henry (1974) cogently explained reading as a concept-formation phenomenon that includes two basic modes of thinking—analysis and synthesis. He contended that traditional views, which suggest that reading is only an analytic process and writing solely a synthetic process, are faulty and limited because they neglect synthetic processing in reading and analytic processing in writing. He explained,

> One of these operations [analysis and synthesis] can never go without the other, but one of them is always in the ascendency only because of our purpose. Logical purpose is an organizing drive. Analysis (separating) encases synthesis (joining) when we want (purpose) to get at the nature of something. . . . On the other hand, synthesis supercedes and embodies analysis when we want to put together into a whole several separate parts or separate relations of a work (poems or stories). (p. 7)

Both reading and writing demand analysis and synthesis as they are occurring. In reading, analysis precedes synthesis, but comprehension will not occur at any level (word, sentence, or passage) until synthesis has been completed. For example, even after children segment *cat* into /k/ /æ/ /t/, they must still synthesize the three phonemes into a single lexical item, mapping the new sound onto a single concept. Conversely, in writing, synthesis precedes analysis (separation); i.e., in most traditional writing systems words are represented by strings of letters which are transcribed individually (this is not to suggest that whole words, sentences, or paragraphs cannot be generated as a single unit through computerized systems).

Reading and Writing as Developmental Phenomena

The development of reading and writing abilities in young children has always been an issue of interest to educators and parents throughout history (cf. Deese's [1970] account of James VI of Scotland's experiment, in which two infants were abandoned on an uninhabited island in the care of a deaf adult to determine the true origins of language).

Individual language development in children has parallels to the historical development of language in civilization. Primitive peoples had no notion of writing or reading (as we currently know it), and even today there are many humans who have no need for it (Flood and Salus 1984). Various aboriginal peoples today seldom venture beyond their tribal territory; voice, gesture, drum, whistle, and horn are used for communicative purposes.

In the past, without writing, it was incumbent upon the wise men or women of the tribe, chosen for their well-developed memories, to remember the tribe's past, its rules, its rites, and the times of the year for sowing, herding from one pasture to another, and harvesting. The development of civilization from small bands to larger groups and from the hunter-gatherer stage to the agricultural stage meant that some kinds of information had to be recorded and that aids to memory had to be devised. The earliest records of attempts to preserve material appear in inventories and trade lists. The earliest precursors of writing are actual physical tokens of the things they represented. Such a system was quickly determined to be both cumbersome and limited in the scope of things that it could represent.

Many countries today use alphabetic systems that evolved from the earliest writing systems, but which, unlike early systems, encode sounds rather than ideas. Two existing writing systems that encode sounds rather than ideas, syllabaries and alphabets, have survived. While our alphabetic system is much more efficient for English than a syllabary would be (it can deal with the unique phonetic features of English, such as consonant clusters), it is a difficult system to learn.

Our writing system is acquired in predictable stages (Baghban 1984, Clay 1975, Henderson and Beers 1980, and Read 1975). As Harste (1984) suggests, young children acquire their knowledge of reading and writing through participation in real-life literacy events: "That participation . . . is its own readiness and that experience, rather than age, is the key to understanding" literacy acquisition and development (p. vi). Harste further contends that "young children know more about reading and writing than any of us ever dared imagined" (p. v). This knowledge seems to be the result of trial and experimentation with language in both oral and written forms. Many young children who become competent readers/writers begin their written language development through a combination of drawing and estimating the conventions of their written language system. (See Figure 1 for an example of drawing that contains figures as well as letters. Note Maria's name on the right-hand side of the drawing).

Figure 1. Child's drawing incorporating figures and letters.

Young children often initially encode orthography from the sounds they know; e.g., in Figure 2 the child initially writes *doll* as "D" or with letters corresponding to the phonemes within the word, "DL." (This does not suggest that children do not hear all of the sounds within the word; rather, they transcribe selected sounds.) For young children, oral and written language are closely related; in fact, the differences are sometimes inseparable.

As children progress in their understanding of standard orthography, their writings more closely match written language conventions and contain examples of words in which spelling and sound are not consistent. Figure 3 is an example of a humorous, well-formed story in which the child is relying on previous oral language knowledge as well as newly acquired knowledge of written language. Both the auditory system and the visual system are at work in this composition.

The growth of literacy in children is not an inexplicable phenomenon; rather, it results from attentive adults in the child's environment (Durkin 1966, Flood 1977, Wiseman 1980, Flood and Lapp 1981, Baghban 1984). All of these researchers note that children who read early have been exposed to many books (especially storybooks) from their earliest years; they have had their questions answered, and they have been asked probing questions. Children who write early also have received instruction from the adults in their environment; they were given materials (paper, writing instruments) and shown how to write letters and words (Baghban 1984,

Figure 2. Initial encoding of orthography: single-letter spelling (*left*) and phonetic spelling (*right*).

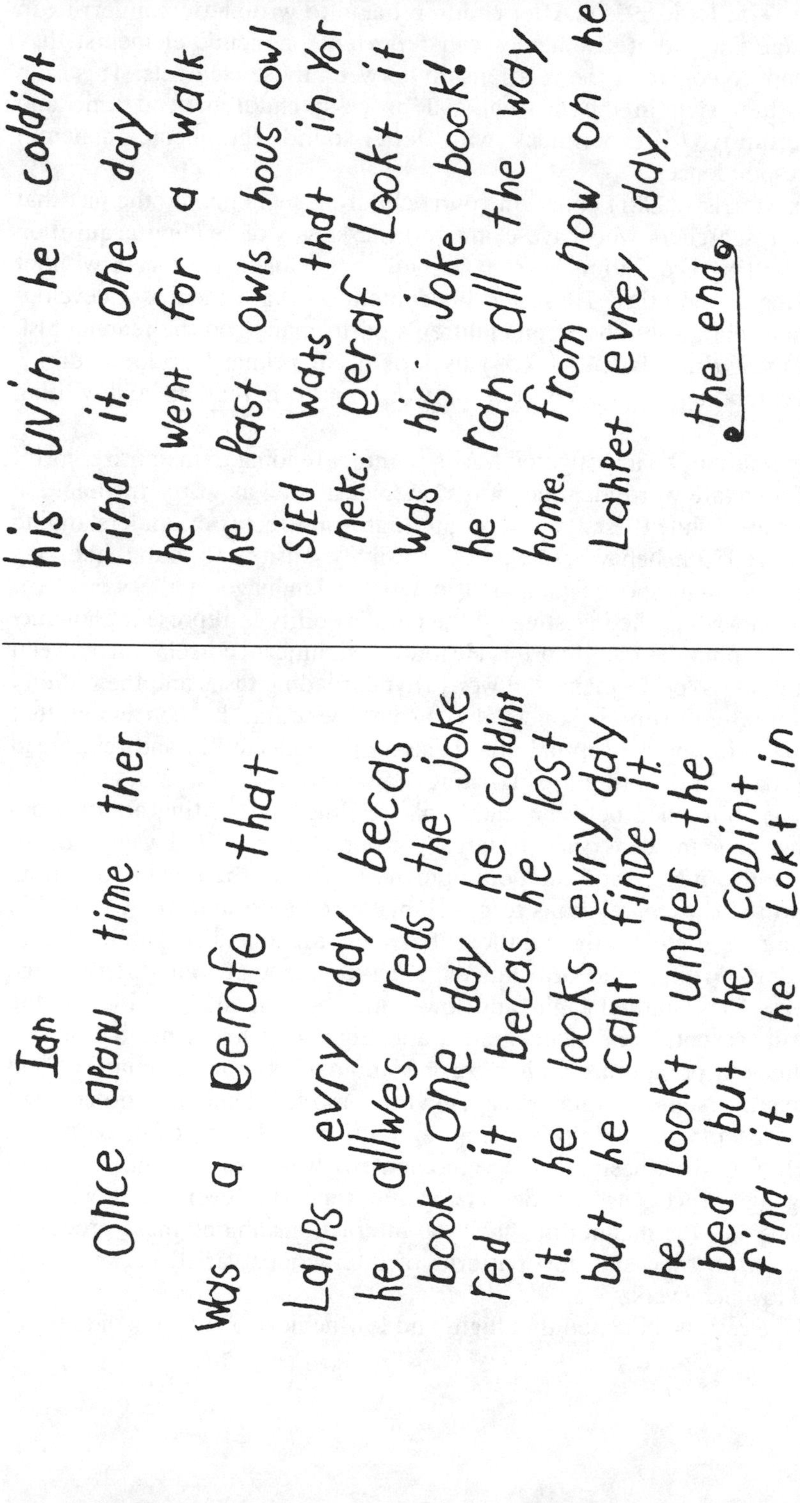

Idn

Once apon time ther

was a Gerafe that

Lahps evry day becas
he allwes reds the joke
book One day he coldint
red it becas he lost
it. he looks evry day
but he cant finde it.
he Lookt under the
bed but he coDint
find it he Lokt in

his uvin he coldint
find it. Ohe day
he went for a walk
he Past owls hous owl
siEd wats that in Yor
neke. Geraf Lookt it
was his joke book!
he ran all the way
home. from now on he
Lahpet evrey ddy.

the end

Figure 3. Composition drawing on both knowledge of oral language and newly acquired knowledge of written language.

Clay 1975, Read 1975). After children begin to write letters, inferring in a limited way that graphemes can represent phonemic elements, they attempt to construct the relationship between these elements. This is an important step in the instructional process; children need time and opportunity to experiment with letter-sound (grapheme-phoneme) correspondences.

In Morris's (1981) paper on young children, he lamented the fact that most researchers who have examined the stages of reading acquisition and writing acquisition have examined each language process without looking at the other. He tested his contention that "there is a developmental relationship between children's performance on the reading task and the writing task" (p. 659) by looking at primary-grade children's understanding of the concept of word in both reading and writing abilities.

In reading, he investigated finger-pointing reading of memorized print and correlate word identification strategies as well as word-rhyming. He noted that while these "measures are highly indirect (i.e., understanding is inferred from behavior) . . . they are highly sensitive to young children's ability to map spoken language to written language at the word" (p. 661). In writing, he investigated the child's ability to represent phonetic/orthographic elements in print. He found a significant correlation between first-graders' performance on word-rhyme reading tasks and their ability to represent words phonetically. From the data, he concluded that "growth in one conceptual area (reading) is reflected in and reinforced by growth in the other area (writing)" (p. 666).

The difference between children's reading and writing abilities becomes magnified as they progress through their school years. In an attempt to understand the developmental nature of reading and writing growth and their relations to oral language, Flood and Menyuk (1983) examined some of the relations between metalinguistic abilities and reading, writing, and oral language achievement at four different age levels. They studied high- and low-achieving students' abilities at the fourth, seventh, and tenth grades and high- and low-achieving adults' abilities to paraphrase and/or correct anomalous, nongrammatical, and ambiguous sentences and passages in three modes of language processing: oral (listening/speaking), reading, and writing. The critical issue in this study was the question of development. It was assumed that all three language-processing abilities change in time; however, what was not known was the manner in which the interactions among these processes changed in time and how patterns of interactions varied between high and low achievers.

The results indicated that high- and low-achieving students did best in reading, then listening, and least well in writing. Performance in writing and listening improved with age for the high achievers, but not for the low achievers.

It can be argued that poor writing performance as compared with oral language processing and reading may be the result of a lack of writing instruction during school years. Most children receive far less instruction in writing than they do in reading.

The lack of significant differences between oral language processing and reading is also intriguing. If the high achievers had performed better on the oral presentation mode, it could have been argued that metalinguistic abilities existed for low achievers in general but not in a specific mode (in this case, reading). However, the lack of significant modal differences between oral language and reading processing precludes the possibility of the presence of metalinguistic abilities in any mode (at least in the age range of this study).

From these limited data, it appears that the current school curriculum is working for students who are language-aware by fourth grade. These students' continual progress in oral language and writing skills matches their reading skills by adulthood. However, the curriculum is working far less well for low-achieving students. For these students, nothing seems to happen from fourth grade to adulthood; in general, the scores that students receive in fourth grade are the same scores that their adult counterparts receive. Continued research is needed in this area to more fully understand the ways in which able and less able students develop their abilities and their awareness of the ways in which reading and writing are related.

Direction for the Future: Instructional Research

The direction for future research in language learning is clear: research must focus on teaching. And the studies that will provide the needed data must involve collaboration between curriculum researchers and curriculum developers.

Research in Basic Processes versus Research in Instruction

While some basic research findings have enlightened instructional practices, it may be unwise at this time to directly apply findings from research conducted for the purpose of understanding basic processes in reading and writing to classroom teaching without direct and comprehensive research in instruction.

Instruction must be our next consuming focus of research. Issues in literacy instruction and subsequent learning need to be isolated for intense scrutiny and structured inquiry in the same way that the relations between reading and writing have been examined in the past few years. The teacher's role, the learner's role, the school's role, and the role of the home need extensive investigation before effective instructional practices can be recommended.

In the last few decades, interaction theorists in the fields of reading and writing have maintained that readers and writers mobilize their resources according to their purposes and the demands of the task (Holmes and Singer 1966, Singer 1983, Hayes and Flower 1980, Rumelhart 1984). Yet few theorists have generated knowledge about the role played by the teacher in enhancing the interactions between the text and the reader (which lead to the construction and storage of meaning), and about the role of the teacher in enhancing the interaction between the writer's knowledge and the construction of text. Interaction theorists in reading and writing are incapable of explaining effective classroom instruction because they do not include the teacher as a critical component in the initial research design.

To date, well-formulated theories of reading comprehension instruction do not exist (Tierney and Cunningham 1984), and few theories are capable of explaining effective writing instruction. Although a great deal of research has been conducted that points the way toward an inclusive theory of instruction (Armbruster and Brown 1984, Flood et al. 1987, Hayes and Flower 1980, Herber and Riley 1979, Rothkopf 1982), the research to date is incomplete and will remain incomplete until the teacher's role is clearly and coherently described and understood. More and varied studies of teachers instructing students in reading and writing need to be conducted by unobtrusive ethnographic observation of teachers and students. After observations are conducted and analyzed, highly controlled manipulation of the behaviors that seem to affect student learning must be conducted and analyzed to determine the characteristics of effective instruction as well as the methods that ensure effective writing/reading instruction for multiethnic, culturally diverse learners.

In designing effective instructional practices, it is important *not* to assume that what the competent learner does can be done by the novice or disabled learner. Frequently, the competent behaviors of able learners are turned into instructional sequences before they have been determined to be the actual steps that were taken in learning to read and write. It is possible that these behaviors are the finely tuned end-product of the process we hope to replicate. What may be necessary is to document the steps of the competent learner's development in order to create opportunities for novices and disabled readers/writers to experiment with different sequences, modifying them to meet individual needs.

The Teacher, the Learner, and the School

Unfortunately, research designed to analyze effective strategies for teaching reading/writing is not extensively conducted because of the difficulty of controlling and manipulating variables. Too often researchers who are interested in instructional research find themselves in classroom situations with intact populations that cannot be changed because of size, space, and time constraints. The results from studies conducted within the boundaries of these limitations reflect significant occurrences. Consequently, a great deal of time can be spent with limited results.

In order to alleviate these problems, curriculum researchers and developers must work together to provide environments in which careful study can be conducted for determining effective instructional practices.

Future studies of reading and writing need to examine issues of curriculum, attending to Harste's (1984) suggestion that the best language learning curriculum is not nearly as tidy as is the one we currently plan for children in schools. We need to implement and test curriculum that has as its core the tenet that functional language learning is rooted in what real language users do with language. We need to design and test an instructional curriculum with theoretically sound teaching procedures that enables students to be involved in real language operations and not the "dummy runs" that Britton (1970) feared. As he suggested, a sound curriculum would be one in which students use language to make sense of the world:

> They must *practise* language in the sense in which a doctor "practises" medicine . . . , and *not* in the sense in which a juggler "practises" a new trick before he performs it. This way of working does not make difficult things easy: what it does is make them worth the struggle. (p. 130)

References

Armbruster, B., and A. Brown (1984). Learning from reading: The role of metacognition. In *Learning to read in American schools: Basal readers and content texts,* edited by R. C. Anderson, J. Osborn, and R. J., Tierney, 273–81. Hillsdale, N.J.: Erlbaum.

Baghban, M. (1984). *Our daughter learns to read and write.* Newark, Del.: International Reading Association.

Bowey, J. (1980). Aspects of language processing in the oral reading of third, fourth and fifth grade children. Unpublished doctoral dissertation, University of Adelaide, Australia.

Britton, J. (1970). *Language and learning*. London: The Penguin Press.

Calfee, R. C., and R. Curley (1984). Structures of prose in content areas. In *Understanding reading comprehension: Cognition, language, and the structure of prose*, edited by J. Flood, 161–80. Newark, Del.: International Reading Association.

Chall, J. S. (1984). Readability and prose comprehension: Continuities and discontinuities. In *Understanding reading comprehension: Cognition, language, and the structure of prose*, edited by J. Flood, 233–46. Newark, Del.: International Reading Association.

Clay, M. (1975). *What did I write?* Auckland, New Zealand: Heinemann.

Deese, J. (1970). *Psycholinguistics*. Boston: Allyn and Bacon.

Durkin, D. (1966). *Children who read early*. New York: Teachers College Press.

Farnan, N. (1983). A perspective on reading and writing as similar cognitive processes. Unpublished master's project, San Diego State University, California.

Flood, J. (1977). Parental styles in reading episodes with young children. *The Reading Teacher* 30, no. 8: 864–67.

Flood, J., and D. Lapp (1981). *Language/reading instruction for the young child*. New York: Macmillan.

Flood, J. and P. Menyuk (1981). *Detection of ambiguity and production of paraphrase in written language. Final report. Revised*. National Institute of Education. ED 204 712.

———— (1983). The development of metalinguistic awareness and its relation to reading achievement. *Journal of Applied Developmental Psychology* 4: 65–80.

Flood, J., P. Menyuk, and S. Gordon (1981). Writing and metalinguistic awareness. Unpublished paper, Boston University.

Flood, J., and P. Salus (1984). *Language and the language arts*. Englewood Cliffs, N.J.: Prentice-Hall.

Flood, J., H. Singer, C. Mathison, and D. Lapp (1987). Reading comprehension performance: The effects of teacher presentations and text features. San Diego State University. Unpublished manuscript.

Goldsmith, S. (1977). Reading disability: Some support for a psycholinguistic base. Paper presented at Conference on Language Developments, Boston University.

Harste, J. (1984). Foreword to *Our daughter learns to read and write*, by M. Baghban. Newark, Del.: International Reading Association.

Hayes, J., and L. Flower (1980). The process of writing. In *Cognitive processes in writing*, edited by L. Gregg and E. Steinberg. Hillsdale, N.J.: Earlbaum.

Henderson, E., and J. Beers, eds. (1980). *Developmental and cognitive aspects of learning to spell*. Newark, Del.: International Reading Association.

Henry, G. H. (1974). *Teaching reading as concept development: Emphasis on affective thinking*. Newark, Del.: International Reading Association.

Herber, H., and J. Riley, eds. (1979). *Research in reading in the content areas: The fourth report*. Syracuse, N.Y.: Syracuse University.

Holmes, J. A., and H. Singer (1966). *Speed and power of reading in high school*. Cooperative Research Monograph, No. 14. Washington, D.C.: Office of Education. ED 038 257.

Indrisano, R. (1984). *Reading and writing revisited.* Ginn Occasional Paper. Lexington, Mass.: Ginn and Co.

Jensen, J. (1984). Introduction. In *Composing and comprehending,* edited by J. Jensen, 1–4. Urbana, Ill.: ERIC Clearinghouse on Reading and Communications Skills and NCRE. ED 243 139.

LaBerge, D., and S. Samuels (1974). Toward a theory of automatic information processing in reading. *Cognitive Psychology* 6: 293–323.

Lapp, D., and J. Flood (1983). *Teaching reading to every child.* 2d ed. New York: Macmillan.

Loban, W. (1976). *Language development: Kindergarten through grade twelve.* Research report no. 18. Urbana, Ill.: National Council of Teachers of English. ED 128 818.

Mattingly, I. (1972). Reading, the linguistic process, and linguistic awareness. In *Language by ear and by eye,* edited by J. Kavanagh and I. Mattingly. Cambridge, Mass.: MIT Press.

——— (1979). Reading, linguistic awareness and language acquisition. Paper written by IRA/University of Victoria International Reading Research Seminar on Linguistic Awareness and Learning to Read, Victoria, B.C., Canada.

Menyuk, P. (1984). Language and development. In *Understanding reading comprehension,* edited by J. Flood, 101–21. Newark, Del.: International Reading Association.

Moffett, J. (1984). Reading and writing as meditation. In *Composing and comprehending,* edited by J. Jensen, 57–65. Urbana, Ill.: ERIC Clearinghouse on Reading and Communication Skills and NCRE. ED 243 139.

Moffett, J., and B. Wagner (1983). *Student-centered language arts and reading, K–13: A handbook for teachers.* 3d ed. Boston: Houghton Mifflin.

Morris, D. (1981). Concept of word: A developmental phenomenon in the beginning reading and writing processes. *Language Arts* 58: 659–68.

Piaget, J. (1952). *The origins of intelligence in children.* Trans. by M. Cook. New York: International Universities Press.

Purves, A. (1979). That sunny dome: Those caves of ice: A model for research in reader response. *College English* 40: 802–12.

Read, C. (1975). *Children's categorization of speech sounds in English.* Research report no. 17. Urbana, Ill.: National Council of Teachers of English. ED 112 426.

Rothkopf, E. (1966). Learning from written instructive materials: An exploration of the control of inspection behavior by test-like events. *American Educational Research Journal* 3: 241–49.

Rothkopf, E. (1982). Adjunct aids and the control of mathemagenic activities during reading. In *Reading expository material,* edited by W. Otto and S. White. New York: Academic Press.

Rumelhart, D. (1984). Understanding understanding. In *Understanding reading comprehension,* edited by J. Flood, 1–20. Newark, Del.: International Reading Association.

Ryan, E. (1980). Meta-linguistic development and reading. In *Language awareness and reading,* edited by L. Waterhouse, K. Fischer, and E. Ryan. Newark, Del.: International Reading Association.

Ryan, E., and M. Semmel (1969). Reading as a constructive language process. *Reading Research Quarterly* 5: 59–83.

Singer, H. (1983). The substrata factor theory of reading: Its history and conceptual relationship to interaction theory. In *Reading research revisited,* edited by L. Gentile, M. Kamil, and J. Blanchard. Columbus, Ohio: Merrill.

Spivey, N. (1983). Discourse synthesis: Constructing texts in reading and writing. *Dissertation Abstracts International* 44: 2699-A.

Squire, J. (1983). Composing and comprehending: Two sides of the same basic process. *Language Arts* 60: 581–89.

Stotsky, S. (1984). Research on reading/writing relationships: A synthesis and suggested directions. In *Composing and comprehending,* edited by J. Jensen, 7–22. Urbana, Ill.: ERIC Clearinghouse on Reading and Communication Skills and NCRE. ED 243 139.

Tierney, R., and J. Cunningham (1984). Research on teaching reading comprehension. In *Handbook of reading research,* edited by P. D. Pearson, 609–55. New York: Longman.

Tierney, R. J., and P. D. Pearson (1984). Toward a composing model of reading. In *Composing and comprehending,* edited by J. Jensen, 33–45. Urbana, Ill.: ERIC Clearinghouse on Reading and Communication Skills and NCRE. ED 243 139.

Vygotsky, L. (1962). *Thought and language.* Edited and translated by E. Hangman and G. Vaker. Cambridge, Mass.: MIT Press.

——— (1978). *Mind in society: The development of higher psychological processes.* Cambridge, Mass.: Harvard University Press.

Welty, E. (1984). *One writer's beginnings.* Cambridge, Mass.: Harvard University Press.

Wiseman, D. (1980). The beginnings of literacy. *Reading Horizons* 29: 311–13.

Wittrock, M. (1983). Writing and the teaching of reading. *Language Arts* 60: 600–606.

The Cognitive Base
of Reading and Writing

Stephen B. Kucer
University of Southern California

During the last several years a renewed interest in the relationships between the reading and writing processes has emerged within a number of academic disciplines. Cognitive psychologists, linguists, and educators—who in the past limited their study to only one of the two processes—have widened their focus to include the examination of both literacy acts. What led to this expanded focus was not the sudden realization that reading and writing are related in some manner but rather that they may be linked in ways not previously considered.

Until recently, our theoretical orientation toward reading and writing limited the extent to which relationships were possible. Discussions of text processing frequently employed the notions of decoding and encoding to explain the operations involved in comprehending and composing. Within this framework, reading was viewed as a bottom-up, linear, and word-by-word phenomenon (Gough 1976, Gray and Rogers 1956, Holmes 1976, Kavanagh and Mattingly 1972, LaBerge and Samuels 1976, Singer 1976). Readers abstracted the author's intended message from print by passively identifying or decoding each word on the page and then linking the words syntactically. Through this sequence of events, the reader was able to "crack" the surface structure of the text and obtain its inner meaning.

In contrast, writing tended to be defined in more constructive—though also somewhat linear—terms (Britton et al. 1975; Emig 1971; Graves 1973; Young, Becker, and Pike 1970). In this apparently top-down process, the writer was the source and creator of meaning, generating and structuring ideas which became encoded into a text. Such activity was thought to require a greater use of cognitive resources than did reading, as the writer had to formulate both the inner meaning of the text and its accompanying surface structure.

Given this theoretical orientation, it is understandable that attempts to build conceptual links between reading and writing were limited at

27

best. The relationship most frequently put forth, though seldom in detail, was that of a mirror image or reverse process (Beaugrande 1979, Marshall and Glock 1978, Page 1974, Ruddell 1969, Sticht et al. 1974). It was proposed that reading as a bottom-up process utilized the same procedures involved in the top-down process of writing, but in reverse order. That is, the process of reading was driven by the input of graphics, with abstracted meaning serving as the output; in writing, the process was reversed, with the generation of ideas preceding the production of print.

Despite this prevailing paradigm, not all researchers felt comfortable with such distinctions. Throughout the last fifty years numerous investigators continued to seek common roots for the two processes (Bagley 1937; Barton 1930; Christiansen 1965; Clark 1935; Diederich 1957; Evans 1979; Evanechko, Ollila, and Armstrong 1974; Loban 1963; Maloney 1968; Monk 1958; Schonell 1942; Stotsky 1975). For the most part, these explorations focused on correlations between reading achievement and writing ability or examined the influence of one process on the other (Stotsky 1983). However, the significance of these studies remained limited until there was a substantial paradigm shift in how the reading process was conceptualized, and until writing was further delineated as an interactive process.

Beginning in the 1960s with the miscue studies (Allen and Watson 1976; K. Goodman 1965, 1969, 1972; K. Goodman and Burke 1973; Y. Goodman 1967; Menosky 1971; Rousch 1972), and continuing through the seventies and eighties with numerous investigations of text comprehension (Adams and Collins 1977; Anderson et al. 1976; Anderson, Spiro, and Montague 1977; Iser 1978; Kintsch 1974; Kintsch and van Dijk 1978; Neisser 1976; Ortony 1980; Pichert and Anderson 1977; Rosenblatt 1978; Rumelhart 1975; Smith 1982; Spiro, Bruce, and Brewer 1980; Stein 1978; van Dijk 1980), researchers began to develop an alternate perspective toward the reading process. Basic to this perspective was the active role of the reader, the interactive and constructive nature of comprehension, and the reader's use of nonvisual information or schemata during text processing. In essence, and in sharp contrast to the traditional paradigm, reading came to be seen as an act of meaning making.

Accompanying the paradigm shift in reading were advances in writing research which further captured the recursive and nonsequential nature of the process (Atwell 1981; Beaugrande 1979, 1982; Flower and Hayes 1981; Matsuhashi 1980; Perl 1979; Pianko 1979; Sommers 1979). Though previous investigators had attempted to conceptualize writing as a process rather than a product, they frequently used sequential stage–model terminology such as *prewriting, writing,* and *revision* to explain the process. To a large extent these attempts at depicting writing as an evolving event simply divided the product into a series of subproducts. Furthermore, much of the terminology failed to fully represent the probability that a number of cognitive operations co-occur during the act of writing. In contrast, the in-process research during the late 1970s and early 1980s provided the data necessary for more interactive theories of writing to emerge.

By the beginning of the 1980s, theories of reading and writing began to interface. Researchers in both fields had reached the point at which their conceptualizations of the two processes were becoming nearly synonymous. Readers as well as writers were depicted as being actively engaged in a search for meaning, attempting to build a cognitive text world through the employment of a variety of mental processes. It was this similarity in perspectives which ultimately led to the realization that alternative connections between reading and writing needed to be considered.

Perhaps one of the most speculative connections to be considered has been the notion that comprehending and composing share key cognitive mechanisms. Though this is not always explicated in detail, readers and writers are frequently depicted as drawing from a common pool of "cognitive basics" during text processing, at least when formulating the mental representation of a text. As numerous investigators have noted (Birnbaum 1982; Bracewell 1980; Beaugrande 1980, 1982; Harste, Burke, and Woodward 1982; Kucer 1983, 1985; Shanklin 1982; Spivey 1983; Squire 1983; Tierney and Pearson 1983; van Dijk 1979, 1980; van Dijk and Kintsch 1983), given that both reading and writing require the building of an internal configuration of meaning, language users are unlikely to have completely separate and independent mechanisms for the two processes. Rather, cognitive efficiency demands a sharing of procedures, with the same basic mechanisms being operable in both reading and writing.

Advantages to a "Cognitive Basics" View of Reading and Writing

The development and eventual acceptance of a set of cognitive basics or universals has direct implications for theory development, research, and literacy instruction. As Beaugrande (1982) has proposed, the formulation of literacy universals would begin to establish the interdisciplinary nature of the linguistic and cognitive sciences. Those presently working exclusively within a particular field could no longer afford to operate in a vacuum, content to ignore advances and accomplishments made by others in related areas. Gains made in one domain would afford the potential for similar gains within the others, making it profitable to build communicative bridges among all parties interested in written language processing.

In particular, the existence of literacy universals might result in the validation, modification, or rejection of existing theories in reading and writing. If theories of text comprehension and of text production were conceived as using some of the same basic processes, each would need to account for key aspects of the other, at least in general ways. For example, both readers and writers utilize information stored in their cognitive structures, make use of the same short-term memory system, and operate within a contextual situation. Given these commonalities, theories of reading and writing should describe in similar or complementary ways such things as information storage and retrieval, short-term memory operations, and the influence of the communicative situation on text processing. Through triangulating theories of reading and writing, purely artificial findings dictated by one belief system would be eliminated since they would not be transferable from one domain to another.

Through triangulating the acts of reading and writing we can also begin to formulate a general theory of written language processing which utilizes the same procedures for comprehension and production. Shanklin (1982), Tierney and Pearson (1983), Tierney (1983), and Kucer (1983, 1985) have already begun to generate such theories. Not only will theories of this nature contribute to a fuller understanding of reading/writing relationships, they also will provide the conceptual base for interpreting both past and present research findings. Theories of text processing might more fully explain the positive correlation between reading and writing abilities, or how and why growth in one process affects growth in the other. In turn, research findings which cannot be explained by or predicted from these theories would result in new conceptualizations of reading and writing connections. It is through this interaction and tension between theory and research that our understanding of the common bonds between reading and writing will be advanced.

For classroom teachers, the discovery of common operating mechanisms would support the development of literacy programs that fully integrate reading and writing instruction. While at best our students are exposed to activities in both areas, each process is usually presented as if it were cognitively and linguistically unrelated to the other (Birnbaum and Emig 1983; Petrosky 1982; Tierney, Leys, and Rogers 1984). However, given a set of cognitive basics, it would be possible to generate instructional activities which highlight key strategies in both literacy events. In these "conceptually related activities" (Kucer and Rhodes 1986), the manner in which language is used in the reading lesson would parallel or be a counterpart to the use of language in the writing lesson. Each activity would fine-tune the use of language in the other and support increased control of both literacy expressions. In this way, literacy curricula would maximize the interrelationships between reading and writing and facilitate student growth in the true basics of literacy (Kucer and Rhodes 1983; Squire 1983).

Processing Universals in Reading and Writing

Given the effects which literacy universals might have on theory, research, and pedagogy, the remainder of this paper will be used to develop four universals which appear to undergird the processes of reading and writing. The universals to be developed represent a synthesis of the current reading/writing literature. No attempt has been made, however, to analyze separate studies of reading and writing; such an analysis is beyond the scope of this paper. It should also be noted that the universals are not distinct and unrelated in nature. Rather, each affects and is affected by the others.

Universal One: Readers and writers construct text-world meanings through utilizing the prior knowledge which they bring to the literacy event.

Almost all recent investigations of reading/writing relationships have addressed, at least in general terms, the role of prior knowledge or schemata in text processing. Simply defined, schemata are complex structures of information which represent the individual's past encounters with the world. They contain the language user's knowledge of objects, situations, and events as well as knowledge of procedures for retrieving, organizing, and interpreting information. The availability of schemata which are relevant to the text under construction and the ability of the language user to mobilize or access the information are perceived as crucial to effective and efficient reading and writing.

Berthoff (1983), Petrosky (1982), Squire (1983), and Wittrock (1983) have all emphasized that the creation of meaning requires the reader and writer to generate relationships or connections between available background knowledge and text. The language user must direct his or her attention to those schemata which are relevant and pertinent to the literacy event and link them with the discourse being processed. The existence of relevant schemata is, therefore, a prerequisite to successful reading and writing. According to Petrosky, this "putting together" of prior knowledge and text is not simply a linear act of information retrieval, of matching each segment of text with a particular schema. Rather, it involves an act of interpretation which Berthoff defines as a process of form-finding and form-creating, or "a matter of seeing what goes with what, how this goes with that" (p. 168).

Tierney and Pearson (1983), Pearson and Tierney (1984), and Tierney (1983) have discussed the role of available background knowledge during reading and writing in terms of the symbiotic relationship which it forms with plans and goals. They propose that to a large extent prior knowledge determines the initial goals and plans which the individual brings to either literacy act. Both readers and writers vary their goals and plans based on what they currently know about the topic. Once text processing is initiated, these goals and plans guide what, how, and when background knowledge is used in the creation of meaning. Through this interplay between background and intentions, schemata are both selected and refined during the process of reading or writing. However, while stating that it is well substantiated that individuals with more background knowledge tend to read with greater comprehension and write more coherently, Tierney and Pearson also note that the individual must access the "right" background knowledge. Goals and plans help assure that the right knowledge is mobilized.

Drawing from the work of schema theorists, Kucer (1983, 1985) has defined the parallel roles which schema location and activation, evaluation, and instantiation play in reading and writing. He suggests that the quest for meaning which permeates all acts of literacy requires the language user to locate background knowledge which is relevant to the communicative situation. In both reading and writing, the location of prior knowledge is accomplished through bottom-up as well as top-down processes. Local meanings which have been generated may trigger the discovery of more global schemata, or previously instantiated schemata may determine which local schemata are available. In either case, as the individual locates schemata during reading or writing, the most salient concepts and relationships within each structure are explored and evaluated. Structures which are found to contain the required information are then instantiated. The reader or writer accepts, if only temporarily, the information within the structure as being appropriate to the situation. Instantiated schemata form a global framework of information from which data are drawn during the construction of the text world.

Shanklin (1982), in her transactional view of text processing, focuses particular attention on the nature of schemata as they are employed in the processes of reading and writing. Using constructs set forth by Neisser (1976) and Iran-Nejad (1980), she characterizes schemata as functional rather than structural systems. As such, schemata do not exist apart from a particular context. Therefore, readers and writers have only potential world knowledge from which they can construct their text worlds. The knowledge structures which are actually created for text processing are the result of an interaction between the language user's potential world knowledge and the environment in which the literacy act evolves. Shanklin also suggests that, based on the context, background is located through schemata activation, instantiation, and refinement, a process she terms "transactional." The information contained within instantiated schemata exists on global and local levels and is used to make, as well as to constrain, global and local predictions about the content of the text world. Extending comprehension principles set forth by Beaugrande (1980), Shanklin develops five theses to explain the operation of transactions in both reading and writing: (1) transactions are privileged if they closely match stored world-knowledge patterns, (2) transactions are privileged if they can be attached to major nodes of applicable schemata, (3) transactions become conflated or confused if they are closely related in world knowledge, (4) transactions are altered to produce a better match with world knowledge, and (5) transactions decay and become unrecoverable if they are neutral or accidental in world knowledge. Finally, Shanklin notes that when readers or writers have little background knowledge, it is difficult for them to simultaneously perform transactions on several levels. This difficulty results in missed transactions or errors.

Van Dijk and Kintsch (1983) have also suggested that the fundamental role of the language user's world knowledge in the comprehension and production of discourse must be recognized. Though not developing parallels between reading and writing to any great extent, they propose that the text world is the result of a "marriage" between prior knowledge and text. Such a marriage requires that the language user continuously consult his or her stock of world knowledge for information appropriate to text-world construction. In this process, the reader and writer are perceived as having recourse to the same or similar procedures for accessing prior knowledge. According to van Dijk and Kintsch, these procedures allow the language user to locate global as well as local information. It is the use of global information which provides the basis for active, top-down processing in both reading and writing. In fact, they suggest that readers and writers might have a global bias in locating world knowledge since it would limit the number of schemata which must be located and explored. Finally, in a discussion of the nature of world knowledge, van Dijk and Kintsch propose that in most cases, pre-established-knowledge schemata will not fit the requirements of the reader or writer. Rather, existing schemata "provide a basis or a background for comprehension (or production), but not more" (p. 304).

Universal Two: The written language system operates by feeding into a common data pool from which the language user draws when constructing the text world.

An essential part of the language user's world knowledge is an understanding of how written language operates as a communicative system. Readers and writers have knowledge of the uses or functions which written language serves, as well as the organizational patterns to which texts must conform. They possess, in addition, an awareness of the semantic, syntactic, and orthographic features within the written language system. As the text world is constructed, the individual employs this knowledge to give form to the evolving meanings. Much of the current reading/writing research has examined the contributions which various literacy encounters make to the individual's schemata for written language processing.

Harste, Burke, and Woodward (1982) and Harste, Woodward, and Burke (1984) have hypothesized that all knowledge of the written language system, be it gained through reading or writing, feeds into a common linguistic data pool. Rather than having separate schemata for written language—one set for reading and one set for writing—the language user possesses a unified understanding of how written language operates. In the process of building such an understanding, the individual uses what is learned about written language in one literacy expression as available data for anticipating the form in which language will be cast in the other expression. This sharing of available linguistic data is cyclic and allows for growth in, and use of, one language expression to support and fine-tune the other.

It is also through engaging in both reading and writing processes that language users come to understand their rights and responsibilities within each communicative system. Tierney and LaZansky (1980) have proposed that there exists an implicit allowability contract between the reader and writer "which defines that which is allowable vis-à-vis the role of each in relation to the text" (p. 2). When either the reader or writer violates this communicative contract, meaning will be lost. In reading, the individual has the right to explore the text for his or her own purposes and to mobilize background knowledge which will support an interpretation of the text. In addition, the reader has the right to employ strategies which will enhance learning from the text and the right to evaluate the author's message. At the same time, the reader must not distort or abandon the author's message and must be sensitive to the author's purpose. Similarly, the writer has the right to communicate his or her meanings to the audience and to mobilize prior knowledge in doing so. The writer also has the responsibility to be sincere and relevant, and to establish points of contact with the reader's background. Because readers and writers are aware of the rights and responsibilities of both parties in this communicative process, they construct their text worlds accordingly.

In attempting to understand the development of schemata for the written language system, a number of researchers have focused on the particular contributions of each process. DeFord (1981) and Eckhoff (1983) examined the influence which instructional reading material had on the writing development of primary school children. Both found that the children's writing reflected features of the materials read in the classroom. Children who encountered reading materials with constrained graphophonic and syntactic patterns produced writing displaying similar patterns. Similarly, children exposed to materials containing more elaborate syntactic structures, complex verbs, and a greater number of words per T-unit tended to include these characteristics in their own writing.

Reading has also been shown to contribute to the language user's schemata for rhetorical structures. A number of researchers have proposed that an awareness of these structures results in their employment during comprehending and composing. Blackburn (1982), Geva and Tierney (1984), and Tierney and Leys (1986) have found that young children will spontaneously incorporate certain textual patterns into their writing after they have encountered the patterns in their reading. This is especially true if the stories read contain predictable organizational sequences. According to Blackburn, the use of such sequences is initiated only after the child's conception of storiness has begun to develop. That is, the beginnings of schemata for story structure in reading precede the use of the structures in writing. The subsequent use of these structures in writing allows the child to "move forward without a lot of organizational decision-making" (p. 3). Finally, Blackburn notes that when children first use a particular story pattern in their writing, they will frequently include meanings from the story so as to help them control the pattern.

Bereiter and Scardamalia (1984) and Gordon and Braun (1982) have also investigated the influence of reading on the construction of schemata for the rhetorical aspects of written language. Bereiter and Scardamalia had students in grades 3 through 7 write in a number of genres, including suspense stories and restaurant reviews, then read one piece of material reflecting the genre, and finally make revisions in their writings. They found that students from all ages were able to abstract some rhetorical knowledge from the readings and use it to improve aspects of their writing. Improvement, however, tended to be oriented toward content rather than toward more global aspects of the rhetorical structure. Similarly, Gordon and Braun found that children were able to improve their writing of stories if the structural aspects of the narratives being read were highlighted.

Frank Smith (1983, 1984) has discussed the role which reading plays in the child's understanding of written language conventions. He asserts that writing requires specialized knowledge of spelling, punctuation, capitalization, and syntax which cannot be learned through writing alone. Hypothesis generating and testing require enormous amounts of information and feedback, and the schools simply do not provide enough writing experiences to support such a process. Instead, children must learn the conventions of written language through the texts which they read. Because all existing texts display the relevant conventions, it is through reading these texts with the eye of a writer that children come to control the conventions.

A second line of research has examined the contribution of writing to the language user's schemata for written language processing. In a number of school-based studies with young children, Graves and Hansen (1983) and Hansen (1983a, 1983b) have found that a developing sense of authorship influenced the stances which children took toward published texts. As the children grew in their ability to reflect on what they had written, they began to reflect on what they read. As they learned to generate options in their production of written language and to make revisions, the children also began to read and reread with a sense of options. According to Graves and Hansen, the children initially approached the reading of a text with a sense of distance and accepted the author's meanings as stated. However, as the children learned to question the meanings in their own texts, they also began to question the meanings in those which they read. Through first engaging in the activity during writing, the children began to read for layered meanings and to look for part-whole relationships in text content.

Newkirk (1982) and Boutwell (1983) have also examined how young children learn to distance themselves from their writing and the effect of this ability on children's ability to distance themselves from what they read. Paralleling the findings of Graves and Hansen, the children in these studies usually had difficulty disembedding the text they wrote from their experiences. Experience and text were fused, and evaluations of the text became evaluations of the experience. Through writing conferences, however, the children learned to distance themselves from what they wrote, and the bonds between experience and text loosened. They learned to become strategic readers of their own texts, rereading to evaluate the sense of what they had written, and rewording, deleting, and adding new information to clarify their meanings. This same sense of strategic reading also became apparent in the children's reading of published texts. They became critical readers and used the same strategies to generate meanings from what they were reading.

Somewhat in contrast to Frank Smith, Bissex (1980), Clay (1975), Dyson (1982), Ferreiro and Teberosky (1982), and Ferreiro (1984) have suggested that writing may play a complementary role to reading in that it helps children discover the alphabetic nature of written language. Clay has proposed that beginning readers rely heavily on their knowledge of the structural aspects of language. If this is the case, the hypotheses which children generate about the inner workings of words may fail to capture the alphabetic nature of words. For example, according to Ferreiro and Teberosky, children initially hypothesize a concrete relationship between words and referents, with a great number of referents being represented by a greater number of letters. When writing, children put into action such conceptualizations, and "in attempting to read or to have others read their writing, they must face the inevitable contradictions between what they thought they were doing and what they in fact did" (in Dyson 1982, p. 833).

Universal Three: Readers and writers utilize common procedures for transforming prior knowledge into a text world.

As well as hypothesizing that schemata are mobilized in similar ways during comprehending and composing, several researchers have suggested that common procedures are employed to transform this knowledge into a text world. Typically, the delineation of these procedures has been accomplished in a metaphoric or abductive fashion: procedures which are known to exist in one process are used as a framework to set forth similar procedures in the other.

Based on their work in text comprehension, van Dijk and Kintsch (1983) have proposed that readers and writers may utilize some of the same global strategies during text processing. Strategies, as defined by van Dijk and Kintsch, are the actions which an individual takes to transform an existing state of affairs into another state of affairs. Strategies are goal-oriented and provide the avenue through which intentions can be realized in the most effective and efficient way possible. In reading and writing, strategies allow the reader or writer to transform background knowledge into an internal representation of meaning. While noting the existence of strategies which are specific to each process, van Dijk and Kintsch hypothesize that top-down processing requires the employment of global strategies in both reading and writing. These global strategies are responsible for generating macropropositions and organizing them into a macrostructure. The macrostructure represents the global content of the text—similar to that of a gist or summary—and assists the reader and writer in going beyond the immediate local information of the discourse. Without the evolvement of a macrostructure during the text processing, the language user would have difficulty in controlling large sequences of semantic content. Therefore, macrostructures are particularly important in reading and writing because they support the creation of coherent meaning, which creation, according to van Dijk and Kintsch, drives all language processing.

Also drawing upon her own research in text comprehension, Meyer (1982) has hypothesized that the text-processing strategies in reading and writing are guided by macro plans. A macro plan serves as a set of directions for how meanings are to be represented within the text. As meanings are generated during reading or writing, the plan facilitates the creation of an overall organizational pattern for the semantic content. Similar to the position taken by van Dijk and Kintsch, Meyer perceives the organization of meaning as crucial to effective reading and writing. In supporting the organization of meaning, plans serve three functions: topical, highlighting, and informing. The topical function provides a hierarchy within which meanings can be embedded, such as antecedent/consequent, comparison, or time-ordered. The highlighting function creates dependencies among subtopics through subordination and signals how blocks of content are to be related. The informing function guides the presentation of new content in relation to the meanings which have already been stated. It would appear likely that van Dijk and Kintsch's macropropositions might be placed at the top of the hierarchy, and in a superordinate position, during the construction of the text world.

Though not discussing the building of coherence in propositional terms, a number of other researchers have also emphasized that reading and writing require the strategic organization of meaning. Salvatori (1983), Moxley (1984), and Wittrock (1983) have noted that a critical procedure in both literacy acts is that of consistency building. Readers and writers must seek to relate elements of meaning to one another so that they form a consistent whole. Moffett (1983) has characterized both reading and writing as mediating processes, as avenues through which inner speech can be modified or transformed. In the attempt to create meaning, the language user must strive for coherence in, and continuity of, content. This requires an intervention in the flow of consciousness, with the reader or writer imposing a structure on inner speech so that a unified meaning can be created.

In their composing model of reading, Tierney and Pearson (1983; also Pearson and Tierney 1984) elaborate on the critical role which coherence plays in text processing. In the process of building a coherent model of meaning, they have proposed that the language user engages in planning, drafting, aligning, revising, and monitoring. During planning, the language user decides (*a*) how the topic will be approached, (*b*) the purpose which the reading or writing will serve, and (c) what meanings need to be constructed. These plans are represented at different levels of specificity, are embedded in one another, and become fine-tuned during reading or writing. Drafting is the process of refining meaning as it is encountered on the page. Drawing upon prior knowledge which has been activated and instantiated, and guided by current plans, the language user strives to build a model of meaning. The model which is built, according to Tierney and Pearson, is greatly influenced by the alignments taken by the reader or writer. Alignments represent both the stance which the language user assumes in relation to the author or audience and the role which the stance requires. Alignments influence the content of the text world by providing the reader or writer with a foothold from which meaning can be negotiated. Permeating the entire process of text-world construction is the revision of meaning. As the language user attempts to draft meanings into a coherent whole, it will be necessary for revisions to be made. All meanings constructed are tentative in nature and frequently require fine-tuning or wholesale revision as the text world evolves. Tierney and Pearson suggest that "the driving force behind revision is a sense of emphasis and proportion" (1983, p. 576). Finally, the reader or writer must monitor the balance of power among the procedures of planning, aligning, drafting, and revising. Monitoring allows the language user to distance him- or herself from the text and to decide which procedures should dominate at given points during text processing.

Birnbaum and Emig (1983), however, have added a note of caution to these attempts at generating common procedures for reading and writing. While acknowledging that both are characterized by the orchestration of certain shared subprocesses, they observe that reading and writing are markedly different as well. In reading, the language user is interacting with a visible text, a text which exists independent of the reader. It is the task of the reader to re-create meaning in the form of a "poem." In contrast to the text, a poem has no independent life of its own; rather, it is each reader's unique response to the text. Writing, on the other hand, involves the generation of an evolving or unfolding text which the writer initiates. In this process, the writer predicts forthcoming meaning and then is required to enact the predictions. During reading, the language user predicts what has already been done.

Universal Four: Readers and writers display common processing patterns or abilities when constructing text worlds.

A number of researchers have also examined the common processing patterns or abilities which individuals display as they read and write. If in fact readers and writers draw from a common pool of data as they process text, it may also be the case that their behavior patterns will be similar in reading and writing. Studies of this type have usually looked for shared behaviors of proficient readers and writers and compared them with the behaviors of individuals who are less proficient.

To a large extent, this line of research arises from Loban's (1963) extensive longitudinal study of children's language development. In general, Loban found that children who were proficient in one language process tended to be proficient in the others, and that this relationship increased as the children grew older. Stotsky (1983), in her review of correlational studies which examined the relationship between reading and writing abilities, also notes that most researchers found reading and writing abilities to be positively correlated. Such a relationship would suggest that processing abilities in reading and writing may emerge from a common source. Current studies in this area have attempted to more fully explore and explain this phenomenon.

Birnbaum (1982) examined the behavioral patterns in the reading and writing of proficient and less proficient fourth- and seventh-grade students. In the study, Birnbaum gathered and triangulated data from a variety of perspectives and then generated hypotheses about processing behaviors common to reading and writing. Each group of students orally and silently read reality-based fiction, fantasy, and factual material, and composed in expressive, poetic, and transactional modes. In addition, all students were observed in the classroom and other school settings. Her findings indicated that there was consistency among individuals in processing behaviors across reading and writing, and that these parallels existed regardless of the mode. Also, while there were some age-related differences, Birnbaum found that students who were proficient in reading and writing "shared a set of characteristics and behaviors that distinguished them from the less proficient" (p. 253). In summary, the behaviors of the proficient language users were grounded in their intent to generate meaning to themselves and to others. They continually monitored the generation of meaning and were able to control the strategies which they employed in each process. Furthermore, the more proficient readers and writers (*a*) had access to a wide range of strategies to support the construction of meaning, (*b*) were sensitive to varying situational demands, and (*c*) reflected on what they read or wrote. In contrast, the students who were less proficient focused their attention on the surface features of the text. They had difficulty monitoring their own processing and tended to rely on graphophonic strategies. These students also demonstrated little concern for the context in which their reading and writing occurred and were oblivious to the overall coherence of the meanings which they generated. In effect, both groups of students which

Birnbaum studied appeared to hold common processing schemata for reading and writing, though the schemata varied with the degree of proficiency.

The processing behaviors found by Birnbaum, however, may not be applicable to all readers and writers. While Loban (1963) found a positive correlation between reading and writing abilities, there were students for whom this relation did not apply. In each grade level which Loban examined, at least 17 percent of the students were ranked as good or superior in one process and below average in the other. Tierney and Leys (1986) have cited similar findings from their own reading/writing research with third graders. Approximately 20 percent of the students whom they studied displayed significant differences in their control of the reading and writing processes. Tierney and Leys suggest that a variety of other factors may influence processing patterns, such as the child's instructional history, the reading and writing opportunities which the school provides, and the extent to which the teacher coordinates reading and writing activities.

Bracewell (1980), in a synthesis of a number of studies (Bereiter and Scardamalia 1982; Bereiter, Scardamalia, and Bracewell 1979; Bereiter, Scardamalia, and Turkish 1980; Scardamalia and Bereiter 1983; Scardamalia and Bracewell 1979), has suggested that not only may abilities in one process not be positively related to abilities in the other, but that initial processing schemata for reading may actually interfere with the development of writing ability. According to Bracewell, children's initial schemata for written language processing are strongly influenced by reading encounters, as well as encounters with oral language. Children therefore have a sophisticated understanding of story and sentence structure, which they use in their comprehension of text. The use of this knowledge, however, tends not to be under the conscious control of the reader. Rather, the perceptual-cognitive processes mediating surface structure and meaning are highly routinized. In contrast, writing requires the child to choose deliberately from among linguistic forms and meanings, and to put together extended sequences of text in a coherent manner. The research cited by Bracewell found that children aged nine to eleven had difficulty employing strategies which gave them access to their knowledge of language forms. The necessary knowledge existed, but the children had not acquired the skills necessary for using the knowledge. Even when they had the ability to talk consciously about discourse forms, or could read and understand certain syntactic structures, they were unable to produce such patterns in their own writing. Bracewell states that this inability is due to the children's attempt to employ reading routines in their writing.

Complementing the research which has explored processing patterns in reading and writing, several studies have examined the relationship of structural components in the two processes. Chall and Jacobs (1983) and Chall et al. (1982) investigated developmental trends in reading and writing among low-socioeconomic-status elementary school children. These students were in the second, fourth, and sixth grades and had above- or below-average reading abilities. Their reading abilities were measured in terms of word recognition, phonics, oral reading, word meaning, silent reading comprehension, and spelling. In the measurement of writing ability, the children were first asked to write for ten minutes in a narrative and expository mode. Writing samples were then evaluated in four general ways: (1) overall: holistic score and rank; (2) syntactic-organizational: organization rating, T-unit length, and sentence length; (3) content rating; and (4) precision in form, handwriting, and spelling. All children were retested in the same manner a year later when they were in grades 3, 5, and 7. Chall and Jacobs found parallels between reading and writing in both ability and in developmental trends. Except for grade 3, in which the writing scores of above- and below-average groups were similar, the above-average readers had better scores on all four writing measures. The biggest contributor to the difference in scores at the upper grades was precision in form. While the content ratings were similar between above- and below-average groups at all grade levels, the below-average readers had more difficulty with spelling, punctuation, and capitalization. However, as Chall and Jacobs note, all students tended "to have 'better ideas' than ways of expressing them" (p. 622). Developmentally, both groups of students made the greatest gains in reading and writing during grade 2; during grades 4 and 6 there was a deceleration of growth in both processes. In reading, the strongest and most consistent growth was in oral and silent reading. Word meaning, spelling, and word recognition showed strong development in grade 2 but decelerated in the later grades. In writing, content ratings showed growth throughout the grades, accompanied by a deceleration in aspects of form, such as grammar and mechanics.

Shanahan (1984) examined the relationship of structural components in reading and writing using multivariate procedures. The procedures allowed for the relationships of several factors in the two processes to be considered simultaneously. Reading and writing abilities of a heterogeneous sample of second and fifth graders were assessed using a variety of instruments. Reading ability was measured in terms of phonetic analysis, comprehension, vocabulary, and cloze. In writing, the students were required to write two narrative-descriptive pieces, which were then evaluated for mean T-unit length, vocabulary diversity, and organizational structure. Finally, a spelling test was administered and analyzed for words spelled correctly, phonemic accuracy, and visual accuracy. Based on these analyses, Shanahan also identified the least and most proficient readers from the second- and fifth-grade samples. In all cohorts, except for the most proficient readers, the overlap between reading and writing was greatest among phonic and spelling measures—what Shanahan described as a "word recognition-word production relationship." For the fifth graders, the importance of vocabulary to the reading/writing relationship was also significant, while the importance of grammatical complexity and a number of idea units in writing decreased. For the proficient readers, however, the overlap between reading and writing factors differed from the other cohorts. The reading comprehension variable was a significant contributor to the relationship, and the importance of phonics declined. In writing, vocabulary diversity increased in importance, as did the ability to structure prose in a variety of ways. Given this changing relationship between reading and writing as proficiency increased, Shanahan proposed that the relationship between reading and writing is not a straightforward one. Rather, "as students learn to read, what can be learned about reading from writing instruction, and vice versa, changes also" (p. 23).

Future Reading/Writing Research: Extending the Connection

During the last five years we have made tremendous gains in our understanding of reading/writing connections. However, because many of us have not been trained in an interdisciplinary manner, we frequently approach the subject with either a reading perspective or a writing perspective. Such bias may limit in unseen ways our ability to discern certain kinds of connections or interactions between the two processes. This may be especially true when we examine the effects which growth in one process has on growth in the other. There may in fact be a more dynamic relationship between reading and writing which has gone unnoticed. To avoid such biases, we need to begin to see ourselves as researchers of literacy rather than as researchers of reading or writing. This alternative perspective can be facilitated if researchers in both fields will collaborate in studies of the reading/writing process.

Furthermore, given the separate lines of inquiry which the reading and writing communities have conducted over the years, there is no reason that each line of inquiry should not be extended to the other discipline. For example, the reading community has made substantial gains in its understanding of the role which prior knowledge plays in text comprehension. Similarly, the writing community has documented the effects which mode and audience have on the production of text. It would now be fruitful for researchers to examine more fully the role of mode and purpose in text comprehension and to then triangulate their findings with those of the writing community. In the same fashion, the role of background knowledge in the writing process should be explored and triangulated with text-comprehension findings. To a certain extent this has been done in the general theories of text processing which Tierney and Pearson (1983), Shanklin (1982), and Kucer (1985) have developed. Langer (1984) has also engaged in this process by examining the role of prior knowledge in the writing process.

Another avenue for extending the lines of research would be to conduct parallel reading/writing studies with the same populations. Rather than triangulating findings from a number of separate reading and writing investigations, researchers would explore the influence of certain variables on both processes within the same study. The role of prior knowledge in reading and writing could be examined with the same group of students, as could the effects of mode or purpose. Studies of this type, especially if conducted jointly by reading and writing researchers, might facilitate the ease with which reading/writing connections could be explored.

There also would be advantages to combining the use of process-oriented procedures, such as those used by Birnbaum (1982), with analyses of structural components as employed by Chall and Jacobs (1983) and Shanahan (1984). The ability of the language user to control certain structural aspects of the reading and writing processes might begin to more fully explain certain in-process behaviors. Key processing patterns might also be related to the individual's control of certain structural aspects. This type of research would be particularly powerful if it examined developmental trends as well as individuals who were proficient and less proficient in their control of the two processes.

Finally, as Tierney, Leys, and Rogers (1984) have recently noted, reading and writing are acts of social negotiation as well as cognition. In both their use and their development, reading and writing are influenced by the social context in which they evolve. The classroom teacher, in conjunction with the curriculum, largely determines the social negotiations which children experience during reading and writing activities. There needs to be a closer examination of these learning environments and the effects which they have on reading/writing development and processing. Investigations of this type would not only extend our understanding of reading/writing connections, but also connect researchers with teachers.

References

Adams, M. J., and A. Collins (1977). *A schema-theoretic view of reading comprehension.* Technical report no. 32. Champaign, Ill.: Center for the Study of Reading, University of Illinois at Urbana-Champaign. ED 142 971.

Allen, P., and D. Watson, eds. (1976). *Findings of research in miscue analysis: Classroom implications.* Urbana, Ill.: National Council of Teachers of English and the ERIC Clearinghouse on Reading and Communication Skills. ED 128 762.

Anderson, R. C., R. E. Reynolds, D. L. Schallert, and E. T. Goetz (1976). *Frameworks for comprehending discourse.* Technical report no. 12. Champaign, Ill.: Center for the Study of Reading, University of Illinois at Urbana-Champaign. ED 134 935.

Anderson, R., R. Spiro, and W. Montague, eds. (1977). *Schooling and the acquisition of knowledge.* Hillsdale, N.J.: Erlbaum.

Atwell, M. (1981). The evolution of text: The interrelationship of reading and writing in the composing process. *Dissertation Abstracts International* 42: 116–A.

Bagley, D. (1937). A critical survey of objective estimates in the teaching of English. *British Journal of Educational Psychology* 7: 57–71.

Barton, W. (1930). *Outlining as a study procedure* (Contributions to Education No. 411). New York: Bureau of Publications, Teachers College, Columbia University.

Beaugrande, R. de (1979). The processes of invention: Association and recombination. *College Composition and Communication* 30: 260–67.

———— (1982). Psychology and composition: Past, present, and future. In *What writers know: Studies in the psychology of writing,* edited by M. Nystrand, 211–67. New York: Academic Press.

———— (1980). *Text, discourse, and process.* Norwood, New Jersey: Ablex.

Bereiter, C., and M. Scardamalia (1982). From conversation to composition: The role of instruction in a developmental process. *Advances in instructional psychology: Vol. 2,* edited by R. Glaser, 1–64. Hillsdale, N.J.: Erlbaum.

———— (1984). Learning about writing from reading. *Written Communication* 1: 163–88.

Bereiter, C., M. Scardamalia, and R. Bracewell (1979). An applied cognitive-developmental approach to writing research. Paper presented at the annual meeting of the American Educational Research Association.

Bereiter, C., M. Scardamalia, and L. Turkish (1980). The child as discourse grammarian. Paper presented at the annual meeting of the American Educational Research Association.

Berthoff, A. (1983). How we construe is how we construct. In *Fforum: Essays on theory and practice in the teaching of writing,* edited by P. Stock, 166–70. Upper Montclair, N.J.: Boynton/Cook Publishers.

Birnbaum, J. (1982). The reading and composing behavior of selected fourth- and seventh-grade students. *Research in the Teaching of English* 16: 241–60.

Birnbaum, J., and J. Emig (1983). Creating minds, created texts: Writing and reading. In *Developing literacy: Young children's use of language,* edited by R. Parker and F. Davis, 87–104. Newark, Del.: International Reading Association.

Bissex, G. (1980). *Gnys at wrk: A child learns to write and read.* Cambridge, Mass.: Harvard University Press.

Blackburn, E. (1982). *Borrowing words: Children use literature to improve writing.* Unpublished manuscript. Great Falls School, Somersworth, New Hampshire.

Boutwell, M. (1983). Reading and writing process: A reciprocal agreement. *Language Arts* 60: 723–30.

Bracewell, R. J. (1980). Writing as a cognitive activity. *Visible Language* 14: 400–22.

Britton, J., T Burgess, N. Martin, A. McLeod, and G. Rosen (1975). *The development of writing abilities (11–18).* London: Macmillan.

Chall, J., and V. Jacobs (1983). Writing and reading in the elementary grades: Developmental trends among low SES children. *Language Arts* 60: 617–26.

Chall, J., C. Snow, W. Barnes, J. Chandler, I. Goodman, L. Hemphill, and F. Jacobs (1982). *Families and literacy: The contributions of out-of-school experiences to the acquisition of literacy: A final report.* Washington, D.C.: National Institute of Education.

Christiansen, M. (1965). Tripling writing and omitting readings in freshman English: An experiment. *College Composition and Communication* 16: 122–24.

Clark, J. D. (1935). A four-year study of freshman English. *English Journal* 24: 403–10.

Clay, M. (1975). *What did I write?* Auckland, New Zealand: Heinemann.

DeFord, D. (1981). Literacy: Reading, writing, and other essentials. *Language Arts* 58: 652–58.

Diederich, P. (1957). *The problem of grading essays.* Princeton, New Jersey: Educational Testing Service. Mimeo.

Dyson, A. (1982). Reading, writing, and language: Young children solving the written language puzzle. *Language Arts* 59: 829–39.

Eckhoff, B. (1983). How reading affects children's writing. *Language Arts* 60: 607–16.

Emig, J. (1971). *The composing processes of twelfth graders.* Research report no. 13. Urbana, Ill.: National Council of Teachers of English. ED 058 205.

Evanechko, P., L. Ollila, and R. Armstrong (1974). An investigation of the relationship between children's performance in written language and their reading ability. *Research in the Teaching of English* 8: 315–26.

Evans, R. (1979). The relationship between the reading and writing of syntactic structures. *Research in the Teaching of English* 13: 129–135.

Ferreiro, E. (1984). The underlying logic of literacy development. In *Awakening to literacy,* edited by H. Goelman, A. Oberg, and F. Smith, 154–73. Exeter, N.H.: Heinemann.

Ferreiro, E., and A. Teberosky (1982). *Literacy before schooling.* Trans. K. Goodman Castro. Exeter, N.H.: Heinemann.

Flower, L., and J. Hayes (1981). A cognitive process theory of writing. *College Composition and Communication* 32: 365–87.

Geva, E., and R. Tierney (1984). Text engineering: The influence of manipulated compare-contrast selections. Paper presented at the annual meeting of the American Educational Research Association.

Goodman, K. (1965). A linguistic study of cues and miscues in reading. *Elementary English* 42: 639–43.

——— (1969). Reading: A psycholinguistic guessing game. *Journal of the Reading Specialist* 4: 125–35.

——— (1972). The reading process: Theory and practice. In *Language and learning to read,* edited by R. Hodges and E. Rudorf. New York: Houghton Mifflin.

Goodman, K., and C. Burke (1973). *Theoretically based studies of patterns of miscues in oral reading performance. Final Report to the U.S. Department of Health, Education, and Welfare.* Washington, D.C.: Office of Education.

Goodman, Y. (1967). A psycholinguistic description of observed oral reading phenomena in selected young beginning readers. *Dissertation Abstracts International* 29: 60–A.

Gordon, C., and C. Braun (1982). Story schemata: Metatextual aid to reading and writing. In *New Inquiries in Reading: Research and Instruction,* edited by J. Niles and L. Harris. Rochester, N.Y.: National Reading Conference.

Gough, P. (1976). One second of reading. In *Theoretical models and processes of reading,* edited by H. Singer and R. Ruddell, 509–35. Newark, Del.: International Reading Association.

Graves, D. (1973). Children's writing: Research directions and hypotheses based upon an examination of the writing process of seven-year-old children. *Dissertation Abstracts International* 34: 6255–A.

Graves, D., and J. Hansen (1983). The author's chair. *Language Arts* 60: 176–83.

Gray, W., and R. Rogers (1956). *Maturity in reading.* Chicago: University of Chicago Press.

Hansen, J. (1983a). Authors respond to authors. *Language Arts* 60: 970–76.

——— (1983b). First grade writers who pursue reading. In *Fforum: Essays on theory and practice in the teaching of writing,* edited by P. Stock, 155–62. Upper Montclair, N.J.: Boynton/Cook.

Harste, J., C. Burke, and V. Woodward (1982). Children's language and world: Initial encounters with print. In *Reader meets author—Bridging the gap,* edited by J. Langer and M. Smith-Burke. Newark, Del.: International Reading Association.

Harste, J., V. Woodward, and C. Burke (1984). *Language stories & literacy lessons.* Portsmouth, N.H.: Heinemann.

Holmes, J. (1976). Basic assumptions underlying the substrata-factor theory. In *Theoretical models and processes of reading,* edited by H. Singer and R. Ruddell, 597–618. Newark: Del.: International Reading Association.

Iran-Nejad, A. (1980). *The schema: A structural or a functional pattern.* Technical report no. 159. Champaign, Ill.: Center for the Study of Reading, University of Illinois at Urbana-Champaign. ED 181 449.

Iser, W. (1978). *The act of reading: A theory of aesthetic response.* Baltimore: Johns Hopkins University Press.

Kavanagh, J., and I. Mattingly, eds. (1972). *Language by ear and by eye: The relationship between speech and reading.* Cambridge, Mass.: MIT Press.

Kintsch, W. (1974). *The representation of meaning in memory.* Hillsdale, N.J.: Erlbaum.

Kintsch, W., and T. A. van Dijk (1978). Toward a model of text comprehension and production. *Psychological Review* 85: 363–94.

Kucer, S. (1983). Using text comprehension as a metaphor for understanding text production: Building bridges between reading and writing. *Dissertation Abstracts International* 44: 3016–A.

———— (1985). The making of meaning: Reading and writing as parallel processes. *Written Communication* 2: 317–36.

Kucer, S., and L. Rhodes (1983). Taking advantage of reading and writing interrelationships. Paper presented at the Colorado Reading Association State Conference.

———— (1986). Counterpart strategies: Fine-tuning language with language. *The Reading Teacher* 40: 186–93.

LaBerge, D., and S. Samuels (1976). Toward a theory of automatic information processing in reading. In *Theoretical models and processes of reading,* edited by H. Singer and R. Ruddell, 548–79. Newark, Del.: International Reading Association.

Langer, J. (1984). The effects of available information on responses to school writing tasks. *Research in the Teaching of English* 18: 27–44.

Loban, W. (1963). *The language of elementary school children.* Research report no. 1. Urbana, Ill.: National Council of Teachers of English. ED 001 875.

Maloney, H. (1968). An identification of excellence in expository composition performance in a selected 9A population with an analysis of reasons for superior performance. *Dissertation Abstracts International* 28: 3564–A.

Marshall, N., and M. Glock (1978). Comprehension of connected discourse: A study into the relationship between the structure of text and information recalled. *Reading Research Quarterly* 14: 10–56.

Matsuhashi, A. (1980). Producing written discourse: A theory based description of the temporal characteristics of three discourse types from four competent twelfth grade writers. *Dissertation Abstracts International* 40: 5035–A.

Menosky, D. (1971). A psycholinguistic analysis of oral reading miscues generated during the reading of varying portions of text by selected readers from grades two, four, six, and eight: A descriptive study. *Dissertation Abstracts International* 32: 6108–A.

Meyer, B. (1982). Reading research and the composition teacher: The importance of plans. *College Composition and Communication* 33: 37–49.

Moffett, J. (1983). Reading and writing as meditation. *Language Arts* 60: 315–22.

Monk, R. (1958). A study to determine the relationship between children's home environments and their school achievement in written English. Unpublished doctoral dissertation, University of Washington.

Moxley, R. (1984). The compositional approach to reading in practice and theory. *Journal of Reading* 27: 636–43.

Neisser, U. (1976). *Cognition and reality: Principles and implications of cognitive psychology.* San Francisco: W. H. Freeman & Co.

Newkirk, T. (1982). Young writers as critical readers. *Language Arts* 59: 451–57.

Ortony, A. (1980). *Understanding metaphors.* Technical report no. 154. Champaign, Ill.: Center for the Study of Reading, University of Illinois at Urbana-Champaign. ED 181 426.

Page, W. (1974). The author and the reader in writing and reading. *Research in the Teaching of English* 8: 170–83.

Pearson, D. and R. Tierney (1984). On becoming a thoughtful reader: Learning to read like a writer. In *Becoming readers in a complex society,* edited by A. Purves and O. Niles. Chicago: National Society for the Study of Education.

Perl, S. (1979). The composing processes of unskilled college writers. *Research in the Teaching of English* 13: 317–36.

Petrosky, A. (1982). From story to essay: Reading and writing. *College Composition and Communication* 33: 19–36.

Pianko, S. (1979). A description of the composing processes of college freshman writers. *Research in the Teaching of English* 13: 5–22.

Pichert, J. W., and R. C. Anderson (1977). Taking different perspectives on a story. *Journal of Educational Psychology* 69: 309–15.

Rosenblatt, L. (1978). *The reader, the text, the poem: The transactional theory of the literary work.* Carbondale, Ill.: Southern Illinois University Press.

Rousch, P. (1972). A psycho-linguistic investigation into the relationship between prior conceptual knowledge, oral reading miscues, silent reading, and post-reading performance. *Dissertation Abstracts International* 33: 6074–A.

Ruddell, R. (1969). Psycholinguistic implications for a system of communication models. In *Psycholinguistics and the teaching of reading,* edited by K. S. Goodman and J. T. Flemming. Newark, Del.: International Reading Association.

Rumelhart, D. (1975). Notes on a schema for stories. In *Representation and understanding,* edited by D. Bobrow and A. Collins. New York: Academic Press.

Salvatori, M. (1983). Reading and writing a text: Correlations between reading and writing patterns. *College English* 45: 657–66.

Scardamalia, M., and C. Bereiter (1983). The development of evaluative, diagnostic, and remedial capabilities in children's composing. In *The psychology of written language: A developmental approach,* edited by M. Martlew, 67–95. London: John Wiley & Sons.

Scardamalia, M., and R. Bracewell (1979). Local planning in children's writing. Paper presented at the annual meeting of the American Educational Research Association.

Schonell, F. (1942). *Backwardness in the basic subjects.* Toronto: Clare, Irwin.

Shanahan, T. (1984). Nature of the reading-writing relation: An exploratory multivariate analysis. *Journal of Educational Psychology* 76: 466–77.

Shanklin, N. (1982). *Relating reading and writing: Developing a transactional model of the writing process.* Monographs in language and reading studies. Bloomington, Ind.: Indiana University Press.

Singer, H. (1976). Substrata-factor patterns accompanying development in power of reading, elementary through college level. In *Theoretical models and processes of reading,* edited by H. Singer and R. Ruddell, 619–33. Newark, Del.: International Reading Association.

Smith, F. (1982). *Understanding reading: A psycholinguistic analysis of reading and learning to read.* 3d ed. New York: Holt, Rinehart & Winston.

—— (1983). Reading like a writer. *Language Arts* 60: 558–67.

—— (1984). The creative achievement of literacy. In *Awakening to literacy,* edited by H. Goelman, A. Obert, and F. Smith, 143–53. Exeter, N.H.: Heinemann.

Sommers, N. (1979). Revision in the composing process: A case study of college freshmen and experienced adult writers. *Dissertation Abstracts International* 39: 5374–A.

Spiro, R., B. Bruce, and W. Brewer, eds. (1980). *Theoretical issues in reading comprehension.* Hillsdale, N.J.: Erlbaum.

Spivey, N. (1983). Discourse synthesis: Constructing texts in reading and writing. *Dissertation Abstracts International* 44: 2699–A.

Squire, J. (1983). Composing and comprehending: Two sides of the same basic process. *Language Arts* 60: 581–89.

Stein, N. (1978). *How children understand stories: A developmental analysis.* Technical report no. 69. Champaign, Ill.: Center for the Study of Reading, University of Illinois at Urbana-Champaign. ED 153 205.

Sticht, T., L. Beck, R. Hauck, G. Kleinman, and J. James (1974). *Auditing and reading: A developmental model.* Alexandria, Va.: Human Resources Research Organization.

Stotsky, S. (1975). Sentence-combining as a curricular activity: Its effect on written language development and reading comprehension. *Research in the Teaching of English* 9: 30–71.

Stotsky, S. (1983). Research on reading/writing relationships: A synthesis and suggested directions. *Language Arts* 60: 627–42.

Tierney, R. (1983). Writer-reader transactions: Defining the dimensions of negotiation. In *Fforum: Essays on theory and practice in the teaching of writing,* edited by P. Stock, 147–51. Upper Montclair, N.J.: Boynton/Cook.

Tierney, R., and J. LaZansky (1980). *The rights and responsibilities of readers and writers: A contractual agreement.* Reading education report no. 15. Champaign, Ill.: Center for the Study of Reading, University of Illinois at Urbana-Champaign.

Tierney, R., and M. Leys (1986). What is the value of connecting reading and writing? In *Convergences: Transactions in reading and writing.* Urbana, Ill.: National Council of Teachers of English. ED 265 568.

Tierney, R., M. Leys, and T. Rogers (1984). Comprehension, composition, and collaboration: Analysis of communicative influences in two classrooms. Paper presented at the Conference on Contexts of Literacy, Snowbird, Utah.

Tierney, R., and P. D. Pearson (1983). Toward a composing model of reading. *Language Arts* 60: 568–80.

van Dijk, T. A. (1979). From text grammar to interdisciplinary discourse studies. Paper presented at the La Jolla Conference on Cognitive Science, University of California at San Diego.

——— (1980). *Macrostructures: An interdisciplinary study of global structures in discourse, interaction, and cognition.* Hillsdale, N.J.: Lawrence Erlbaum Associates.

van Dijk, T. A. and W. Kintsch (1983). *Strategies in discourse comprehension.* New York: Academic Press.

Wittrock, M. (1983). Writing and the teaching of reading. *Language Arts* 60: 600–606.

Yoos, G. (1979). An identity of roles in writing and reading. *College Composition and Communication* 30: 245–250.

Young, R., A. Becker, and K. Pike (1970). *Rhetoric: Discovery and change.* New York: Harcourt Brace Jovanovich.

Commentary

Alan C. Purves
State University of New York at Albany

What strikes me as particularly felicitous in the Flood and Lapp and Kucer papers is that neither title uses what to me is the most problematic aspect of the assigned topic, the word *processes*. I would like to suggest that their avoidance of the term in their titles should be a caution to us all. The problem with *process* is that it implies a linearity, a finiteness, and a rule-governed structure that many researchers have suggested simply does not exist. Reading and writing are not to be seen as analogous to the digestive process.

I would suggest that reading and writing be considered *activities*, a term suggested by the Russian psychologists Vygotsky and Galparin, and applied to language by Leontiev. An activity consists of a number of *acts*, which in turn consist of *operations* about which the individual is not necessarily conscious. The individual may or may not be conscious of an act. The acts comprising an activity may not necessarily occur in a fixed sequence or order, but operations often occur as sequences. Leontiev suggests that in language learning what becomes an operation may have begun as an activity. For a young child, letter formation is an activity, but for an adult it is clearly an operation. The process by which activities become operations is what George Miller calls *chunking*. Leontiev goes on to suggest that a person who is *adept* at operations has developed a *habit;* a person who is adept at an act is *skilled.*

I believe that this set of terms is useful for research in reading and writing, because it clarifies the unease that Kucer and Flood and Lapp suggest about reading and writing relationships. As activities, reading and writing are distinct in that they have different aims. However, they may have certain acts and operations in common. And as both papers suggest, what they have in common are certainly not the psychomotor acts and operations but—possibly—the mental ones.

The two activities share the fact that they have goals, but as Kucer suggests, these goals are not the same. The goal of a writer writing a letter is not the same as the goal of a reader reading a letter. The letter-writer's goal may be to persuade, but the reader does not have as a goal to be persuaded. Both writers and readers select from a range of goals, but as I. A. Richards and other reader-response theorists have suggested, the two groups make quite different selections.

When we compare the acts and operations of readers and writers, then, I think we must look carefully at their similarities and differences. I do not think it is enough to say, as Kucer does, that "for the classroom teacher, the discovery of common operating mechanisms would support the development of literacy programs that fully integrate reading and writing instruction." I think I see the two activities as complementing one another, but I am unsure of their integration. They may be *analogous,* as Flood and Lapp, I believe, correctly suggest, and an analogy may prove enlightening.

Kucer's "universals" and Flood and Lapp's "generalizations" have much in common. Reading and writing are comparable in that both involve the individual's use of prior knowledge, both involve language and thereby a knowledge of language, both involve some general procedures and ends, both involve monitoring as they proceed, and both have some relation to other uses of language, particularly the oral ones of speaking and listening. To a certain extent the three major pieces of news for research in this list are that knowledge is an important antecedent of reading and writing, that when people read and write they monitor their acts, and that language knowledge goes beyond words and sentences. Each of these suggests a major change in focus for research in both reading and writing.

As I read through the detailed review of the studies that support these universals and generalizations, I found myself pausing less at the generalizations than at the particulars cited to relate reading and writing. Two persistent items give pause. The first is that there is little evidence of parallelism at the operational level: the parallels occur at the level of intention (e.g., to make meaning) and strategy or at such a high level of abstraction, such as that dealing with prior knowledge and schemata or that dealing with the language pool, that the studies appear to be belaboring the obvious.

The second item that the studies cited give rise to is an issue of measurement. The studies that look at readers and writers (Chall et al., Shanahan) use sets of measures to establish relationships, but on inspection the logical connections between supposedly parallel or complementary measures are tenuous at best, and the modest correlations support that tenuousness. On the face of it, the closest correspondence can be found in the measures of vocabulary, but even there studies have suggested differences between word recognition and word use.

In summary, I heartily agree with the caution expressed in both papers and in the call for reading researchers to talk to writing researchers and vice versa and to stop the over-compartmentalization of research. I would urge great caution in doing so by a reductionist approach. Just as language research did a number of years ago, I think educational research should adopt the metaphor of competence and performance, or *langue* and *parole*, to see that there are many activities that involve language as a representation of meaning. Though the activities share this general characteristic, their other similarities and their differences need to be systematically examined.

Commentary

Julie M. Jensen
University of Texas at Austin

The last time I was invited to a research conference planned by Jim Squire was in 1972. We numbered sixty then—twice the number here. At that conference, six papers—not a hefty collection of twelve—served as the basis for discussion. Along with the papers of an anthropologist, a psychometrist, a philosopher, a technologist, and a Swede was only one from an American researcher in English education. At the present conference, the most common job description is "professor of education." My fellow discussant then, as today, was Alan Purves. But we were joined by Jimmy Britton. I wish he could add some of his good sense to the topic at hand as he did thirteen years ago when we discussed Swedish researcher Gunnar Hansen's work on response to literature. We have no "working parties" here; there were seven then, dealing with (1) language development, (2) interdisciplinary studies, (3) literature, (4) method and curriculum, (5) composing and speech, (6) reading, and (7) sociolinguistics, psycholinguistics, and reading.

From the diverse roles of the papers' authors—anthropologist, psychometrist, philosopher, technologist, and English educator—we built interdisciplinary bridges, as has been suggested at this conference, and we learned that the very definition of research differs according to one's professional vantage point. We also learned about available perspectives on research, and about extending the boundaries of research in English education. More than one conferee observed that it wasn't the papers at all that became our content; it was the people there—their actions, their opinions, the effect of their responses on one another. I expect the same at this seminar.

I have reminisced at length neither to deceive you about the quality of my memory—for I revived that long-ago conference by using the Fall 1973 issue of *Research in the Teaching of English* (Purves 1973)—nor because I envisioned in the early seventies the current intensity of the search for relationships between reading and writing. Remember, this was the era of a revolutionary new study by Janet Emig (1971) on writers while they were writing, using case-study methods. And it was the era of Frank O'Hare's NCTE best-seller (1973) on sentence combining. The link between reading and writing was hardly a conference theme in 1972. That would have to wait at least a decade.

I bring up the past because of that single American researcher in English education, Dwight Burton, and a haunting memory of his paper, "Research in the Teaching of English: The Troubled Dream" (1973). I will argue that today's research on composing and comprehending is, in some respects, an appropriate referent for Burton's "troubled dream."

Let me begin with the "dream" part by deferring to four respected colleagues:

> On the long, hard, never-ending trail to the improvement of education, research does play an important role. (James Squire, 1976, p. 63)

> Why all this reliance on research in the improvement of English teaching . . . ? Education, like politics or religion or economics, must have recourse to some form of authority to lend stability to it as an institution. Education at present has no Supreme Court, no Vatican Council. (George Henry, 1966, p. 230)

> One of the benefits expected from educational research is unimpeachable evidence for or against the usefulness of this or that school practice. (Harry Broudy, 1973, p. 240)

> We have great hopes for what research can do for us in the teaching of English. Though at the moment, we acknowledge that research has had little to do with curriculum structure and teaching methods in English, we have the feeling that answers are just around the corner if we could but design the right studies. (Dwight Burton, 1973, p. 160)

Conferences like this one tell me that the "dream" is not illusory.

But, on to the word *troubled* in Burton's "troubled dream." I take my cue this time from James Moffett (1984), who said recently, "We're preoccupied with research as a way to improve practice. But lack of knowledge is *not* what blocks curricular improvement. In the last twenty years knowledge has moved forward while practice has moved backward."

None of us would dispute the premise that knowledge has moved forward in the past twenty years. For example, we can't ignore growth in knowledge about writing. I enjoyed Donald Murray's observation that during the last two decades there has come to be "a new discipline of composition theory with its own theoretical base, its own research methods, its own academic groups and journals, its own academic leaders, its own jargon, its own arrogance and snobbery" (1984, p. 21). Murray went on to call the reintegration of reading and writing "the most important development in the field of English in the last five years" (p. 21). I want, though, to call attention, as did Kucer and Flood and Lapp, to the *re* before *integration*. Interest in reading and writing relationships is renewed, not new; continuing, not beginning; and, in most instances, reaffirmed and popularized, not recently discovered or invented. Those who have always maintained an integrative spirit are now having a day in the sun, along with countless newcomers.

As in 1972, researchers with diverse traditions have come together to learn more about what unifies listening, speaking, reading, and writing as meaning-making experiences. The reading theorists at this conference can enrich our understanding of how readers and writers comprehend text; the writing theorists can describe how texts are made and how we learn to read our own texts. That is all to the good, but back to Moffett's "practice has moved backward." The explanation here is less clear-cut. It has been said that zippers, television sets, and heart pacemakers took fifty years from invention to mass use. How, then, can we expect anything as complex as classroom teaching to keep pace with educational theory and research? Dismissing the state of current practice so easily is not an approach taken by dreamers, however—regardless of whether you think practice is moving backward, holding its own, or moving ahead; whether you think it is doing so because of, in spite of, or apart from advances in knowledge over the past twenty years; or whether you think that a sound determination can't be made on such a global scale and that even if it could we should attend at this conference to the perceptions of the Moffetts among us. We might consider how we could respond to forces not only outside the research community but outside the profession—political, social, and economic influences on the potential of research to affect the quality of classroom practice. More centrally, we might discuss forces within our ranks that diminish our impact on practice. I'll conclude with two of these internal challenges.

First, I wish we could encourage a redefinition of the word *researcher.* To the ranks of thesis and dissertation writers, assistant professors seeking tenure, and the small crowd that we represent, let's recruit anyone who has a question and a disciplined approach to finding an answer. The gap between theory and practice is fed by many other gaps: to name but a few, there are researchers who aren't readers, researchers who don't value clear writing, researchers who don't know children or how they learn, researchers who have not experienced life in classrooms, teachers who don't do research, and teachers who are neither readers nor writers. Membership in the club of reading/writing researchers needs to be broad enough to encompass those who read, who write, who know children, and who know classrooms. Anyone who encourages or collaborates with a classroom teacher gets extra points.

Second, I wish we could encourage a redefinition of the term *research report*. Research reports with even a slim chance of affecting classroom practice are in the minority. Granted, it is at times appropriate for researchers to address their work to other researchers, but most often it is essential that we speak to teachers. If research has had little effect on practice, it may be because researchers forget that classrooms are practical places where teachers make countless decisions daily. Studies of minute aspects of language clothed in complex prose and undertaken by researchers removed from all the complexities of teaching a particular classroom of students are unlikely to have import for teachers, no matter how much we might wish that instructional decisions were influenced by research findings.

Several years ago a colleague asked me to substitute-teach her graduate course entitled "Secondary School Reading." My job was to listen to each of a dozen or so students as they reported on a piece of reading research, to join in follow-up discussions about the research, and to take notes on each student's performance for the benefit of the course instructor.

During those weeks I learned less about reading and about research than I did about the interaction between a small group of students, mostly inservice teachers, and a small body of research drawn from the most respected journals and textbooks in the field. My memory is vivid, not of the skills those teachers brought to the reading of reading research, but of their attitudes toward that research.

The teachers' presentations, coupled with their responses to follow-up questions, led me to this profile of their view of published research in reading:

—It's in print; it must be important.

—It appeared in [such and such publication]; it must be good.

—[So and so] said it; it must be right.

—Who am I to criticize [so and so]; he/she is a researcher and I'm just a teacher.

—These ideas must be very complex because the language is so difficult to read.

—This article must be profound because I can't understand it.

—I get so bored trying to read this.

—I don't understand what this has to do with my classroom.

While a self-effacing attitude has its charms, it does little to serve a teacher's cause of returning to graduate school so that secondary school students may become better readers. Well, we translated and we groped for meaning. And I asked them to reconsider the focus of their confusion and condemnation, believing that more important than knowing the attributes of a few reading studies was their understanding that it is the writer's responsibility to communicate with the reader, that research articles need not be either dull or difficult, that complex prose is not the mark of a superior mind, that every word should be written to build meaning for the reader, and that no one should know that better than a reading researcher.

If we hope to improve the teaching of reading and writing, we bear the burden of understanding, if not having insight into, classroom teaching; further, we must demonstrate skill, if not artistry, in the use of language. The obvious and prevalent alternative is failure to communicate with those who can give our work life.

Clearly we do not yet know the precise nature of the relationships among oral language, reading, and writing. But the gaps in our knowledge distress me less than the false dichotomy between "those who teach" and "those who research." My "dream" is sustained by growing interest and knowledge about links among the language arts, and by educators of all stripes who are designing and evaluating programs that support growth of all the language arts. It is "troubled" because the vast majority of language learners in schools remains untouched.

References

Broudy, H. S. (1973). Research into imagic association and cognitive interpretation. *Research in the Teaching of English* 7: 240–59.

Burton, D. L. (1973). Research in the teaching of English: The troubled dream. *Research in the Teaching of English* 7: 160–89.

Emig, J. (1971). *The composing processes of twelfth graders.* Research report no. 13. Urbana, Ill.: National Council of Teachers of English. ED 058 205.

Henry, G. H. (1966). English teaching encounters science. *College English* 28: 220–35.

Moffett, J. (1984). Paper presented at the meeting of the International Federation for the Teaching of English, East Lansing, Michigan. See also Moffett, J. (1985). Hidden impediments. In *Language, schooling, and society,* edited by S. Tchudi. Upper Montclair, N.J.: Boynton/Cook Publishers.

Murray, D. (1984). Facets: The most important development in the last five years for high school teachers of composition. *English Journal* 78, no. 5: 21.

O'Hare, F. (1973). *Sentence combining: Improving student writing without formal grammar instruction*. Research report no. 15. Urbana, Ill.: National Council of Teachers of English. ED 073 483.

Purves, A., ed. (1973). The 1972 Minnesota NCTE seminar of research in English education. *Research in the Teaching of English* 7: 144–290.

Squire, J. R. (1976). Research can make a difference. *Research in the Teaching of English* 10: 63–65.

II Texts with Different Structures and Different Content: Implications for Teaching Comprehension and Composition

Introduction

Recent years have seen growing interest in studying the relationship between thought structures and language structure in discourse. Both linguistic/rhetorical and cognitive dimensions have received attention, the more so as interest in viewing reading and writing as interactive activities has grown. The two papers presented here focus on contrasting concerns. Schallert concerns herself largely with response to texts. She reveals not only present knowledge of domain-specific texts—including specific patterns of generalizations as well as linguistic structures—but also knowledge of how socio-personal factors influence reader perceptions. Calfee, in contrast, focuses mainly on the design of texts which in popular parlance are "user-friendly" and contribute to comprehensibility. He suggests important linkages between current studies of readability and modern rhetorical analyses of English prose. Indeed, Calfee suggests that lack of consideration of text may be at the root of current problems in tracking higher-order skills and processes in comprehension. He finds in such rhetoric suggestions for teaching children to comprehend texts. Both authors and both respondents note that present knowledge concerning the teaching and learning of narrative is far more widespread than knowledge of the teaching and learning of expository text.

Thought and Language, Content and Structure in Language Communication

Diane Lemonnier Schallert
University of Texas at Austin

All of the important problems associated with communication seem to be the result of an unalterable fact of human nature: we live alone inside our skin, with our thoughts, wishes, and feelings coursing through the shimmering mass of neural matter locked inside our skulls. When we formulate messages that we wish to express or actions that we need others to perform, we often choose to fashion our thoughts into language. The texts we produce act as road maps or recipes that others like us can use to reconstruct what they believe we intended. Thus we say that composing and comprehending are interpretive-constructive processes by which the inherently private thoughts that humans entertain can be recovered and shared (though the recovery is never perfect).

In this paper, I want to analyze the multidimensional relationship between content and structure in any communication act involving language. I will proceed by attempting to clarify what is meant by *content* and *structure* before discussing research findings that help elucidate how the two influence composition and comprehension. I will then close with my response to the charge that we identify critical gaps in our current understanding that we believe would benefit from systematic consideration.

Before dealing with the topic proper, I want to make explicit the theoretical propositions (or prejudices, if you will) that underlie my understanding. I will take as givens the following principles reflected in the current psychological and educational literature:

1. Reading is an activity that involves the coordination of interactive perceptual and cognitive processes, sharing the resources of a limited-capacity processor, with the goal of making sense of a message (e.g., Goodman 1967, Lesgold and Perfetti 1981, Roser and Schallert 1983, Rumelhart 1977).

2. Reading comprehension in particular is a meaning-making activity, a purposeful process by which a reader takes the print as clues for

reconstructing the author's message. Included in this view is the reader's apprehension of not only the sense but also the significance of the message (e.g., Anderson 1984, Goodman and Goodman 1979, Roser and Schallert 1983, Tierney and Pearson 1983).

3. Writing is on the one hand the reverse of reading—i.e., a process by which an author makes ideas explicit and renders them into text form—and, on the other hand, the same as reading—involving as it does the construction of meaning influenced by existing knowledge and salient goals for communication (e.g., Eckhoff 1983; Nystrand 1982; Olson, Mack, and Duffy 1981; Squire 1983; Tierney and Pearson 1983; Wittrock 1983).

4. For both reading and writing, theorists have been most interested in describing the underlying processes involved—exactly how we coordinate the subprocesses and respond to the constraints inherent in meaning making (e.g., Flower and Hayes 1981, 1984; Just and Carpenter 1984; Kintsch and van Dijk 1978; Matsuhashi 1982; McCutchen 1984; Scardamalia, Bereiter, and Goelman 1982).

5. The above interest has accompanied a new view of text. Texts are no longer taken as having single stable, correct meanings. Nor is the term *text* reserved only for external realizations of language extending beyond a sentence in length. Instead, *text* refers to language in use, printed or spoken, by an author with an authentic purpose. Texts can be of any length ranging from single words to whole volumes (e.g., Beaugrande 1982, Beaugrande and Dressler 1981, Nystrand 1982).

6. Reading and writing, like other communicative acts, are influenced profoundly by the social situation in which they occur. Thus, context, purpose, task, and social function are all relevant variables that will determine how composition and comprehension proceed and what form of text results (e.g., Bransford 1979; Faigley 1986; Gundlach 1982; Odell and Goswami 1984; Schallert, Alexander, and Goetz 1984; Wilkinson 1982).

Having made clear the theoretical approach I take to the processes of comprehension and composition, I am now ready to address the topic of structure and content in text.

Toward a Definition of Content and Structure

My goal in this section is to make clear how unclear is the distinction between content and structure and how intertwined are the two concepts.

My hope is that from such an appreciation we might develop better descriptions of how language participates in composition and comprehension processes.

The Content of Text

When we are talking about the content of a text, we are in fact using a shorthand phrase for referring to the topics, concepts, and relations in the minds of authors and readers as they meet each other through print. The "content of the text" refers both to the meaning that the author hoped to express and to the meaning that the reader will construct from the print. Thus there are at least two contents to any text—one in the sender's mind and one in each recipient's internal constructions of the text. Particular word choices and word orders, insofar as they act to invite the instantiation of particular concepts in the language users, become surface representatives of the text content.

There are a number of constructs that can be useful in characterizing further what we mean by content. For example, Nystrand's (1982) idea of "textual space" refers to the realized communication that is possible between a reader and an author. A text has meaning only insofar as it allows two people to communicate. "To speak of texts coming to life is to note that they are meaningful—not mere objects in the world as for nonreaders. They are intention-filled expressions of others in the world. To read is to dwell in textual space, to transcend the material text—seeing through this text to the 'expression of others' " (p. 82). As Nystrand adds, textual space is accessible to the degree that the language chosen by the author is transparent. Truly opaque texts remain objects that are unintelligible; that is, they do not allow us to make sense of them. In terms of our current consideration of the content of text, "textual space" refers to the field of constructs that an author wishes to explore. As with any terrain, the field is characterized by focus-ground distinctions. As the author focuses on some constructs, others recede in a continuous gradation to ground. Furthest from focus they melt into the sea of tacit knowledge from which explicated intentions and conceptions are formed.

Such a metaphor for the content of a text is also evident in current conceptions of coherence. As Beaugrande and Dressler (1981) define it, coherence "concerns the ways in which the components of the textual world, i.e., the configuration of concepts and relations which underlie the surface texts, are mutually accessible and relevant" (p. 4). A coherent text is one that allows us to build a sensible textual space, furnishing it with conceptual objects in particular configurations that make sense to us. So far, so good. The content of a text seems to be clearly distinct from its structure and comprises generally the concepts and relations between concepts that are the topic or point of the text. A first hint of trouble is evident when we begin to describe further what we mean by concepts. One popular notion (Anderson 1977, Rumelhart and Ortony 1977, Schallert 1982) is that explicit knowledge is made up of schemata: abstract *structures* that are interrelated and made up of subschemata. The subschemata represent variables that have different degrees of importance for instantiating the schema and that are themselves each associated with a range of typical values. (For example, one type of schema typically called a script has an important variable related to the order of events to be expected.) Further, nearly all schemata require particular configurations of instantiated variables. Two wheels, a tubular frame, pedals, and a seat must be in a particular relationship to each other before one is comfortable in calling the object a bicycle.

Thus, concepts are said to have form, which means that they are made up of elements in particular relationships to one another. Such configurations may influence the order or structure of attempts to communicate a particular conception. That this is so is evident in writers' reports of struggles to make texts follow one line of development when the topics seem instead to follow their own patterns. It is difficult to imagine a coherent text that is intended to describe a bicycle that would jump from spokes to handlebar covers to gear ratios. We know that such a text would be difficult to understand (Bransford and Johnson 1972).

The problem becomes immensely more complex when the topic of a text is some concept more complicated and abstract than a physical object. An example is the variety of informative texts students read in content-area classrooms. Though the knowledge the authors possess can still be described in terms of schemata, the whole complex of schemata that each domain expert can call upon is specifically shaped by the types of concepts and relations central to that domain. Thus in history, patterns of events that predict the rise and fall of nations are quite salient, and it is very difficult to find a history text that doesn't follow a chronology (i.e., later events being influenced by earlier events) and that doesn't mention wars (frequent proximal causes of rises and falls). At the same time it is easy to identify history texts that seem less successful than others in letting the reader understand the basic multidimensional causality that is the point of the discipline (Anderson and Armbruster 1984). Good historians have a chance of being good writers of history. Poor historians are doomed to write poor history.

The above description of the domain-specific organization shared by domain experts might encourage us to describe the structure of disciplines and to prescribe that texts be written accordingly. I do not believe that this would be fruitful. Though it may be true that domain experts agree on certain patterns of concepts, these seldom hold for more than rather circumscribed "areas," corresponding to no more than a subunit in a college-level textbook. This is what I found when looking through geology, history, biology, and psychology textbooks.

The variety among experts makes sense when one realizes that schemata are said to represent the momentary construction one has chosen from one's tacit knowledge. This idea is confirmed by the results of an intriguing study reported by Bazerman (1985). Physicists were observed and interviewed so as to reveal what influenced them in selecting what to read in their field. Though they were all likely to follow the same general rule (i.e., "I read articles that have titles that refer to constructs or that have authors I am currently interested in"), the particular words in titles that would trigger an individual to read further were very different. Bazerman describes their comments in words very similar to those describing the textual space introduced earlier: "The working physicist's map applied to his or her reading is a dynamic exploratory one built on the problems on which the field is working, the way the problems are being worked, and which individuals are working on what. . . . This map, moreover, is seen through the perspective of the reader's own set of problems and estimate of the best ways to solve these problems, so that the map changes as the reader's own problems and guesses about the best approach or technique change" (p. 10). Experts in a field, particularly those who are immersed in developing the field, vary tremendously in how they organize the field.

Instead of attempting to identify domain-specific patterns of organization to serve as the basis of new, improved textbooks, I recommend exploring a suggestion put forth by Bruner (1960). In talking about the structure of different subject matters, Bruner describes fundamental principles or ideas that allow one to relate many different phenomena within a discipline. In a sense, the structure he is describing is in fact a higher-level concept that represents a generalization of other concepts. Bruner recommends that experts identify a relatively small set of these fundamental ideas in their field and use them explicitly, clearly, and frequently when instructing nonexperts. Thus the lifelessness of textbooks that Crismore (1983) reports might disappear, as well as the sense that textbooks are more lists of facts compiled by committee rather than the excited messages of experts sharing a coherent view of their field.

Let us see where we are in our discussion of the content of text. We started out by considering what was meant by text content and determined that the label referred to the meanings authors and readers construct when involved in using language. Such meanings are often described as having structure. We then explored the issue of discipline-specific structure (note the singular form) and drew the conclusion that such a view used to prescribe the writing of content-area textbooks might not be as useful as Bruner's notion of fundamental ideas (concepts, once again) that represent important generalizations in a field. We are nearly ready to move on to a consideration of structure. There is one more confounding of structure with content that we need to mention first, however.

Not only does knowledge have structure, but authors and readers are said to have knowledge *of* structure. One example is the story schema that has been shown to predict the quality and quantity of comprehension of simple stories (Mandler and Goodman 1982, Stein and Policastro 1984). Another example comes from the Flower and Hayes (1981, 1984) models of the writing process. One important kind of knowledge authors are said to invoke is knowledge of writing plans. Another is knowledge of audience, by which is meant knowledge of what the intended audience knows and feels about the topic, as well as knowledge of the language that will work for that audience. Thus, in distinguishing structure from content, we must keep in mind the hybrid construct of knowledge of structure—of structural information now represented as content.

The Structure of Text

Generally when researchers from a psychological tradition refer to the structure of text, they mean the discourse-level plan or overall organization of ideas. Until fairly recently, and with some exceptions, views of these discourse-level plans were rather underdeveloped. If one were to characterize the early views, one would say that organization of text was seen as resembling the hierarchical structures of word-list experiments of the early fifties and sixties (e.g., Bousfield 1953, Tulving 1962), now extrapolated to the discrete concepts represented by sentences in texts. That such views were held makes sense when one considers the explicit interests, empirical tradition, and implicit theories of language held by many psychologists up until at least 1975. First, the focus was much more on memory and on the psychological consequences of information processing than on language per se. Language was of secondary interest, serving as a frequent but not special vehicle for presenting information to human processors. Second, a tradition existed of (*a*) rigorously controlling input materials used in experiments to prevent the influence of unaccountable individual differences and (*b*) unitizing the input to allow one to count discrete responses that could then be subjected to parametric statistical tests. Thus, materials were lists of sentences or very short artificial passages. Third, psychologists held an implicit theory of language that reflected vestiges of Chomsky's influence. Though the Chomskian focus on competence at the expense of performance was not in favor, still psychologists were suspiciously interested in the processing of *sentences*, not longer texts, and in informal features of the language, not in its pragmatic socio-functional features.

And so, conceptions of text structure were at first very simple in psychological literature. As I mentioned, there were exceptions. One example was the prolific work of individuals involved in developing a story grammar. As Kintsch (1982) recounts, psychologists were influenced by the work of linguists and anthropologists dealing with folk tales. What captured their interest was the thesis that a grammar complete with rewrite rules and transformations could be developed for stories just as had been done for sentences (Johnson and Mandler 1980, Mandler and Goodman 1982, Mandler and Johnson 1977, Rumelhart 1975, Stein and Glenn 1979, Thorndyke 1977). The crucial consequence of such a thesis was that the story grammar or structure was said to have psychological importance in guiding comprehension and production.

What happened next in the development of this idea is relevant to my point that structure and content are difficult to distinguish. A number of theorists such as Black and Wilensky (1979) and Black and Bower (1980) have argued that the idea of a story structure is superfluous in explaining how people understand stories. As they demonstrate, people must understand a story, i.e., determine the semantic relations that hold between the concepts mentioned, before they can identify parts of the story as examples of components of the story grammar. In order to understand the structural role that little Sambo's act of placing his grandmother's butter on his head plays in the story, one must know what is likely to happen to butter in the hot sun. Bruce (1980) has shown how crucial is knowledge of human goals, motives, and actions in explaining how we understand stories. Finally, there is a provocative study by Bisanz and Voss (1981) which demonstrates that young children who lack experience with certain motives construct much more simple narratives than older children reading the same story. Yet the narratives of both groups exhibit characteristics of good story form. Thus it seems that unless one can see that certain concepts being alluded to can fit into a story organization, they are not included in one's constructed understanding. It is concepts, then, that underlie the structure of stories.

Before leaving story structure, I want to mention one last point of view that I find particularly valuable in understanding how structure participates in language use. Kintsch (1982) presents a third position one can take in the controversy over the usefulness of the idea of story grammars. This is that a comprehender who held such a concept for the organization of a story would use it as he or she would any other schema to make predictions about the story being processed. Kintsch acknowledges the importance of knowledge of goals, plans, and actions. But, he adds, knowledge that one is dealing with a story "makes available to the comprehender (or producer of stories) an important set of story-specific problem-solving strategies. . . . Knowing what to expect helps in locating and identifying important pieces of information in the text. Knowing what sort of relations to look for in a story helps finding them" (p. 96). Thus story structure is not a characteristic of the text per se but is a concept that a language user possesses about the typical relationship between elements in a story.

One other example of psychological explanations of overall text types is represented by the work of Meyer (1975, 1977, 1984, 1985), who has extended conceptions of text structure beyond simple stories. Based on an adaptation of Grimes's idea of rhetorical predicates (1975), Meyer (e.g., 1985) classifies texts into five major categories: description, collection, causation, response, and comparison. These text types have been found to influence comprehension and production, as demonstrated by the degree to which the decomposed versions or unpacked hierarchies of each structure predict the recall of subjects. Though Meyer's work is generally considered seminal in the psychological literature, it is nevertheless criticized on the grounds that the texts subject to analysis are artificial. In particular, studies in which an attempt was made to hold content (topic) constant while structure was varied probably distorted typical language use to such a degree that their results should be considered cautiously. (I have, however, noticed that Meyer's latest text-structure manipulations leave the text much more natural.)

I have described what psychologists were generally doing with text structure up until very recently. In the meantime, what were reading researchers and educators saying? Two points need to be made. The first is derived from a comprehensive paper by Moore, Readence, and Rickelman (1983) on the history of content-area reading instruction. One main concern of reading educators over the years has been the balance to be struck between informational and literary passages when choosing materials for instruction. Though there have been many fluctuations, young readers have generally been provided literary passages (of more or less authentic literary value!), even though most of their reading then and later is of an informative sort. Second, a look at research studies that allude to different types of text reveals a simple binary classification scheme: texts are either narrative or expository. The major conclusions drawn from the implied comparison are not usually that people deal with the two types of text differently because of text *structure* elements.

Rather, the overriding conclusion is that readers learn less from, and do less well with, expository texts than with narratives. Quantity is stressed over quality. Similar variables such as background knowledge are said to influence the processing of the two kinds of text.

The conclusion I draw about the reading field's view of text structure is that it is remarkably similar to that of the psychology field. Though a transactional view of reading and of comprehension and production is espoused, and though the process is loudly touted to be influenced by the reader's and writer's contributions, the view of structure is most often insidiously reactionary. Structure is represented as being a characteristic of texts that exists apart from the people involved in producing and comprehending them. Furthermore, a relatively small number of variations are deemed important.

A more useful view of text structure, I argue, is available from modern rhetoric. As Faigley and Meyer (1983) tell us, the concern with text types in rhetoric has a 2,400-year history. Though there have been many fluctuations in how text types are portrayed, the major swings have gone from an emphasis on modes or forms to an emphasis on aims or purposes (Connors 1984, 1985). Modes—which traditionally distinguish between narration, description, exposition, and argumentation—represent the less helpful classification system. "The major objections to these four traditional 'modes' center on the confusion of the purpose of discourse with text type" (Faigley and Meyer 1983, p. 308). For example, argumentation might easily make use of narration, description, and exposition in order to serve the pragmatic aim of persuading the reader.

The emphasis on aims, by contrast, offers an intriguing view of text structure, one that fits better with our transactional description of language use. The best example is Kinneavy's (1971) system of discourse structure, which differentiates between texts in terms of their functions. These functions are based on the theoretical components of communication: the speaker/writer, the audience, the subject matter, and the text itself. On any occasion of communication, all four components exist, though one component is usually emphasized over the others. Thus, expressive text emphasizes the author; persuasive text emphasizes the audience; referential text emphasizes subject matter; and literary text emphasizes the text itself. In terms of influencing text production, it is the aim or purpose of the author that determines which concepts will be mentioned; how they will be tied together; what words will actually be used in the discourse; and how narration, description, classification, and evaluation will be combined. Most of all, it is the author's purpose that determines the point of the communication, the function that it is supposed to serve.

Thus, from rhetoric we have a view of structure that is based squarely back inside the heads of authors and speakers. Structure is represented not simply as concepts with parameters to be filled, but rather as guiding plans that determine the selection of concepts and of words to express them.

Gaps in Our Current Understanding and Future Directions for Filling Them

Based on my current understanding of how structure and concepts interact in composition and comprehension processes, I have three suggestions to make about the questions future work should address.

1. What are the fundamental understandings and conceptions of reality worth learning and writing about?

Let me admit from the start that I am not about to provide my own list of the great thoughts of human culture, or even of the fundamental concepts of the psychology of language use. I do believe that researchers interested in the language-cognition connection and, even more so, educators of all kinds, need to be concerned with getting discipline experts to identify important generalizations in their fields. It is interesting to me that as adults, when we have the freedom to choose, we typically read texts that say interesting things to us, that give us new insights and conceptions of our world. This is true even when we are not reading explanatory text. Similarly when we write, we choose what we struggle with to make clear a point we feel needs communicating. Students, on the other hand, particularly young ones, not only are told what to read and what to write about but they must suffer through texts and topics that are often bland compilations of ideas, devoid of significance and purpose. How much more careful should we be about choosing what people read and compose when they are "forced" to obey us!

2. How exactly does language get mapped onto thought, and most particularly, how do the actual words and surface orderings get chosen to render meaning?

Here I am asking about the lexicalization process. This particular problem is one I have alluded to but perhaps not directly enough. When we describe communication, we are referring to a four-part phenomenon. One component is the socio-functional system within which the communicants exist and which filters communication through the purposes and goals of the participants. The next three components are the author (speaker), the text, and the reader (listener). The problem with these components is that while two are quite similar (author and reader), the link between the two (the text) is of a different sort. A person has a point to make, a conception to express. That point or concept is a complex, multidimensional, nonlinear structure of ideas, colored by feelings and moved by intent. Now the person wants another person to entertain a similar conception, similar in its complex, multidimensional structure and "color." If the person chooses to communicate through spoken or written language, the conception must be squeezed into a sequential, one-unit-at-a-time system. Words must be expressed one after the other. The ideas of the author can never be presented holistically, capturing at once the complex web of their interconnections. The success of the transaction depends in large part on the particular words chosen—in other words, on the thought-language connections.

What is surprising to me is how little researchers have to say about how these choices are made. For example, the translating box in the model of the writing process of Flower and Hayes (1984) is uniquely empty. Another example is Kintsch's (Kintsch and van Dijk 1978) system of micro- and macro-propositions, which stops short of explaining how surface forms get turned into propositions in comprehension. A rare exception is McCutchen (1984), who argues that views of writing as a problem-solving activity have led to an emphasis on the planning component of the process. As she says, "Planning is certainly important in writing, but a well-planned text is not necessarily a well-written one" (p. 226). She recommends that we pursue writing as a linguistic activity, not solely as a cognitive one:

> Only so much planning of a composition . . . can be done in the abstract, even by skilled writers. Relatively early the writer is forced to define variables (i.e., to actually write a sentence or a few words), and this often occurs before every paragraph is fully planned. With such early constraints on variables, the writer loses the power of the hierarchical planners. The writer is forced, at some point in the actual generation of sentences, to follow the linearity assumption typical of nonhierarchical planners, choosing to begin with something and following it, sometimes to a preplanned next idea, sometimes to a newly discovered thought, and sometimes to a dead end. (p. 228)

McCutchen thus illustrates what she means by analyzing the protocols of writers in terms of the linguistic problems they express.

Though McCutchen is one person addressing herself exactly to my second question, I believe we need much more work in this area. One result I envision is a clearer idea of how surface language forms and the rules for their proper use are represented.

3. What do we mean by the "functional aspect of communication," and how do people's purposes and goals influence language use?

After all, language is a primary way for humans to locate themselves in social space. Here our analyses of language use might benefit from making clearer how people interpret their tasks as they communicate through language (Faigley 1986; Schallert, Alexander, and Goetz 1984). Bound up with context/task variables are ideas related to audience awareness and social cognition (Rubin 1984). And so, theoretical considerations of language use connect with the broader issues of personality, awareness, and the nature of the human condition.

As I see it, I have come full circle back to my first statement concerning our inherent aloneness and individuality. Before closing, I would like to say one more thing about the tension between *n*-dimensional thought and one-dimensional language. There is one great advantage to a system such as I have described. If we could communicate through a system that captured vertically the full conception we wanted to express, we could then transfer directly our thoughts into each other's heads. Gone then would be the problems of misunderstandings. Communicating would be like the copying of files in a word processor. Instead, we communicate through a system that forces us to make a myriad of choices both as we beat our conceptions into the linear rendering of language and as we construct conceptions from a linear-sequential recipe. The room for error in such a system is tremendous, and that is certainly not its great advantage. Rather, what satisfies my existential soul is the idea of the freedom and creativity that such a system necessitates.

References

Anderson, R. C. (1977). The notion of schemata and the educational enterprise. In *Schooling and the acquisition of knowledge,* edited by R. C. Anderson, R. J. Spiro, and W. E. Montague. Hillsdale, N.J.: Erlbaum.

——— (1984). Role of the reader's schema in comprehension, learning, and memory. In *Learning to read in American schools; Basal readers and content texts,* edited by R. C. Anderson, J. Osborn, and R. J. Tierney, 243–57. Hillsdale, N.J.: Erlbaum.

Anderson, T., and B. Armbruster (1984). Content-area textbooks. In *Learning to read in American schools: Basal readers and content texts,* edited by R. C. Anderson, J. Osborn, and R. J. Tierney. Hillsdale, N.J.: Erlbaum.

Bazerman, C. (1985). Physicists reading physics: Schema-laden purposes and purpose-laden schema. *Written Communication* 2: 3–23.

Beaugrande, R. de (1982). Psychology and composition: Past, present, and future. In *What writers know,* edited by M. Nystrand, 211–67. New York: Academic Press.

Beaugrande, R. de, and W. Dressler (1981). *Introduction to text linguistics.* London: Longman.

Bisanz, G. L., and J. F. Voss (1981). Sources of knowledge in reading comprehension: Cognitive development and expertise in a content domain. In *Interactive processes in reading,* edited by A. M. Lesgold and C. A. Perfetti. Hillsdale, N.J.: Erlbaum.

Black, J. B., and G. H. Bower (1980). Story understanding as problem solving. *Poetics* 9: 223–50.

Black, J. B., and R. Wilensky (1979). An evaluation of story grammars. *Cognitive Science* 3: 213–29.

Bousfield, W. A. (1953). The occurrence of clustering in the recall of randomly arranged associates. *Journal of General Psychology* 49: 229–40.

Bransford, J. D. (1979). *Human cognition: Learning, understanding, and remembering.* Belmont, Calif.: Wadsworth.

Bransford, J. D., and M. K. Johnson (1972). Contextual prerequisites for understanding: Some investigations of comprehension and recall. *Journal of Verbal Learning and Verbal Behavior* 11: 717–26.

Bruce, B. C. (1980). Plans and social actions. In *Theoretical issues in reading comprehension,* edited by R. Spiro, B. Bruce, and W. Brewer, 367–84. Hillsdale, N.J.: Erlbaum.

Bruner, J. S. (1960). *The process of education.* New York: Random House.

Connors, R. J. (1984). The rhetoric of explanation: Explanatory rhetoric from Aristotle to 1850. *Written Communication* 1: 189–210.

——— (1985). The rhetoric of explanation: Explanatory rhetoric from 1850 to the present. *Written Communication* 2: 49–72.

Crismore, A. (1983). Metadiscourse in social studies texts: Its effect on student performance and attitudes. Paper presented at meeting of the National Reading Conference.

Eckhoff, B. (1983). How reading affects children's writing. *Language Arts* 60: 607–16.

Faigley, L. S. (1986). Nonacademic writing: The social perspective. In *Writing in nonacademic settings,* edited by L. Odell and D. Goswami. New York: The Guilford Press.

Faigley, L. S., and P. C. Meyer (1983). Rhetorical theory and readers' classifications of text types. *Text* 3: 305–25.

Flower, L., and J. R. Hayes (1981). Plans that guide the composing process. In *Writing: The nature, development, and teaching of written communication,* edited by C. H. Frederiksen and J. F. Dominic, 39–58. Hillsdale, N.J.: Erlbaum.

——— (1984). Images, plans, and prose: The representation of meaning in writing. *Written Communication* 1: 120–60.

Goodman, K. S. (1967). Reading: A psycholinguistic guessing game. *Journal of the Reading Specialist* 4: 126–35.

Goodman, K. S., and Y. M. Goodman (1979). Learning to read is natural. In *Theory and practice of early reading,* Vol. 1, edited by L. B. Resnick and P. A. Weaver, 137–54. Hillsdale, N.J.: Erlbaum.

Grimes, J. E. (1975). *The thread of discourse.* The Hague: Mouton.

Gundlach, R. A. (1982). Children as writers: The beginnings of learning to write. In *What writers know,* edited by M. Nystrand, 129–47. New York: Academic Press.

Johnson, N. S., and J. M. Mandler (1980). A tale of two structures: Underlying and surface form in stories. *Poetics* 9: 51–86.

Just, M. A., and P. A. Carpenter (1984). Reading skills and skilled reading in the comprehension of text. In *Learning and comprehension of text,* edited by H. Mandl, N. L. Stein, and T. Trabasso, 307–29. Hillsdale, N.J.: Erlbaum.

Kinneavy, J. (1971). *A theory of discourse: The aims of discourse.* Englewood Cliffs, N.J.: Prentice-Hall.

Kintsch, W. (1982). Text representations. In *Reading expository material,* edited by W. Otto and S. White. New York: Academic Press.

Kintsch, W., and T. van Dijk (1978). Toward a model of text comprehension and production. *Psychological Review* 85: 363–94.

Lesgold, A. M., and C. A. Perfetti, eds. (1981). *Interactive processes in reading.* Hillsdale, N.J.: Erlbaum.

Mandler, J. M., and M. S. Goodman (1982). On the psychological validity of story structure. *Journal of Verbal Learning and Verbal Behavior* 21: 507–23.

Mandler, J. M., and N. S. Johnson (1977). Remembrance of things parsed: Story structure and recall. *Cognitive Psychology* 9: 111–51.

Matsuhashi, A. (1982). Explorations in the real-time production of written discourse. In *What writers know,* edited by M. Nystrand, 269–90. New York: Academic Press.

McCutchen, D. (1984). Writing as a linguistic problem. *Educational Psychologist* 19: 226–38.

Meyer, B. J. F. (1975). *The organization of prose and its effects on memory.* Amsterdam: North-Holland.

——— (1977). The structure of prose: Effects on learning and memory and implications for educational practice. In *Schooling and the acquisition of knowledge,* edited by R. C. Anderson, R. J. Spiro, and W. E. Montague. Hillsdale, N.J.: Erlbaum.

——— (1984). Text dimensions and cognitive processing. In *Learning and comprehension of text,* edited by H. Mandl, N. Stein, and T. Trabasso, 3–51. Hillsdale, N.J.: Erlbaum.

——— (1985). Prose analysis: Purposes, procedures, and problems. In *Understanding expository text,* edited by B. K. Britton and J. B. Black, 11–64. Hillsdale, N.J.: Erlbaum.

Moore, D. W., J. E. Readence, and R. J. Rickelman (1983). An historical exploration of content area reading instruction. *Reading Research Quarterly* 18: 419–38.

Nystrand, M. (1982). The structure of textual space. In *What writers know,* edited by M. Nystrand, 75–86. New York: Academic Press.

Odell, L., and D. Goswami (1984). Writing in a nonacademic setting. In *New directions in composition research,* edited by R. Beach and L. S. Bridwell. New York: The Guilford Press.

Olson, G. M., R. L. Mack, and S. A. Duffy (1981). Cognitive aspects of genre. *Poetics* 10: 283–315.

Roser, N., and D. L. Schallert (1983). Reading research: What it says to the school psychologist. In *Advances in school psychology,* Vol. III, edited by T. R. Kratochwill. Hillsdale, N.J.: Erlbaum.

Rubin, D. L. (1984). Social cognition and written communication. *Written Communication* 1: 211–45.

Rumelhart, D. E. (1975). Notes on a schema for stories. In *Representation and understanding,* edited by D. G. Bobrow and A. Collins. New York: Academic Press.

———— (1977). Toward an interactive model of reading. In *Attention and performance,* Vol. VI, edited by S. Dornic, 573–603. Hillsdale, N.J.: Erlbaum.

Rumelhart, D. E., and A. Ortony (1977). The representation of knowledge in memory. In *Schooling and the acquisition of knowledge,* edited by R. C. Anderson, R. J. Spiro, and W. E. Montague. Hillsdale, N.J.: Erlbaum.

Scardamalia, M., C. Bereiter, and H. Goelman (1982). The role of production factors in writing ability. In *What writers know,* edited by M. Nystrand, 173–210. New York: Academic Press.

Schallert, D. (1982). The significance of knowledge: A synthesis of research related to schema theory. In *Reading expository material,* edited by W. Otto and S. White. New York: Academic Press.

Schallert, D. L., P. A. Alexander, and E. T. Goetz (1984). Implicit instruction of strategies for learning from text. Paper presented at a conference on Learning and Study Strategies: Issues in Assessment, Instruction and Evaluation. College Station, Texas.

Squire, J. R. (1983). Composing and comprehending: Two sides of the same basic process. *Language Arts* 60: 581–89.

Stein, N. L., and C. G. Glenn (1979). An analysis of story comprehension in elementary school children. In *New directions in discourse processing,* Vol. 2, edited by R. O. Freedle, 53–120. Norwood, N.J.: Ablex.

Stein, N. L., and M. Policastro (1984). The concept of story: A comparison between children's and teachers' viewpoints. In *Learning and comprehension of text,* edited by H. Mandl, N. L. Stein, and T. Trabasso, 113–55. Hillsdale, N.J.: Erlbaum.

Thorndyke, P. W. (1977). Cognitive structures in comprehension and memory of narrative discourse. *Cognitive Psychology* 9: 77–110.

Tierney, R. J., and P. D. Pearson (1983). Toward a composing model of reading. *Language Arts* 60: 568–80.

Tulving, E. (1962). Subjective organization in free recall of "unrelated" words. *Psychological Review* 69: 344–54.

Wilkinson, L. C. (1982). Introduction: A sociolinguistic approach to communicating in the classroom. In *Communicating in the classroom,* edited by L. C. Wilkinson. New York: Academic Press.

Wittrock, M. C. (1983). Writing and the teaching of reading. *Language Arts* 60: 600–606.

The Design of Comprehensible Text[1]

Robert C. Calfee
Stanford University

In *Goodbye, Darkness,* William Manchester (1979) gives us the memoirs of his experiences as a Marine platoon sergeant in the South Pacific during the Second World War. At one level, the book is an engaging narrative, intense in its description of Manchester's experiences, terrifying in its portrayal of the insanity of war. At another level, it is a weaving together of history and autobiography, as the author places his individual experience within the broader context of global events. From yet another perspective, the book is a psychological exploration. The twenty-year-old Marine—naive, frightened, burdened with unexpected and unwanted leadership against forces unfamiliar and overwhelming, driven by the passionate idealisms of that time in American society—is drawn in contrast with the sixty-year-old author—haunted by memories that will not fade, distraught by a world under the threat of nuclear war (no "war to end wars" this time), feeling the onset of old age and the loss of hope.

So much for the content of the book. For Manchester, there was the technical chore of composing an essay that engages the reader at all of these levels. His goal was not only the working through of a personal need (the book was explicitly therapeutic in its intent) but the creation of an exposition that would communicate, that would share, and that would sell! Manchester uses a variety of devices to accomplish this task—for instance, in the juxtaposition of past, present, and future, one is reminded of *A Christmas Carol.*

Consider next the reader's response. On the one hand the text can be understood as an adventure story, grist perhaps for the screenwriter's

---

1. This essay is part of a longer paper that was prepared for the seminar. I have selected the portions of the original document that provide the theoretical foundation for studying the comprehensibility of a text. The original document also contained examples of the analysis sketched in this essay. A parallel paper provides a review of the literature on text comprehension. The lengthier treatment is available on request. In keeping with the purpose for which this paper is intended, I have kept references to a bare minimum.

mill *(Roots, Shogun, Thornbirds, Winds of War)*. It also provides a vicarious thrill, an entertaining collection of anecdotes, a diversion during the flight home. Or again, it might be assigned to a high school or college student for a book report—"summarize the main ideas, and prepare a critique."

I suspect none of these reactions is a good match with the author's intentions. Here we have a carefully constructed text, a complex inter-mingling of content and structure that, when thoroughly analyzed and reconstructed by the reader, leads to an experience paralleling the author's. By standing in his shoes (or boots) for a few hours, the reader gains a new perspective on the world. It is as though Manchester had learned from Mr. Spock how to "meld minds."

One can also examine Manchester's work—and the response of the reader—from various psychological perspectives. For example, how would the behaviorist describe what Manchester has done, and the reactions of different readers? Some behaviors are certainly observable, but it strikes me that to limit one's analysis to these is to leave the most interesting psychological questions untouched.

What about the information-processing psychologist? The model of the reader's experience would begin with the entry of letters into a short-term memory register, and would end (presumably) in the contact with larger schemata in long-term memory. Here the description of Manchester's activities might be a bit more problematic.

Finally, what about the curriculum expert? There appears to be notable variation in this field at present, so the response is a bit difficult to predict. On the one hand, terms like *main idea, inference, fact-versus-opinion,* and *character description* would probably be invoked. On the other hand, the book might wind up on California's list of "one hundred important literary works" which are to be read "in depth" (California State Department of Education 1985). Pursuing the comprehension of these works includes such activities as "comparing-contrasting, summa-rizing, drawing inferences, and making judgments." In any event, the focus would probably be on student activities rather than the nature of the text and the work of the author.

The Comprehension Problem

What I have been mulling over thus far is an approach to the topic of comprehension. By beginning with a "qualitative" account of my personal experience with a particular text, I have departed from the more popular contemporary approaches to research on comprehension, with the goal of laying a foundation for the material that follows.

Before getting to my main point, one more digression. As the heading suggests, we appear to have a comprehension problem today. To be sure, the water is rather muddy. Some experts (e.g., Farr and Fay 1982) have argued that reading achievement has not declined in this country, and may actually be on the rise. But others claim that America has too many illiterates. The causes for the problem are debated with great fervor. Some experts would handle the situation by a greater emphasis on phonics instruction—teach students to crack the code, and all will be well. Other experts see this "solution" as part of the problem—too much emphasis on "skills" has rendered reading a boring, meaningless, and unlearnable task.

Reports from the National Assessment of Educational Progress provide one of the few gauges we have to assess reading nationally. The picture from summary reports (NAEP 1981) is relative rather than absolute, but the picture emerging over the past decade or so is of a steady improvement in multiple-choice test scores in the primary grades for the most basic skills, coupled with a decline at the upper grades that is most pronounced in the more demanding tasks of comprehension and interpretation.

Durkin's (1979) classroom observations revealed little systematic instruction in anything that she could identify as comprehension. Durkin admitted to a problem of definition—what should she be looking for? Indeed, Hodges's (1980) critique of Durkin's work argued that she underestimated the amount of time spent in comprehension because she failed to include all relevant activities in her definition.

So we may have a problem. The difficulty in gaining a consensus from experts about the nature of the problem is rather disturbing. It may be that poor student performance reflects the uncertainty about what is to be taught, and that for this and other reasons students do not receive sufficient instruction in comprehension.

I will argue in this paper that we do have a problem—and a rather serious one. Moreover, I think that the lack of a clear definition may be largely at fault. But before rushing to recommend more time on comprehension objectives (or more comprehension questions on tests, or more staff development on comprehension objectives), I want to explore a facet of this topic that receives remarkably little consideration in the various debates—*the text*.

Research on text analysis has grown exponentially during the past decade or so (Meyer and Rice 1984). Several methods for analyzing texts now exist, for both narrative writing (Stein and Glenn 1979) and expository writing (Britton and Black 1985). Empirical research has begun to point to the textual factors that influence the comprehensibility of a passage, and we may even be approaching the time when text design can be grounded in both theory and data. In pursuing this goal, I will combine something old (the rhetoric), something new (cognitive psychology), and something borrowed (principles of experimental design). I have yet to find something blue.

Design and the Rhetoric

The primary purpose of this essay is to sketch a theoretical framework for thinking about the design of texts—more specifically, the design of texts intended for instruction. I will begin by considering what is entailed in creating a coherent design of any sort. Next I will discuss the application of the principles of the rhetoric as a basis for the design of school texts. This foundation will allow me to make some suggestions for creating narrative and expository passages for more effective comprehension instruction. It also generates a methodology for evaluating the passages in school texts. To the degree that these methods are persuasive, they have relevance for the design of texts in the future and for the training of teachers in text analysis. The paper ends with some speculations about these possibilities.

Principles of Design

According to Webster's, a *design* is "a mental project or scheme in which means to an end are laid down"; to design is "to conceive and plan out in the mind." As Simon (1981) notes, the preparation of a design is one of the key distinctions between the *natural* and the *artificial,* between those things that "just happen" and the artifices of humankind.

As I reflect on my past experiences, I see many ways in which design has intruded—sometimes without announcement (in childhood, erector sets, model airplanes, and crocheting), and sometimes quite explicitly (working with the builder on my first house, and the courses on experimental design in graduate school). What binds these experiences? What is the underlying concept? The dictionary definition is probably right as far as it goes, but it does not go very far. Simon is articulate and laudatory, and gives some helpful clues, but he does not attempt to conceptualize the term. Neither do the instructions to the erector sets nor the texts on experimental design make any such effort. Perhaps if I had become an architect . . .

In any event, during the past few years I have continued to grapple with the question "What is a design?" It now seems to me that all designs have three essential ingredients. First, you need *a set of fairly distinctive elements.* Simon refers to these as "nearly decomposable" components.

The elements may not be as separable as the parts of an erector set, but you can't prepare a design if the pieces are comprised of mush. Second, you need *something to link the elements,* something to hold the pieces together. Nuts and bolts do the job in the erector set; knots handle the task in crocheting. Third, there must be *an overall theme.* The young child hooking Lego blocks together at random is not working out a design.

A couple of parenthetic remarks: First, might not the theme itself comprise "the design"? I think not. Certainly we can find constructions that appear to lack any unifying theme, with results that are especially troubling to our aesthetic reasoning. The individual who begins a project without a theme is like the child linking a set of play blocks at random. On the other hand, a child may have a clear thematic vision and yet fail in the project because of a failure at the implementation stage, which relies on design principles to guide the transformation of a dream into a reality. Second, my examples have tended to be fairly physical. The fundamental tools of design (the elements and the methods of linking) need not be "concrete," however, and it makes sense to speak of a mathematician *designing* the proof of a theorem.

I have found this conception of design personally helpful over a range of situations, from Tinkertoys to factorial experiments. For example, one problem with courses in experimental design (based on the notes that I have taken and the courses I have taught) may be that they typically focus on the details of bolting one piece to another but have seldom tackled the more fundamental question "How do you *design* a research study?" The technical side is important, but technique without knowledge of the underlying mechanisms can lead to silliness.

The preceding remarks are primarily to set the stage for the discussion of text design that follows—they certainly do not provide a comprehensive exploration of the topic of design. One final conjecture merits comment, however, even in this limited treatment. *Good designs are simple.* Simon (1981) speaks to this point: any apparently complex entity can be represented by a small number of relatively separable elements, linked by sturdy (i.e., thematic) threads into a structure that is coherent.

It is interesting to speculate about the importance of simplicity in this context. Perhaps an evolutionary advantage accrues to the simple design (Simon seems to suggest as much at some places in his essay). Whether this conjecture is true, parsimony seems essential in many human enterprises (Peters and Waterman 1982); the limited capacity of our attentional focus ensures that any "complication" that cannot be *represented* (the key word) in a simple and parsimonious fashion will elude us. That is, if anything is represented to a human being in a truly complicated way, it will prove incomprehensive because of our limited capacity to deal with complexity (Calfee 1981).

The Rhetoric as a Basis for Text Design

It may seem strange to talk about "designing a text." Indeed, in none of the books on text research that are readily within my grasp do I find any reference to design (nor do most include *rhetoric* in the index). Designing, however, is a formal activity, requiring intention and forethought. If it is not talked about and made explicit, it is unlikely to happen.

I would argue that design is essential for composing textbooks, because the overriding goal in reading instruction is to help students acquire command of language as a formal system for thinking and communicating (Freedman and Calfee 1984). Natural language serves these purposes, but in ways that are uncertain and idiosyncratic, and which depend on local context and shared experiences to be effective. The natural tendency is to organize experiences; from repeated experiences in any situation comes the development of a prototype or schema. Visit a restaurant enough times and you will create an implicit mental structure that contains the basic features of the institution.

While these naturally formed images meet individual needs by organizing new experiences (through analogy and metaphor), they lack generality and they cannot be articulated (in current jargon, they have not attained a metacognitive level). This observation is not to depreciate the value of natural language capacities. To the contrary, these capacities make the difference between humans and other animals, and they retain their significance even when overlaid by more formal capabilities. As Kinneavy (1980) says, "No use of language is considered superior to any other. . . . Each achieves a different *and* valid purpose. . . . Persuasion is bad science, but good rhetoric; and science may be good reference discourse but bad literature" (p. 66). Indeed, the fully literate person not only has control—both natural and formal—over language, but has the good sense to know when each kind of control is appropriate. Don't lecture a friend when relaxing at a bar . . .

If students are to be taught to use language as a tool, so my argument goes, then it will be important to *design* a set of language experiences that highlight the dimensions of this technology. Presenting the material in the form of printed passages is a convenience for storing the information. In principle, there is nothing unique about the printed form, and a teacher could use properly designed experiences with spoken language to accomplish the same end. In fact, I would argue that, in comprehension instruction, well-designed discussion is an essential accompaniment to well-designed text. The *medium* can be important: the physical stability of the printed text makes possible analytic work that is difficult to parallel with more ephemeral speech. Likewise the *message:* what is being talked or written about does make a difference, especially in the later years of schooling.

What may be most critical in literacy, however, is neither the medium nor the message, but the *method*—the process used to analyze language. In natural language, these processes occur by happenstance. In formal language, they reflect methods shared by the literate community, methods that exemplify good design and a significant enhancement in intellectual power.

The foundational principles for the technical analysis of language are generally referred to as *the rhetoric.* This term, though it is most likely to show up as a term in freshman composition courses in college, has its etymological roots in the Greek art of oratory. Webster's gives as a meaning "the art of speaking or writing effectively." Brooks and Warren (1972) stress the same point:

> What is this course [on rhetoric] about? Is it concerned with punctuation, figures of speech, and participial phrases? Does it have to do with outlining themes, constructing topic sentences, and studying the principles of unity, coherence, and emphasis? Obviously the answer to these questions is yes. But such matters are not studied for their own sake. They are studied because they contribute to the effective use of language. (p. 5)

What is the substance of the rhetoric, and how does it provide a basis for text design? The history is fascinating. *Rhetors,* as they were called by the Greeks, were professional persuaders, trained in the principles of oratory. Corax, who produced one of the earliest rhetorics to survive (472 B.C.), divided the subject into five segments—poem, narrative, arguments, additional remarks, and peroration—that in combination yielded an appropriate speech. Aristotle later brought together the knowledge of his time, expanded it, and published the results in 322 B.C. His analysis, highly "scientific" in tenor, divided the rhetorical domain into three parts: deliberative, forensic, and epidictic. The first part had to do with the analysis of the object of presentation (invention), the second with the organization of the presentation, and the third with the character of the delivery (style). Aristotle's work superceded Corax and is viewed by many scholars as the basis for present-day treatments (and for psychological research on text; see Meyer and Rice 1984). Interestingly, Aristotle's highly analytic and formal approach was opposed in his own time by a large camp of orators who decried "scientific principles" and relied instead on intuition and "practice."

One of the handiest sources for studying modern rhetoric is a good text for the freshman course in composition. I cannot claim to have examined this entire genre, but I have relied on several texts recommended to me by colleagues. In Table TOC (see next page), I have placed the contents of three of these texts side by side to allow comparison. At first it may appear that they have little in common. Can the rhetoric serve as the basis for text design when it is apparently without any framework itself?

The fact that commonalities do not leap out from Table TOC, does not mean that there is no design. A design is a representation. Used to *create* an entity, it may or may not be obvious to the senses (just as the plumbing and air conditioning in a building may or may not be visible). Used to *perceive* an entity, it may or may not reflect the intentions of the creator. For instance, we can't be sure who or what was responsible for making turkeys. Nonetheless, if one is to handle the carving chores on Thanksgiving, it is important for the person handling the knife to have an adequate mental representation of the bird. The carver must, as it were, impose a design on the turkey.

Likewise, just because a design is not apparent in Table TOC does not mean that the authors did not have one in mind, nor does the appearance of variability mean that the different authors used different designs. Rather, it means that the reader must search for a representation meeting the criteria given earlier, one that brings order out of the apparent chaos.

This point has broad applicability. Here I am using it in an analysis of the rhetorical foundations of text design. It applies with equal force to analysis of the design for a particular text. Because the design of a text is not immediately obvious does not mean that no design exists. In a sense, the essence of comprehension is the search for a design. In some instances, the author will have created a structure that is clear-cut, in which case the informed reader has relatively little to do. (An important aside: just because the structure is clear-cut does not mean that all readers have the technical knowledge needed to handle the material.) In other instances, the design may be obscured, intentionally or otherwise. The reader then has a bigger job. Finally, there are instances in which a text may not possess any coherent design; some texts are simply badly written. The reader's task in such cases is difficult and may entail a virtual rewriting of the text, taking whatever cues may be available. (Some of my experiences with instructions for assembling computer hardware fall into this latter category.)

The Elements

In Table TOC, I do not find the task of representation especially difficult. What elements are available to the writer for composing a text? Certainly

Table TOC

Table of Contents from Three College Texts on the Rhetoric

Brooks and Warren (1972)	Baker (1977)	Perrin (1950)
PART ONE: MAKING A BEGINNING	THESIS	THE ACTIVITY OF WRITING
Language, thinking, feeling, and rhetoric	STRUCTURE (Beginning, middle, end)	VARIETIES OF ENGLISH (Formal vs. colloquial)
The problem of making a beginning (The subject; the divisions)	PARAGRAPHS	
	DESCRIPTION, NARRATION, PROCESS	PROBLEMS IN ENGLISH GRAMMAR
Organizing the composition		
	EVIDENCE	GOOD ENGLISH (Appropriateness to situation and audience)
PART TWO: THE FORMS OF DISCOURSE	WRITING GOOD SENTENCES	
The main intention (form and function)	CORRECTING WORDY SENTENCES	PUNCTUATION AND OTHER CONVENTIONS OF WRITING
Methods of exposition (identification, comparison, etc.)	WORDS	
		SPELLING
Argument	RESEARCH	
Persuasion	THE HANDBOOK (Grammar, verbs, pronouns, modifiers, punctuation, usage)	WRITING PARAGRAPHS
Description		KINDS AND QUALITIES OF PARAGRAPHS
Narration		
PART THREE: SPECIAL PROBLEMS OF DISCOURSE		SENTENCE FORM
The paragraph and the sentence		QUALITIES OF SENTENCES
Diction (Words: general and specific, formal and informal)		THE MEANINGS OF WORDS
Metaphor		QUALITIES OF WORDS
Tone and other aspects of style		THE REFERENCE PAPER
PART FOUR: THE RESEARCH PAPER		

the most fundamental answer to this question is *words,* the topic of one or more chapters in each of the textbooks. A second elemental basis is *the sentence,* again found in one or more chapters. The third building block is *the paragraph,* which I think has some characteristics in common with the sentence, though it is generally treated as a separate topic. Finally, there is *the text* itself. It may seem strange to talk about "the text" as a building block for composing, but texts of any significant length generally prove to be combinations of more basic subtexts.

Each of these elements is separable from the others, in the sense that they comprise unique sets of subcategories and analytic tools. These properties are the key to understanding the advantages of separability.

Consider the domain of *texts,* for example. Each textbook addresses this issue at some point, and the taxonomy is reasonably similar over the three. Brooks and Warren are "out front" in their presentation. Under "Forms of Discourse" they list four main types of texts, with emphasis on the classical areas of *argument* and *persuasion.* Baker is equally obvious, listing *description* and *narration* in common with Brooks and Warren, adding the category of *process,* and leaving out *argumentation.* Perrin "hides" the topic under the heading "Kinds and Qualities of Paragraphs," where he discusses *narration* and *description* (which are more typically considered texts rather than paragraphs), along with *supporting* and *climax* paragraphs (which are more paragraphic in function).

For better or worse, these textbooks (and most others) leave some work for their readers in organizing the concept of text genre. I have argued elsewhere (Calfee and Curley 1984) that there are three basic genres—description, sequence, and argument-persuasion—each of which can assume a more or less natural or formal appearance. Thus, many narratives can be viewed as a relatively natural sequential portrayal, whereas the operation of a four-cycle engine requires a more formal treatment of sequence.

To view text genre in this way is to emphasize the *design aspects* of the topic. I realize that this is not the perspective of many textbook writers, but it may serve a useful purpose for those who are interested in schooling. As an aside, let me suggest that this perspective may reflect movement toward an integration of cognitive psychology and the elements of curriculum and instruction (Calfee 1981).

Problems for the reader also arise when the writer intermingles subcategories from different domains—whether in the pursuit of understanding the design of a composition textbook or in understanding a text on some other topic. Perrin "intermingles" when he treats text types under the heading of paragraphs. To be sure, a text may occasionally comprise a single paragraph, for example, the writer introduces a brief description or characterization in the midst of a larger text, or the elementary student writes a one-paragraph story. Nonetheless, good design probably separates form and function, in the sense of not confusing one for the other. The paragraph is a formal entity in writing: my dictionary suggests that it is a division of a composition that expresses a thought relevant to the whole but which is complete in itself. It is, however, distinct from the text as a whole.

Linkage

Each of the textbooks in Table TOC also addresses the issue of linkage. For the text as a whole, the most fundamental issue is the serial arrangement—how to begin, the "middle game," and how to conclude. In one of the simplest constructions—the "five-paragraph" system often taught in high school—the structure consists of an opening, three main points, and a closing. In more complex passages, the writer is still advised to begin with an overall arrangement comprising a relatively small number of discernible topics, each of which may then be subdivided into a relatively small number of subtopics, and so on.

The writer is directed next to the paragraph level. Here the textbooks discuss a variety of paragraph types, each designed to serve particular functions within the larger structure of the text. Some paragraphs are designed to give an overview, others to summarize; transitional paragraphs help the reader move from one segment to the next in a passage. Within a paragraph, the linkages depend in part on the function of the paragraph. Most composition textbooks deal with this matter quite explicitly, presenting examples of how to begin and end the paragraph and describing the use of devices such as "signal words" that help the reader move from segment to segment within the paragraph.

The basic element for creating a paragraph is the sentence. Natural sentences differ in several ways from those in formal writing. The latter are also built of words, to be sure, but there is extensive use of clauses and phrases to modify and to show relations. In a sense, one of the most important features in the design of written sentences is again the use of linking devices—prepositions, relative pronouns, conjunctions, and punctuation.

The Theme

Finally, each textbook gives considerable attention to the thematic substance of a composition. Brooks and Warren talk about "making a beginning," in which they discuss the importance of framing a topic that makes sense to the writer. Baker also introduces the notion of a thesis: find your thesis, sharpen your thesis, believe in your thesis.

> You can usually blame a bad essay on a bad beginning. If your essay
> falls apart, it probably has no primary idea to hold it together. . . .
> The central idea, or thesis, is your essay's life and spirit. If your
> thesis is sufficiently firm and clear, it may tell you immediately how
> to organize your supporting material. . . . If you do not find a thesis,
> your essay will be a tour through the miscellaneous. (p. 2)

Perrin speaks to this issue under "The Activity of Writing," in which he
discusses how to focus on a subject.

There is no substitute for "the beef" in writing. In composition
instruction, numerous observers have commented about the emphasis on
the technical side of writing (grammar and punctuation) to the neglect
of methods for thinking about the topic. Students may need explicit
instruction in the *tools of thought.* As Kinneavy has noted, "The
segregation of thought from expression by the exile of logic, dialectic,
and rhetoric from the field of English is probably the most serious defect
of the present composition situation in both college and high school"
(1980, p. 32). I am tempted to address this issue at greater length, but
will leave it for another time. Suffice it to say that without a substantive
and reflective thematic core, rhetorical methods come to naught. This
problem appears most pressing in the so-called content areas of social
studies and science, where students are typically presented with large
quantities of unadorned and unorganized facts. A thematic core is
generally hard to identify. The problem appears in a different guise in
materials for the elementary grades.

None of the composition textbooks gives much attention to a matter
that many of us would consider a significant part of the development of a
theme—a *sense of audience.* To be sure, there is some truth to the notion
that the writer is his or her most important audience (Zinsser 1980). If
you, the composer, do not feel interest in the topic, then the result is
likely to be hackneyed and dull for most audiences. Nevertheless, the
writer is well advised to consider the readers: what is their background,
why should they want to read the passage, what are their literary skills?

Application of Rhetorical Principles to Text Design

In this section, I will explore how the rhetorical analysis of passages that
is described above can yield strategic approaches for use in comprehension
instruction. In this task, the goal is more than a set of prescriptions for
"good writing." Rather, the aim is to consider the nature of materials
that will help the student to move from the natural processes of
understanding to the formal techniques of comprehension.

This section covers four topics. First are considerations of simple texts
and more complex combinations of the basic building blocks. Next is a
discussion of the canonical structures that comprise the "middle" portion

of a complex text. Finally is a presentation of methods for the rhetorical analysis of a text; these methods, admittedly still in preliminary form, have nonetheless proven useful to me as frameworks for training teachers in text analysis and for aiding students in handling complex passages.

Simple Texts

It is important at the beginning to distinguish between *simple* and *complex* text structures. A simple text will be defined as one with a single generic structure, whereas a complex structure is one that combines two or more text components.

A simple narrative, for instance, consists of the bare bones of a story-grammar structure: a setting, one or more episodes, and a resolution. Bare bones though it may be, the structure should nonetheless be complete and coherent. Experts may disagree about certain details of proper story grammar, but for the tale without ending or resolution, where the problem or reactions are missing or scrambled, one need not be an expert to sense that something is wrong with the overall structure.

Story fragments, for instance, generally strike the reader as unsound. The listener's response in natural settings is straightforward enough. Suppose you enter during the middle of a personal tale; you may be confused, but you can usually ask for context. In writing, and more generally in the formal texts used for teaching comprehension, the passage should be sufficient to carry the message in the absence of interactions with the author. It is the essence of formal language (whether as utterance or text) that the presentation is sufficiently explicit to carry its own weight, given the author's assumptions about the audience. The young student's introduction to the comprehension of formal texts, usually in the form of narratives, should presumably be based on passages of transparent clarity, completeness, and coherence.

Present reality is unfortunately not up to this standard. Primary grade texts, because of assumptions about the limited decoding skills of students, often provide only shadowy glimpses of the total discourse, relying on the accompanying pictures to support understanding. Also in the effort to reduce the decoding demands, these passages often use sentence structures that challenge the beginning reader because of their incompleteness and unfamiliarity.

As the teacher of beginning readers, I would expect to find in a simple narrative a bare-bones structure with clear signals in the paragraphs and sentences about the major elements of the text, with complete and appropriate sentences, and with simple but proper word choices. Given that my concern is to help a child learn techniques for *comprehending* the text, then decoding difficulty and sentence length will be a minor consideration. Rather, I want a story in which the structure is simple and obvious, so that extracting the basic plot is an easy task. The content of the narrative should be familiar, interesting, and "comfortable." These characteristics of the tale allow me to concentrate my attention (and that of my students) on processes for analyzing the text and on the structure revealed by the application of these processes.

I would make a similar request for simple types of text other than the narrative. At first glance this request might seem unreasonable—the number of "models" might be too great. In fact, if my analysis of the rhetoric is valid, the number of distinctive text genres is not great. The division by Calfee and Curley (1984) into sequential, descriptive, and argumentative provides a basic framework. Each of these genres contains in turn a relatively small number of subcategories. Descriptive writing, for instance, appears to include the following distinctive subtypes: definition, illustration, comparison and contrast, classification, and analysis. One might argue about how to refine these categories (each is described in the composition textbooks listed earlier), and one or two additions might prove desirable. Nonetheless, the list does not boggle the mind by its extent or complexity. Incidentally, although the literature suggests that there is a single "grammar" for narratives, I suspect that there are actually a small number of distinctive subtypes within this genre (e.g., the adventure, the fairy story, the fable).

A simple descriptive text features a structure that clearly exemplifies one subtype. Writing within such tight structural constraints requires care, but we have identified models that show it can be done. To begin with, the reader should be given clues during the introduction of the passage about the structural approach being taken:

Comets are among the more unusual of heavenly bodies.

Mermaids appear in legends from around the world.

Chicks and ducklings—how are they the same and how are they different?

The introduction should be followed by a small number of elements that fulfill the introductory statement. The finale should restate the original theme. This organization comprises the essence of exposition: "Tell what you are going to say, say it, then tell what you have said." The model for the primary grades may not excite the creative writer, but it can serve an important function for comprehension instruction:

Today we traveled. First we rode in a van. Then we went in a truck. After that we got on a train. We had a lot of rides.

In recommending simple, streamlined texts, I am not arguing that they necessarily comprise the best writing for all occasions. Rather, the point is that they can serve an important role in introducing the reader to the basic rhetorical building blocks used to create more complicated passages.

Complex Texts

Most writing (and talking) is structurally complex. The reason is that most of the topics that interest us are multifaceted. Structure follows purpose. The person who constructs a model of the Empire State Building from a Lego set must deal with a complicated topic; the building blocks are nonetheless individually simple. (The analogy is actually misleading. What is relevant is the ability of the constructor to divide the Empire State Building into a set of subcomponents that can in turn be subdivided into sub-subcomponents, down finally to the level of the block).

Goodbye, Darkness illustrates the point. Manchester's opening (labeled "Preamble") is a prototypical narrative setting:

> Our Boeing 747 has been fleeing westward from darkened California, racing across the Pacific toward the sun, the incandescent eye of God, but slowly, three hours later than West Coast time, twilight gathers outside, veil upon lilac veil.

The construction of the sentence and the choice of words show numerous instances of rhetoric at work. My present purpose is to note the "once upon a time" character of the lines. We are off on an adventure.

In the next two sentences, without a break in the paragraph, Manchester switches style:

> This is what the French call *l'heure bleue*. Aquamarine becomes turquoise; turquoise, lavendar; lavendar, violet; violet, magenta; magenta, mulberry.

This handful of words shifts the informed reader to an expository palette; again, sentence structure and word choice mesh to the purpose, a steady progression of color, with other senses (lavendar and mulberry) adding to the intensity. Is this text a happy accident of free association? Probably not.

As the page unfurls before the reader, Manchester continues to reminisce: "Old memories, phantoms repressed for more than a third of a century. . . . " Some seem pleasant, as "the rhythm of surf on distant snow-white beaches." But, without a break in the paragraph, our passenger-author moves to "one of my worst recollections . . . back with a clarity so blinding that I surge forward against the seat belt. . . . "

Against this shifting and moody backdrop, Manchester frames his second paragraph: a single stark line:

> I am remembering the first man I slew.

And so the tale is on its way. The several hundred pages that follow continue with a mixture of styles and devices. To the reader who can track the movements, the writing is marvelously constructed. For Manchester to have restricted himself to a "plain" autobiography would have probably failed his purpose. Complexity intrigues and attracts partly through novelty, but even more so when the viewer can trace the design underlying the text.

And therein lies the key to the comprehension of complex passages. Students need to learn to read not only the simple texts that model the basic building blocks of the rhetoric. They also need to study the more complex texts that do full justice to more complex topics. For instruction, however, these passages should be well-designed to illustrate the way that the author uses the various elements and links them together, such that when the whole is comprehended the student can grasp the theme as it was construed by the author. There is a big difference between a complex but well-crafted text and a passage that is simply messy.

What does one look for during an analysis of the structure of text? To remind you, my test in this chapter is from the student's perspective: can I as a beginning reader easily "unpack" the text into chunks that are *topically and structurally distinctive*? My focus here is on structural clarity and coherence; a subject-matter specialist would have to confirm that the topic of the passage has also been appropriately represented.

In examining a passage, I have found that a relatively simple approach works with certain passages. These are the ones that I would recommend for comprehension instruction. First, the opening segment of the passage gives a clear message about the main topic and overall structure. Second, the ending segment provides an equally clear resolution or summary. Between the opening and the closing, the reader can easily divide the text into a small number of chunks that are, again, topically and structurally distinctive. The main work of comprehension comes in the "middle game," to which I turn in the segment below.

Before proceeding, however, let me reemphasize the importance of establishing the overall structural form at the outset of a passage, whether the text be simple or complex. The beginning reader should not be left uncertain about the genre. Most of the reading selections that I have examined are reasonably direct when presenting the narrative form: the "Once upon a time" introduction of a setting is readily apparent in such texts, at least those from the second grade and afterward. Similarly, the "happy ending" expected by most students is in fact characteristic of virtually all stories in basal series. Problems are more likely to occur in expository passages, both in reading series and in content-area texts. These passages often begin and end in a confusing manner, with a variety of genres in between, and sometimes even varying from sentence to sentence within a paragraph. The result is almost certain to pose a challenge in interpretation for both students and teacher.

The comment above about topical and structural distinctiveness seems important to me, given my review of textbook passages. A switch in text genre is seldom an accidental matter. In most instances, the author wants to address a subtopic, expand a point that is incidental to the main theme, or illustrate a concept that would otherwise remain abstract. For maximum effectiveness, the text should provide clear signals about these departures from the main theme. Even so, one must assume that the reader knows how to use these signals or is in an instructional situation where guidance is provided to help the reader in detecting and applying the cues. Most of this action takes place between the beginning and the end of the passage.

Structure in the Middle of a Text

Writing, like a speech, is inherently linear. Word follows word in sequence, and likewise sentences, paragraphs, chapters, and so on. Hence the emphasis in composition books on beginning, middle, and end. Unlike speech, however, print allows both the writer and the reader to escape from a strictly straight-line progression. The author does not even have to present the introduction first nor the conclusion last, though that is my recommendation about texts designed for the early stages of comprehension instruction.

What about structural considerations for the middle of a text? The answer depends to a degree on the primary genre. For a narrative, the series of episodes is the primary determinant of the middle structure. In *The Three Billy Goats Gruff,* for instance, the division into the three crossings can be identified by most first graders. In many trade book versions of this tale, this division is supported by other textual devices: each crossing occupies one or two separate pages with accompanying pictures. The stories in basal series are sometimes "marked" in this fashion, but not always. Thus, one may find the first sentence or two of a new episode tagged onto the bottom of a page; it appears that typographic considerations may outweigh the need to give definite clues about the partitioning of the text along structural lines. Basal texts seldom direct the student's attention to the structural features of a passage, and so the absence of marking devices is consistent with the pedagogy—unfortunately so.

Within the narrative form, the author may switch to another genre for elaborative purposes. Such switches are often marked by paragraphing. Thus, the writer may pause in the midst of a story to paint a descriptive picture of the surroundings, or to enter a character's mind to show the working out of a problem or reflections on a situation. For comprehension instruction, it is helpful if such digressions are clearly identified, and if the genre within a given paragraph is consistent. To be sure, this advice is often "broken" in literary works: in the example from Manchester presented earlier, the first paragraph was a mixture of styles—partly narrative, partly descriptive, partly historical, tentative as to tone. The mixture serves Manchester's purpose, but it puts a burden on the reader and is not a passage suitable for the beginner.

In expository writing, the author has a much freer palette, which can be either blessing or curse. In my examinations of textbook examples, I find that most non-narrative passages comprise a melange of styles and topics, varying from paragraph to paragraph, and without any clear markers to guide the reader. The result is that the reader winds up with a structureless list of items, which overwhelms short-term memory and provides little guidance for retrieval of the information.

The structural considerations in the middle of a text are determined to some degree by the author's decisions about the basic rhetorical structure—definition, illustration, comparison, process, and so on. These in turn may be shaped by the topic under consideration. The latter is often of secondary importance in passages in basal readers, but may be critical in content-area texts.

Beyond the standard rhetorical structures, I think that four primary arrangements of information can account for most cases. Figure STR (see next page) shows these four in diagrammatic form. Two of them— the *topical net* and the *linear string*—are fairly primitive. The natural tendency to cluster frequently co-occurring associations is the basis for the topical net. Suppose you ask a person to think about the words/ images that come to mind in response to a term like *dog;* the task can be easily performed if the word is commonplace, and with a high degree of predictability in the associations. In particular, most of the words will be "first-order" associations, fairly directly linked to the original stimulus word.

The linear string is also a familiar structure. Perhaps because time is such an important dimension in our lives, we have little trouble remembering a temporal sequence—as long as there is a meaningful link from one item to the next and the list is not too long. The narrative form can be thought of as having a list structure, in most instances. If meaningful links do not exist, then repeated experience or practice on the sequence is essential: it takes quite a few repetitions of the "ABC" song before the child masters the order.

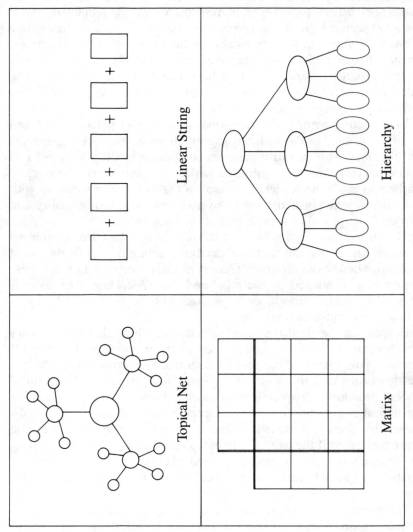

Figure STR. Basic structures for mid-text exposition.

The *matrix* and the *hierarchy* are the structures most formalistic in character, and they require instructional guidance. These two arrangements may be less natural, but it appears that they are critical tools for topical analysis in most of the content areas: again and again in the social and physical sciences, one finds instances in which the products of analysis are expressed in one or the other of these two forms, or in various combinations thereof.

Here again the notion of design comes to bear. The easiest way to construe the structures in Figure STR is as patterns for linking elements to serve some thematic purpose. They are building blocks that can be hooked to one another to generate larger structures of unlimited complexity. For the designer and for the comprehender of a design, it continues to be important that the complexity be separable at each level into a small number of relatively independent components. *Small* in this instance probably means Miller's (1956) "magical number 7 +/− 2."

Hence my recommendations for creating the middle portion of a text designed for comprehension instruction. First, the author should clearly establish the overall structural form of the passage. The number of distinctive elements in this structure should be limited—no more than five to nine segments, depending on the familiarity of the topic. The text should be organized around this structure, with departures clearly marked and for an obvious purpose.

At several points I have talked about "marking." It seems to me that textbook passages are especially flawed in this respect. In the "real world," most writing makes extensive use of markers to the structure. Long narratives are divided into chapters, often with a chapter title. Within a chapter, episodes are often marked by extra spaces or a "super capital" letter at the beginning of a paragraph.

In expository writing, the technical character of the topic and the variety of structures available to the writer increase the need for clear markers to the structure. Headings are especially important for this purpose. In some domains of technical writing, the basic headings are determined by longstanding convention; reports of empirical research in the behavioral sciences illustrate this point. More often, it is up to the author to decide on a skeletal framework for the passage. Unfortunately, headings are absent in many of the expository passages found in basal series, and the headings in content-area texts often present a confused and idiosyncratic character—reflecting an underlying incoherence in the material.

Technical writing can also be supported by a variety of other marking devices, including "boxes," figures, tables, and graphs. The importance of cogent overviews and summaries should not be underestimated. The goal is, in a sense, to help the reader "see" as well as "read." This aim is most easily realized when the topic is simply represented and clearly marked.

A Methodology for Text Analysis

Theory is a good starting point for solving problems, but translation into practice is also important. How can the ideas sketched in the preceding sections be put into a practical format? I have wrestled with this question over the past several years, and while much work remains ahead, I think we are converging on a set of techniques that can be implemented in a variety of settings while preserving the underlying principles of the rhetoric.

Before proceeding, let me set this activity in juxtaposition to other ongoing work in text analysis. In doing so, I will rely on Rumelhart's (1977) distinction between *bottom-up* and *top-down* processes in comprehension. Bottom-up processes emphasize working from details to overall structure, whereas top-down models impose overall structure as a framework for organizing details. Both processes are undoubtedly important to the reader, each in its own proper place.

Most current work on text analysis by psychologists focuses on the bottom-up aspects of comprehension, aspects that I would identify as important for the comprehension of sentences and paragraphs, but of less utility in the comprehension of complete texts. For instance, in Britton and Black (1985) all of the analytic systems presented for explanatory (i.e., expository) text take the *proposition* as their point of departure (a proposition is an *idea unit*, usually a sentence or less). These systems have their origin in the work of Crothers (1972), Frederiksen (1972) and Kintsch and van Dijk (1978), among others. All begin with analysis of the microstructure of a passage, and then work toward a macrostructural representation. Without making any claims about the relative merits of different approaches, let me simply note that the approach in the present paper begins with a search for a macrostructural representation, based on an analysis of introduction, summary, and headings, and followed by an examination of paragraphs. Seldom do I resort to looking at sentence or subsentence units.

My presentation to the Mid-Decade Seminar included a number of examples of such a top-down analysis of passages from basal readers and content-area textbooks. I will comment only that these examples represented a first effort to look at a variety of texts from the primary through the secondary grades using a macrostructural perspective, working mostly with the paragraph as the smallest unit of analysis. This analysis revealed a wide variety of styles and a predominance of complex texts—some for the better and some for the worse. Narratives tended to come off reasonably well; exposition was notable for its lack of coherence.

In a project with a local high school, I have taken a different tack toward rhetorical analysis. The focus for the remedial students with whom I am working begins with their book reports. One task assigned to these students is to prepare a book report once a month. They begin by selecting a book from the library—almost always a paperback narrative. After reading the book, they write a report. We found that the students tended to read the text in a "natural fashion"; lacking any analytic tools, they began at the beginning and continued to the end. At that point, they were then suddenly faced with the challenge of organizing a report.

To aid them in this effort, we designed the Story Notes form shown in Figure SN (see next page). This form, which is built upon the major elements that comprise a book-length narrative, is for the purpose of guiding the student during the reading of the text to organize the information along lines suggested earlier. *Setting* (where, when, conditions, the overall problem), *characters, plot,* and *resolution* are the structural elements highlighted in this method.

The process is fairly straightforward. The students are given direct instruction in the basic elements; they analyze sample stories according to this framework; and then are encouraged and supported to use the format when reading other narrative texts. The importance of limiting the number of significant events is stressed: not everything that happens in a story is equally important.

The Story Notes were designed with a specific goal in mind, but the approach has broader applicability. In particular, it provides a methodology for critical analysis of a wide variety of narrative passages. The process requires some modification if the goal, for example, is to assess the opportunities for instruction provided by a particular passage. A teacher might be interested not only in the general structural characteristics of the narrative, but also in the digressions (a particularly well-written descriptive segment, or samples of word usage that merit attention).

The process, as we have used it, operates in the following fashion. We begin with the assumption that the reader (student, teacher, or researcher) has a structural model in mind; the individual knows what he or she is looking for. In addition, we assume that if the setting, major characters, and primary problem are not immediately apparent at the outset of a story, then something is wrong with the passage. Once these basic elements are established, the reader looks for the big chunks: story-grammar concepts suggest that the reader should examine each episode

STORY NOTES

How does the story begin? (setting, time)

Who are the main characters? (briefly describe)

What is/are the main problems or conflicts to be solved?

The Plot: (use abbreviations to label information: p = problem/ r = response/
            a = action/ o = outcome)

#1 _____

_____

#2 _____

_____

#3 _____

_____

#4 _____

_____

#5 _____

_____

#6 _____

_____

How does the story end? (resolution)

Other remarks? (e.g., use of description)

Figure SN. Form for text analysis of a narrative passage.

for a problem, a response by the protagonist, and an outcome. The resolution is generally rather obvious; the critical reader may also inquire into the *point* of the tale. Some stories are for entertainment only; others entail a moral.

Examination of an expository passage proceeds in a similar fashion, with a few significant variations. A form for analysis of an expository passage is shown in Figure EXP (see next page). As can be seen, the categories of analysis are different from those for stories. In addition, the sequence is different. One does not ordinarily leap to the end of a story; it spoils the fun. On the other hand, checking the end of an exposition makes a great deal of sense. Headings in a narrative are uncommon; in an exposition, they should be available to guide the reader in organizing the material. Pictures for a narrative are more often decorative; figures and tables can be critical elements of an exposition, however, without which the text may be incomprehensible.

The method of expository analysis thus proceeds more or less as follows. First establish that you are dealing with an exposition. Since expository material is not uncommonly embedded in a narrative frame, this decision may not be a simple one. Second, check the beginning and the end of the text for hints about topic and structure. Third, look for headings and other markers of the primary elements of the middle of the text. Finally, proceed through each paragraph of the text, searching for the major point of the paragraph and the relation of the paragraph to what precedes and to the overall structure of the text (digressions do occur in expository writing). The form in Figure EXP is designed to facilitate recording the analysis—assuming the text is well-written and coherent. It is hard for me to imagine a process or a form that will handle the task of analyzing a poorly crafted text.

Implications

As noted at the beginning of this essay, the work described herein is preliminary. Nonetheless, I think that some fairly straightforward suggestions spring from the analysis. I have not made much effort to relate the material to the empirical research on comprehension, but the investigation does build on a tradition of trustworthy scholarship.

At the same time, the recommendations are subject to some caveats. First, it would be informative to have a broader empirical research base on (*a*) the effect of text structure on comprehension and (*b*) the effect of training in rhetorical techniques on comprehension. We have the beginnings of such a research base, but the texts and the training have tended

EXPOSITORY TEXT ANALYSIS NOTES

What does the title indicate about the content and the text structure?

_____

_____

Is there an introductory section? _____ yes   _____ no

If yes, please comment on the content and structure indicated:

_____

_____

Is there a conclusion section? _____ yes   _____ no

If yes, please comment on the content and structure indicated:

_____

_____

What type of expository text does the passage seem to be?

(descriptive, sequential, argument-persuasion) _____

Are there headings or other markers? _____ yes   _____ no

If yes, give a brief sketch: _____

_____

_____

Figure EXP. Form for text analysis of an expository passage.

to be microcosms of the "real thing." Second, the emphasis in this paper has been on text structure. The complete rhetoric covers a broader domain: word usage and the parsing of sentences and paragraphs are among the significant areas neglected in the present paper.

Textbook Design

The materials available for instruction in today's schools tend to be content-oriented. For reading and language arts, the content is referred to as "skills." Most of these are fairly low-level details—specific letter-sound correspondences, the meaning of the "new words" in a passage, word compounds, comma usage, and so on. Comprehension is covered by terms like *main idea, literal details, inference,* and *fact versus opinion.*

Figure EXP. (*continued*)

Divide the text into seven or fewer chunks, using any markers available. Write paragraph numbers for each segment, indicate function using legend at bottom of page, and write synopsis of content.

Paragraphs

____ Function: _____

_____

_____

____ Function: _____

_____

_____

____ Function: _____

_____

_____

____ Function: _____

_____

_____

____ Function: _____

_____

_____

____ Function: _____

_____

_____

____ Function: _____

_____

_____

Legend: i = introduction/ s = summary/ t = transition/ d = definition/
c = comparison/ p = problem + solution/ e = explanation

While these terms can be interpreted with reference to rhetorical principles, the parallels are strained and something is lost in translation.

When the topic is English, social studies, or science, the content is determined by prevailing topics in the field. English has been subject to wide variations in recent years. Social studies has a set of classic dimensions—history, geography, economics, political science—but is also beset by doubts as to the proper foci for public education. In the physical and biological sciences, the disciplines are well-established; problems arise in translating the rapidly evolving content and methods of modern science into a form suitable for the schools.

Neither in the reading curriculum nor in the content areas do I find much attention to rhetorical principles. In language arts, some consideration is given to relatively low-level concepts of formal language usage, mostly in connection with "proper usage." Discussion of text forms, whether for reading or writing, is rare.

The shortcomings, from my perspective, exist at two distinctive levels. First, the concentration seems to be on what I have labeled *content,* with less consideration of the techniques for text analysis and the structures that emerge from application of these techniques. In my examinations of basal readers, I find few instances in which students are led to inquire into character and plot: they are not instructed in the questions that yield answers about these issues, nor are they shown the well-formed shapes taken by these answers.

Second, whatever the concerns to ensure the adequacy of the content of modern textbooks, less attention seems to be given to the rhetorical quality of the materials. To put it bluntly, many of these materials are not well-written (Anderson, Armbruster, and Kantor 1980). Previous analyses have intermingled problems of content and structure. The purpose of this paper has been to highlight the latter.

Textbook publishers must deal with a multitude of constraints in the design of a series. Many of these constraints reflect the conventions of the marketplace. Others spring from concerns about values—for example, proper respect for individuals from all parts of the society. Some appear rather silly, such as the restrictions on readability. A few verge on censorship.

Nonetheless, it seems a reasonable request that texts provide rhetorical models that, if not ideal, are at least adequate. In addition, I would argue that reading series should include a variety of simple models of the various genres that teachers can use to instruct students in the techniques of comprehension. My investigations of basal readers suggest that, while many of the contemporary series contain good literature, samples of "clean" expository writing are harder to identify.

Textbook Selection

A few states stand as the primary gatekeepers in the designation of those textbook series that will thrive in the marketplace. I have participated as a member of several groups responsible for selecting reading series. My experience suggests that these decisions are generally negligent with regard to writing quality. The background and qualifications of the committees generally do not emphasize this dimension: committee members are often talented in their own fields, and the groups have been diligent. However, I cannot remember a discussion that systematically focused on the writing quality of the texts.

This difficulty can be solved partly by considering the matter in the appointment of groups responsible for textbook selection. I can also imagine alternations in the ubiquitous paper form that serves to tally opinions during this process. Changes in the methodology, however, are likely to matter only if the people understand the issues.

Teacher Training

Elementary teachers generally have to take one or two courses on "how to teach reading." In some states, all teachers must submit to this requirement. In examining a dozen or so books of the sort used for these courses, I have yet to find any that include any references to rhetorical principles. None of the examples in my library even draws the basic distinction between narrative and expository forms. Text comprehension is described according to the terms used in test construction and in scope-and-sequence charts—*main idea* and so on.

I would suggest that we have a problem, in that many of the teachers in elementary classrooms and most of those at the secondary level may lack knowledge of some fundamental principles in the technical use of language. To be sure, many of these individuals may have encountered a freshman English course in which these principles were reviewed. I am not greatly reassured by this possibility. First, the content and impact of such courses vary widely. Second, we should make explicit the link between these principles and the young student's ability to read and write. The tendency is to view rhetorical concepts as the province of the elite, whereas in fact, every one of us has to wrestle with the 1040 tax form and other afflictions of the modern world.

Formal language, the language of the rhetoric, provides the foundation for dealing with the modern world. Thinking, problem solving, and communication are the basic skills for survival today. Learning the tools for handling these tasks is the job of our schools. I see no reason why we cannot ensure that all students possess these tools at the end of thirteen years of schooling. We must be clear in our purpose, and explicit in the message we present to students. The essential elements for designing a curriculum to achieve this goal are available. The job ahead is to make the best use of what we already know.

References

Anderson, T. H., B. B. Ambruster, and R. N. Kantor. (1980). *How clearly written are children's textbooks? Or, of bladderworts and alfa.* Reading education report no. 16. Champaign, Ill.: Center for the Study of Reading, University of Illinois at Urbana-Champaign. ED 192 275.

Baker, S. (1977). *The complete stylist and handbook.* New York: Thomas Y. Crowell.

Britton, B. K., and J. B. Black (1985). *Understanding expository text.* Hillsdale, N.J.: Erlbaum.

Brooks, C., and R. P. Warren (1972). *Modern rhetoric.* 2d ed. N.Y.: Harcourt Brace Jovanovich.

Calfee, R. C. (1981). Cognitive psychology and educational practice. *Review of Research in Education* 9: 3–72.

Calfee, R. C., and R. G. Curley (1984). Structures of prose in the content areas. In *Understanding reading comprehension,* edited by J. Flood. Newark, Del.: International Reading Association.

California State Department of Education (1985). *State curriculum frameworks.* Sacramento, Calif.: California State Department of Education.

Crothers, E. J. (1972). Memory structure and the recall of discourse. In *Language comprehension and the acquisition of knowledge,* edited by J. B. Carroll and R. O. Freedle, 247–83. Washington, D.C.: Winston.

Durkin, D. (1979). What classroom observations reveal about reading comprehension instruction. *Reading Research Quarterly* 14: 481–533.

Farr, R., and L. Fay (1982). Reading trend data in the United States: A mandate for caveats and cautions. In *The rise and fall of national test scores,* edited by G. R. Austin and H. Barber. New York: Academic Press.

Frederiksen, C. H. (1972). Effects of task-induced cognitive operations on comprehension and memory processes. In *Language comprehension and the acquisition of knowledge,* edited by J. B. Carroll and R. O. Freedle. Washington, D.C.: Winston.

Freedman, S. W., and R. C. Calfee (1984). Understanding and comprehending. *Written Communication* 1: 459–90.

Hodges, C. A. (1980). Toward a broader definition of comprehension instruction. *Reading Research Quarterly* 15: 299–306.

Kinneavy, J. L. (1980). *A theory of discourse: The aims of discourse.* New York: W. W. Norton & Co.

Kintsch, W., and T. A. van Dijk (1978). Toward a model of text comprehension and production. *Psychological Review* 85: 363–394.

Manchester, W. (1980). *Goodbye, darkness: A memoir of the Pacific War.* Boston: Little, Brown and Company.

Meyer, B. J. F., and G. E. Rice (1984). The structure of text. In *Handbook of reading research,* edited by P. D. Pearson, 319–51. New York: Longman.

Miller, G. A. (1956). The magical number seven, plus or minus two: Some limits on our capacity for processing information. *Psychological Review* 63: 81–97.

National Assessment of Educational Progress (1981). *Three assessments of reading: Changes in performance 1970–1980.* Report no. 11-R-01. Denver, Colo.: Education Commission of the States.

Perrin, P. G. (1950). *Writer's guide and index to English.* Revised ed. Chicago: Scott, Foresman & Company.

Peters, T. J., and R. H. Waterman Jr. (1982). *In search of excellence.* New York: Harper & Row.

Rumelhart, D. E. (1977). Toward an interactive model of reading. In *Attention and performance,* Vol. 6, edited by S. Dornic, 573–603. Hillsdale, N.J.: Lawrence Erlbaum Associates.

Simon, H. A. (1981). *The sciences of the artificial.* 2d ed. Cambridge, Mass.: MIT Press.

Stein, N. L., and C. G. Glenn (1979). An analysis of story comprehension in elementary school children. In *New directions in discourse processing,* Vol. 2, edited by R. Freedle, 53–120. Norwood, N.J.: Ablex.

Webster's ninth new collegiate dictionary (1983). Springfield, Mass.: Merriam-Webster.

Zinsser, W. K. (1980). *On writing well.* N.Y.: Harper & Row.

Commentary

Judith A. Langer
Stanford University

The papers are interesting and very different. Essentially they represent the tensions in our field between form and function, and how these relate to readability and well-written text. Each author has interpreted "text" in a different way: Schallert deals with textual discourse in general, while Calfee has focused on constructed texts, particularly those used for reading instruction. He seems to see texts as essentially constructed, while she seems to view them as essentially interpersonal and discursive. While Calfee goes on to explore ways in which text can be manipulated to improve readability, Schallert would likely look toward changes in the social context or functional intent that invokes the writing in the first place. These obvious differences aside, my reaction focuses on (1) their papers in general, (2) some apparent points of agreement and disagreement, and (3) some general issues their papers raise for the field to consider.

Both Schallert and Calfee indicate that a text is an interactive enterprise between reader and author which requires an awareness of the other as well as the topic, and that it is function-driven—its creation driven by guiding purpose. Further, they see text structure as being guided by these factors. Schallert develops the notion of function-driven text in some detail, while Calfee goes on to other things.

Schallert argues for an interpersonal and socio-communicative view of text, while Calfee focuses on the design of the text—on the logically predictable and generalizable structures associated with particular genres and discourse modes. Schallert describes text in terms of an abstract framework that grows out of how things are perceived and organized in a particular domain, and hence sees text as an amalgam of content and structure—the blueprint and its ideas, with an understandable message to an intended audience.

Schallert shows how the purposes and underlying rules of the message help shape the text, and she calls for a diminution of focus away from domain-specific texts and toward a focus on fundamental principles or ideas. While on the whole I find the argument she develops in this paper to be strong, and I agree with most of what she has said, I sense one issue concerning domain-specific texts. She argues against the use of such texts because "even experts cannot agree on a certain pattern of concepts," so how can they be used to guide text patterns? I think we can look at the same issue another way—not on the pattern of concepts, but on ways in which people approach problems and seek evidence in a particular field. It may be that the set of underlying principles of logic or rules of evidence people use to make sense of ideas and judge concepts is domain-specific, and an understanding of these domain-specific approaches to knowledge may make texts more comprehensible to readers who understand these approaches.

Schallert has presented the complexity of the interrelationships between content and structure within socio-functional underpinnings, and aptly argues that beyond topic familiarity, even well-written and logically "rule-abiding" texts are less comprehensible to someone who is unfamiliar with that particular discourse form or rule of logic. However, in developing this social-interpersonal notion of meaningful text, she loses her focus on its relationship to structure.

Calfee, on the other hand, while stating that each text must have a guiding purpose, does not develop this notion but focuses instead on what he calls the essence of comprehension—the text design. He has shared his work-in-progress—his beginnings of a design for readable text—and in doing this has given me a chance to impose my own design upon it.

I see Calfee as working toward a broader definition of what well-readable, and therefore well-written, approaches to text should be. He seems to use a text-semantic approach by taking into account what well-written text must include and the way it is processed by the reader. In doing this he sees writing, like Schallert, as an interactive (as well as functional) exchange between writer and audience.

Calfee's text types may not be so different from the traditional types, if you think of the traditional categories as strategies in the service of some larger communicative goal. In particular, his simple/complex text notion may be a very helpful distinction. However, the distinction may be a bit more complicated than is described in his paper. The strategies he speaks of may seldom be pure, even in their simplest forms.

In his conclusion, Calfee asks why teachers don't complain about badly written texts. Perhaps I can begin to answer that. For the past four years, Arthur Applebee and I have been studying writing in secondary school classrooms. To do this, we spend a few days a week in particular subject-area classes. The teachers we worked with have all but given up on texts. They teach the concepts first, in their lectures, and use the textbooks as a supplement, afterwards. Comprehension becomes the focus of discussions; reading is for review and extension of ideas.

Some Questions for the Field

1. Although Schallert and Calfee both focus on readable texts, to some degree each seems to approach the issue from the viewpoint of the author reaching toward the reader and manipulating something in an effort to be understood. However, neither really questions the extent to which "well-formed" texts make a difference from the point of view of the reader, or under what circumstances this does or does not make a difference. Before the field engages in widespread text reform, such questions need to be explored.

2. Given well-structured text (and Calfee has made a nice step in identifying functionally well-structured text), we need to address one other issue important for purposes of readability of text: how important is it to teach children those structures?

3. Both Schallert and Calfee begin with a sense of the importance of interweaving notions of function and structure in their views of text. However, the relationships between the two get lost; each author moved on to develop one or the other of the pair. Just as with process/product distinctions, socio-functional and structural relationships may not yet be sufficiently conceptualized. It may take time to develop models of how they work together in the development of more readable texts.

4. My last question is one that isn't really addressed by either Schallert or Calfee, but one that I think needs asking. And that has to do with how the orchestration of structure and purpose changes with such variables as topic, task, and age—within and across individuals. Although it is necessary to develop a model indicating the general interplay of purpose and structure, more useful for the field would be descriptions of the roles that purpose and structure play in the service of producing different kinds of texts.

Commentary

Robert J. Tierney
Ohio State University

In the first half of the eighties, attempts to account for reading comprehension in terms of text structure fell into ill repute as a result of the theoretical criticisms of Morgan and Sellner (1980) and the empirical work of Brewer and others (Brewer and Lichtenstein 1981, Jose and Brewer 1983, Hay and Brewer 1983, Tierney and Mosenthal 1983). In the past year, we have seen some thoughtful responses to these criticisms in the discussions of the role of text structure by Trabasso, Secco, and Van Den Broek (1984), Stein and Policastro (1984), and Meyer (1984). As these researchers move away from what proved to be purely structural accounts of understanding text, we are seeing the emergence of new insights. The papers by Calfee and Schallert are an attempt to begin to apply these new views to text or, at least, to raise our consciousness to them. Their attempts to apply these views do not occur without the emergence of some tensions. It is a few of these tensions which I wish to articulate in my discussion of their papers.

One tension relates to a reader's purpose. Sometimes Calfee and Schallert give the impression that readers should be viewed as learners whose charge in life is to match the author's representation of meaning. At other points Calfee and Schallert refer to notions such as Nystrand's textual space, the overriding influences of context, and the generalization that "no text has a single stable correct meaning." The latter point of view is apparent in Schallert's conclusion (veiled in cautious optimism) that texts have "open" rather than "closed" meaning potentials. Unfortunately, both authors tend to retreat from the view that text is more "open" than "closed." And, as a result, they base their comments about comprehension and the "ideal" text upon the notion that text should be read with the goal of gleaning a representation of the author's ideas.

A second tension involves how Schallert and Calfee view the structure of knowledge. In both papers, but especially Calfee's, there is a tendency to assume that expository text is best structured in accordance with how ideas are logically outlined or organized hierarchically. At other points in their discussion of structure, Calfee and Schallert defer to Aristotle's modes. At still other points, both Calfee and Schallert cite research by cognitivists who have dealt with issues such as limited capacity, schema activism, etc. Unfortunately, the authors never draw together these considerations. For example, they never relate the findings of schema theorists to the discussion on how texts might be structured. Nor do they address Miller's 7 +/− 2 research on imagery, perspective taking, but instead retreat to models of knowledge which emphasize structural considerations and tend toward an advocacy of a linear model of discourse processing. I would posit that readers are not tied to the text in such a manner. Readers can skip around, take time out, refer to other sources— that is, they can control the rhythm and nature of their approach to text.

A third tension follows from the attempt to model meaning by enlisting arguments about form which disregard function. Calfee mentions that as a result of thinking about his courses in experimental design he is very sensitive to the need for emphasizing design. My experience differs from Calfee's. I find I have students who have more difficulty specifying research questions after taking such courses, and part of their difficulty arises as a result of placing a design before their purposes. I feel Calfee's reference to architecture is plagued with an appreciation of form which disregards issues of function. Despite the homage given rhetoricians, both Calfee and Schallert appear to place more credence in the text frame or mode as an end rather than a possible means.

The struggle between function and form should not be viewed as a minor area of concern nor an issue which will be resolved in simple terms. If we are to understand text, we must grapple with issues of the intentionality of authors and readers. In discussions of what makes a text considerate or what purposes a text are intended to serve, we often unwittingly and naively approach text with a view to function and form which ignores the complexities involved in form's alignment with function. Oftentimes, as teachers, we may attribute intentions to authors with the reckless abandon of an officious editor and require students to be held accountable to our interpretations.

I close where Robert Calfee began his paper. Calfee presented a rich and enlightening discussion of the multidimensional nature of his encounter with *Goodbye, Darkness*. I jotted down a note to myself: "I love this excursion into the reality of his own reading experience. Too often our analyses of text reflect disembodiments due to our lack of appreciation of the multifaceted and personal nature of such encounters." I believe it is from an appreciation of reading as involving such phenomena that our understanding of the role played by structure will be defined. It is then that we will understand the delicate balancing act which takes place between form, concepts, points of view, characters' beliefs, narrator's view, author's intentions, readers' purposes, and text potentials. Maybe such analyses will enable us to appreciate the politics underlying our view of the world through text. Maybe it will force us to reconsider our metaphors—pipelines to knowledge, process, information retrieval—and generate others which capture the reader's varied experiences with the text.

References

Brewer, W. F., and E. H. Lichtenstein (1981). Event schemas, story schemas and story grammar. In *Attention and performance IX,* edited by J. Long and A. Baddeley. Hillsdale, N.J.: Erlbaum.

Hay, A. E., and W. F. Brewer (1983). *Children's understanding of the narrator's role in stories.* Technical report no. 294. Champaign, Ill.: Center for the Study of Reading, University of Illinois at Urbana-Champaign.

Jose, P. E., and W. F. Brewer (1983). *The development of story liking: Character identification, suspense, and outcome resolution.* Technical report no. 291. Champaign, Ill.: Center for the Study of Reading, University of Illinois at Urbana-Champaign.

Meyer, B. J. F. (1984). Text dimensions and cognitive processing. In *Learning and comprehension of text,* edited by H. Mandl, N. L. Stein, and T. Trabasso, 3–51. Hillsdale, N.J.: Erlbaum.

Morgan, J., and M. Sellner (1980). Discourse and linguistic theory. In *Theoretical issues in reading comprehension,* edited by R. Spiro, B. Bruce, and W. Brewer, 165–200. Hillsdale, N.J.: Erlbaum.

Stein, N. L., and M. Policastro (1984). The concept of story: A comparison between children's and teachers' viewpoints. In *Learning and comprehension of text,* edited by H. Mandl, N. L. Stein, and T. Trabasso, 113–55. Hillsdale, N.J.: Erlbaum.

Tierney, R. J., and J. Mosenthal (1983). Cohesion and textual coherence. *Research in the Teaching of English* 17: 215–29.

Trabasso, T., T. Secco, and P. Van Den Broek (1984). Causal cohesion and story coherence. In *Learning and comprehension of text,* edited by H. Mandl, N. L. Stein, and T. Trabasso, 83–111. Hillsdale, N.J.: Erlbaum.

III Oral Language: Its Relation to Writing, Reading, and Response to Literature

Introduction

Speaking and listening are important strands of the language arts curriculum even if sometimes overlooked in the current zeal for connecting reading and writing. The two papers presented here remind us of important research too often overlooked in planning school programs, and they point to critical avenues of inquiry yet to be undertaken. Miles Myers presents a valuable historical perspective and a clear analysis of the shared features of oral and written language. One intriguing dimension of his paper is the suggestion that experiences with speech events lead to inevitable consequences with written language.

David Dickinson summarizes studies in interactive learning, particularly studies in early childhood education, and explains why kindergarten and first grade teachers attend more to oral language than those who follow. Because the two papers tap diverse fields of study, they complement one another.

In her commentary, Roselmina Indrisano stresses the importance of oral language to disabled learners and vigorously argues for the future interaction of researchers and teachers, a theme that aroused many participants at the seminar. David Dillon, also, seeks a reorientation of research efforts, and, in focusing on purpose and meaning, he issues a clarion call for change, a change mandatory in many ways if studies of learning beyond the primary school level are to come to grips with the importance of oral language in learning.

The Shared Structure of Oral and Written Language and the Implications for Teaching Writing, Reading, and Literature

Miles Myers
University of California at Berkeley

Humans are primarily, over and above their biological needs, makers and users of symbols (Whitehead 1927, Langer 1942, Cassirer 1944), and it is through oral and written language that humans most frequently interpose a network of signs between the world and themselves and then use those signs to construct and master their world (Gusdorf 1965). For example, mathematical (6,7), visual (○,□), and action (☞) signs can all be translated into oral and written language (six, seven, circle, square, and pointing), thus making oral and written language the primary mediums for using sign systems and for knowing the world. One question to be addressed is whether oral and written language are themselves different ways of knowing—a different consciousness. The answer to this question can have important implications for the way oral and written language are taught in the classroom.

A Historical Perspective on Oral and Written Language

Plato answers the question with both a yes and a no. On the one hand, in the *Phaedrus* and in the *Seventh Letter* he draws a sharp distinction between oral and written language and attacks writing in terms quite similar to those sometimes used today against computers: writing destroys the memory; it is a thing pretending to do outside the mind what can only be done inside the mind; and it is an unresponsive, garbage-in/garbage-out device (Ong 1982).

On the other hand, Plato, who formulated his ideas in writing, also attacked the old oral tradition (excluding poets from his Republic) and praised alphabetic writing as analytic, abstract, and visual (Ong 1982, Havelock 1963). Plato's inconsistency is not a simple issue. Havelock and Ong believe that Plato's oral/written ambivalence results from the fact that oral and written language represent different types of consciousness: the oral is additive, cumulative, situational, and participatory; the written is subordinate, analytic, detached, and objectively distanced. Plato cannot decide whether he favors the participatory consciousness of oral language or the analytic objectivity of written language.

Myron Tuman finds some of this same ambivalence in Ong's work (Tuman 1983). On the one hand, Ong argues that in writing and print literacy, we gain a "phenomenological sense of existence [that] is richer in its conscious and articulate reflection than anything that preceded it" (Ong 1982, p. 155). On the other hand, he observes, "By removing words from the world of sound where they had first had their origin in active human interchange and relegating them definitively to visual surface . . . print encouraged human beings to think of their own interior conscious and unconscious resources as more and more thing-like, impersonal and religiously neutral" (pp. 131–32). For Ong, ultimately, oral language is primary: "The interiorizing force of the oral word relates in a special way to the sacral, to the ultimate concerns of existence" (p. 74).

Plato's problems with oral/written differences continue in the writing of information-processing theorists, who also give a mixed response to the oral/written question, depending upon whether the theory emphasizes assimilation and early acquisition or accommodation and later acquisition. From a gradualist perspective, which emphasizes assimilation, oral language is primary because it is the bridge to writing. Learners learn by reducing new problems, such as writing, to problems previously solved, such as oral language. From the stages and structuralist perspective, which emphasizes accommodation, oral and written language represent two radically different structures in the mind of the competent user of language. In other words, learning to write requires a fundamental change in internal mental schemes for language so that mental structures are available to fit the new realities of writing.

These two themes, the gradualist and structuralist, appear in a number of studies of interactive language development in children (Harrell 1957; O'Donnell, Griffin, and Norris 1967; Golub 1969; Emig 1971; O'Donnell 1974; Graves 1975; Loban 1976; Falk 1979; Flower and Hayes 1970; and Perl 1979). Dyson (1983), taking a gradualist perspective, found that kindergarten children initially use talk to invest written graphics with meaning and eventually view talk as the substance of written language. As Vygotsky and others have indicated, in the early stages of acquiring writing skills, oral/written correspondence is crucial:

> In speaking, he is hardly conscious of the sounds he pronounces and quite unconscious of the mental operations he performs. In writing, he must take cognizance of the sound structure of each word, dissect it, and reproduce it. . . . (1962, p. 99)

Bereiter (1980), taking a structuralist perspective and emphasizing the differences between oral language and written language, found in writing acquisition that the "incorporation of a new skill requires reorganization" of the mental process, creating stages of development (p. 154). Loban has a dual perspective, describing how at first oral language appears to be the source of structure for writing and then later writing appears to be structurally different:

> From grades one through seven the *oral* average words per unit tends to be slightly higher than the *written* average. In grades seven through nine a rapprochement seems to be occurring, and in grades ten through twelve longer units occur in writing. (1976, p. 34)

The gradualist perspective, emphasizing developmental history, sometimes gives a primary status to oral language. De Saussure argued that writing exists "for the sole purpose of representing" oral language because the basis of written language is the "associative" bond between an oral sound and a concept ([1916] 1966), and Bloomfield argued, "Writing is not language, but merely a way of recording language by means of visible marks" (1933, p. 21). For both de Saussure and Bloomfield, the oral is language, and writing a mere reflection of the oral.

The structuralist perspective, emphasizing differences, sometimes gives priority to written language. Olson first argues that oral and written language have fundamentally different ways of defining meaning:

> Chomsky provides a theory of sentence meaning in which the meaning of the sentence is independent of its function or context. Chafe, in contrast, offers a theory of intended meaning that encompasses both the intentions of the speaker and the interpretations the hearer constructs on the basis of the sentence, its perceived context, and its assumed function. . . . Chomsky's assumption is that language is best represented by written texts; Chafe's is that language is best represented by oral conversational utterances. (1977, p. 260)

He then argues that learning to write is a process of learning to decontextualize information and that because modern literacy puts a high value on decontextualizing information, writing is of primary importance.

Olson's description of the cultural relationships of oral and written language follows closely the description proposed by Emig. For her, writing is learned, talk natural; writing is a technological device, but talk is organic (Emig 1977). The separatist arguments of Emig, Olson, and others seem to have three main problems. First, these arguments ignore the fact that there is nothing inherently "natural" about oral language. Both oral and written language are learned sign systems which mediate experience and which put forth masks for both speakers and writers. Ong, arguing that the writer's audience is a fiction, says, "Masks are inevitable in all human communication, even oral" (1977, p. 80), and Derrida takes the argument one more step in his claim that oral language, in the sense that it recreates texts (roles for speakers and listeners) and uses signs, is a kind of writing (Derrida 1976).

Second, many of the separatist arguments assume one direction of influence, from oral to written. But Goody challenges this assumption: "Is it not likely that as speech is the major determinant of writing, so writing to a lesser degree will influence speech and the associated cognitive processes?" (1977, p. 76). This question calls attention to the fact that much of the oral language that contemporary students hear and bring to classrooms as background information is what Ong calls "secondary orality"—TV news, plays, discussions, lectures, and documentaries which all began as planned and written prose and then secondarily became oral language on radio or television (Ong 1982). This shift of direction, from written to oral, means that the primary differences between one kind of language and another become matters of context, not oral/written differences.

Third, many of the separatists' arguments have a Piagetian perspective which ignores context and culture. Information-processing researchers like Flower and Hayes (1970) usually include a box for context in their flow charts, but they do not specify its details. However, Margaret Donaldson (1978), among others, has shown persuasively that when the context of a Piagetian task is changed, the children's response changes:

> The way a situation is described will have an effect on how the child construes it. . . . We do not in ordinary conversations with one another attend to "pure linguistic meaning." . . . We have repeatedly seen that young children's interpretations of language may be powerfully influenced by context. (pp. 69, 71)

Donaldson argues that the primary problem for children may not be an understanding of conservation but an understanding of the differences among speech situations: "The child has not learned to distinguish between situations where he is supposed to give primacy to the langauge and situations where he is not" (1978, p. 70).

In other words, the way one solves a problem is determined by context; the context is mediated or shaped by the language or sign system; and the child must be able to "read" the language or sign system in order to know what kinds of contexts are signified and thus what kinds of answers are appropriate. Vygotsky has explained how contexts get internalized and how oral-language versions of these contexts are turned into written versions. In doing so, he provides an important modification of Piagetian theory. Piaget (1926) argued that a child's talking-aloud-to-self behavior was an instance of egocentricism and that this kind of oral language disappeared as the child became less egocentric and able to talk to others. Vygotsky (1978), on the other hand, argued that this external egocentric speech is a step in the process of internalizing language and contexts. In the first step of internalizing contexts, according to Vygotsky, the learner begins with the help and assistance of another, usually through oral language exchanges (Bruner 1979, Snow 1977) in which the learner's partner in the exchange is someone who structures the language of the exchange at a level *slightly* ahead of the learner's level of development. Dialogues between children at a similar stage of development fail to produce improvement in performance (Herber 1979, Sonstroem 1966, Wood 1980).

Later, as the learner attempts to use a sign system without the help of others, the learner "starts conversing with himself as he has been doing with others" (Vygotsky 1962, p. 19) and uses talking-aloud-to-self or egocentric speech as a scaffold or supporting aid to remind the self of what to do (Vygotsky 1962, Graves 1975). "At three," says Vygotsky, "the difference between egocentric and social speech equals zero" (1962, p. 134).

Next, between the ages of three and seven, this external talking-aloud-to-self is slowly internalized and changed into inner speech, a new speech form which is semantically abbreviated and which contains the basic forms of social interaction in which the language occurs. Thus, the learner transfers "social, collaborative forms of behavior to the sphere of inner-personal psychic functions" (Vygotsky 1962, p. 19). These internalized forms of social interaction represent quite different contexts—conversations, lectures, sermons, graduation speeches. In other words, language learners learn to converse with themselves, to give themselves lectures and sermons, and even to present to themselves graduation speeches and ceremonies. Once the context is internalized through language signs, whether oral or written, the signs become analogous to a tool which is manipulated within some functional activity, being used for internal and external problem solving and for the control of self and others (Vygotsky 1978). Vygotsky has diagramed this relationship as in Figure 1.

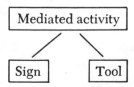

Figure 1. (From L. S. Vygotsky, *Mind in Society,* p. 54. Cambridge: Harvard University Press. Reprinted by permission.)

This position of a fundamental oral/written similarity in underlying forms is supported by evidence from a number of sources. Studies of the written language of deaf children seem to have established rather conclusively that there is an important functional connection between hearing and using oral language and learning to write (Templin 1950, Ruddell 1966, Kyle 1981, Charrow 1981). Tannen argues that "features that have been associated exclusively with spoken or written language are often found in discourse of the other mode" (1982, p. x), and Cooper finds that the "fundamental communicative process" is the same in both oral and written language (1982, p. 109).

The essential difference, then, is not the oral/written contrast but the contrasts of different contexts or styles. Blankenship concluded that her study "indicates that syntactic structure is determined by an individual's style" rather than the oral/written distinction (1962, pp. 419–22), and Chafe (1982) found that spoken ritual, as observed among Senecan Indians, shares many features with written language, suggesting that the essential distinction is between ritual and colloquial contexts within the same societies, not oral/written differences. Exploring a similar problem, Olson compared written textbooks in literate societies to ritualized speech in oral societies, and concluded that the two forms served the same purpose in the different societies (1980b). What Olson did not do is to examine how the ritualized speech of oral societies was also replaced in the ritualized speech of literate societies. In other words, do the written texts of literate societies have analogous forms in the oral language of these literate societies? The argument I am making is that these oral/ written analogies exist and are functional (Myers 1982).

But not all researchers agree that the oral and the written are similar forms used to signify such different contexts as rituals and conversations. Drieman (1962), Gruner et al. (1967), Kroll (1977), and Higgins (1978) are examples of studies which emphasize the structural differences between oral and written language. But Kroll provides no statistical tests of her counts of subordinators and coordinators in oral and written discourse, and Drieman's analysis of vocabulary differences suffers from a small *n,* eight subjects, and a graphics analysis in which frequency was *not* based on dividing a given word count by total words.

The Gruner and Higgins studies present different problems. Gruner's oral/written contrast is based on differences between an assigned essay and an assigned "extemporaneous" speech. The fact that the speech had to be extemporaneous and the essay did not creates an important difference of context that was not controlled for. The question is whether extemporaneous contexts for writing and extemporaneous contexts for speaking require significantly different language. Keenan (1977) has examined this question and found that the distinction between planned and unplanned contexts is critical in both writing and oral language.

Murphy (1981) notes that the Higgins oral/written contrast is based on oral and written samples from students in grades 4, 5, 6, and 8, without any controls for developmental differences—raising the question of whether the study was examining trends in the acquisition of oral and written skills, not differences between the oral and written forms per se among accomplished performers. One would certainly expect significant oral/written differences in the language of students just beginning to write.

At least two researchers have changed their minds about oral/written differences. In an early study, Collins and Williamson argued that the semantic abbreviation of the inner language could not be adequately elaborated in writing by writers in grades 4, 8, and 12 because these writers depended too heavily on their oral experiences and did not recognize the fundamental structural differences of writing (1981). But in a follow-up study of writers in grades 8 and 12, these two researchers arrived at a different conclusion, modifying the findings of their 1981 study: weak writers are not characterized by a higher rate of semantic abbreviation but by an inability to vary the use of semantic abbreviation for different contexts (Collins and Williamson 1984).

Collins and Williamson's finding that the difference of fundamental importance is the difference among different forms of inner speech, capturing differences in social interaction, is the position taken by this paper. Oral and written language, although having obvious differences which must be overcome in acquisition, share fundamental mental sign systems which internalize different rhetorical forms from culture. It is the differences of context within oral and written versions that must be understood. The critical question is "What is the cultural unit which gets internalized and shapes both oral and written language?" This question has been at the center of frame semantics (Fillmore 1976), speech act theory (Searle 1969), anthropology (Bateson 1972), and sociolinguistics (Berger 1963). Hymes (1974) and Ricoeur (1979) have given the most perceptive responses to this question.

Hymes has distinguished between the speech act (such as a joke), the speech event (such as a conversation or lecture), and the speech situation (such as eating, political gatherings, and weddings). Hymes says that speech acts are rule-governed and are embedded in speech events. Speech events are the maximum set of speech activities "directly governed by rules or norms for the use of speech." And speech situations, "in contrast to speech events . . . are not themselves governed by . . . one set of rules throughout" (1974, pp. 51–52).

In Ricoeur, this speech event is the "discourse" which underlies both speaking and writing: "It is as discourse that language is either spoken or written" (1979, p. 74). For Ricoeur (and Hymes), discourse has four traits: text or instance of discourse, speaker, subject, and audience. Says Ricoeur, "These four traits taken together constitute speech as an event" (1979, p. 75). The speech event is shaped out of language, which has as its basic unit the sign, the basic "construct between socially organized persons in the process of interaction" (Volosinov 1973, p. 21).

For Ricoeur, a speech event or discourse underlies both oral and written language, despite the fact that oral and written language have differences. This position is similar to Goody's, in which "language" is related to both speech and writing (1977, p. 77), as shown in Figure 2.

The Nature of the Speech Event

Within the speech event, there are three relationships—speaker-audience, speaker-subject, and speaker-text—all organized around the sign (or word). These three relationships are explicit or implicit in studies of audience and subject (Moffett 1968, Himley 1980, Kantor and Rubin 1981); poetic and transactional writing (Britton et al. 1975, Applebee 1977); the social and logical (Olson 1980a); the interpersonal, ideational, and textual (Halliday and Hasan 1976); and the continuum from telephone calls to prayers and lectures (R. Lakoff 1982).

In this analysis, the three relationships are co-occurring features, not separate features. The division of the speech event into separate features such as audience and function in Britton et al. (1975) and even audience alone in Rubin (1984) runs counter to the empirical evidence on how people classify things in natural language. Neither writers nor speakers separate audience from subject or other matters when actually engaged

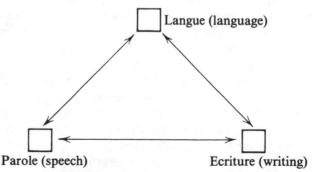

Figure 2. (From J. Goody, *The Domestication of the Savage Mind.* © 1977 Cambridge University Press. Reprinted by permission.)

in the act of speaking or writing. Rosch (1977) reports that people use common prototypes with central tendencies and co-occurring features to anchor classifications, not a list of separate features, and that people group things as more or less distant from the imagined prototype— providing a fuzzy, more-or-less distinction between classifications, not an either/or distinction.

The separation of audience and function does not work—even in the data of Britton et al. (1975). They report "the overriding association of 'pupil to examiner' with transactional writing," "a strong association of the 'child to trusted adult' audience with expressive writing," and "the strong association of all informative categories (taken together) with the 'pupil to examiner audience' " (p. 184). These strong associations suggest that audience and subject or function are co-occurring features within a larger speech-event framework—not separate, isolated features.

The three co-occurring relationships—shown in Figure 3 (see next page)—are (*a*) *distancing:* between speaker and audience, from personal to impersonal, involving both personal relations and subject matter, signaled by such signs as first, second, and a third person; (*b*) *processing:* between speaker and subject, from participant to spectator, signaled by such signs as "alot," "kinda," and, "however," "although," and "consequently;" and (*c*) *modeling:* between speaker and text, from transitory to permanent texts, signaled by presence or absence of titles, abstracts, institutional identification, and types of conclusions.

Moffett's use of co-occurring features, speaker-audience relations, and speaker-subject relations is the correct direction (Moffett 1968), but his failure to organize these features around a few stable intermediate prototypes resulted in a project with a proliferation of disconnected forms, which in turn resulted in an enormous management and explanation problem for teachers when the project reached the classroom. The need for a few stable intermediate forms is not just a matter of simplifying classroom management. Herbert A. Simon has argued that these forms are essential for development: "We have shown thus far that complex systems will evolve from simple systems much more rapidly if there are stable intermediate forms than if there are not" (1981, p. 209).

In the model proposed here (see again Figure 3), there are four fundamental prototypes of contexts, each with a set of co-occurring features around which are organized four distinctive speech events— *acquisition events, conversations, presentations* (lectures, sermons), and *rituals* (oaths of office, presentations of academic papers at conferences) (Myers 1983). According to Goffman, the critical distinction among all forms is between talk (acquisition events and conversations) and lectures (presentations and rituals) (1981).

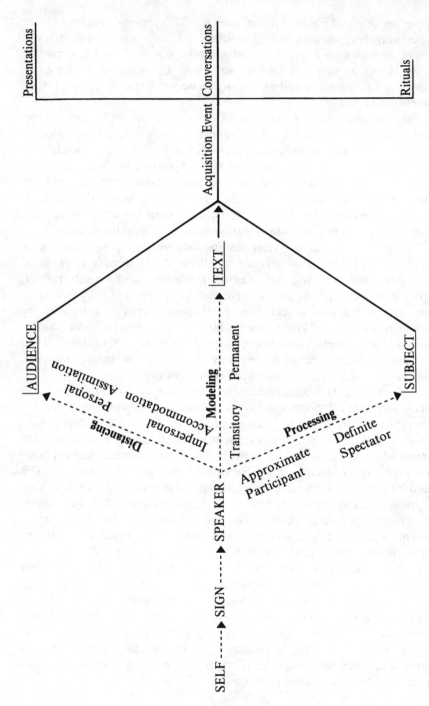

Figure 3. Distancing, processing, and modeling within the speech-event framework.

It is important to note that this approach to culture is in terms of speech events, not social classes. An example of the latter is Bernstein's study of restricted language in lower classes and elaborated language in middle classes (Bernstein 1971), and an example of the former is Richard Ohmann's study of rhetorical situations (1982). Ohmann sees Bernstein's position as an argument for static social continuity, sorting people into class and code users, and sees his own position as allowing "choice at every point" among a variety of roles: "The participants create the social relations of each encounter, in addition to inheriting them" (p. 17). Speech events are the forms that speakers and writers use to create contexts and, in the process, create new roles for themselves in their culture. Cultural events are embedded within the larger framework of sign systems and participatory, observational, and analytic practices, including different writing, reading, and literature activities, as shown in Figure 4.

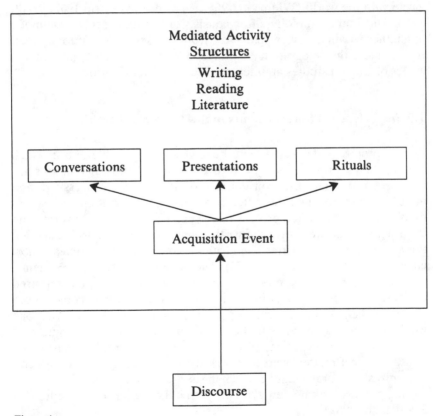

Figure 4.

In this cultural framework, individual conscious experience is made possible by the symbol systems or semiotics of various collectives (Durkheim 1954), societies (Shibutani 1955), interpretive communities (Fish 1972), and cultural institutions (Culler 1975). In other words, there is no strict inherent correspondence between words and things. The correspondence that exists is established by each culture for different contexts, and within our culture different speech events establish different rules of correspondence.

Signs of various types (linguistic, mathematical, visual) mediate and shape our understanding and insight in at least three ways: First, understanding consists of reducing or translating one type of reality or sign system into another—say, from visual signs to words (Marx 1911, Freud 1943, Lévi-Strauss 1963). Second, understanding consists of using signs for a continual interplay—possibly through dreams—between an inner, isolated self, which remains unconscious and does not communicate with the world, and an outer self, which is conscious and does communicate with the world (Winnicott 1965; Klein 1960; Guntrip 1961; Pradl, n.d.). Third, understanding often consists of translating from one mode to another within a sign system—say, from one speech event to another. In summary, the integration of oral and written language puts at the center of English studies an interest in semiotics and culture.

The Importance of Speech Events in the Teaching of Writing

What is proposed here is that texts be analyzed as speech events in which writing shares with oral language three sets of rhetorical relationships established through the conventions of distancing, processing, and modeling, and in which the differences among conversations, presentations, and rituals—whether oral or written—are more important than the differences between oral and written language. For English educators, this emphasis on oral/written similarities is consistent with studies of how children learn to write (Dyson 1983). The same is true of adults. Williams, in examining the writing processes of university freshmen, has reported an increase in covert verbalization as the writing task becomes more abstract (1983). Williams's finding seems to be the opposite of what one would expect if one were to believe those theorists who argue that abstract texts are decontextualized, separated from oral language experiences. Even Bereiter, who sees writing as a separate symbol system, recognizes that oral language exchanges are an important step in the writing process, linking new symbols with old experiences (Bereiter and Scardamalia 1982).

Some observers, of course, believe that oral experiences interfere with learning to write: "Unaware of the ways in which writing is different from speaking, he [the basic writer] imposes the conditions of speech on writing" (Shaughnessy 1977, p. 79). But researchers also emphasize the collaborative relationship of oral and written language:

> The findings of this study indicate that some analogues and parallels do appear to exist between the two modes of discourse, particularly when the writer has not yet fully achieved mastery of skills needed to generate written language effectively. . . .
> Tentative as the findings of the present study must be regarded, they do indicate some evidence of the adult basic writer's reliance on the oral repertoire when communicating in the written mode. (Cayer and Sacks 1979, pp. 126–27)

The collaborative relationship between oral and written language is outlined in many pedagogical studies. Zoellner has called for a "vocal-scribal" weld (1969, p. 307), and Radcliffe (1972) has argued that saying things aloud and then writing them helps students write better. Bartholomae (1980) has argued that writing and then reading one's text aloud helps students correct their mistakes. In fact, students who do not recognize errors in their papers correct these errors while reading their papers aloud. As an explanation for this, Bartholomae makes a critical distinction between students' reading of someone else's text and "students' oral reconstruction of their texts":

> Since fluent readers are reading for meaning, they are actively predicting what will come and processing large chunks of graphic information at a time. They do not read individual words, and they miscue because they speak what they expect to see rather than what is actually on the page. . . .
> The situation is different when a student reads his own text, since this reader already knows what the passage means and attention is drawn, then, to the representation of that meaning. Reading also frees a writer from the constraints of transcription, which for many basic writers is an awkward, laborious process, putting excessive demands on both patience and short-term memory. (1980, p. 267)

In other words, students have in their heads a model of discourse easily translatable between oral and written forms. What interferes is not the differences between the forms but the memory overload of unpracticed transcription. Bartholomae, however, in another part of his study appears to want to separate oral and written forms in the teaching of writing:

> One of the most interesting results of the comparisons of the spoken and written versions of John's texts is his inability to *see* the difference between "frew" and "few" or "dementic" and "demerit." . . . When I put *frew* and *few* on the blackboard, John read

them both as "few." The lexical item "few" is represented for John by either orthographic array. He is not, then, reading or writing phonetically, which is a sign . . . of a high level of fluency, since the activity is automatic and not mediated by the more primitive operation of translating speech into print or print into speech. When John was writing, he did not produce "frew" or "dementic" by searching for sound/letter correspondences. . . . He went to stored print forms and did not take the slower route of translating speech into writing. (1980, p. 263)

It is not clear to me why Bartholomae in the passage above argues that speech and writing can only be interacting when there is evidence of phonetic analysis, particularly given the success of his read-aloud approach in other areas. There is, after all, evidence of a whole-word sound, the learner knowing the whole-word sound without attending to the phonetic units of a word. If one were guessing words, why not retrieve whole-word sounds based on an opening sound? Phonetic analysis may be evidence of sound-to-letter sequences in learners struggling with a problem of acquisition, but performers may chunk speech-writing relationships as co-occurring, automatic relationships. In other words, what Bartholomae calls "stored print forms" may be for the student "stored oral-print" forms.

My own study of the writing of ninth graders in a school district proficiency exam found evidence of both underlying conversational events and presentational events, with conversational features having their highest frequency in the bottom-half papers and presentational features having their highest frequency in the upper-half papers (Myers 1982). Furthermore, the lowest-scoring students in the two-year sample averaged more words on letters than they did on essays. However, all the other score groups averaged more words on essays than on letters. The point is that students at the beginning stages of writing acquisition need the close audiences and personal subjects of letters in order to develop the necessary fluency—a situation very much like Bruner's joint-action format (1979) or Dore's proto-conversation (1979), both stages of early acquisition in oral language.

My own examination of the writing of many students who fall just below minimum competency in writing is that these students have misinterpreted the speech event called for in a proficiency exam. They think that a conversational event is the required underlying structure, not realizing that a presentational event is required. Sometimes teachers and researchers point to the topic as "misleading" these students, but the fact is that the students who know better are not misled. In fact, the successful students know that the conventions of the proficiency exam are signaled by more than simply the topic.

I believe that a speech-event analysis of writing has the distinct advantage of connecting the writing taxonomy with language structures in everyday life, thereby naturalizing the text and avoiding the invalid separation of audience and subject. A speech-event definition of taxonomies in writing also brings to composition courses the possibility of a critique—something now missing. Conversations, which serve a social function, call for close speaker-audience relations, approximations and coordinations in information, and transitory texts. On the other hand, presentations, which serve a logical function, call for distant speaker-audience relations, definite information with clear thesis sentences, hierarchical relations in information, and permanent texts.

Clear thesis sentences help produce the politics of presentational speech events, in which the speaker stands as an authority. Unclear thesis sentences, such as those required in conversational speech events, can produce social equality and camaraderie among participants, and also turn information into approximations and social entertainment. Conversational talk is not neutral, despite the claims of those who propose teacher-student rap groups for all classes. In fact, there is some evidence that teacher-student conversational discussions in class contradict the values of cultures which place teachers always in the position of authority. I am convinced that this is a central problem for some teachers of American Indians.

The introduction of contrasting speech events with contrasting "rules" is a way to bring to writing classrooms some insight into the pleasure of words and style. Says Lanham:

> What we have now is a tedious, repetitive, unoriginal body of dogma—clarity, sincerity, plainness, duty—started up every week. . . . The dogma of clarity, as we shall see, is based on a false theory of knowledge; its scorn of ornament, on a misleading taxonomy of style; the frequent exhortations to sincerity, on a naive theory of the self. . . . (1974, p. 19)

Speech events are a way to explain how knowledge, style, and self are constructed out of the conventions we use to organize our discourse and thus our social relations with others. Oral language events can provide powerful analogues for illustrating what is happening in written texts.

The Influence of Speech Events on Teaching Reading

In reading, Harste and his associates (1984) have outlined many of the teaching approaches associated with different attitudes toward the relationship of oral and written language. In the behaviorist oral-language-is-supreme-and-separate approach, the assumption is that oral language is a prerequisite to reading and that neither reading nor writing should happen in preschool and kindergarten programs until oral language is fully under control. Even within the formal reading programs of the first grade, oral activities are given the initial priority, and "some teachers delay writing until the second half of first grade" (Hill 1980, cited in Harste et al. 1984, p. 98).

The oral language supremacy argument often appears to be based on the simple fact that oral language occurs first. A number of studies have found that the lag from oral to written language is also present in oral to reading development. By presenting the same material in both oral and written forms to students in first through eighth grade, Durrell (1969) found that sentence-paragraph comprehension in listening surpassed comprehension in reading in the first grade, but in the eighth grade reading comprehension was 12 percent superior to listening comprehension. Ruddell, in fact, says, "The research reviewed indicates that oral language development serves as the underlying base for the development of reading and writing achievement" (1966, p. 16). The argument presented in this paper (see Figure 2) is that there are basic speech event forms which underlie development in both oral and written language and that although oral experience comes first and provides the basic prototypes of speech events for writing development, the writer ultimately reaches a point at which writing experience begins to shape what happens in oral experience. For this reason it would seem that writing and oral language should start interacting early.

In the writing-is-primary-and-separate position of the rationalists and the writing-is-a-separate-stage position of the information processors, students are not ready for reading or writing as a *result* of their oral language experiences. Rather, in these approaches, according to Harste et al., "The trick in teaching children to read and write is . . . to teach them print cues upon which to depend as opposed to the contextual clues they used in oral language" (1984, p. 99).

These two approaches, derived as they are from Chomsky and Piaget, also ignore the pervasive influence of cultural settings on a reader's or listener's interpretation of meaning. Donaldson, as noted earlier, has pointed out that when an adult tests a child, the situation tends to be one in which the reader/listener is supposed to give primacy to language as an objective entity:

> We do not, in our ordinary conversations with one another, attend to "pure linguistic meaning." Ziff, in a book called *Understanding Understanding*, gives a number of examples of this. For instance, if we heard the following statement made about a game of football:

"No one got in without a ticket," we would not interpret this with strict attention to "the meaning" of "no one." In other words, we would not be led to conclude that all employees and players had tickets or else were refused entry. (1978, p. 68)

We are not led to this conclusion in a conversation, but we might be led to this conclusion in a ritual speech event—that is, in the formal, stylized oral exam of the type conducted by Piaget in his experiments. The point is that students need to learn the different rules of speech events in order to understand what it is they are being asked to do.

An example of a research project in this general area is Fillmore's investigation of the response of third and fifth graders to items from the CTBS, Level 1, Form S, and the Metropolitan Achievement Tests, Reading Instructional Tests, Form J1, Elementary. Fillmore has found that the ideal reader of tests must learn an institutionalized genre: "The testing industry, we have come to realize, has created a new genre for English written language . . . dictated, I presume, by the intention to test knowledge of particular vocabulary items, the need to produce something which fits accepted readability formulas [and] . . . satisfies copyright laws" (1982, p. 251).

Within a speech event perspective, Fillmore is merely outlining some of the characteristics of ritual speech events, particularly the way they are governed by institutional formulas, codes, and intentions. These events are not new. They can be found in oaths of office, wedding ceremonies, graduation ceremonies, and journals of academic disciplines. What students need to understand is how these events underlie many different kinds of oral and written language. In this way, they can use what they know from other sources to learn to read tests.

Another example of a speech event orientation to reading problems is Murphy's (1984) examination of how second graders differ in their comprehension of diectic terms in oral and written language—pronouns (I, you), locatives (this, here), and motion verbs (come, go). She finds that these terms present special reading problems for beginning readers and suggests that terms marking space and time in context have been ignored in considerations of the readability of texts.

Speech Events and the Teaching of Literature

The question is "How does a speech event analysis influence the teaching of literature?" First, as Culler has indicated, a theory of literary interpretation must overlap with a theory of reading: "A literary interpretation taxonomy should be grounded on a theory of reading. The relevant categories are those which are required to account for the range of acceptable meanings which works can have for readers of literature" (1975, p. 120).

A speech event analysis can help one understand some of the problems that readers encounter in literature (Myers 1982). For example, the close distancing and approximations of the conversational event underlying Mansfield's "The Garden Party" require a conversational reader who is cooperative, accepting both the ambiguity of the ending, Laura's uncertain values, and the transitory nature of the text. The reader of this story is not to play the role of critic, not to analyze the events too closely.

A different reader role is called for in the history or ritual speech event. Here the reader must play the role of critic, analyzing points of view carefully and establishing one's own perspective. Faulkner's "Barn Burning" is an example of the ritual or history speech event in which the reader must play the role of critic. The mistake that students sometimes make with Faulkner's story is an uncritical acceptance of either the position of the young boy, who defends his father as a brave man who fought in the War, or the position of the narrator, who argues that the boy's defense is unjustified. In other words, these students act like conversational readers in a ritual setting.

Sometimes the literary work is not anchored in one speech event prototype but in boundary cases between one speech event and another. Salinger's *The Catcher in the Rye* and Ring Lardner's "I Can't Breathe" are both conversational prototypes, requiring cooperative, friendly readers. But *The Great Gatsby* is a boundary case between conversation and presentation, less conversational than the other two stories but not as strictly presentational as a Hemingway story. Thus, the reader of *The Great Gatsby* is required to be more suspicious and uncooperative toward the narrator than the reader of either the Salinger or the Lardner story.

Finally, in addition to specifying different roles for the readers, speech event analysis draws a distinction between the roles played by writer and narrator in literature (see Figure 5).

This general approach of embedding literature within speech events, with analogues in oral language, is implicit or explicit in much of the literary work of Booth (1961), Gibson (1966), Chatman (1975), Pratt (1977), and Barthes (1968). But some researchers take strong exception to this approach. Banfield, for example, argues that speech occurs in time and "is structured by this subservience to time," but that writing "can free itself from the structure imposed by time, by sequence, and by order of production" (1982, p. 272). She points to the indirect style as an example of what she calls "unspeakable sentences."

CONVERSATIONS

Writer: Stenographer
Recorder

Narrator: Conversational partner
Sharing burden of
communication and
expression

World: Approximate
Loosely constructed

Reader: Conversational partner
Cooperatively sharing
burden of communi-
cation and expression

Text: Transitory and
impermanent
Social taboo against
public sharing of text

REPORTS

Writer: Plays role of narrator
(may be same or dif-
ferent values)

Narrator: Reporter or detective
Fact collector and
distributor

World: Factually certain
Ideologically uncertain
or not immediately
visible to the
uneducated eye

Reader: Accepts facts
Speculates on generali-
zations and overall
meaning

Text: Archive of fact
No storage of ideas

EXPOSITIONS

Writer: Plays role of narrator

Narrator: Authority figure
Generalizer about ideas
based on itemized
facts

World: Rational
Logically ordered
Complex
Hierarchical
Hard to know

Reader: Critic of ideas and
estimator of weights
and validity of facts

Text: Archive of ideas supported by facts
A monument to our
eternal rationality

Figure 5. The projected roles and participants in different speech events.

Fillmore gives an example of this situation in the following three sentences (1974, p. 97):

He lived there many years ago.

He had lived there many years earlier.

He had lived there many years ago.

The last sentence is an example of a sentence that "cannot be contextualized within normal conversational language" (Fillmore 1974, p. 97). But the fact is that this last sentence can be contextualized within a ritual speech event in which the speaker stands outside a set of events, generalizes about them, and summarizes in indirect speech the direct speech from a given community of learning. Thus, "he had lived there many years ago" means "My research community tells me that Lincoln said, 'I lived in this place in the 1870s.' " My argument is that legal codes, articles in academic journals, and various ceremonial forms, in addition to fictional narratives, make use of this indirect style, and they do so because they are anchored in an underlying speech event in which an indirect style is used and sometimes required.

The separation of literature from speakable situations has in general led to a pervasive separation of composition classes from literature classes, of transactional studies from poetic studies. Pratt, in her comments on speech act theory, basically argues that the study of literature as speech event is a way of integrating the study of literature and other kinds of discourse:

> A speech act approach to literature enables and indeed requires us to describe and define literature *in the same terms* used to describe and define all other kinds of discourse. . . . Similarities between literary and nonliterary utterance types . . . can be linked quite naturally to similarities in the linguistic context and the communicative purposes of the participants. . . . In short, a speech act approach to literature offers the important possibility of integrating literary discourse into the same basic model of language as all our other communicative activities. (1977, p. 88)

Conclusion

This paper has argued that the critical difference occurs not between oral and written language but among different speech events. This view has practical benefits for the curriculum. Speech events offer a way of organizing an integrated curriculum in which problems of comprehending literature and reading provide helpful insights for language production in writing. For example, understanding why a conversational reader must be cooperative while reading helps the writer understand how to invoke and create the conversational reader through appropriate distancing, processing, and modeling in writing.

Much of a student's experience in schools is mediated through some kind of speech event. One very important question left untouched in this paper is how these speech events change the ways students think about problems. Do conversational rules call for one kind of problem-solving strategy and presentational rules another? Thus, for example, I have found that teachers who think they are in a test situation will not use drawing to solve a math problem even though drawing will produce a good answer. The teachers report that they think drawing does not look "smart" in a test situation. This question of how speech events influence problem solving takes us deeper into the structure of sign systems, proving once again that oral/written issues are among the most important in contemporary English education.

References

Applebee, A. (1977). The elaborative choice. In *Language as a way of knowing: A book of readings,* edited by M. Nystrand, 82–94. Toronto: The Ontario Institute for Studies in Education.

Banfield, A. (1982). *Unspeakable sentences: Narration and representation in the language of fiction.* Boston: Routledge & Kegan Paul.

Barthes, R. (1968). *Writing degree zero,* trans. A. Lavers and C. Smith. New York: Hill and Wang.

Bartholomae, D. (1980). The study of error. *College Composition and Communication* 31: 253–69.

Bateson, G. (1972). *Steps to an ecology of mind.* New York: Ballantine.

Bereiter, C. (1980). Development in writing. In *Cognitive processes in writing,* edited by L. W. Gregg and E. R. Steinberg, 73–93. Hillsdale, N.J. Erlbaum.

Bereiter, C. and M. Scardamalia (1982). From conversation to composition: The role of instruction in a developmental process. In *Advances in instructional psychology,* Vol. 2, edited by R. Glaser, 1–64. Hillsdale, N.J.: Erlbaum.

Berger, P. (1963). *Invitation to sociology.* Garden City, N.Y.: Doubleday.

Bernstein, B. (1971). *Class, codes, and control,* Vol. 3. London: Routledge & Kegan Paul.

Blankenship, J. (1962). A linguistic analysis of oral and written style. *Quarterly Journal of Speech* 48: 419–22.

Bloomfield, L. (1933). *Language.* New York: Holt, Rinehart & Winston.

Booth, W. (1961). *Rhetoric of fiction.* Chicago: The University of Chicago Press.

Britton, J., T. Burgess, N. Martin, A. McLeod, and H. Rosen (1975). *The development of writing abilities, 11–18.* London: Macmillan.

Bruner, J. (1979). From communication to language: A psychological perspective. In *Language development,* edited by V. Lee. New York: John Wiley & Sons.

Cassirer, E. (1944). *An essay on man.* New Haven, Conn.: Yale University Press.

Cayer, R. L., and R. K. Sacks (1979). Oral and written discourse of basic writers: Similarities and differences. *Research in the Teaching of English* 13: 121–28.

Chafe, W. (1982). Integration and involvement in speaking, writing, and oral literature. In *Spoken and written language,* edited by D. Tannen, 35–53. Norwood, N.J.: Ablex.

Charrow, V. (1981). The written English of deaf adolescents. In *Variation in writing,* edited by M. Farr Whiteman. Hillsdale, N.J.: Erlbaum.

Chatman, S. (1975). The structure of narrative in transmission. In *Style and structure in literature,* edited by R. Fowler. Ithaca, N.Y.: Cornell University Press.

Chomsky, N. (1957). *Syntactic structures.* The Hague: Mouton.

——— (1964). Comments on Project Literacy meeting. *Project Literacy Reports* 2. Ithaca, N.Y.: Cornell University.

——— (1965). *Aspects of the theory of syntax.* Cambridge, Mass.: MIT Press.

Collins, J., and M. Williamson (1981). Spoken language and semantic abbreviations in writing. *Research in the Teaching of English* 15: 23–35.

——— (1984). Assigned rhetorical context and semantic abbreviation in writing. In *New directions in composition research,* edited by R. Beach and L. Bridwell. New York: Guilford Press.

Cook-Gumperz, J., and J. Gumperz (1981). From oral to written culture: The transition to literacy. In *Variation in writing,* edited by M. Farr Whiteman, 89–109. Hillsdale, N.J.: Erlbaum.

Cooper, M. (1982). Context as vehicle: Implications in writing. In *What writers know,* edited by M. Nystrand, 105–28. New York: Academic Press.

Culler, J. (1975). *Structuralist poetics.* Ithaca, N.Y.: Cornell University Press.

Derrida, J. (1976). *Of grammatology,* trans. by G. Spivak. Baltimore: The Johns Hopkins University Press.

de Saussure, F. (1966). *Course in general linguistics,* trans. by W. Baskin, edited by C. Bally and A. Sechehaye. New York: McGraw-Hill.

Donaldson, M. (1978). *Children's minds.* New York: W. W. Norton & Co.

Dore, J. (1979). Conversational acts and the acquisition of language. In *Developmental pragmatics,* edited by E. Ochs and B. Schieffelin. New York: Academic Press.

Drieman, G. H. (1962). Differences between written and spoken language: An exploratory study. *Acta Psychologica* 20: 36–57.

Durrell, D. D. (1969). Listening comprehension versus reading comprehension. *Journal of Reading* 12: 455–60.

Durkheim, E. (1954). *The elementary forms of the religious life,* trans. by J. Swain. Glencoe, Ill.: Free Press.

Dyson, A. (1983). The role of oral language in early writing processes. *Research in the Teaching of English* 17: 1–30.

Emig, J. (1971). *The composing processes of twelfth graders.* Urbana, Ill.: National Council of Teachers of English. ED 058 205.

——— (1977). Writing as a mode of learning. *College Composition and Communication* 28: 122–28.

Falk, J. S. (1979). Language acquisition and the teaching and learning of writing. *College English* 41: 436–47.

Fillmore, C. (1974). *Frame semantics and the nature of language.* Berkeley Studies in Syntax and Semantics. Berkeley, Calif.: Department of Linguistics, University of California, Berkeley.

———— (1976). The need for a frame semantics within linguistics. In *Statistical methods in linguistics,* edited by H. Karlgren, 5–29. Stockholm: Skriptor.

———— (1982). Ideal readers and real readers. In *Analyzing discourse: Text and talk,* edited by D. Tannen, 248–70. Washington, D.C.: Georgetown University Press.

Fish, S. (1972). *Self-consuming artifacts: The experience of seventeenth-century literature.* Berkeley, Calif.: University of California Press.

Flower, L., and R. Hayes (1970). *A process model of composition.* Pittsburgh: Carnegie-Mellon University.

Freud, S. (1943). *A general introduction to psychoanalysis.* Garden City, N.Y.: Garden City Publishing Co.

Gardner, H. (1983). *Frames of mind: The theory of multiple intelligences.* New York: Basic Books.

Gibson, W. (1966). *Tough, sweet, and stuffy: An essay on modern American prose styles.* Bloomington, Ind.: Indiana University Press.

Goffman, E. (1981). *Forms of talk.* Philadelphia: University of Pennsylvania Press.

Goody, J. (1977). *The domestication of the savage mind.* New York: Cambridge University Press.

Golub, L. S. (1969). Linguistic structures in students' oral and written discourse. *Research in the Teaching of English* 3: 70–85.

Graves, D. (1975). An examination of the writing process of seven year old children. *Research in the Teaching of English* 9: 227–41.

Gruner, C., R. Kibler, and W. Gibson (1967). A quantitative analysis of selected characteristics of oral and written vocabularies. *Journal of Communication* 17: 152–58.

Guntrip, H. (1961). *Personality, structure, and human interaction.* London: Hogarth Press.

Gusdorf, G. (1965). *Speaking,* trans. by P. T. Brockelman. Evanston, Ill.: Northwestern University Press.

Halliday, M. A. K., and R. Hasan (1976). *Cohesion in English.* London: Longman.

Harrell, L. E., Jr. (1957). A comparison of oral and written language in school age children. *Monographs of the Society for Research in Child Development* 27, 3, serial no. 112.

Harste, J. C., V. A. Woodward, and C. L. Burke (1984). Examining our assumptions: A transactional view of literacy and learning. *Research in the Teaching of English* 18: 84–108.

Havelock, E. (1963). *Preface to Plato.* Cambridge, Mass.: Belknap Press of Harvard University Press.

Heider, F. K., and G. M. Heider (1940). A comparison of sentence structure of deaf and hearing children. *Psychological Monographs* 52, no. 1: 42–103.

Herber, M. (1979). Effective features of dialogue: The influence of speech on progress in seriation of children of 5–6 years. Paper presented at the annual conference of the British Psychological Society, Nottingham.

Higgins, E. T. (1978). Written communication as functional literacy: A developmental comparison of oral and written communication. In *Perspectives on literacy,* edited by R. Beach and P. D. Pearson, 130–52. Minneapolis: College of Education, University of Minnesota.

Hill, M. (1980). Preschoolers' print awareness: An in-depth study of 3- and 4-year old children. In *Perspectives in reading research and instruction,* edited by M. L. Camile and A. J. Moe. Washington, D.C.: National Reading Conference.

Himley, M. (1980). Text and content: A dynamic interaction. Chicago: University of Illinois at Chicago. ED 193 640.

Hymes, D. (1974). *Foundations in sociolinguistics.* Philadelphia: University of Pennsylvania Press.

———— (1979). On communicative competence. In *Language development,* edited by V. Lee. New York: John Wiley & Sons.

Kantor, K., and D. Rubin (1981). Between speaking and writing: Processes of differentiation. In *Exploring speaking-writing relationships,* edited by B. M. Kroll and R. J. Vann. Urbana, Ill.: National Council of Teachers of English. ED 204 794.

Keenan, E. (1977). Unplanned and planned discourse. In *Discourse across time and space,* edited by E. O. Keenan and T. L. Bennett. California Occasional Papers in Linguistics, No. 5. Los Angeles: Department of Linguistics, University of Southern California.

Klein, M. (1960). On mental health. *British Journal of Medical Psychology* 33: 237–41.

Kroll, B. (1977). Combining ideas in written and spoken English: A look at subordination and coordination. In *Discourse across time and space,* edited by E. O. Keenan and T. L. Bennett. California Occasional Papers in Linguistics, No. 5. Los Angeles: Department of Linguistics, University of Southern California.

Kyle, J. G. (1981). Written language in a visual world. In *Exploring speaking-writing relationships,* edited by B. Kroll and R. Vann. Urbana, Ill.: National Council of Teachers of English. ED 204 794.

Lakoff, R. (1977). What can you do with words: Politeness, pragmatics, and performatives. In *Papers from the Austin, Texas Conference on Performative Speech Acts.* Berkeley, Calif.: University of California Press.

———— (1982). Some of my favorite writers are literate: The mingling of oral and literate strategies in written communication. In *Spoken and written language,* edited by D. Tannen, 239–60. Norwood, N.J.: Ablex.

Langer, S. K. (1942). *Philosophy in a new key.* New York: The New American Library.

Lanham, R. (1974). *Style: An anti-textbook.* New Haven, Conn.: Yale University Press.

Lévi-Strauss, C. (1963). *Structural anthropology,* trans. by C. Jacobsen and B. Schoepf. New York: Basic Books.

Loban, W. (1976). *Language development: Kindergarten through grade twelve.* Research report no. 18. Urbana, Ill.: National Council of Teachers of English. ED 128 818.

Marx, K. (1911). *A contribution to a critique of political economy,* trans. by N. I. Stone. Chicago: Charles H. Kerr & Co.

Moffett, J. (1968). *Teaching the universe of discourse.* Boston: Houghton Mifflin.

Murphy, S. (1981). Language differences in speech and writing. Paper prepared for Language and Literacy Division, University of California, Berkeley.

——— (1984). Children's comprehension of deictic categories in oral and written language. Paper presented at annual convention of the American Educational Research Association.

Myers, M. (1982). *Fictional narrative as speech event.* ED 252 857.

——— (1983). The speech events underlying written composition. *Dissertation Abstracts International* 44: 92–93A.

O'Donnell, R. C. (1974). Syntactic differences between speech and writing. *American Speech* 49: 102–10.

O'Donnell, R. C., W. Griffin, and R. Norris (1967). *Syntax of kindergarten and elementary school children: A transformational analysis.* Research report no. 8. Champaign, Ill.: National Council of Teachers of English. ED 017 508.

Ohmann, R. (1982). Reflections on class and language. *College English* 44: 1–17.

Olson, D. R. (1977). From utterance to text: The bias of language in speech and writing. *Harvard Education Review* 47: 257–81.

——— (1980a). Some social aspects of meaning in oral and written language. In *The social foundations of language and thought,* edited by D. R. Olson. New York: W. W. Norton & Co.

——— (1980b). On the language and authority of textbooks. *Journal of Communication* 30: 186–95.

Ong, W. J. (1977). *Interfaces of the word: Studies in the evolution of consciousness and culture.* Ithaca, N.Y.: Cornell University Press.

——— (1982). *Orality and literacy: The technologizing of the word.* New York: Methuen.

Perl, S. (1979). The composing processes of unskilled college writers. *Research in the Teaching of English* 13: 317–36.

Piaget, J. (1926). *The language and thought of the child.* London: Kegan Paul, Trench, Trubner, & Co.

——— (1928). *Judgment and reasoning in the child.* New York: Harcourt, Brace and Co.

Pradl, G. (n.d.). *Object relations and the creation of self.* Unpublished document.

Pratt, M. L. (1977). *Toward a speech act theory of literacy discourse.* Bloomington, Ind.: Indiana University Press.

Radcliffe, T. (1972). Talk-write composition: A theoretical model proposing the use of speech to improve writing. *Research in the Teaching of English* 6: 187–99.

Ricoeur, P. (1979). The model of the text: Meaningful action considered as a text. In *Interpretive social science,* edited by P. Rabinow and W. M. Sullivan. Berkeley, Calif.: University of California Press.

Rosch, E. (1977). Human categorization. In *Advances in cross-cultural psychology*, Vol. 1, edited by N. Warren. London: Academic Press.

Rubin, D. (1984). Social cognition and written communication. *Written Communication* 1: 211–45.

Ruddell, R. B. (1966). Oral language and the development of other language skills. In *Research in oral language*, edited by W. Petty, 10–20. Urbana, Ill.: National Council of Teachers of English. ED 026 370.

Searle, J. (1969). *Speech acts: An essay in the philosophy of language*. London: Cambridge University Press.

Shaughnessy, M. (1977). *Errors and expectations*. New York: Oxford University Press.

Shibutani, T. (1955). Reference groups as perspectives. *American Journal of Sociology* 60: 562–69.

Simon, H. A. (1981). *Sciences of the artificial*. Cambridge, Mass.: MIT Press.

Snow, C. (1977). Mother's speech research: From input to interaction. In *Talking to children: Language input and acquisition*, edited by C. Snow and C. A. Ferguson. Cambridge, England: Cambridge University Press.

Sonstroem, A. M. (1966). On the conservation of solids. In *Studies in cognitive growth*, edited by J. S. Bruner et al., 208–44. New York: John Wiley & Sons.

Tannen, D., ed. (1982). *Spoken and written language: Exploring orality and literacy*. Norwood, N.J.: Ablex.

Templin, M. (1950). *The development of reasoning in children with normal and defective hearing*. Minneapolis: University of Minnesota Press.

Tuman, M. (1983). Words, tools, and technology. *College English* 45: 769–79.

Volosinov, V. N. (1973). *Marxism and the philosophy of language*, trans. by L. Matejka and I. R. Titunik. New York: Seminar Press.

Vygotsky, L. S. (1962). *Thought and language*, edited and trans. by E. Hanfmann and G. Vakar. Cambridge, Mass.: MIT Press.

——— (1978). *Mind in society: The development of higher psychological processes*. Cambridge, Mass.: Harvard University Press.

Whitehead, A. N. (1927). *Symbolism: Its meaning and effect*. New York: Macmillan.

Williams, J. D. (1983). Covert language behavior during writing. *Research in the Teaching of English* 17: 301–12.

Winnicott, D. W. (1965). *The maturational processes and the facilitating environment: Studies in the theory of emotional development*. New York: International Universities Press.

Wittgenstein, L. (1968). *Philosophical investigations*. New York: Macmillan.

Wood, D. (1980). Teaching the young child: Some relationships between social interaction, language, and thought. In *The social foundations of language and thought*, edited by D. R. Olson. New York: W. W. Norton & Co.

Zoellner, R. (1969). Talk-write: A behavioral pedagogy for composition. *College English* 30: 267–320.

Oral Language, Literacy Skills, and Response to Literature

David K. Dickinson
Tufts University

The National Council of Teachers of English has long endorsed the position that there is a close relationship between oral language, reading, writing, and response to literature. As we entered the decade of the 1980s, this position was bolstered by the emergence of psycholinguistic models of the reading process and by research on the early, spontaneous acquisition of reading and writing skills. However, at the same time, correlational studies cast doubt on the directness of the relationship between oral language skills and literacy skills, and new thrusts in writing and reading research emphasized cognitive and strategic aspects of reading and writing.

Given our increasingly sophisticated knowledge about literacy skills, it is possible to analyze in a relatively fine-grained fashion the connections among these abilities. With greater sophistication comes greater complexity. Global conclusions that apply to all developmental levels and all processes simply cannot reflect adequately the complexity of the issues. Two separate clusters of issues can be identified. First, one can ask whether the cognitive processes and the knowledge structures employed when speaking, listening, reading, and writing are similar. Secondly, the acquisition process can be examined, considering similarities in how oral language and literacy skills are acquired and ways in which these skills are related at different points in development. These clusters of issues will provide a backdrop for examining the varied research traditions.

The scope of the issues involved is immense, the length of this paper limited, and the knowledge of its author finite; therefore, several restrictions were necessary. I concentrate on early acquisition because it is here that the parallels are strongest, and therefore the point at which denial of the intimacy of the oral language/literacy linkages is most significant. Evidence cited is drawn heavily from major existing reviews, except for in less well-known areas. Cognitive-process models in reading will be dealt with in a superficial manner and writing models will not be

147

discussed. Research on language as the vehicle for education will not be discussed.

Processing: Reading and Oral Language Relationships

Studies of orthographic systems, models of the reading process, and good/poor reader differences have all indicated that oral language provides a base required for reading to occur; that is, reading depends upon oral language processing capacities.

Orthographic Systems

Orthographic systems are closely tied to the oral language systems they represent (Tzeng and Hung 1981, Wang 1981). The link to the oral language system may occur via the sound system, as in alphabetic systems; via a combination of semantic and phonological information carried by phonograms, as in the Chinese logographic system (Tzeng and Hung 1981); or directly to the semantic system, as in a pictographic system. The level at which an orthography connects with a language appears to depend upon characteristics of that language. Wang (1981) described the differences between Chinese logographies and two Japanese scripts (Kanji and Kana) and found that differences in the scripts could be attributed to differences in the spoken languages. If, as Wang claims about written systems, "their development (and probably their emergence as well) is largely based on speech" (p. 223), then we should find similar intimate relationships in the processing of oral and written language.

Reading Models

Cognitive models of the reading process attempt to describe how graphic images are miraculously transformed into meaningful propositions and entire texts. Initial receptive stages of reading and listening obviously differ because the transducer systems are not the same. Receptor system differences may have important implications for the processing of printed and written language, because the ear may be innately programmed to discriminate speech segments and assign them to discrete categories (Fowler 1981, Nickerson 1981). The problems some children have matching phonemes to graphemes may result from the use of vision to process speech (Gleitman and Rozin 1977). Modality-related differences also arise as a result of the concrete nature of print. During later stages of reading development (Chall 1983), print allows skilled readers to sample information in any order and to adopt differential strategies (Nickerson 1981).

A matter of great controversy among modelers of the reading process is the role of auditory images in the retrieval of meaning. One position is that reading is "parasitic" upon oral language (Gough 1972, Liberman and Shankweiler 1979). Print first is decoded into internal speech (I use this phrase to avoid issues surrounding the exact nature of the representation) which accesses lexical and syntactic representations. An intermediate position is that, in the reading of text, speech-code representations are retrieved after words have been accessed (Banks, Oka, and Shugarman 1981). Finally, some believe that speech-code representations can be bypassed by accessing entire words directly (Johnson 1981) or by using orthographic cues (Taft 1979). Currently most theorists believe that multiple techniques are used to construct meaning, that internal speech is employed at some point (Banks, Oka, and Shugarman 1981; Fowler 1981), and that oral language and reading processes share lexical, syntactic, and discourse knowledge and the world knowledge used for making inferences (Nickerson 1981).

Good/Poor Reader Research

The largest body of research on language processing bearing directly on the question of a link between reading and oral language skills is that describing differences between good and poor readers. Poor readers are usually poor decoders, and this problem generally has been attributed to difficulties constructing speech-code representations (for reviews, see Perfetti and Lesgold 1979, Liberman and Shankweiler 1979, Vellutino 1977, Wolf and Dickinson 1984). Even as they improve their reading, disabled readers continue to be troubled by difficulties constructing speech-code representations. Snowling (1980) compared the ability of dyslexic readers from four reading levels to read pronounceable four-letter nonsense words and found no improvement on this demanding decoding task. Normal readers improved significantly.

Evidence also is accumulating that poor readers are slow to retrieve speech-code information (Backman 1984, Barron 1981, DeSoto and DeSoto 1983, Jackson and McClelland 1981, Lesgold and Curtis 1981, Perfetti and Roth 1981). Wolf (1982, 1984) has found high correlations among reading abilities, speed of alternately naming letters and numbers, and performance on a task requiring children to think of words beginning with f (requiring speech-code information). Of most immediate interest, she found her results (1982) were almost identical to those found by Goodglass and Kaplan (1972) in an aphasic population, indicating that the retrieval problems of poor readers reflect a language-based problem.

Being able quickly to retrieve and employ an internal speech code is important for several reasons: first, automatic retrieval limits the cognitive load imposed on the child, reducing the chances of a cognitive "bottle-neck" developing (Perfetti and Lesgold 1979); second, it increases the precision of the retrieval process (Barron 1981); third, it helps one to retain information in memory until the information gets recoded into deeper representations, resulting in improved comprehension (Barron 1981, Liberman and Shankweiler 1979, Perfetti and Lesgold 1979). Finally, the speech code may help one sense intonation and prosody, thus helping one disambiguate meanings, construct syntactic representations, and appreciate style (Banks, Oka, and Shugarman 1981).

Poor readers also have difficulty constructing complex representations of text. Weak syntactic skills are associated with poor reading in deaf readers (Quigley and Paul 1984) and hearing children (for reviews, see Huggins and Adams 1980, Ryan 1981, Vellutino 1977), and these problems seem not to be simply the result of difficulties using phonological representations (Byrne 1981). Poor readers also have problems integrating information beyond the sentence level. They tend not to mark the ends of sentences and phrases when reading aloud, indicating they are not adequately processing the syntax (Clay and Imlach 1971, Huggins and Adams 1980). When retelling stories, compared with normal readers, dyslexic readers are prone to omit temporal or causal markers (e.g., *because, next*), whereas good readers tend to add these markers (Weaver and Dickinson 1982). Poor readers' difficulties in recognizing what is important in a text (Smiley et al. 1977) and producing concise and appropriate summaries (Winograd 1984) also suggest that they are constructing less adequate textual representations of stories than normal readers.

Summary: Process and Knowledge Factors

Models of the reading process indicate that once past the acoustic level, the process employs the same knowledge structures as oral language. However, among skilled readers the processes used for meaning construction may be less like those employed with spoken language because of increasing use of reading strategies. Research on good and poor readers shows that reading is a language-based process: weakness in normal oral language functioning results in reading problems.

Inefficient processing of print and language accounts for many reading problems, but knowledge factors also affect reading. Reading ability is related to vocabulary size in deaf children (Quigley and Paul 1984) and hearing children (Anderson and Freebody 1981; Johnson, Toms-Bronowski, and Pittelman 1981), and also to familiarity with discourse structure (Fitzgerald 1984, Langer 1982, Taylor and Beach 1984) and background knowledge (Anderson 1977, Lipson 1983, Reynolds et al. 1982). Processing problems or limitations in language-related knowledge result in impaired reading, but we are only beginning to be able to identify which children suffer from different types of reading problems. Equally important, we do not yet know what can be done to remedy processing problems, and we are only beginning to develop techniques for fostering the development of needed knowledge structures.

Correlational Evidence from Normal Readers

Recent studies have raised questions as well as reported data on the relationships between oral language and other linguistic skills.

Raising Questions

Despite the apparent dependence of reading upon oral language processing and knowledge structures, questions have been raised about the significance of this relationship in children with normal language-processing abilities. Lundsteen (1977) described nine respects in which learning to read is different from learning to speak, including social and affective factors such as anxiety about learning and cognitive factors such as differences in the need for conscious control and in the comprehensibility of the different activities. Hammill and McNutt (1980) synthesized the results of eighty-nine studies done between 1950 and 1978 that gave correlations between measures of listening comprehension, speaking (grammatical usage, sentence imitation, oral vocabulary), and writing (spelling, mechanics). They found a strong relationship between reading and writing variables but limited relationships between reading and language measures. Recently another correlational study has found that global measures of oral language proficiency in young children predict academic success less well than IQ (Gray et al. 1980). These findings raise questions about the directness of the oral language/literacy relationship, but caution is advisable. The grammatical measures used were diverse and global, and ages, social classes, reader groups, and ethnic groups were all merged in the analysis.

Groff (1978a) reviewed literature linking oral language to writing and also concluded that the relationships are tenuous. He supported the commonly reported observation (e.g., Gundlach 1982, Loban 1976, Stotsky 1983) that oral language complexity is greater than that of written language until the middle grades or junior high, and noted that by the middle grades, dialect-related and second language–related writing errors decrease. They do not necessarily disappear because they still are evident in the writing of dialect-speaking adults (Whiteman 1981). Groff concluded that by the middle grades children do not "write as they speak." Groff also noted that children do not always use speech when writing, and when used it is not always helpful in planning or proofreading.

A New Look at the Oral/Written Distinction

Relationships between spoken and written language are more complex than had previously been supposed. Numerous linguists, sociolinguists, and psychologists have begun to study the nature of spoken and written language. One general conclusion is that there is a continuum of forms extending from essayist written language to forms that show little influence of written language. The poles of the continuum are not defined by modality, but by the forms and communicative strategies usually associated with formal writing (literate-style) or casual face-to-face conversation (oral-style). These poles also are associated with a focus on conveying decontextualized information as opposed to a more rhetorical and interpersonal focus.

Oral styles are found in the most pure form in cultures with no or little history of literacy, such as the early Greeks (Goody 1977) and Athabaskan Eskimos (Scollon and Scollon 1979). Heavy use of oral-style strategies when telling stories also is common among groups in Western societies having histories of limited access to literacy (Erickson 1984, Michaels 1981), though oral-style strategies also are found among highly literate groups such as Jewish Americans in New York City (Tannen 1985).

Clusters of features have been found that characterize speech from opposite ends of the continuum. Among these clusters are the following:

1. Literate-style narratives tend to have a single, explicitly identified topic; such narratives may be called "topic-centered" stories (Green and Morgan 1981, Michaels 1981). Oral-style narratives tend to have an implicit theme that is illustrated using concrete examples; these narratives may be called "topic-chaining" stories (Erickson 1984, Michaels 1981).

2. Literate-style discourse uses lexical resources and syntax to signal shifts in perspective, to indicate the speaker's opinion about the material being conveyed, to mark thematic progressions, and to clarify the referents to pronouns; oral-style narratives, in contrast, rely heavily on prosody for these functions (Cook-Gumperz and Gumperz 1981; Erickson 1984; Gumperz 1982; Gumperz, Kaltman, and O'Connor 1984; Michaels and Collins 1984).

3. Literate-style discourse relies minimally on shared knowledge, leaves little to be inferred by the audience, and concentrates on factual accuracy; oral-style narrative encourages collaboration by the audience (Olson 1977; Scollon and Scollon 1979, 1984; Tannen 1982).

4. Literate-style narrators tend to stand apart from their story, treating it in a more impersonal manner; oral-style narrators tend to become more personally involved and are more concerned with interpreting the personal significance of reported events (Tannen 1982).

5. Literate-style discourse is more carefully planned and packs more information into fewer words than oral-style language by using syntactic devices such as different kinds of subordinate clauses and information-bearing relative clauses (Beaman 1984, Chafe 1982, Redeker 1984).

In general, literate-style discourse reflects its origins: it can be understood out of the context in which it is produced; it does not assume mutual negotiation of meaning; and it conveys information in as concise a manner as possible.

Acquisition of Literate-Style Strategies

Work on oral and literate styles has shown that essayist-style literacy (i.e., that used for communicating decontextualized information) within a culture results in the development of specialized uses of oral language among at least some members of that culture. The literate nature of speech in even very young children was first noted by Scollon and Scollon (1979, 1984), who found that their two-year-old used language in ways unlike her Chippewyan Eskimo friends. For example, she was comfortable answering test questions; her stories had internal cohesion and did not presume audience response; and she took a distanced third-person stance toward her own life when recounting her own adventures (fictionalization of self).

Preschool children develop considerable awareness of the differences between oral and literate styles of language use. One important development leading toward literacy is the ability of nonreaders to "pretend read" (emergent reading) in ways that closely approximate the style and content of a story (e.g., Holdaway 1979; Schickedanz 1981; Sulzby 1981, 1983). This development can be seen as movement from interactive discussion or first-person enactment of texts toward disengaged construction of a self-contained text. Children who rate high on Sulzby's (1985) emergent reading classification scheme distinguish between using language for conversing and using it to construct literate-style texts. They restrict conversational features to stories they tell (1982), give evidence of planning what they will say before producing a monologue (Cox and Sulzby 1981), vary the type of prosody and the lexical density they use, and prosodically mark places where commas and periods would appear if the text were written (Sulzby 1986a, 1986b). Scores on emergent reading scales predict later reading success (Clay 1979, Sulzby 1983).

Differences between oral and literate styles of storytelling appear in "Sharing Time" narratives. Some first graders—especially black girls— tell topic-chaining stories (i.e., illustrate an implicit theme with concrete instances) and use rhetorical styles containing many oral-style strategies (Michaels 1981). These children often are misunderstood by their teachers, who are more able to help children who tell literate-style, topic-centered stories. Topic-chaining narratives are appreciated more by black adults than by whites, supporting the suggestion that these stories reflect a culturally accepted way of telling stories (Cazden, Michaels, and Tabors 1985).

Implications for Writing

Differences between oral and literate styles have special importance for writing. Michaels and Collins (1984) analyzed written and spoken narratives of black and white first and fourth graders and found that the oral-style narrators had difficulties with writing in precisely those places where their rhetorical styles meshed poorly with the demands of writing. For example, where prosodic cues would disambiguate multiple characters in oral stories, in written versions these were points where stories were confusing. Also, the child with the most oral-style features in his speech failed to use complex syntax in his writing, signaled transitions poorly, had difficulty with paragraphing, and used a limited lexicon. Other researchers (Cayer and Sacks 1979; Gumperz, Kaltman, and O'Connor 1984; Meier and Cazden 1982; Wolf and Dickinson 1984) have also reported examples of importation of oral-style strategies into children's writing.

Developmental study of children's writing shows a movement toward creating more decontextualized texts (King and Rentel 1981). Between kindergarten and second grade, children from different classes and racial backgrounds begin producing more cohesive texts, increase their use of complex conjunctions, use more text-referring pronouns (endophora), and decrease their use of pronouns referring to things outside the text (exophora). Middle-class children create substantially more cohesive texts than lower-class children, possibly reflecting differences in control of literate-style strategies. Other researchers have also found that children's writing becomes progressively more cohesive, syntactically complex, and explicit (e.g., Collins 1984; Pellegrini, Galda, and Rubin 1984; Rutter and Raban 1982), approximating the decontextualized essayist ideal.

Ambiguities are a common source of problems in children's writing, and pronouns are a primary source of ambiguities. Such problems are particularly likely to bother children who do not control literate-style strategies, because in speech pronominal reference can be signaled prosodically. Use of pronouns is probably acquired slowly in spoken language (Webber 1980), and it causes many problems in writing. Bartlett and Scribner found that the majority of third to seventh graders failed to disambiguate two same-sex characters when writing stories (Bartlett and Scribner 1981, Bartlett 1984). Even if they do detect the presence of a problem, children often fail to correct it, probably because they do not adequately understand how spoken or written text works (Bartlett 1982).

Implications for Reading

Recently two groups of researchers have begun probing the relationships between oral language skills and early reading success. Wells (1979, 1981, 1985) followed a group of children from different socioeconomic classes from preschool years into the third year of schooling. Measures of spontaneous oral language ability during the preschool years revealed few class-related differences (only in oral comprehension and the variety of auxiliary verbs used). However, teacher assessments of oral language and tests of language comprehension, vocabulary, and knowledge of literacy administered during the first term of school and at age seven revealed strong social class differences. These tests and assessments predicted reading and math achievement at age seven. Overall academic success was most strongly related to children's knowledge of literacy measured using Clay's (1979) Concepts About Print Test, and with parental responses to questions about children's exposure to and enjoyment of reading. Questionnaire responses also correlated highly with social class. Finally, children's reading comprehension at age seven correlated with the frequency of having a story read or told to them when they were younger. Book experiences were also strongly related to reading success in data from another study (Moon and Wells 1979).

Wells noted that lower-class children had particular difficulty responding to teacher questions requiring them to demonstrate knowledge about a school-related topic. These difficulties came, he believes, not from children's discomfort in answering test questions, as Mehan has suggested (1979), but from difficulty using talk that does not relate to their own experiences. At home these children frequently named pictures in books on request, but they were not accustomed to responding to questions unrelated to continuing activities or personally relevant experiences. Wells concluded that children learn to deal with decontextualized, literate-style language before entering school by being read to and discussing stories.

Torrance and Olson followed a group of working-class and middle-class children from kindergarten to third grade. They administered a variety of tests measuring oral language ability and reading skill (Torrance and Olson 1984a, 1984b), and devised measures of conversational ability. These measures included the ability of a speaker to pick up and extend a prior speaker's meaning (a turnabout), the number of turns a child had speaking, and the types of topics introduced. The strongest correlate of reading was the number of cognitive psychological verbs (e.g., *think, know, believe*) the children used. Also correlated with reading were the mean length of utterance for independent clauses and the frequency of use of dependent clauses. Measures of conversational ability revealed two clusters of skills. One set included measures such as the number of turns, interpreted as reflecting interpersonal aspects of conversational ability. A second type of conversational ability emerged from indices such as the types of topics introduced and the number of turnabouts. These logical-structural characteristics were more often used by children who also used a number of cognitive psychological verbs, but there were no direct correlations between conversational ability and reading.

Olson (1984) concludes that the use of cognitive psychological verbs suggests that children of highly literate parents learn to stand apart from language and view it as an artifact. Literate parents assume they need to make special efforts to "teach" their children to talk. Although these efforts are not necessary, they may inculcate an attitude that language can be objectified, thus preparing children for dealing with the objectification of language required in early reading instruction.

Reading to Children

A major difference between learning to speak and learning to read is the fact that reading requires children to use language that allows others not present to construct the message being conveyed. Such language, called decontextualized language (e.g., Snow 1983), allows listeners or readers to use language to recreate the interpersonal and intellectual contexts needed to understand the speaker's intended meaning. Reading and talking about books is an excellent way for children to begin developing language skills needed for success in school. Snow (1983) and Wells (1985) believe that it is the interaction that occurs while books are being read that is critical, because parents adopt different styles of book reading which may not be equally successful in preparing children for reading.

Variations in book reading are best documented in Heath's ethnographic study (1983) of three groups in the Piedmont of the Carolinas. Heath found that middle-class parents prepare their children for the type of question answering and decontextualized-language use expected in schools, but poor white parents engage in little elaboration of the text. Poor blacks do not regularly read to their children, and when one mother did try to begin reading to her child she needed considerable external support (Heath and Thomas 1984). Heath found that how parents read to children is consistent with their uses of and attitudes toward language in general; therefore, changes require more than simply learning a new "technique" for talking to children (see Philips 1975 for a similar observation).

While maximal benefit may come from parent-child interaction around books, considerable benefit can also be derived from school programs that expose children to large numbers of books. Chomsky (1972) showed the beneficial effects of reading on language development, and several subsequent studies also have found gains in vocabulary level and reading achievement from reading children large numbers of books (reviewed by Johns 1984, Goldfield and Snow 1984, Teale 1984). In an experimental study, Elley and Mangubhai (1983) examined Fijiian children's learning of English using different approaches. They compared the effect of Holdaway's (1979) Shared Book technique, silent sustained reading (SSR) of many high-interest books, and a traditional structured approach to teaching English to Fijiian children. The two literature-based programs resulted in greater learning of English structures and greater gains in reading comprehension than the structured drill program both at the end of the program and one year later. These results are probably more dramatic than one would expect from children who have available good models of standard English, but they do highlight the extent to which children can learn language from books.

When children are read to by parents who help them extend the meaning of the story, they may learn ways of taking meaning from books. Regardless of the social interaction, school-age children also may benefit because they gain sensitivity to literate-style language, control of more vocabulary, knowledge of different discourse styles, and broadened world knowledge.

Summary

Clearer descriptions of the nature of the language associated with literacy reduce reliance upon global reference to modality when considering how spoken competence is related to reading and writing skills. The correlational evidence of Wells, Torrance, and Olson suggests there may be only special aspects of oral language competence that are related to reading success, possibly explaining why Hamill and McNutt found low correlations when global measures were used. Also, we see that Groff's finding of progressive divergence between spoken and written forms merely reveals a growing ability to shift style, not a basic discontinuity between spoken and written language. This divergence highlights the influence of print experiences on language development.

While the claims about the importance of decontextualized language are provocative, we need consensus on what is being referred to—specific structural features and special strategies? Particular knowledge about language? A general orientation to language? Also we need much more precise descriptions of how decontextualized language skills affect early reading, where the emphasis is on decoding and stories often deal with familiar topics (Chall 1983). Michaels and Collins's work established somewhat more clearly the importance of oral language strategies for writing, but we need many more descriptions of how oral and literate styles do and do not transfer into writing, as well as studies of instructional techniques for dealing with these transfer problems. Finally, the importance of exposure to books is clear, but we still know little about how teachers read to children or about the benefits different children derive from varied styles of oral reading by teachers.

Acquisition: Parallels and Interdependencies

Close relationships among oral language, reading, and writing are apparent during initial phases of acquisition. Parallels in how acquisition occurs in the different modalities suggests that the same competencies and learning mechanisms are employed. Such parallels include examples of spontaneous development of literacy skills, the importance of function to early use, and development and spontaneous creation and refinement of rule systems. A second type of relationship is that of support of literacy activities by speech. As children learn to read and write, they depend on oral language for communication and for self-direction.

Spontaneous Acquisition

Many who believe that there is an intimate relationship between oral language and learning to read and write claim that acquisition of literate skills is as natural (or nearly so) as learning to speak (Clark 1984, K. Goodman 1982, Goodman and Goodman 1982, Hoskisson 1979, Smith 1984, Snow 1983, Teale 1982). Some preschool-age children have surprisingly sophisticated knowledge about print (Harste, Burke, and Woodward 1981), and they move into reading and writing without concentrated or direct parental tuition (e.g., Bissex 1980, Schickedanz and Sullivan 1984, Taylor 1983). For example, Harste, Burke, and Woodward (1981) found that regardless of race or social class children as young as three could distinguish between writing and drawing.[1] These children had attempted to convey meaning with print, had developed conventions of their own, could give pragmatically relevant responses to environmental print presented in context (e.g., labels, signs), and had a variety of strategies for responding to print.

Function and Early Writing

Since the mid-1970s many child-language researchers have stressed the importance of the social context in which oral language develops. Especially important has been the functionalist claim that linguistic forms are acquired to perform previously available communicative functions (e.g., Bates and MacWhinney 1982). Research on early literacy development has picked up the spirit of these approaches, emphasizing the social context of literacy acquisition. For example, Smith (1984) has argued that young children can learn to read because reading poses communication problems similar to those encountered in learning to talk, and that problems in acquiring facility with print result from its functional differences from oral language.

Descriptions of children's initial attempts to write show that they want to communicate to a specific audience. Frequently notes and letters are among children's first written productions (Bissex 1980, Gundlach 1981). Studying preschool writers, Lamme and Childers (1983) found that children's work was more mature when they wrote cards than when they wrote small books. Having a specific audience seems to have been the critical variable. In the past year, teachers in Tufts' Eliot-Pearson Children's School have begun encouraging writing among their kindergartners and have found card writing to be the most successful activity (Beardsley, Kennedy, and Wachler, class presentation 11/28/84).

For young children, writing also is attractive because its permanence enables it to do things that speech cannot do. For example, notes can be slipped to parents who are ignoring you, letters sent to absent friends and relatives, warnings left for intrusive siblings, lists of possessions compiled, and reminders left to jog one's own memory (Bissex 1980, Taylor 1983).

Children remain sensitive to the function of writing after they enter school. Edelsky and Smith (1984) found major differences between what

---

1. Others would disagree; cf. Donaldson 1984 and Dyson 1982.

they called "authentic writing" and "inauthentic writing." In contrast to assignments, writing that had a real purpose for children flowed easily and included a broad array of functions such as flattery and promises. Function also is a crucial determinant of the type of speech acts encoded in writing (Staton 1982) and of children's enthusiasm for writing (Florio 1979, Florio and Clark 1982). Function actually may define the activity; Dyson (1984b) has found that children approach tasks involving varied types of writing such as copying and free writing differently and do not see them as related. Bissex (1980) even found that her son, a precocious writer, used entirely different sentence structures, spelling, and content at home from that used at school.

Oral Language as a Support for Writing

During the early stages of learning to write, oral language often supports the child's initial attempts. Many children talk to themselves while they write, and this speech has been found to serve varied functions. Young writers initially introduce voice into their writing by speaking expressively as they write; later they use punctuation such as exclamation points and underlining to represent graphically their intonation (Graves 1982). Self-directed talk also has been found to be used for self monitoring and idea generating, and for analyzing spoken language and written products (Dyson 1981, Graves 1979).

There are developmental patterns in how children use self-directed language while writing. Scardamalia, Bereiter, and Goelman (1982) found that second and third graders tend to dictate to themselves as they write, but fourth graders tend to do more mouthing of words during pauses. Graves (1979) also found a decline in vocalizing as children develop facility. However, speech does not disappear entirely, and subvocalizing is positively related to the quality of compositions among fourth graders (Scardamalia et al. 1982) and adults (Williams 1983).

Overt interpersonal talk also is common during writing times; talk surrounds writing and helps children figure out how to write (Dyson 1981). Some children use oral language as a tool to get information, and some use it to give information (Dyson and Genishi 1982). Dickinson (1985) has found that when first and second graders write collaboratively at a computer, the amount of language dealing with monitoring, planning, and evaluating is greater than when they write alone. Such collaborative writing might help children develop a sense of planning and audience. Structured talk in groups in the form of writing "Sharing Time" also provides important opportunities for children to develop their writing skills and their understanding of the process (Graves and Hansen 1983).

Finally, talk between adults and children provides assistance to young writers. As they tell stories, children practice conventions necessary for writing narratives, such as how to distance themselves from the action of the story and how to keep different characters distinct (Rubin and Wolf 1979). Writing instruction in the form of conferences between teachers and children is, of course, another important influence on writing development (Cordeiro, Giacobbe, and Cazden 1983; Estabrook 1982; Graves 1982).

Spelling and Punctuation: Evolving Rule Systems

Children rely on knowledge of spoken language as they try to spell, and they construct rules in ways similar to rule construction during language acquisition. Chomsky (1970) and Read (1971, 1975) demonstrated that there is consistency in young children's invented spellings, partly because they attend to the articulatory features of words. Subsequent work on spelling development has revealed that development moves through regular stages, beginning with analysis of articulatory features of spoken language and slowly incorporating regularities of written English (Beers 1980, Beers and Henderson 1977). The generality of this finding is illustrated by Stever's (1980) finding that, despite coming from different classes and speaking different dialects of English, all the second graders she tested used the same spelling strategies.

Children also develop their own systems for punctuation, which reveal implicit knowledge of language structures. If young children divide words at all, they may use spaces as well as dots, strips of paper, or dashes (Bissex 1980, 1984; Sulzby 1981), and these segmentations reflect use of phonological, morphological, or syntactic structures (Edelsky 1983). Edelsky found that, without instruction, the segments delineated by spaces became smaller while the units marked by other punctuation became larger, revealing simultaneous growth in understanding of multiple levels of language structure. Although there was little within-child consistency in strategy use, Edelsky (1982) did find that the segmentation of work written in English (the children's second language) was more conventional than that of work written in Spanish. Proportionately more of the English input to these children was in written form, indicating that exposure to conventional forms results in learning that is at least initially restricted to the language in which it is learned. Cordeiro, Giacobbe, and Cazden (1983) also found that the learning of punctuation reflects children's analysis of language. They compared two different types of punctuation, those with a semantic base (e.g., quotations, possessive) and those delimiting formal linguistic units, and found that those that segment words into formal units (e.g., periods) are hardest to learn. They suggest that to learn to use these types children must become sensitive to the structures of their language.

Punctuation and spelling research shows that children construct rule systems that draw upon knowledge of language structures. An interesting and more exact parallel in acquisition has emerged. In both modalities children avoid taking advantage of the plurifunctionality of language. King and Rentel (1981) identified a point at which children over-mark cohesion to avoid having the same words serve multiple functions. Similarly, Ferreiro (1984) describes a three-year-old who refused to believe that the letter *m* could appear in more than one word. This resistance to accepting the plurifunctional nature of language has also been observed in oral language, when children fail to understand the multiple meanings carried by determiners (Karmiloff-Smith 1979).

Summary

Under ideal supportive conditions, reading and writing may emerge spontaneously as children use them to serve valued functions. In an accepting classroom, children develop progressively more mature rule systems for spelling and punctuation in ways similar to those observed during speech acquisition. Oral language also can provide valuable support to developing competencies in reading and writing. The excitement of these examples of naturally developing competencies is that they suggest that children's powerful language-acquisition mechanisms can be activated to assist the learning of reading and writing. What we understand far too poorly is whether all or most children can learn in this manner, and how writing systems evolve and function in classrooms (but see Cazden, Michaels, and Watson-Gegeo 1984 for discussion). It is especially important to discover how well children acquire the modality-specific knowledge needed for reading and writing.

What is Special about Learning to Read and Write

Few would dispute that reading and writing are language-based processes, but teachers are concerned with what accounts for variations among children. Several lines of research suggest that it is the special knowledge and cognitive-processing requirements of reading and writing that present the stumbling block to the acquisition and perfection of literacy skills. Reading and writing differ from oral language in the need to learn sound-symbol correspondences and orthographic regularities and in the importance of language awareness.

Learning How Print Works

Growing up in an environment filled with print enables some children to move seemingly effortlessly into reading and writing. But in literate societies, most homes of all classes and ethnicities have some printed matter in them (Anderson and Stokes 1984, Harste et al. 1981, Wells 1985). Families also engage in activities influenced by literacy, and children see signs and labels everywhere. Nonetheless, only a small percentage of children learn to read conventionally before they enter school. One reason for this failure may be that writing is an unnatural representational system for children. They may think of letters as other objects (Y. Goodman 1984), and tend to associate a letter with a single word or object (Ferreiro 1984). Donaldson (1984) also suggests that children find it natural graphically to represent objects, but have great difficulty representing events such as addition, subtraction, and speech.

Beginning Reading

Since Chall's review (1967), many publishers and school systems have concluded that children need to be taught sound-symbol correspondences directly. This position is bolstered by the previously reviewed evidence that poor readers are weak at decoding. But if learning to read is like learning to talk, simple exposure to environmental print should result in children learning to map sounds to discrete symbols. This is not always the case; rather there seems to be a discontinuity between being able to respond to environmental print and having flexible knowledge of sound-symbol correspondences.

Mason (1980) found three stages in the development of knowledge about early print: (*a*) recognition of print when situated in its environmental context (context dependency), (*b*) ability to recognize the entire word (visual recognition), and (*c*) letter-sound analysis of words. She also found the oft-reported result that there is a strong correlation between knowledge of the alphabet and level of reading. Similar results were obtained by Ehri and Wilce (1985). These researchers taught new words to three groups ranging from "prereaders" to "veterans" (those who could read several words) and found that prereaders relied more heavily upon visual cues; novices and veterans relied more on phonetic cues. Those unable to read environmental signs often even failed to notice when the first letters in words were altered. Similar results were reported by Masonheimer, Drum, and Ehri (1984), suggesting that initial reading requires children to shift how they approach print. This may not happen simply as a result of being exposed to environmental print.

Spelling

The importance of sensitivity to graphic characteristics for early reading
is supported by the finding that spelling skills at the beginning and in the
middle of first grade strongly predict word-recognition scores in the
spring (Morris and Perney 1984). Schwartz (1983) also found strong
correlations between spelling of nonsense words and reading ability
between the ages of eight and ten.

As children learn to read and write, they move away from reliance
upon spoken language for spelling because they begin learning with the
orthographic regularities of their written language. Research with dialect
speakers makes this point most clearly. At second grade, relationships
have been found between pronunciation and spelling among dialect
speakers, but considerable speech-spelling variation is also evident. For
example, Cronnell (1979) found that dialect speakers varied in deletion
of final consonants depending upon whether or not deletion would create
a homophone. In spelling, no such variation was noted. Similar results
were obtained on a reading task in which first-grade dialect speakers
were asked to say whether or not the word they were looking at was the
same as what an experimenter read them (Hart, Guthrie, and Winfield
1980). No dialect-related differences in accuracy were found, suggesting
that recognition of the special nature of print-speech relationships
emerges quite early. By the later elementary school years, spelling is only
minimally associated with features of spoken dialect (Groff 1978b).

Language Awareness and Learning to Read

As children learn to speak, they focus on accomplishing things with
language. They are concerned about the success of their attempts and
oblivious to the vehicle conveying their message. When learning to write
and read, children must at least temporarily turn their attention from
establishing communication to considering the sounds used for speaking.
This distinction between speaking and writing was first noted by Vygotsky
(1962) and more recently has been important to research on language
awareness. I will focus on later manifestations of language awareness and
will assume that it is conscious awareness that is important for early
reading (Downing 1984, Valtin 1984a).

Early Reading and Language Awareness

Since Mattingly's influential paper (1972), many have assumed that
language awareness is a prerequisite to learning to read: in order to learn
to read, children must be able to turn their attention to the speech

stream, segment it into phonemes, and understand that these units are related to letters. If language awareness is needed in order to learn to read and if it requires special knowledge or instruction, then it introduces a major difference between oral language and literacy skills. In the mid-1970s a flurry of correlational research provided overwhelming evidence that poor readers have limited language awareness. Using a variety of techniques, researchers repeatedly demonstrated that poor readers have difficulty focusing on the phonemic structure of words (Valtin 1984b) and the syntactic structure of phrases and sentences (Hirsch-Pasek, Gleitman, and Gleitman 1978; Menyuk and Flood 1981; Ryan and Ledger 1984). Despite the correlational evidence and the strong conceptual support for the claim that language awareness is required for learning to read, no one has successfully shown a causal relationship. For example, a recent study of early spontaneous readers (Backman 1983) failed to find that these children were particularly advanced in their ability to attend to the sound structure of words.

The lack of causal relationships between measures of language awareness and reading could be interpreted as indicating that language awareness is unnecessary for early reading, or as suggesting that language awareness is a product of learning to read. In either case, increases in language awareness appear as children begin to read, and this improvement is correlated with successful reading.

Knowledge and Language Awareness

Language awareness has sometimes been assumed to emerge naturally as a more or less general ability unaffected by experiential factors (see Valtin's 1984a review of current French work). Such a developmental course would link it closely with language development, seeing it as a natural extension of the child's linguistic curiosity and language learning. But evidence suggests that knowledge about language structures such as phonemes, words, and sentences results from experiences with print. For example, learning spellings of words influences how children hear the sounds, how they segment words, and how they pronounce and recall words (Ehri 1979, 1984). Ehri claims that providing a concrete representation of sound objectifies spoken language, making it easier to reflect upon and construct concepts about language. Similarly, Templeton (1980) found that seeing the spelling of words increases children's understanding of the relationships between derived versions of the same word (e.g., *profane, profanity*). Added evidence of the importance of literacy to the development of language awareness comes from the finding that an illiterate neolithic tribe in New Guinea, the Eipo, have no terms for language structures such as *word* or *sentence* (Heeschen 1978).

While language awareness is fostered by experiences with print, at least some language awareness may be important as children begin reading instruction. Downing (1984) has proposed that beginning readers need a degree of cognitive clarity about language (especially structural terms such as *word*) and about the nature of reading. Children who lack this clarity may become overwhelmed in the early stages and give up. Support for this hypothesis comes from the previously cited correlational evidence linking early language awareness with later reading.

Cognitive Control and Language Awareness

A two-factor approach to language awareness is emerging, with knowledge factors being separated from more general cognitive factors. Although no conclusive proof of the separability of knowledge and cognitive factors has been advanced, several researchers have found relationships between measures of cognitive development and measures of language awareness (Downing 1984, Ryan and Ledger 1984, Watson 1984). Some evidence also suggests that the spelling of elementary school children is related to cognitive development (Hiebert 1980, Zutell 1980). The relationships found between cognitive development, language awareness, and reading suggest that general cognitive abilities facilitate the emergence of language awareness by providing the operational capacities needed to focus on language.

Summary

Many children fail to learn to read or write without great difficulty. These problems usually are attributed to failures to acquire modality-specific knowledge, especially knowledge of sound-symbol correspondences. One often-cited reason for problems learning to decode is that some children lack the necessary language awareness. Tantalizing correlations between language awareness and reading acquisition have been found, but we are not yet certain whether language awareness is necessary for learning to read. Even less is known about the relationship between early writing and language awareness. Certain concepts of language appear to be important to early reading, but we do not know whether these draw upon knowledge already available to competent language users, whether they require special instruction or information, or whether they require the prior development of general cognitive capacities. Equally important, we do not know whether they can emerge or be constructed by average children without the aid of direct instruction.

Oral Language and Responding to Literature

Literacy appears in many forms and serves diverse functions in the lives of adults and children (Anderson and Stokes 1984, Heath 1983, Schickedanz and Sullivan 1984), but teachers of English have special interest in the uses children make of literature. A strong motive for learning to read is the opportunity books provide for children to move beyond the here and now by entering into many different possible worlds (Bruner 1984). Early writing also holds special appeal because it offers children an opportunity to control imaginary worlds (Britton 1982). Unfortunately we know very little about developmental progressions in children's response to stories and even less about how language abilities influence children's response to literature; Applebee (1977) found only a few unpublished dissertations linking ability or comprehension factors to literary response and none examining oral language competence and literary response.

We do know that elementary school children have limited understanding of literature. For example, there is a regular increase between ages six and nine in the realization that stories are "made up" (Applebee 1976). Even fifth graders from private schools do not necessarily understand that events in a story are under the control of the author (Galda 1982). The ability to stand back from stories, taking a spectator stance (Britton 1982), is a hallmark of a mature approach to literature. In fifth graders such an attitude is not always present even in girls from advantaged backgrounds. For example, Galda (1982) found one girl (out of a group of three) who evaluated story characters by comparing them to her own experiences and was quite bothered by events that did not fit her conception of the world. Children in Galda's study also gave evidence of knowing terms such as *style* and *theme,* but to the children these were essentially empty terms. Facile but empty use of such words characterizes children in discussion of literature throughout the school years, according to the 1979–1980 National Assessment of Educational Progress (Langer 1982).

Although many classrooms probably do little to foster the ability to view literature aesthetically, some elementary classrooms stand as examples of what is possible. In a rare ethnographic study of mixed-aged classrooms, Hickman (1980) found great variety in the physical and verbal responses of children to books. At times children would make brief comments to each other and at other times they would read to each other, pointing out what they especially liked. These verbal interactions were important to maintaining the children's enthusiasm for reading, and they illustrate that oral language is a natural part of children's response to literature (Y. Goodman 1984).

Probably the most exciting approach to building respect for literature is through group discussions about children's writing. In classrooms where children write frequently and share their work in meetings, they can assume the author and critic roles regularly (Hansen 1983). In such rooms children learn that, as authors, they control events in their stories and choose how to recount their narratives. As audience members, they learn to listen appreciatively, to relate personal experiences to the work being presented, and to consider written pieces as imperfect, mutable artifacts representing the effort of individuals. In such rooms children begin learning to assume a spectator stance toward the writing of peers and adult authors as they learn to take that stance toward their own writing.

We know relatively little about how children learn to appreciate literature and nearly nothing about links between oral language and literary appreciation. It is somewhat ironic that research on children's responsiveness to literature ignores the relationship between oral language and literary appreciation. As was pointed out earlier, oral-style strategies are rhetorically based and are well suited to aesthetic uses of language (see especially Bennett 1983, Gee 1985). I suspect that teachers and researchers unintentionally have been seduced into viewing literature in too literate a manner, ignoring the power of the spoken word that is the bedrock of literature. Considerable benefit could come from better appreciating the literary capacities of children—especially those children from homes where parents do not give intensive early training in the use of literate-style language.

A Typology of Language/Literacy Relationships

Four kinds of relationships between oral language and reading, writing, and response to literature can be identified: (*a*) dependence upon language-processing capacities, (*b*) interdependence of knowledge structures, (*c*) support of acquisition of literacy with speech, and (*d*) independence of the different modalities.

Dependence on Language-Processing Abilities

Literacy skills are dependent upon the language system used to process ideas. This dependence is described by reading models and research with disabled readers which shows that inefficiencies or breakdowns in language processing result in reading problems. A relationship of dependence might also characterize the mechanisms that enable children to learn to read and write spontaneously. Although controversy still surrounds the question of whether special-purpose abilities enable children to learn language, I assume that not all language learning can be accounted for in terms of general cognitive abilities (Gleitman and Wanner 1982). To the extent that special abilities for language learning are involved in acquiring oral language, those same abilities might be recruited for literacy acquisitions, with the possible exception of auditory mechanisms. Examples of similar rule-construction abilities in acquisition support this suggestion (see also Mattingly 1984).

Interdependence of Knowledge Structures

Oral language and literacy skills also are interdependent in certain respects; abilities required for one activity are drawn upon by another and experiences in one modality influence performance in other modalities. Most knowledge structures required for reading and writing fall under this heading. We have seen that literacy experiences shape children's vocabularies, syntax, and knowledge of discourse forms, and that control of these knowledge structures is necessary for reading and writing. A more subtle form of interdependence can be seen in the influence of reading and writing experiences on children's language awareness. A certain amount of cognitive clarity probably is necessary for children to begin learning to read, but the experience of reading greatly facilitates the development of language awareness, which then facilitates reading and writing.

There are developmental shifts in the balance of importance of the contribution of the different modalities, with young children being more dependent upon oral language experiences for constructing knowledge structures and older children more dependent upon literacy experiences. Phonological rules provide the most extreme example of such shifting. Beginning readers and writers are heavily dependent upon knowledge of the sound system, but as they are exposed to print they become progressively less reliant upon speech-code representations and more able to rely upon graphic representations (Barron 1981, Ehri and Wilce 1985).

Support by Oral Language

Oral language also may support development in other modalities. Self-directed language can be useful for monitoring oneself and guiding thought and action during writing. Social uses provide an even more important support to reading and writing. Informal conversations and structured group discussions provide children opportunities to learn how to read and write, to reflect on what they have read, to learn new ways of approaching reading and writing, and to share their enthusiasm. The importance of oral language as a support of literacy skills most often has been demonstrated among young children, but given the diverse uses of oral language, it is likely that older children would also benefit.

Independence of Modalities

Some processes, knowledge, and skills are modality-specific. For example, pairing graphic symbols to sounds and forming letters correctly require modality-specific knowledge. Other kinds of modality-specific knowledge such as reading strategies and techniques for organizing and presenting ideas in writing become more important with age. Also, at least in early processing stages, these activities are independent because they rely upon different receptor systems.

Abilities that are independent of oral language are generally taught explicitly and consume large amounts of instructional time. Interestingly, the extent to which skills actually are independent of an oral language base may vary depending upon how they are fostered. For example, we noted that children are able to develop their own spelling and punctuation systems once they have learned some modality-specific information (e.g., letters of the alphabet, types of punctuation marks). Teaching that stresses memorization of conventional forms is not likely to encourage children to use this knowledge.

Research Directions

Examination of the relationships among oral language, reading, and writing reveals support for the longstanding assumption that oral language competence is essential to the acquisition of literacy skills. Many traditions have been discussed, each of which has its own set of research problems, but I see two general directions for research examining oral language/ literacy relationships that could be especially worthwhile. We can examine whether particular language-based competencies (e.g., literate-style language strategies) provide a foundation for development of skills in reading and writing. Second, we can attempt to understand better whether, within the institutional restrictions imposed by schools, children can learn to read and write in ways that approximate how they learn oral language.

We do not know whether—except for breakdowns in language-processing abilities—any other oral language–related problems account for significant numbers of reading failures. We know even less about what accounts for writing problems. One hopeful direction for research is to examine the relationships between ability to use decontextualized language and skills in reading and writing. We know that, compared with good readers, poor readers often have less control of varied aspects of language structure (e.g., Squire 1983, Stotsky 1983, Tierney and Pearson 1983), and exposure to books influences language and writing (Britton 1982) development. We do not know whether all of these pieces might fit together, reflecting competence with using decontextualized language. It could be that correlates to reading problems indicate limited knowledge of the language of books and minimal understanding of the literate approach to language. On the other hand, reading problems could result from many unrelated problems. Separate clusters of problems may be related to diverse language-related problems, including both process-based problems such as speed of access to verbal information and more knowledge-related problems such as limited vocabulary and world knowledge, limited control of complex syntax, minimal grasp of high-level discourse structures, and weak understanding of reading and language.

Undoubtedly there are multiple causes of reading and writing failures, but at present sufficient evidence suggests the importance of decontextualized language to warrant study of how limited control of literate-style language does and does not affect a child's reading and writing at different stages of development. We also need to research-test the hypothesis that development of literate-style language-using abilities translates into improved reading and writing. Such research might take the form of clearer specification of the nature and importance of decontextualized contact in work on language awareness, research on language use in the classroom (e.g., Cazden 1986), good/poor reader research, and research on techniques for improving reading comprehension (e.g., Beck, Omanson, and McKeown 1982).

A second general avenue for research is exploration of whether it is effective and efficient to foster reading and writing development in ways that attempt to mimic oral language learning in school environments. "Spontaneous acquisition" of literacy skills usually refers to acquisition that occurs seemingly without effort (e.g., that is enjoyable, functional, and involves little overt study), without didactic instruction imposed upon the child, without correction of errors of form, and in the context of close interpersonal relationships. We have case studies of classrooms that exemplify several of these components in the teaching and learning of functional writing, and rooms where oral language supports reading and writing. Approaches becoming popular that also approximate this model include programs encouraging large amounts of writing using invented spelling (e.g., Graves 1982) and programs using the Shared Book technique described by Holdaway (1979).

Unfortunately we have little generalizable understanding of how exceptional classrooms function. What teacher and administration attitudes, child behaviors, skill levels, and classroom routines and rules are needed to create such environments? Equally important, in such rooms can we observe unusual development in mastery of the skills being inculcated? For example, in rooms that allow much time for writing and discussion, language awareness could be heightened, writing ability elevated, literacy appreciation and the ability to assume a spectator stance fostered, and at least normal reading development maintained. Careful study of the educational progress of children from all skill levels is needed to discover whether all children benefit equally from such programs.

Advances in theory and shifts in pedagogy enable us to begin examining in detail what oral language competencies are important to learning to read and write and also how to create settings that maximize the chances that children will utilize their language-learning abilities as they learn to read and write. There is considerable pressure toward fragmented instruction of discrete skills (Cazden and Dickinson 1981). Research specifying how oral language competence and literacy skills are related might help teachers resist this pressure by providing clearer guidance about what oral language skills should be encouraged.

References

Anderson, A. B., and S. J. Stokes (1984). Social and institutional influences on the development and practice of literacy. In *Awakening to literacy,* edited by H. Goelman, A. Oberg, and F. Smith, 24–37. Exeter, N.H.: Heinemann.

Anderson, R. C. (1977). The notion of schemata and the educational enterprise. In *Schooling and the acquisition of knowledge,* edited by R. C. Anderson, R. J. Spiro, and W. E. Montague, 415–31. Hillsdale, N.J.: Erlbaum.

Anderson, R. C., and P. Freebody (1981). Vocabulary knowledge. In *Comprehension and reading,* edited by J. T. Guthrie. Newark, Del.: International Reading Association.

Applebee, A. N. (1976). Children's construal of stories and related genres as measured with repertory grid techniques. *Research in the Teaching of English* 10: 226–38.

——— (1977). The elements of response to a literary work: What we have learned (ERIC/RCS report). *Research in the Teaching of English* 11: 255–71.

Backman, J. (1983). The role of psycholinguistic skills in reading acquisition: A look at early readers. *Reading Research Quarterly* 18: 466–79.

——— (1984). Acquisition and use of spelling-sound correspondence in reading. *Journal of Experimental Child Psychology* 38: 114–33.

Banks, W. P., E. Oka, and S. Shugarman (1981). Recoding of printed words to internal speech: Does recoding come before lexical access? In *Perception of print: Reading research in experimental psychology,* edited by O. J. L. Tzeng and H. Singer, 137–70. Hillsdale, N.J.: Erlbaum.

Barron, R. W. (1981). Reading skill and reading strategies. In *Interactive processes in reading,* edited by A. M. Lesgold and C. A. Perfetti, 299–327. Hillsdale, N.J.: Erlbaum.

Bartlett, E. J. (1982). Learning to revise: Some component processes. In *What writers know: The language, process, and structure of written discourse,* edited by M. Nystrand, 345–64. New York: Academic Press.

——— (1984). Anaphoric reference in written narratives of good and poor elementary school writers. *Journal of Verbal Learning and Verbal Behavior* 23: 540–52.

Bartlett, E. J., and S. Scribner (1981). Text and context: An investigation of referential organization in children's written narratives. In *Writing: The nature, development, and teaching of written communication,* Vol. 2, edited by C. H. Fredriksen and J. F. Dominic, 153–68. Hillsdale, N.J.: Erlbaum.

Bates, E., and B. MacWhinney (1982). Functionalist approaches to grammar. In *Language acquisition: The state of the art,* edited by E. Wanner and L. R. Gleitman, 173–218. New York: Cambridge University Press.

Beaman, K. (1984). Coordination and subordination revisited: Syntactic complexity in spoken and written narrative discourse. In *Coherence in spoken and written discourse,* edited by D. Tannen, 45–80. Norwood, N.J.: Ablex.

Beck, I. L., R. C. Omanson, and M. G. McKeown (1982). An instructional redesign of reading lessons: Effects on comprehension. *Reading Research Quarterly* 17: 462–81.

Beers, J. W. (1980). Developmental strategies of spelling competence in primary school children. In *Developmental and cognitive aspects of learning to spell,* edited by E. H. Henderson and J. W. Beers, 36–45. Newark, Del.: International Reading Association.

Beers, J., and E. Henderson (1977). A study of developing orthographic concepts among first graders. *Research in the Teaching of English* 11: 133–48.

Bennett, A. T. (1983). Discourses of power: The dialectics of understanding, the power of literacy. *Journal of Education* 165: 53–74.

Bissex, G. L. (1980). *GNYS at WRK.* Cambridge, Mass.: Harvard University Press.

——— (1984). The child as teacher. In *Awakening to literacy,* edited by H. Goelman, A. Oberg, and F. Smith, 87–101. Portsmouth, N.H.: Heinemann.

Britton, J. (1982). Spectator role and the beginnings of writing. *What writers know: The language, process, and structure of written discourse,* edited by M. Nystrand, 149–72. New York: Academic Press.

Bruner, J. (1984). Language, mind, and reading. In *Awakening to literacy,* edited by H. Goelman, A. Oberg, and F. Smith, 193–200. Exeter, N.H.: Heinemann.

Byrne, B. (1981). Deficient syntactic control in poor readers: Is a weak phonetic memory code responsible? *Applied Psycholinguistics* 2: 201–12.

Cayer, R. L., and R. K. Sacks (1979). Oral and written discourse of basic writers: Similarities and differences. *Research in the Teaching of English* 13: 121–28.

Cazden, C. B. (1986). Classroom discourse. In *Handbook of research on teaching,* 3d ed., edited by M. C. Wittrock. New York: Macmillan.

Cazden, C. B., and D. K. Dickinson (1981). Language in education: Standardization vs. cultural pluralism. In *Language in the U.S.A.,* edited by D. Hwang, C. A. Ferguson, S. B. Heath, and J. Tollefson, 446–68. New York: Cambridge University Press.

Cazden, C. B., S. Michaels, and K. Watson-Gegeo (1984). *Microcomputers and literacy project.* Fourth Quarterly Report, National Institute of Education (NIE-G-83-0051).

Cazden, C. B., S. Michaels, and P. Tabors (1985). Spontaneous repairs in sharing time narratives: The intersection of metalinguistic awareness, speech event and narrative style. In *The acquisition of written language: Revisions and response,* edited by S. W. Freedman. Norwood, N.J.: Ablex.

Chafe, W. (1982). Integration and involvement in speaking, writing, and oral literature. In *Spoken and written language,* edited by D. Tannen, 35–53. Norwood, N.J.: Ablex.

Chall, J. S. (1967). *Learning to read: The great debate.* New York: McGraw-Hill.

——— (1983). *Stages of reading development.* New York: McGraw-Hill.

Chomsky, C. (1970). Reading, writing, and phonology. *Harvard Educational Review* 40: 287–309.

——— (1972). Stages in language development and reading exposure. *Harvard Educational Review* 42: 1–33.

Clark, M. M. (1984). Literacy at home and at school: Insights from a study of young and fluent readers. In *Awakening to literacy,* edited by H. Goelman, A. Oberg, and F. Smith, 122–30. Exeter, N.H.: Heinemann.

Clay, M. (1979). *The early detection of reading difficulties.* 2d ed. Exeter, N.H.: Heinemann.

Clay, M., and R. M. Imlach (1971). Juncture, pitch, and stress as reading behavior variables. *Journal of Verbal Learning and Verbal Behavior* 10: 133–39.

Collins, J. L. (1984). The development of writing abilities during the school years. In *The development of oral and written language in social contexts,* edited by A. Pellegrini and T. Yawkey, 201–11. Norwood, N.J.: Ablex.

Cook-Gumperz, J., and J. Gumperz (1981). From oral to written culture: The transition to literacy. In *Variation in writing,* edited by M. Farr Whiteman, 89–109. Hillsdale, N.J.: Erlbaum.

Cordeiro, P., M. E. Giacobbe, and C. Cazden (1983). Apostrophes, quotation marks, and periods: Learning punctuation in the first grade. *Language Arts,* 60: 323–32.

Cox, B., and E. Sulzby (1981). Evidence of planning in dialogue and monologue by five-year-old emergent readers. *NRC Yearbook* 31: 124–30. ED 218 585.

Cronnell, B. (1979). Black English and spelling. *Research in the Teaching of English* 13: 81–90.

DeSoto, J. L., and C. B. DeSoto (1983). Relationship of reading achievement to verbal processing abilities. *Journal of Educational Psychology* 75: 116–27.

Dickinson, D. K. (1985). Collaborative writing at the computer. Paper presented at the annual meeting of the American Educational Research Association.

Donaldson, M. (1984). Speech and writing and modes of learning. In *Awakening to literacy,* edited by H. Goelman, A. Oberg, and F. Smith, 174–84. Exeter, N.H.: Heinemann.

Downing, J. (1984). Task awareness in the development of reading skill. In *Language awareness and learning to read,* edited by J. Downing and R. Valtin, 27–55. New York: Springer-Verlag.

Dyson, A. H. (1981). Oral language: The rooting system for learning to write. *Language Arts* 58: 776–84.

——— (1982). The emergence of visible language: Interrelationships between drawing and early writing. *Visible Language* 16: 360–81.

——— (1984a). Emerging alphabetic literacy in school contexts: Toward defining the gap between school curriculum and child mind. *Written Communication* 1: 5–55.

——— (1984b). Learning to write/learning to do school: Emergent writers' interpretations of school literacy tasks. *Research in the Teaching of English* 18: 233–64.

Dyson, A. H., and C. Genishi (1982). "Whatta ya tryin' to write?": Writing as an interactive process. *Language Arts* 59: 126–32.

Edelsky, C. (1982). Writing in a bilingual program: The relation of L1 and L2 texts. *TESOL Quarterly* 16: 211–28.

——— (1983). Segmentation and punctuation: Developmental data from young writers in a bilingual program. *Research in the Teaching of English* 17: 135–56.

Edelsky, C., and K. Smith (1984). Is that writing—or are those marks just a figment of your curriculum? *Language Arts* 61: 24–32.

Ehri, L. C. (1979). Linguistic insight: Threshold of reading acquisition. In *Reading research: Advances in theory and practice,* Vol. 1, edited by T. G. Waller and G. E. MacKinnon. New York: Academic Press.

——— (1984). How orthography alters spoken language competencies in children learning to read and spell. In *Language awareness and learning to read,* edited by J. Downing and R. Valtin, 119–47. New York: Springer-Verlag.

Ehri, L. C., and L. S. Wilce (1982). Recognition of spellings printed in lower and mixed cases: Evidence for orthographic images. *Journal of Reading Behavior* 14: 219–30.

——— (1985). Movement into reading: Is the first stage of printed word learning visual or phonetic? *Reading Research Quarterly* 20: 163–79.

Elley, W. B., and F. Mangubhai (1983). The impact of reading on second language learning. *Reading Research Quarterly* 19: 53–67.

Erickson, F. (1984). Rhetoric, anecdote, and rhapsody: Coherence strategies in a conversation among Black American adolescents. In *Coherence in spoken and written discourse,* edited by D. Tannen, 81–154. Norwood, N.J.: Ablex.

Estabrook, I. W. (1982). Talking about writing—Developing independent writers. *Language Arts* 59: 696–706.

Ferreiro, E. (1984). The underlying logic of literacy development. In *Awakening to literacy,* edited by H. Goelman, A. Oberg, and F. Smith, 154–73. Exeter, N.H.: Heinemann.

Fitzgerald, J. (1984). The relationship between reading ability and expectations for story structures. *Discourse Processes* 7: 21–41.

Florio, S. (1979). The problem of dead letters: Social perspectives on the teaching of writing. *The Elementary School Journal* 80: 1–7.

Florio, S., and C. M. Clark (1982). The functions of writing in an elementary classroom. *Research in the Teaching of English* 16: 115–30.

Fowler, C. A. (1981). Some aspects of language perception by eye: The beginning reader. In *Perception of print: Reading research in experimental psychology,* edited by O. J. L. Tzeng and H. Singer, 171–96. Hillsdale, N.J.: Erlbaum.

Galda, L. (1982). Assuming the spectator stance: An examination of the responses of three young readers. *Research in the Teaching of English* 16: 1–20.

Gee, J. P. (1985). The narrativization of experience in the oral style. *Journal of Education* 167: 9–35.

Gleitman, L. R., and P. Rozin (1977). The structure and acquisition of reading, I: Relations between orthographies and the structure of language. In *Toward a psychology of reading,* edited by A. S. Reber and D. L. Scarborough, 1–53. Hillsdale, N.J.: Erlbaum.

Gleitman, L. R., and E. Wanner (1982). Language acquisition: The state of the state of the art. In *Language acquisition: The state of the art,* edited by E. Wanner and L. R. Gleitman, 3–48. New York: Cambridge University Press.

Goldfield, B. A., and C. E. Snow, (1984). Reading books with children: The mechanics of parental influences on children's reading achievement. In *Understanding reading comprehension,* edited by J. Flood, 204–15. Newark, Del.: International Reading Association.

Goodglass, H., and E. Kaplan (1972). *The assessment of aphasia and related disorders.* Philadelphia: Lea & Febinger.

Goodman, K. S. (1982). The reading process. In *Language and literacy: The selected writings of Kenneth S. Goodman,* edited by F. V. Gollasch, 5–18. Boston: Routledge & Kegan Paul.

Goodman, K. S., and Y. M. Goodman (1982). Learning to read is natural. In *Language and literacy,* Vol. 2, edited by F. V. Gollasch, 251–70. Boston: Routledge & Kegan Paul.

Goodman, Y. (1984). The development of initial literacy. In *Awakening to literacy,* edited by H. Goelman, A. Oberg, and F. Smith, 102–9. Exeter, N.H.: Heinemann.

Goody, J. (1977). *The domestication of the savage mind.* New York: Cambridge University Press.

Gough, P. G. (1972). One second of reading. In *Language by eye and ear,* edited by J. F. Kavanagh and I. C. Mattingly, 331–58. Cambridge, Mass.: MIT Press.

Graves, D. (1979). What children show us about revision. *Language Arts* 56: 312–19.

———— (1982). *A case study observing the development of primary children's composing, spelling, and motor behaviors during the writing process. Final report to the National Institute of Education.* NIE-G-78-0174. ED 218 653.

Graves, D., and J. Hansen (1983). The author's chair. *Language Arts* 60: 176–83.

Gray, R. A., J. Saski, M. E. McEntire, and S. C. Larsen (1980). Is proficiency in oral language a predictor of academic success? *Elementary School Journal* 80: 260–68.

Green, G. J., and J. L. Morgan (1981). Writing ability as a function of the appreciation of differences between oral and written communication. In *Writing: The nature, development, and teaching of written communication,* Vol. 2, edited by C. H. Frederiksen and J. F. Dominic, 177–88. Hillsdale, N.J.: Erlbaum.

Groff, P. (1978a). Children's oral language and their written composition. *Elementary School Journal* 78: 180–91.

———— (1978b). Children's spelling of features of Black English. *Research in the Teaching of English* 12: 21–28.

Gumperz, J. J. (1982). *Discourse strategies.* New York: Cambridge University Press.

Gumperz, J. J., H. Kaltman, and M. C. O'Connor (1984). Cohesion in spoken and written discourse: Ethnic style and the transition to literacy. In *Coherence in spoken and written discourse,* edited by D. Tannen, 3–19. Norwood, N.J.: Ablex.

Gundlach, R. (1981). On the nature and development of children's writing. In *Writing: The nature, development, and teaching of written communication,* Vol. 2, edited by C. H. Frederiksen and J. F. Dominic, 133–52. Hillsdale, N.J.: Erlbaum.

———— (1982). Children as writers: The beginnings of learning to write. In *What writers know: The language, process, and structure of written discourse,* edited by M. Nystrand, 129–48. New York: Academic Press.

Hammill, D. D., and G. McNutt (1980). Language abilities and reading: A review of the literature on their relationship. *Elementary School Journal* 80: 269–77.

Hansen, J. (1983). Authors respond to authors. *Language Arts* 60: 970–76.

Harste, J. C., C. L. Burke, and V. A. Woodward (1981). *Children, their language and world: Initial encounters with print. Final Report.* NIE-G-79-0132. ED 213 041.

Hart, J. T., J. T. Guthrie, and L. Winfield (1980). Black English phonology and learning to read. *Journal of Educational Psychology* 72: 636–46.

Heath, S. B. (1983). *Ways with words: Language, life, and work in communities and classrooms.* New York: Cambridge University Press.

Heath, S. B., and C. Thomas (1984). The achievement of preschool literacy for mother and child. In *Awakening to literacy,* edited by H. Goelman, A. Oberg, and F. Smith, 51–72. Exeter, N.H.: Heinemann.

Heeschen, V. (1978). The metalinguistic vocabulary of a speech community in the highlands of Irian Jaya (West New Guinea). In *The child's conception of language,* edited by A. Sinclair, R. J. Jarvella, and W. J. M. Levelt, 155–87. New York: Springer-Verlag.

Hickman, J. (1980). Children's response to literature: What happens in the classroom. *Language Arts* 57: 524–29.

Hiebert, E. H. (1980). The relationship of logical reasoning ability, oral language comprehension, and home experiences to preschool children's print awareness. *Journal of Reading Behavior* 12: 313–24.

Hirsch-Pasek, K., L. Gleitman, and H. Gleitman (1978). What did the brain say to the mind? A study of the detection and report of ambiguity by young children. In *The child's conception of language,* edited by A. Sinclair, R. J. Jarvella, and W. J. M. Levelt, 97–132. New York: Springer-Verlag.

Holdaway, D. (1979). *The foundations of literacy.* Exeter, N.H.: Heinemann.

Hoskisson, K. (1979). Learning to read naturally. *Language Arts* 56: 489–96.

Hudson, R. A. (1980). *Sociolinguistics.* New York: Cambridge University Press.

Huggins, A. W. F., and M. J. Adams (1980). Syntactic aspects of reading comprehension. In *Theoretical issues in reading comprehension: Perspectives from cognitive psychology, linguistics, artificial intelligence, and education,* edited by R. Spiro, B. Bruce, and W. Brewer. Hillsdale, N.J.: Erlbaum.

Jackson, M. D., and J. L. McClelland (1981). Exploring the nature of a basic visual-processing component of reading ability. In *Perception of print: Reading research in experimental psychology,* edited by O. J. L. Tzeng and H. Singer, 125–36. Hillsdale, N.J.: Erlbaum.

Johns, J. L. (1984). Students' perceptions of reading: Insights from research and pedagogical implications. In *Language awareness and learning to read,* edited by J. Downing and R. Valtin, 57–77. New York: Springer-Verlag.

Johnson, D. D., S. Toms-Bronowski, and S. D. Pittelman (1981). *An investigation of the trends in vocabulary research and the effects of prior knowledge on instructional strategies for vocabulary acquisition.* Theoretical paper no. 95. Madison, Wis.: Wisconsin Center for Education Research, University of Wisconsin.

Johnson, N. (1981). Integration processes in word recognition. In *Perception of print: Reading research in experimental psychology,* edited by O. J. L. Tzeng and H. Singer, 29–63. Hillsdale, N.J.: Erlbaum.

Karmiloff-Smith, A. (1979). Language development after five. In *Language acquisition,* edited by P. Fletcher and M. Garman, 307–24. New York: Cambridge University Press.

King, M., and V. M. Rentel (1981). *How children learn to write: A longitudinal study. Final report.* NIE-G-79-0137. Columbus, Ohio: Research Foundation, Ohio State University. ED 213 050.

Lamme, L. L., and N. M. Childers (1983). The composing processes of three young children. *Research in the Teaching of English* 17: 31–50.

Langer, J. A. (1982). Reading, thinking, writing . . . and teaching. *Language Arts* 59: 336–41.

——— (1984). Examining background knowledge and text comprehension. *Reading Research Quarterly* 19: 468–81.

Lesgold, A. M., and M. E. Curtis (1981). Learning to read words efficiently. In *Interactive processes in reading,* edited by A. Lesgold and C. Perfetti, 329–60. Hillsdale, N.J.: Erlbaum.

Liberman, I. Y., and D. Shankweiler (1979). Speech, the alphabet, and teaching to read. In *Theory and practice of early reading,* Vol. 2, edited by L. B. Resnick and P. A. Weaver, 109–34. Hillsdale, N.J.: Erlbaum.

Lipson, M. Y. (1983). The influence of religious affiliation on children's memory for text information. *Reading Research Quarterly* 18: 448–57.

Loban, W. (1976). *Language development: Kindergarten through grade twelve.* Research report no. 18. Urbana, Ill.: National Council of Teachers of English. ED 128 818.

Lundsteen, S. W. (1977). On developmental relations between language-learning and reading. *Elementary School Journal* 77: 192–203.

Mason, J. M. (1980). When do children begin to read: An explanation of four year old children's letter and word reading competencies. *Reading Research Quarterly* 15: 203–27.

Masonheimer, P. E., P. A. Drum, and L. C. Ehri (1984). Does environmental print identification lead children into word reading? *Journal of Reading Behavior* 16: 257–71.

Mattingly, I. G. (1972). Reading, the linguistic process, and linguistic awareness. In *Language by eye and ear,* edited by J. F. Kavanaugh and I. G. Mattingly, 133–48. Cambridge, Mass.: MIT Press.

———— (1984). Reading, linguistic awareness, and language acquisition. In *Language awareness and learning to read,* edited by J. Downing and R. Valtin, 9–25. New York: Springer-Verlag.

Mehan, H. (1979). *Learning lessons: Social organization in the classroom.* Cambridge, Mass.: Harvard University Press.

Meier, T. R., and C. B. Cazden (1982). A focus on oral language and writing from a multicultural perspective. *Language Arts* 59: 504–12.

Menyuk, P., and J. Flood (1981). Linguistic competence, reading, writing problems and remediation. *Bulletin of the Orton Society* 31: 13–28.

Michaels, S. (1981). "Sharing Time": Children's narrative styles and differential access to literacy. *Language in Society* 10: 423–42.

Michaels, S., and J. Collins (1984). Oral discourse styles: Classroom interaction and the acquisition of literacy. In *Coherence in spoken and written discourse,* edited by D. Tannen, 219–44. Norwood, N.J.: Ablex.

Moon, B. C., and C. G. Wells (1979). The influence of home on learning to read. *Journal of Research in Reading* 2: 53–62.

Morris, D., and J. Perney (1984). Developmental spelling as a predictor of first-grade reading achievement. *Elementary School Journal* 84: 440–57.

Nickerson, R. S. (1981). Speech understanding and reading: Some differences and similarities. In *Perception of print: Reading research in experimental psychology,* edited by O. J. L. Tzeng and H. Singer, 257–89. Hillsdale, N.J.: Erlbaum.

Olson, D. R. (1977). From utterance to text: The bias of language in speech and writing. *Harvard Educational Review* 47: 257–81.

———— (1984). "See! Jumping!" Some oral language antecedents of literacy. In *Awakening to literacy,* edited by H. Goelman, A. Oberg, and F. Smith, 185–92. Exeter, N.H.: Heinemann.

Pellegrini, A. D., L. Galda, and D. L. Rubin (1984). Context in text: The development of oral and written language in two genres. *Child Development* 55: 1549–55.

Perfetti, C. A., and A. M. Lesgold (1979). Coding and comprehension in skilled reading and implications for reading instruction. In *Theory and practice of early reading,* Vol. 1, edited by L. B. Resnick and P. A. Weaver, 57–84. Hillsdale, N.J.: Erlbaum.

Perfetti, C. A., and S. Roth (1981). Some of the interactive processes in reading and their role in reading skill. In *Interactive processes in reading,* edited by A. M. Lesgold and C. A. Perfetti, 269–97. Hillsdale, N.J.: Erlbaum.

Petrosky, A. R. (1980). The inferences we make: Children and literature. *Language Arts* 57: 149–56.

Philips, S. U. (1975). Literacy as a mode of communication on the Warm Springs Indian Reservation. In *Foundations of language development,* Vol. 2, edited by E. H. Lenneberg and E. Lenneberg, 367–82. New York: Academic Press.

Quigley, S. P., and P. V. Paul (1984). *Language and deafness.* San Diego, Calif.: College-Hill Press.

Read, C. (1971). Pre-school children's knowledge of English phonology. *Harvard Educational Review* 41: 1–34.

———— (1975). Lessons to be learned from the preschool orthographer. In *Foundations of language development,* Vol. 2, edited by E. H. Lenneberg and E. Lenneberg, 329–46. New York: Academic Press.

Redeker, G. (1984). On differences between spoken and written language. *Discourse Processes* 7: 43–55.

Reynolds, R. E., M. A. Taylor, M. S. Steffensen, L. L. Shirey, and R. C. Anderson (1982). Cultural schemata and reading comprehension. *Reading Research Quarterly* 17: 353–66.

Rubin, S., and D. Wolf (1979). The development of maybe: The evolution of social roles into narrative roles. *New Directions for Child Development* 6: 15–28.

Rutter, P., and B. Raban (1982). The development of cohesion in children's writing: A preliminary investigation. *First Language* 3: 63–75.

Ryan, E. B. (1981). Identifying and remediating failures in reading comprehension. In *Reading research: Advances in theory and practice,* Vol. 3, edited by G. E. MacKinnon and T. G. Waller, 223–61. New York: Academic Press.

Ryan, E. B., and G. W. Ledger (1984). Learning to attend to sentence structure: Links between metalinguistic development and reading. In *Language awareness and learning to read,* edited by J. Downing and R. Valtin, 149–72. New York: Springer-Verlag.

Scardamalia, M., C. Bereiter, and H. Goelman (1982). The role of production factors in writing ability. In *What writers know: The language, process, and structure of written discourse,* edited by M. Nystrand, 173–210. New York: Academic Press.

Schickedanz, J. (1981). "Hey! This book's not working wright." *Young Children* 36: 18–27.

Schickedanz, J., and M. Sullivan (1984). "Mom, what does U-F-F spell?" *Language Arts* 61: 7–17.

Schieffelin, B., and M. Cochran-Smith (1984). Learning to read culturally: Literacy before schooling. In *Awakening to literacy,* edited by H. Goelman, A. Oberg, and F. Smith, 3–23. Exeter, N.H.: Heinemann.

Schwartz, S. (1983). Spelling disability: A developmental linguistic analysis of pattern abstraction. *Journal of Applied Psycholinguistics* 4: 303–16.

Scollon, R., and S. B. K. Scollon (1979). *Linguistic convergence: An ethnography of speaking at Fort Chipewyan, Alberta.* New York: Academic Press.

———— (1984). Cooking it up and boiling it down: Abstracts in Athabaskan children's story retellings. In *Coherence in spoken and written discourse,* edited by D. Tannen, 173–97. Norwood, N.J.: Ablex.

Smiley, S. S., D. D. Oakley, D. Worthen, J. C. Campione, and A. L. Brown (1977). Recall of thematically relevant material by adolescent good and poor readers as a function of written versus oral presentation. *Journal of Educational Psychology* 69: 381–87.

Smith, F. (1984). The creative achievement of literacy. In *Awakening to literacy,* edited by H. Goelman, A. Oberg, and F. Smith, 143–53. Exeter, N.H.: Heinemann.

Snow, C. E. (1983). Literacy and language: Relationships during the preschool years. *Harvard Educational Review* 53: 165–89.

Snowling, M. J. (1980). The development of grapheme-phoneme correspondence in normal and dyslexic readers. *Journal of Experimental Child Psychology* 29: 294–305.

Squire, J. R. (1983). Composing and comprehending: Two sides of the same basic process. *Language Arts* 60: 581–89.

Staton, J. (1982). *Dialogue journal writing.* Washington, D.C.: Center for Applied Linguistics.

Stever, E. F. (1980). Dialect and spelling. In *Developmental and cognitive aspects of learning to spell,* edited by E. H. Henderson and J. W. Beers, 46–51. Newark, Del.: International Reading Association.

Stotsky, S. (1983). Types of lexical cohesion in expository writing: Implications for developing the vocabulary of academic discourse. *College Composition and Communication* 34: 430–46.

Sulzby, E. (1981). Kindergartners deal with word boundaries. Paper presented at the annual meeting of the National Reading Conference. ED 216 333.

——— (1982). "Text" as an object of metalinguistic knowledge: A study in literacy development. *First Language* 3: 181–99.

——— (1983). *Children's emergent abilities to read favorite storybooks.* Final report to Spencer Foundation. ED 236 557.

——— (1985). Children's emergent reading of favorite storybooks: A developmental study. *Reading Research Quarterly* 20: 458–81.

——— (1986a). Children's development of prosodic distinctions in telling and dictation modes. In *Writing in real time: Modelling production processes,* edited by A. Matsuhashi. New York: Longman.

——— (1986b). Writing and reading: Signs of oral and written language organization in the young child. In *Emergent literacy: Writing and reading,* edited by W. H. Teale and E. Sulzby. Norwood, N.J.: Ablex.

Taft, M. (1979). Lexical access via an orthographic code: The basic orthographic syllabic structure (BOSS). *Journal of Verbal Learning and Verbal Behavior* 18: 21–39.

Tannen, D. (1982). Oral and literate strategies in spoken and written narrative. *Language* 58: 1–21.

——— (1985). Relative focus on involvement in oral and written discourse. In *Literacy, language, and learning: The nature and consequences of reading and writing,* edited by D. Olson, N. Torrance, and A. Hildyard, 124–47. New York: Cambridge University Press.

Taylor, B., and R. W. Beach (1984). The effects of text structure instruction on middle-grade students' comprehension and production of expository text. *Reading Research Quarterly* 19: 134–46.

Taylor, D. (1983). *Family literacy: Young children learning to read and write.* Exeter, N.H.: Heinemann.

Teale, W. H. (1982). Toward a theory of how children learn to read and write naturally. *Language Arts* 59: 555–70.

—————— (1984). Reading to young children: Its significance for literacy development. In *Awakening to literacy,* edited by H. Goelman, A. Oberg, and F. Smith, 110–21. Exeter, N.H.: Heinemann.

Templeton, S. (1980). Spelling, phonology, and the older student. In *Developmental and cognitive aspects of learning to spell,* edited by G. H. Henderson and J. W. Beers, 85–96. Newark, Del.: International Reading Association.

Tierney, R. J., and P. D. Pearson (1983). Toward a composing model of reading. *Language Arts* 60: 568–80.

Torrance, N., and D. Olson (1984a). Oral language competence and the acquisition of literacy. In *The development of oral and written language in social contexts,* edited by A. Pellegrini and T. Yawkey, 167–81. Norwood, N.J.: Ablex.

—————— (1984b). Oral and literate competencies in the early school years. In *Literacy, language, and learning: The nature and consequences of reading and writing,* edited by D. Olson, N. Torrance, and A. Hildyard, 256–84. New York: Cambridge University Press.

Tzeng, O. J. L., and D. L. Hung (1981). Linguistic determinism: A written language perspective. In *Perception of print: Reading research in experimental psychology,* edited by O. J. L. Tzeng and H. Singer, 237–55. Hillsdale, N.J.: Erlbaum.

Valtin, R. (1984a). Awareness of features and functions of language. In *Language awareness and learning to read,* edited by J. Downing and R. Valtin, 227–60. New York: Springer-Verlag.

—————— (1984b). The development of metalinguistic abilities in children learning to read and write. In *Language awareness and learning to read,* edited by J. Downing and R. Valtin, 207–26. New York: Springer-Verlag.

Vellutino, F. R. (1977). Alternative conceptualizations of dyslexia: Evidence in support of a verbal-deficit hypothesis. *Harvard Educational Review* 47: 334–54.

Vygotsky, L. S. (1962). *Thought and language.* Cambridge, Mass.: MIT Press.

Wang, W. (1981). Language structure and optimal orthography. In *Perception of print: Reading research in experimental psychology,* edited by O. J. L. Tzeng and H. Singer, 223–36. Hillsdale, N.J.: Erlbaum.

Watson, A. J. (1984). Cognitive development and units of print in early reading. In *Language awareness and learning to read,* edited by J. Downing and R. Valtin, 93–118. New York: Springer-Verlag.

Weaver, P. A., and D. K. Dickinson (1982). Scratching below the surface structure: Exploring the usefulness of story grammars. *Discourse Processes* 5: 225–43.

Webber, B. L. (1980). Syntax beyond the sentence: Anaphora. In *Theoretical issues in reading comprehension: Perspectives from cognitive psychology, linguistics, artificial intelligence, and education,* edited by R. Spiro, B. Bruce, and W. Brewer. Hillsdale, N.J.: Erlbaum.

Wells, G. (1979). Variation in child language. In *Language acquisition,* edited by P. Fletcher and M. Garman, 377–96. New York: Cambridge University Press.

———— (1981). *Learning through interaction: The study of language development.* New Rochelle: Cambridge University Press. ED 218 965.

———— (1985). Preschool literacy-related activities and success in school. In *Literacy, language, and learning: The nature and consequences of reading and writing,* edited by D. Olson, N. Torrance, and A. Hildyard, 229–55. New York: Cambridge University Press.

Whiteman, M. Farr (1981). Dialect influence in writing. In *Variation in writing,* edited by M. Farr Whiteman, 153–66. Hillsdale, N.J.: Erlbaum. ED 214 204.

Williams, J. D. (1983). Covert language behavior during writing. *Research in the Teaching of English* 17: 301–12.

Winograd, P. N. (1984). Strategic difficulties in summarizing texts. *Reading Research Quarterly* 19: 404–25.

Wolf, M. (1982). The word-retrieval process and reading in children and aphasics. In *Children's language,* Vol. 3, edited by K. Nelson, 437–93. New York: Erlbaum.

———— (1984). Naming, reading, and the dyslexias: A longitudinal overview. *Annals of Dyslexia* 34: 87–115.

Wolf, M., and D. Dickinson (1984). From oral to written language: Transitions in the school years. In *Language development,* edited by J. Berko-Gleason. Columbus, Ohio: Charles E. Merrill.

Zutell, J. (1980). Children's spelling strategies and their cognitive development. In *Developmental and cognitive aspects of learning to spell,* edited by E. H. Henderson and J. W. Beers, 52–73. Newark, Del.: International Reading Association.

Commentary

David Dillon
University of Alberta

Fortunately, these two thorough and careful reviews provide us with different perspectives on the research topic we are considering. One, I believe, shows us clearly where (or how) we have been. The other provides an alternative vision of where (or how) we might go. Paradoxically, both reviews—one implicitly and the other explicitly—lead me to consider abandoning, or moving beyond, this topic of oral/written relationships as a major focus for educational research.

First, Dickinson's review reflects what has been the status quo of language arts research in this area, not merely in content, but also in the structure of knowledge in the area. Above all, we see not only a complex area, but also a fragmented and disjointed one. Dickinson is faithful to the descriptors and classifications existing in the field, but despite his effort to pull the many research aspects together into a coherent whole, we are left with a series of juxtaposed mini-reviews, sitting tentatively and uncomfortably side by side. I point this out not necessarily as a deficiency on the reviewer's part, but as an accurate reflection of research efforts in this area.

Many of the pieces fail to fit together, I believe, because of deep structural differences in basic assumptions and starting points embedded in the reviewed surface structure. For example, parts of Dickinson's review seem to assume that psycholinguistic processes of use in acquisition are largely uniform (with the exception of good and poor reading). Yet, other work he reviews focuses on the major impact of purpose and context on the process. Some of the work has a built-in middle-class bias. Other does not. Much of the reviewed work is based on a deficit perspective of children and implies a teacher-dominated instructional model. Other work suggests that resourceful children can only implicitly learn what cannot be taught directly.

Given these differences, Dickinson's review shows us a field preoccupied largely with psycholinguistic processes as well as stylistic and structured comparisons between oral and written modes, surrounded by a constellation of correlational factors which are assumed to affect and determine in some way the nature of the oral/written relationship. The field's preoccupation with the *how* of language use leaves little attention for its *what* and *why;* the processes are treated as if they were acontextual. Much of the reading research seems based on a text-driven model of comprehension. My concern, obviously, is that so much of the work reviewed and the way in which Dickinson has reviewed it fail to be explicit about implicit, deep-structure assumptions, beliefs, and values upon which the research is based. It is as if we are seeing only the low-level details of hierarchical, multidimensional frameworks for viewing this topic. The oral and written modes which are the primary focus of this review strike me as part of the lower level of subheadings, while topics of purpose, meaning, and context of language would be major, superordinate determinants. Yet when these high levels of our conceptual and attitudinal frameworks remain implicit and tacit, it is akin to "flying blind" or missing forests while attending to the detail of trees. I readily agree with Dickinson that the oral/written relationship is a complex one. Yet complexity does not preclude integration and wholeness. Becoming more critically aware of the underlying, superordinate constructs embedded in our research may be extremely helpful for us all in yielding clearer insight into the mass of detail now characterizing the field.

I sense a further problem in operating primarily at such a detailed surface level with little awareness of deep-structure principles. Dickinson, remaining within the paradigms he has perceived in the field, hopes for discovery of ever-further details as the way of creating greater integration among the research findings. My concern centers on what value the new details (as well as many of the details we already have) would be to language educators. I am reminded of several examples which James Britton often uses. One comes from Ed Henderson, who points out that knowing all the detailed rules or skills of the process of horseback riding was of no help to him in learning to ride a horse (indeed, it may even have been a hindrance). The other example comes from Michael Polanyi who explains that, while many of us learn to ride a bicycle, the rules by which we perform this process so successfully are generally unknown. In a like manner, much oral and written language use occurs successfully although we know little about how it occurs. And the more detail we learn about oral and written language processes and their relationship, the more doubtful I am that the detailed knowledge will help us or others learn to listen, speak, read, or write well.

As educational researchers, we must ask ourselves, I believe, about the value of pursuing research focusing primarily on what I've called lower-level details of the oral/written relationship. (I am surprised by the small amount of pedagogical research here at this conference.) Would the results help us become more effective language teachers by helping us understand the heart or essence of oral and written language use—or would it merely provide a Trivial Pursuit game for other researchers in this area? Thus, I have inferred from Dickinson's review that we should abandon or move beyond the oral/written dimension as a research topic of major importance to use.

Myers's review begins to shift us away from the current orientation by structuring a perspective around what I perceive to be higher-level and more basic constructs of sociocultural contexts, thus rendering the oral/written distinction a minor subheading. Myers argues explicitly for abandoning or de-emphasizing this research topic. He offers us a more coherent (yet admittedly more general) vision of language as a shaper of our experience particularly within social, cultural, and interpersonal contexts. He is also explicit about deep-level starting points embedded in a different research and scholarly tradition.

The difference in the two reviews is indicated, I believe, by how well they do—or do not—reflect current research. I have already indicated that I believe Dickinson's does. Myers's perspective seems not to be characteristic of current research in this area—at least within educational circles. Imagine the kind of research we would be engaged in if it were. Rather than being preoccupied with how to ride our analogous horse or bicycle, we would be concerned primarily with the circumstances of the riding and how those circumstances determine its nature.

Yet, although I feel that Myers has shown us steps in the right direction, his perspective still falls short of the deep-structure principles I referred to earlier. While he refers in his review to superordinate headings of purpose and meaning of language use generally, his framework fails to engage with them fully and explicitly (to carry my analogy further, that concern would be with *why* we are riding the horse or bicycle and where we want to go or happen to end up on it). Again, this lack is not entirely on the reviewer's part but reflects a dearth of research in the field with that orientation. Awareness of the deep, overriding importance of purpose and meaning for language use and development (both oral and written) has been with us at least since the Dartmouth Seminar, but has not yet characterized our research efforts. We have embraced psycholinguistics as a shape of our research, but Dartmouth's legacy of the philosophical and social aspects of language use has failed to move us. I offer this reflection to you because I think our research should deal explicitly with these deep-structure headings of purpose and meaning, rather than allow them to remain implicit and tacit, for they are always present.

I have already tried to point out some of the conflicting ideologies I perceive in the research Dickinson reviewed, some of which strikes me as reactionary and even oppressive. I wonder if the underlying ideology embedded in Myers's review values conforming to intersubjective understanding of circumstances, as well as behaving appropriately in a cultural context, thus emphasizing the reproductive, conforming aspects of culture and downplaying the iconoclastic, transforming, and creating potential on the culture of its individual members.

I am still uncertain myself about the nature of these deep-structure ultimates, but will offer you a few possibilities to consider. Both reviewers dealt with literacy but dealt with it largely as if it were neutral. Yet Paulo Freire, among others, points out that literacy is always used to oppress or to liberate the human spirit and body, that becoming truly literate means that a person discovers he or she has a voice. Does the research reviewed by Dickinson and Myers support literate oppression or liberation? J. Krishnamurti suggests that the ultimate purpose of education should be to free us from fear rather than to create fear. Does the current research tend to dissipate or create fear for learners, teachers, ourselves? My own concerns lately about ultimate purposes of language and literacy center around our lives evolving toward a higher good, discovering and defining ourselves, and finding meaning in our existence. How do these concerns fit into our research? I cannot help but think of literature, a topic both reviewers dealt with. Consider how a view of literature as an experience to define ourselves, to grow toward a higher good, and to find meaning in our existence would make us see the details of hearing or reading or writing literature differently than would a view of literature as a process of response or of psycholinguistic strategies built on an oral language base.

All of our research contains a view of humanity which shapes us ever so subtly, to enhance or erode our own humanness. In sum, what appears to be missing in both reviews—at least explicitly—is the treatment of these ultimates underlying the details, particularly ultimates which I would call political and ideological as well as philosophical and epistemological. Our research can never be neutral and pure. If we think it is, we are like Pilate, insidiously supporting the dominant ideology embedded in an area or a field, an ideology which has much to answer for in North American schools. I end by suggesting that we try to discover more the underlying assumptions and beliefs—what I hope I've called "ultimates"—embedded in what Dickinson and Myers have reviewed for us, for it seems that those are the things we are ultimately and most pervasively learning.

References

Freire, P. (1970). *Pedagogy of the oppressed.* Trans. Myra Bergman Ramos. New York: Herder and Herder.

Krishnamurti, J. (1970). The function of education. In *Think on These Things,* edited by J. Krishnamurti. New York: Harper and Row.

Commentary

Roselmina Indrisano
Boston University

In the tradition of reasoned inquiry, each of the researchers who addresses the topic "Oral Language: Its Relations to Writing, Reading, and Response to Literature" reviews and analyzes research evidence and philosophical perspectives, describes or develops a theoretical base, and presents conclusions, implications, and/or recommendations. The process is similar, but the outcomes are quite different. As is so often the case, it is the differences that give texture to the discussion.

David Dickinson concentrates on "early acquisition because it is here that the parallels are strongest." In reviewing and interpreting the literature, he makes clear distinctions between what is known, what can logically be inferred, and what remains a mystery locked within the processes and the learners. Dickinson's investigation and insights result in a typology of language/literature relationships. In his paper, important questions are raised; thoughtful observations and analyses are generated. The perspective of a researcher of child language and learning is evident in the work.

Miles Myers's primary purpose is "to critique the assumption . . . that oral and written differences are the key distinctions between one way of thinking and another and/or between the literate and the illiterate." Beginning with a historical review of definitions of oracy and literacy, Myers next reviews the relevant major language and learning theories and offers a theory of interactive sign systems to explain the relation between oral and written language. He concludes with suggestions for applying his theory of shared structure to "new and productive ways for teaching writing, reading, and literature." An intriguing theory is built; new instructional approaches are offered. The perspective of a researcher of the teaching process is evident in this work.

For those who read with pen in hand, Dickinson's text is a document of evidence. Underlining, mapping, notes in the margin—all attest to a personal view of significance. Notes on the Dickinson paper suggest that his comprehensive review of literature on the acquisition and early development of oracy and literacy is a valuable contribution to the field. The typology of language/literature relationships reflects Dickinson's interpretation of the evidence gathered in the review and the implications of the conclusions. The typology is a promising beginning and will provide a useful structure for discussion and study. Perhaps it will lead to a paradigm of reading/writing relationships for development levels beyond the early stages and ultimately inform evaluative, instructional, and remedial practices.

Regarding the role of oral language in young students' learning, Dickinson suggests, "There are developmental shifts in the balance of importance of the contribution of the different modalities, with young children being more dependent on oral language experience for constructing knowledge structures and older children more dependent on literary experiences." Given the research evidence summarized by Anderson and Pearson (1984), relevant knowledge structures emerge as paramount in comprehending and composing. For the young learner, it is indeed the voice of the teacher—whether parent, professional, or peer—that is the primary medium for joining objects and ideas with language. Ultimately, it is language that makes it possible for teachers to guide learners in constructing, organizing, and relating relevant knowledge structures. While young learners are certainly more dependent on oral language for developing knowledge structures, older children, and even adults, benefit from oral explanation and discussion of complex concepts. While older children are indeed more dependent on literary experiences, young children benefit from listening to literature that provides opportunities for discussion of story concepts. (A more complete justification will be offered later in this discussion.)

Another contribution of oral language to young learners' education is its power to initiate them into the community of the school. It is the language of instruction that serves as a code between teachers and learners. It is the language of instruction, too, that has the potential to alienate learners whose roots are in a different language community.

In summarizing the impact of oral language on teaching and learning, Martha King suggests that "language plays a complex and crucial role in schooling because it pervades the entire process. It is much more than the medium for conveying the message; it helps to form the message" (1985, p. 20). For the disabled reader/writer, oral language is medium and message. In his review of good/poor reader research, Dickinson describes the acknowledged difficulties experienced by disabled readers: decoding, memory and retrieval, and language awareness. The newer research on disabled readers/writers appears to have been influenced by recent developments in reading/writing process research. Given the findings of these studies of disability, it may be concluded that what is known to be important for effective readers is all the more important for the disabled reader: background knowledge, familiarity with discourse structure, and language-related knowledge.

At Boston University's Assessment Center, students are tested in a teaching mode and are encouraged to participate actively in the assessment. Oral language is the primary medium for assessing knowledge structures, vocabulary, language awareness, and understanding of the processes of reading and writing, including the structure of story and informative text. To assess students' understanding of reading/writing processes, they are asked to explain to a young child what to do when you read and write. The findings suggest that most disabled readers/writers view reading and writing from the surface structure only, since they advise students to "sound out the words" or "figure out the letters to write." Have disabled readers/writers learned what they have been taught? If the more contemporary approaches to reading instruction were used, would disabled students learn what they were taught and ultimately view reading and writing as communication processes rooted in meaning?

If it can be agreed that oral language interaction contributes to the development of knowledge structures for all types of learners, is there reason to be concerned with the effects of the pervading visual media in the lives of children? Estimates of time spent with television, video systems, and electronic games vary, but each figure is higher than any estimate of time spent reading or writing. Does the validated effect of time on task apply in this situation? Would the development of knowledge structures applicable to comprehending and composing be enhanced by including time in the school day for students to engage in sustained reading and writing activities that also offer opportunities to apply what they have learned in reading and writing instruction?

Related to knowledge structures are the text structures of story or exposition that serve to organize elements or to reflect thought processes. Dickinson's review suggests that young learners benefit from listening to stories before they are formally taught to read. Baker and Stein (1981) indicate that children use what they know of story structure when they read stories. Would listening to informational text help learners, young and older, to become more familiar with the structures of exposition, or with knowledge structures relevant to the content areas? Would discussing expository text help older children to perceive the relationship between knowledge structures and text structures?

In concluding the discussion of Dickinson's paper, it seems appropriate to consider whether future investigators will discover the same circular relationship between imagining and knowing as is now being described with regard to composing and comprehending. R.L. Gregory, a neuro-psychologist, offers this insight:

> The success of science shows the power of hypotheses as fictions of limited truth. The methods of science demonstrate several extremely effective ways for generating and testing fictional accounts of possible realities, and applying them to win over the environment.
>
> This may suggest that cognitive psychology might learn even more from the methods and philosophy of science than from what science has discovered about objects. Objects are different from us, because they are all fact: we are works of fiction. (from *New Society*, 23 May 1974, p. 398; see also Gregory 1978)

This reader's markings on the paper by Miles Myers reflect a former philosophy student's appreciation for the opportunity to refine familiar ideas and to reflect on them from a new perspective. This philosophical base for the concept of a "shared structure" of oracy and literacy brings to mind the words of Suzanne Langer, who offers this view of relationships among the forms of language:

> Language is much more than a set of symbols. . . . Its forms do not stand alone, like so many monoliths, each marking its one isolated grave; but instead, they tend to integrate, to make complex patterns, and thus to point out equally complex *relationships* in the world, the realm of their meanings. (p. 135, 1957)

The case for Myers's theory of shared structure is most convincing when related to the reading of texts that were specifically written to be rendered orally: poetry, plays, and the language of humor, jokes, and puns. In these reading experiences, an awareness of pragmatics is required for the appropriate oral interpretation of the cognitive and affective dimensions of meaning. In these instances also, "oral and written language are used to represent the same underlying contexts within significantly different sign systems."

Miles Myers's paper also invites questions. Three issues seem appropriate for discussion: the younger learner, the relationship between the oral and written modes, and the differences between texts read for pleasure and those read for information.

In describing the possibilities for translating the theory of shared structure to instructional practice, Myers cites examples of texts and teaching objectives. Neither the books nor the cognitive demands of the instruction seem applicable to younger learners, yet reference is made throughout the paper to studies of young readers. Can readers who are still "glued to print" or "reading from a single viewpoint" (Chall 1983) gain the understanding and the distance to perceive "contrasts of different contexts or styles"? Is there a metacognitive demand, as well, when both process and processing require the learner's attention? Should the theory and approach be tested with readers to determine whether *The Secret Garden* and *The Wind in the Willows* are more appropriate than "The Garden Party" and *The Catcher in the Rye?*

Volumes have been written about the relationships between oral and written modes of communication. Beginning with Louise Rosenblatt's premiśe that "a text, once it leaves its author's hands, is simply paper and ink until a reader evokes from it a literary work" (1978, p. ix), there has been renewed interest in explaining the nuances of the reader/writer relationship. The most comprehensive current publication on the topic, *Composing and Comprehending* (1984), was cosponsored by the National Conference on Research in English and edited by Julie Jensen. Several contributions to the volume offer theories on the relationship between reading and writing. James Squire suggests that "composing and comprehending are two sides of the same process"; Tierney and Pearson offer the premise that both processes are acts of composing; and Wittrock proposes a generative theory of comprehending and composing.

How does the theory of shared structures relate to these theories on the relationships between comprehending and composing? Does the process approach to teaching writing and reading (Graves and Hansen 1984) advance the learner's understanding of the "speech act," affirm the theory of shared structure?

To conclude this discussion, the matter of the characteristics and demands of various texts will be considered in relation to response to literature. It seems appropriate to suggest that response to literature is a sophisticated act of comprehending and composing. The respondee must first comprehend the text and then reflect on its meaning to author and to reader. The ultimate response is a new creation, "composed" by the reader.

When the response is offered within the context of a group discussion, the individual is given the opportunity to test the validity and depth of the response. The insights of other members of the group may serve to verify or alter these impressions. Once again, oral language makes a significant contribution to the development of the reader. For the young child or the disabled learner, there is an added advantage to oral discussion of responses. When the mode of communication is oral, the students can usually offer any idea they wish to share, unencumbered by the challenges of writing and spelling.

One of the text types that offers opportunity for creative response from the reader is the literature read for the purpose Robert Probst (1984) calls "self-indulgence." Most often, the author of such a text invites the reader to create visions and dreams, to become the character, to live in a different time and place. Contrast this freedom to "own" the story with the precision required when the major purpose for reading is to learn, to be informed. When the reader opens *Where the Wild Things Are* (1969), there is an invitation to experience the terrifying nightmares described by Maurice Sendak, and even to imagine visions more fearful. When the reader opens a biography such as *Martin Luther King, Jr.* (1969), the fears experienced by this historic figure must be comprehended within the reality of the events and the times described by the author, D.H. Millender. The reader is invited to imagine the feelings of the hero, but these feelings are evoked from the facts of the biography.

How does the concept of "speech events" help readers to predict the author's purpose, relate the purpose to text genre, or determine the most appropriate approach to reading the text? How does the theory of shared structure inform theories of literary response in developing readers?

Future Directions

Perhaps there can be no more valuable outcome of this seminar than the creation of a plan for communication between researchers, who generate and validate new insights, and teachers, who apply the findings in instructional settings. The plan may hasten the day when students are taught by teacher-scholars.

Preliminary evidence gathered by this observer suggests that the teacher-scholar is an active learner and a keen observer. The teacher-scholar considers process and pupils before selecting procedures, asks "why" before deciding "how," and monitors the effectiveness of instruction before making judgments about the learners. The teacher-scholar is skilled in ethnography, however informal the design of the experiment.

The behaviors of the teacher-scholar seem to mirror those cited by Baker and Brown (1984) when they describe the characteristics of the metacognitive learner. Critical to metacognition—whether the learner is student or teacher—is the capacity to be aware of process, and thus to exert control over performance. For the teacher-scholar, the capacity for metacognitive teaching is likely to be related to knowledge of process, teaching and learning, and oracy and literacy. The Mid-Decade Seminar has made available to researchers a comprehensive review of research and theory on teaching and learning the language arts. It remains for participants of this seminar to make the knowledge synthesized here available to teachers in a form that permits them to test the conclusions and recommendations in the school setting with the diverse group of learners that gather in a unit called a "class."

At mid-point in the decade of the eighties, two significant developments are worthy of consideration. First, there continues to be an unprecedented volume of basic and applied research in the language arts that can serve to improve teaching and ensure learning in ways not yet realized. At the same time, there is a plethora of reports on excellence in education which offer varied perspectives on problems, causes, and solutions. The diverse recommendations serve, at times, to divide rather than to unite the many constituencies concerned with quality education. Another potential outcome of this seminar is to bring together those who seek to improve education with the knowledge base upon which to make decisions about enlightened change.

In this place, at this time, it is well to recall that researchers, teachers, and all who are learners share a common quest, a journey made possible by the miracle of common language in both oral and written forms. In the language of Frank Jennings,

> Learning and teaching and study are the triple strands of the examined life. They are secure against accidental privilege. They shield solitude against loneliness. They enhance our uniqueness, defend our differences and place the power of equality at the service of the individual.

References

Anderson, R. C., and P. D. Pearson (1984). A schema-theoretic view of basic processes in reading comprehension. In *Handbook of reading research,* edited by P. D. Pearson, 255–91. New York: Longman.

Baker, L., and A. Brown (1984). Metacognitive skills and reading. In *Handbook of reading research,* edited by P. D. Pearson, 353–94. New York: Longman.

Baker, L., and N. Stein (1981). The development of prose comprehension skills. In *Children's prose comprehension,* edited by C. Santa and B. Hayes. Newark, Del.: International Reading Association.

Chall, J. S. (1983). *Stages of reading development.* New York: McGraw-Hill.

Graves, D., and J. Hansen (1984). The author's chair. In *Composing and comprehending,* edited by J. M. Jensen, 69–76. Urbana, Ill.: ERIC Clearinghouse on Reading and Communication Skills and NCRE. ED 243 139.

Gregory, R. L. (1978). Ways forward to the psychologist's alternative fictions. In *The cool web: The pattern of children's reading,* edited by M. Meek et al. London: The Bodley Head Ltd.

Jennings, F. J. This is reading, too. Unpublished paper. No date.

Jensen, J., ed. (1984). *Composing and comprehending.* Urbana, Ill.: ERIC Clearinghouse on Reading and Communication Skills and NCRE. ED 243 139.

King, M. L. (1985). Language and language learning for child watchers. In *Observing the language learner,* edited by A. Jaggar and M. T. Smith-Burke. Newark, Del.: International Reading Association and National Council of Teachers of English.

Langer, S. K. (1957). *Philosophy in a new key.* 3d ed. Cambridge, Mass.: Harvard University Press.

Millender, D. H. (1969). *Martin Luther King, Jr., Boy with a dream.* New York: Bobbs-Merrill.

Probst, R. E. (1984). *Adolescent literature: Response and analysis.* Columbus, Ohio: Charles E. Merrill.

Rosenblatt, L. M. (1978). *The reader, the text, the poem.* Carbondale, Ill.: Southern Illinois University Press.

Sendak, M. (1969). *Where the wild things are.* New York: Scholastic Book Services.

Squire, J. R. (1984). Composing and comprehending: Two sides of the same process. In *Composing and comprehending,* edited by J. M. Jensen, 23–31. Urbana, Ill.: ERIC Clearinghouse on Reading and Communication Skills. ED 243 139.

Tierney, R., and P. Pearson (1984). Toward a composing model of reading. In *Composing and comprehending,* edited by J. Jensen, 33–45. Urbana, Ill.: ERIC Clearinghouse on Reading and Communication Skills and NCRE. ED 243 139.

Wittrock, M. C. (1984). Writing and the teaching of reading. In *Composing and comprehending,* edited by J. M. Jensen, 77–83. Urbana, Ill.: ERIC Clearinghouse on Reading and Communication Skills. ED 243 139.

IV Studies of Classroom Practice, Classroom Interaction, and Instructional Materials: What Have We Learned? What Needs to Be Done?

Introduction

Recent years have seen a substantial increase in our knowledge of classroom behaviors. Studies of teaching practices, classroom interaction, instructional sequences in schoolbooks, and teacher uses of time have been examined by researchers with varied points of view and methodological approaches. An increased interest in ethnographic studies has been particularly notable. The two papers reviewing these studies for the seminar reflect how discrete bodies of research, such as the teaching-effectiveness studies, have emerged during recent years, yet how seldom results from one body of research have informed another or even teaching practice. In a sense Fillion and Brause outline the conflicting open-classroom and structured-teaching views, and Smith-Burke shows how similar differences permeate discrete research studies. Whether classroom learning should be relatively open, whether language learning should be studied in relation to function or only to content, whether high test scores on presently assessed low-level skills offer an adequate basis for distinguishing effective teaching—these are among the critical issues. But perhaps even more critical is awareness that the very diversity of approaches requires development of a theory of language teaching to help interpret the theories and practices in language learning. The issue raised by Applebee in his commentary affords Durkin opportunity to reflect on ethical behavior in conducting and interpreting research in the language arts.

Research into Classroom Practices: What Have We Learned and Where Are We Going?

Bryant Fillion and Rita S. Brause
Fordham University at Lincoln Center

Language is learned in virtually all human environments, but none of these has been investigated as thoroughly as has the classroom. This paper considers how studies of classroom practices may contribute to the overriding, long-range purpose of all research in language education: the improvement of learners' language development and use.

The Nature and Purposes of Classroom Research

Classroom-process studies are usually intended to serve one of five purposes: (1) To increase our general understanding of classrooms as educational environments: e.g., what teachers and pupils actually do during reading, writing, or literature lessons, or how students spend their time in classrooms, as in the two Squire and Applebee surveys (1968, 1969) of U.S. and U.K. practices in the teaching of English; (2) to identify and describe classroom factors likely to influence children's linguistic development and achievement of other desired outcomes, as in Dyson's (1984) study of individual primary pupils' response to specific teacher-set tasks; (3) to determine whether and how predetermined constructs, such as "comprehension instruction" or "composition instruction," are manifested in classrooms, as in Durkin (1979) and Applebee (1981); (4) to examine the relationship between actual practices and particular outcomes, as in Galton and Simon's (1981) U.K. studies relating teacher styles to pupil performance in primary schools and Southgate, Arnold, and Johnson's (1981) study of teaching practices related to improved reading performance in British junior schools; or (5) to detail language processes and developments as they occur in school, as in Graves's (1982) study of writing developments in grades 1 through 4.

Classroom research includes a wide range of studies, only some of them specific to language education. Language-education researchers may not be aware of the large body of observational research on teaching, often classed as "interaction analysis," though most are probably familiar with the work of Flanders (1964, 1965, 1970). Other related research, generally associated with the "teacher accountability" and "competency-based education" movements in the 1970s, dealt with various aspects of teacher evaluation (see Adams and Biddle, 1970, Borich 1977, and Good and Brophy 1978). Much of this research involves the study of specific classroom variables, such as organizational patterns and teacher behaviors, as these relate to instructional outcomes and student achievement. A third body of research, in many ways antithetical to the other two (Harste, Woodward, and Burke 1984, Heap 1982), and occasionally overlapping with language-education research, has grown up around ethnomethodological approaches to classroom observation. In the U.K., there is a growing body of ethnographic classroom research that may be largely unknown to U.S. researchers (see Chanan and Delamont 1975, Delamont 1976, and Sinclair and Coulthard 1975).

A fourth body of literature dealing with classrooms, teaching, and learning might be excluded on the grounds that it is not conventional research. Classroom-process studies are among the few types of educational research that have a widely familiar counterpart in classical and popular fiction, and many popular accounts of actual classrooms and schools, such as Dennison's *The Lives of Children* (1969), Lopate's *Being with Children* (1975), and Herndon's *The Way It Spozed to Be* (1968), approach literary writing in their style and impact. Whatever their status as research, there can be little question of their potential influence, as N. L. Gage complained in 1978:

> Since *Summerhill* appeared in 1960, we seem to have been more than ever at the mercy of powerful and passionate writers who shift educational thinking ever more erratically with their manifestos. The kind of research I have been describing [on classroom practices related to achievement] is a plodding enterprise, the reports of which are seldom, I regret to say, as well written as the pronouncements of authors unburdened by scientific method. But, in the long run, the improvement of teaching . . . will come in large part from the continued search for a scientific basis for the art of teaching. (p. 235).

Nevertheless, given that a central function of all educational research must be to inform and improve practice, we perhaps need to weigh the relative benefits to practice of fictional accounts such as *Up the Down Staircase* (1966), quasi-journalistic accounts such as Miriam Wasserman's *The School Fix, NYC, USA* (1971), and more conventional research reports such as Goodlad's *A Place Called School* (1984), or Rutter et al.'s U.K. study, *Fifteen Thousand Hours: Secondary Schools and Their Effects on Children* (1979). What are acceptable data in classroom research, and how do different kinds of data influence practice? At issue is not whether researchers should abandon the classroom to poets, writers, or others "unburdened by scientific method," but whether researchers should be more like poets in their approach to and reporting of classroom data.

The Changing Face of Classroom Research

The bulk of classroom observational research has been conducted since 1960 and has been jointly influenced by development in research technology, such as instruments for interaction analysis and the emergence of ethnographic approaches, and by increased understanding of classroom processes and the nature of learning. The focuses of such research have also changed. Traditional experiments testing the effects of specific methods and materials on particular performance measures have broadened to include the observation and analysis of teaching behaviors related to more general outcomes. Techniques of meta-analysis have allowed us to overcome the limitations of design flaws and small samples in individual studies of similar phenomena and to benefit from the combined force of pooled data. Ethnography and discourse analysis have produced a deeper appreciation of classrooms as dynamic environments in which participants and processes interact in complex ways to influence both instruction and learning. In language education, the burgeoning research into cognitive and linguistic development has shifted attention from the teacher to the learner, and from learning as the retention of information or performance of discrete skills to learning as an active, dynamic process.

As recently as twenty-five years ago, few researchers visited classrooms except to retrieve data, usually consisting of standardized test measures. The world of educational research and the world of the classroom operated independently, despite the frequently voiced belief that there should be a strong relationship between the two. Classroom research, often conducted without benefit of direct observation, consisted largely of hypothesis testing to determine whether particular curriculum or teaching practices produced measurable improvements in student performance. For instance, Singleton, Diederich, and Hill (1961) identified such important research questions for English teachers as the following:

> Would my pupils make fewer errors in punctuation and capitalization if they wrote three 100-word themes each week instead of one 300-word theme?

> Would my pupils' handwriting improve faster through five minutes of practice each morning or one 30-minute period once a week? (pp. 34–35)

The problems addressed in these studies were important, practical concerns for classroom teachers, and the practitioners who participated in the research probably benefited from a heightened awareness of the relationship of practice to outcome. But the narrow focus of the studies virtually precluded attention to or control of critical variables, such as the classroom interactions and learner behaviors by which the instructional techniques influenced learning. After hundreds of such investigations failed to produce clear, consistent findings, teachers and many teacher educators began to question whether research could ever produce sufficiently reliable results to inform educational practice.

Prompted largely by the work of Medley and Mitzel (1963) and Flanders (1964, 1965), various educational researchers began to investigate teaching and its relationship to student achievement using systematic observations of classroom behavior. Most of these studies were experimental or correlational, using conventional hypothesis-testing designs and relying on predetermined coding systems to insure the reliability and comparability of data. However, several researchers, such as Berliner and Tikunoff (1977), used ethnographic approaches in which interpretation and classification of behaviors and events followed from post hoc analysis of holistic observations. Although this research did draw researchers into the classroom, the studies focused mainly on teacher behaviors and teacher-student interactions as these correlated with summative achievement measures. They did not tell us very much about how students learned.

Much of the observational research on teaching has been concerned with various dimensions of the progressive/traditional education controversy, comparing the effects of lecture and discussion, student-centered and teacher-centered instruction, open and informal versus traditional and formal, and the like. The effects on attitude and achievement of particular instructional approaches, such as mastery learning and programmed instruction, have been investigated, as have been such organizational factors as time-on-task and class size, and particular teaching variables such as clarity, enthusiasm, indirect influence, and levels of questioning.

Many of the studies investigating these variables have yielded statistically insignificant, contradictory, or inconclusive findings, leading to the frequent charge that classroom research has produced negligible and undependable results. Using variations of meta-analysis, permitting the results of different studies to be pooled and analyzed together, various research reviewers have argued against this charge of insignificance, pointing out that when the studies are examined in clusters there are frequently very consistent directions indicated. For example, Gage (1978) asserts that through testing the combined results of clusters of studies on similar factors, statistically significant or nonchance results give definite support to direct versus open teaching in the early grades, and to the following "teacher should" statements: Teachers should (1) establish rules that allow pupils to proceed independently with their needs and work without checking with the teacher; (2) move around, monitoring pupils' work and communicating with them and attending to individual needs; (3) insure that pupils' independent work is on interesting, worthwhile, and sufficiently easy tasks; (4) reduce direction giving; (5) call children by name before asking questions; (6) insure that slower pupils give some response to a question; and (7) provide fast-paced, drill-type activities and brief feedback in reading-group instruction (p. 234).

Using a meta-analysis of recent studies on related variables, Walberg, Schiller, and Haertel (1979) argue that there is significant research support for such practices and factors as time on learning, innovative curricula, smaller classes, personalized systems of instruction, mastery learning, programmed instruction, adjunct questions, direct instruction, lecture, student-centered discussion, factual versus conceptual questions, and open versus traditional education. Certainly one of the most striking features of the findings presented in Walberg's "Selective Summary of a Decade of Educational Research" (p. 180) is the seeming contradiction evident in the factors presented as having positive results. For instance, four studies of direct instruction showed a 100 percent positive effect on learning, and thirty-one studies showed positive effects of lecture over discussion on achievement, retention, and attitudes. But twenty-six studies showed a 54.8 percent positive effect of open (versus traditional) education on student achievement. One explanation for such apparent contradictions may be that in many of the studies the control treatments were disorganized or haphazard instruction rather than well-defined alternative methods, and in such conditions the carefully modeled and monitored experimental method would have a natural edge. Similarly, the outcome measures of achievement in these studies were often biased in favor of the experimental method.

Glass and Smith (1978) conducted an exacting meta-analysis of seventy-six class-size studies, concluding that pupils in classes of twenty or less achieve significantly more than pupils in classes larger than twenty, with the overall differences between a class size of twenty and of forty being 0.3 grade equivalent. However, as a recent NCTE review of class-size studies by Albritton (1986) points out, the Glass and Smith analysis and findings have been vigorously questioned and criticized. Albritton's own review of the literature concludes that although class size has demonstrated effects on such factors as teacher morale and some aspects of classroom quality, its effect as an isolated variable on student achievement is uncertain at best, until class size reaches unrealistically low levels. One general conclusion of several class-size researchers is that although smaller class size makes instructional improvement possible, it does not insure that such improvement will occur.

Most of the foregoing research could be characterized as "product" or "hypothesis-testing" studies (Applebee 1984b; Berliner 1984; Brause, forthcoming; Macmillan and Garrison 1984), designed to test possible solutions to particular teaching problems. Very often the learning theories underlying the hypotheses were derived from behaviorist educational psychology, suggesting that learning and student achievement were primarily responses to particular educational stimuli. The research often failed to account or control for the complexity of influences operating in the classroom, or for the role of the learners in their own learning. Cognitive and linguistic theory suggest that influences affecting language development and learning will often be mediated through changes in students' language, but such changes are seldom examined in conventional classroom research.

The personal, informal accounts of such writers as Herndon (1968), Holt (1964, 1967), Kohl (1967), and Kozol (1967) convey convincingly the complexity of classrooms as living environments, where learning is often inhibited by a host of important contextual factors ignored in typical research studies. Although perhaps less systematic and rigorous than the formal studies of teaching, these accounts and criticisms of life in classrooms often incorporated the perspectives of the learners and provided considerable insight into the realities of teaching and learning in schools. Subsequent confirmation of the importance of context (Bakhtin 1981, Vygotsky 1978), and systematic observation by language theorists such as Barnes (1976) and ethnographers such as Delamont (1976) have increased our understanding of those complex realities, as will be discussed below.

By the late 1960s, the behavioral learning theories that had dominated earlier research were being replaced by cognitive learning theories (Bruner 1984), especially in language education. These theories, and the findings of research into language development and processes, stressed the active intellectual involvement of the learners in their learning and the need to understand cognitive processes and strategies. For classroom researchers, these developments suggest a change in focus and methodology. The learner and learning behaviors are as much in need of attention as are teacher behaviors. Student language, both oral and written, and in all parts of the curriculum, becomes as important as teacher or textbook language in any one subject. Many of the techniques of classroom observation developed for hypothesis-testing studies are clearly inadequate for the task of investigating these more complex variables and their interactions in the classroom. However, new approaches to researching the issues (Goetz and LeCompte 1984) and guidelines for interpreting data consistent with the viewpoints of participants in social environments (Erickson 1979, McDermott, Gospodinoff, and Aron 1978, Morine-Dershimer and Tenenberg 1981) have contributed to the increased scope of recent classroom research.

In addition to earlier hypothesis-testing studies, classroom research now includes hypothesis-generating observational and descriptive studies, using qualitative as well as quantitative data, and identifying and interpreting processes and activities in naturally occurring situations. Bolster (1983) emphasizes the important potential of hypothesis-generating research for informing educational practice. Figure 1 on page 208 summarizes the differences between the two research constructs.

Focuses and Findings of Classroom Research

Classroom-process studies have usually focused either on social interactions ("pre-instructional factors"), or on learning ("during-instruction factors") (Berliner 1984). This distinction is one teachers and administrators suggest when they advise attending first to "discipline" and "management" and then to "learning."

Social Interactions in Classrooms

Numerous studies on classroom interactions have used variations of Flanders's (1970) interaction analysis, in which classroom behaviors are coded using a predetermined system, often at the time of observation. Such studies have been criticized by American researchers (Heap 1982, Mehan 1979) and British researchers (Stubbs 1983, Stubbs and Delamont 1976) for overlooking important patterns, events, and student functions in the classroom. This same criticism has been leveled against the spate of American reports reviewed in Cazden (1986) and Green (1983), in which classroom interactions were the intended focus but the teacher's perspective was the only one reported.

Recent informal and ethnographic studies have attempted to meet these criticisms by using more intensive observations and a wider range of data. These studies have focused on both small groups (Allington 1983, McDermott 1978) and whole classes (Brause and Mayher 1984, Cahir and Kovac 1981, Mehan 1979). Most of the studies have focused on teacher-directed activities in which the students are seated facing the teacher, discussions are teacher-led and teacher-dominated, and the teacher orchestrates all movements. Since such classrooms seem to predominate in American schools (Cuban 1984), they are an appropriate subject of considerable research attention.

	HYPOTHESIS-TESTING	**HYPOTHESIS-GENERATING**
Intent	Test validity of pre-determined, explicit hypotheses, theories, or assumptions using statistical significance as the method of evaluation.	Explore a phenomenon/process to understand factors which influence the accomplishment of a task. Explore assumptions. Discover components of a process.
Procedures	Systematically manipulate hypothe-sized variables. Collect data limited to spe-cifically focused, pre-determined variables. Hold constant, or exclude, extraneous factors	Systematically and intensively collect extensive, context-driven holistic data on process. Numerous instances with same participant involved in the same process over time.
Analysis	Intensive, pre-determined analysis based on stated hypotheses. Quantita-tive reduction of data. Statistical significance of data analyzed.	Exploratory—based on identification of significant events from the participant's per-spective. Qualitative reduction of data.
Outcomes	Accept or reject hypotheses. Generalize to larger populations.	Describe how a phenomenon occurs. Identify potential variables/factors in need of continued, systematic testing. Presentation of "stories." Identifi-cation of theories that explain data.
Perspective	Seek similarities among group members.	Discover individual differences.

Figure 1. Comparisons between hypothesis-testing and hypothesis-generating research.

Various observational studies conducted in American classrooms (Brause and Mayher 1984, McDermott 1978, Cahir and Kovac 1981, Brause 1985) support the following general observations:

1. Activities in classrooms are systematically organized.
2. Rules which prevail during each activity are context-sensitive and implicitly conveyed.
3. Participants often display differing familiarity with the rules.
4. Cooperative principles which organize conversation also organize classroom interactions.
5. Teachers and students negotiate rules and help each other save face with those rules.

The predictable nature of classrooms makes them comfortable places for those who have inferred the rules. The most adept students identify ways to use the context-sensitive rules for their own advantage, to obtain or avoid turns-at-talk at will, to avoid participation as desired, and to divert the flow of classroom lessons. Most students apparently become quite adept at avoiding participation, especially with the assistance of the teacher, who negotiates face-saving techniques with them (Dore and McDermott 1982). Fewer students are aware of the procedures for successfully competing for turns-at-talk or for diverting the focus of a lesson. In general, teachers directly control students' behaviors and tell them what to do, and student compliance and physical passivity are rewarded. Only the troublesome few deviate from the teacher's explicit rules, and a smaller subset of these are held accountable for their intransigence.

McDermott (1978) and Dore and McDermott (1982) present a persuasive ethnographic analysis of how Rosa, a nonreading student, negotiates her participation with the teacher and other group members. She avoids turns-at-talk through a complex dance that all participants orchestrate. The student saves face, and the others avoid the task of helping her learn to read. Allington (1983) also analyzed the ploys used by a group of poor readers to avoid turns-at-talk. All of their acts were accepted by the teacher, thus documenting the collaboration among the participants which allows students to avoid learning while remaining cooperatively involved in school tasks.

Questions are a staple of classroom discourse and have often been examined in studies of classroom interactions documenting the "low level" of teacher questions (Dillon 1983, Sinclair and Coulthard 1975). The productivity of much of this research has been questioned by Cazden (1986) as being superficial and misleading. Teachers are assumed to make educational decisions about student knowledge based on students' answers to questions, but Buike (1981) reports that teachers' decision making was less for purposes of instruction than for control and management.

Although classroom organization and management vary considerably within and among schools, the predominant pattern appears to be the teacher-directed classroom, in which students are most of the time expected to work independently and to interact primarily with the teacher and the instructional materials. Researchers contend that families and cultures vary considerably in the extent to which they prepare children for such settings. Children who are accustomed to assisting others in accomplishing tasks, collaborating on projects and generally working together, are comfortable in the cooperative classrooms in which these activities are rewarded, but are ill-at-ease in more typical classrooms. Hispanic homes are characterized by Tikunoff and Ward (1983) as fitting into the cooperative format. Similarly, Philips (1982) found that American Indian children were accustomed to independent activities and were unaccustomed to the noise and competition pervasive in American classrooms. Differences between their home values and classroom values were so extreme as to alienate the children from their teachers and their classmates—perhaps explaining why Indian children rarely complete their formal education.

Further evidence of cultural differences influencing classroom interaction and teacher evaluation is provided by Michaels and Collins (1984), who document differential treatment of children based on their culturally influenced narrative styles during "Sharing Time." Students who used "associative" narrative styles were viewed as not knowing how to tell a story, whereas those who told "hierarchically organized" stories were praised and encouraged. These findings are consistent with Rist's (1973) study of grouping in kindergarten and its effects three years later.

Classroom-interaction research involving students from various cultural, linguistic, and socioeconomic backgrounds must be a high priority for the decade ahead, since these "minority" students are very rapidly becoming the majority in many schools, especially in America's cities.

Learning in Classrooms

Although reports on "the nature of the teaching-learning processes" (Green 1983) have filled journals and anthologies, the findings generally tell us far more about teaching than about learning. For example, Travers (1984) identifies behaviors good poetry teachers display, such as enthusiasm and flexibility, but we do not know how these behaviors influence the learners and what they do. Given the teacher-dominated nature of most classrooms, it is far easier to observe and describe what teachers do than what and how students learn. In many studies, learning appears to be equated with expected and acceptable student behaviors, but interaction studies have demonstrated how students may contrive to appear cooperative while actually avoiding the intended learning. Similarly, Dyson's (1984) study has demonstrated how the learning of teacher-imposed literacy tasks may involve "learning to do school" more than learning language, and may in fact inhibit genuine language development.

Recent classroom studies of reading and writing instruction indicate that there is very limited direct instruction or scaffolding (Bruner 1978) to assist students in completing or learning from the activities and tasks set for them. Durkin (1979) cites the practice of "mentioning" as the way that reading teachers most frequently offer instruction. Once a topic or term is "mentioned," subsequent uses are considered "review," and there is little time or assistance for children to develop their understanding of technical terms the teacher uses in reading activities. Applebee (1981), studying classroom instruction in writing, also observed limited assistance to students in ways to approach assigned tasks, or in the provision of models which might assist them to develop their own models of writing process or products. Michaels and Collins (1984) found that although teachers apparently had definite—if narrow—expectations of narrative formats to be used by children in oral sharing times, these expectations and ways to achieve them were never made explicit to the students. There is little indication in classroom research that teachers either facilitate or monitor the processes and strategies students use in accomplishing tasks or in learning.

A central problem in classroom research is that some of the most important events in educational environments, such as cognitive activity and the learning process itself, are not directly observable. In classrooms where student language is narrowly restricted, observable evidence of cognitive activity and learning is virtually nonexistent, except perhaps on measures of outcomes (Fillion 1983). Johnston (1984) suggests that "instead of a concern over response outcomes, right or wrong, there needs to be greater concern over the reasons behind the responses. The bottom line is that we need to worry more about the assessment of process in the individual, and the process of assessment in context" (p. 175).

What is genuine learning behavior? And how is it manifested in classrooms? What evidence might indicate that students' writing and reading processes are improving, even if such improvements are not yet reflected in their finished compositions or reading test results? What should we accept as evidence that students are in the process of cognitive growth and the development of reflective, critical thinking? Although we may see the effects of such growth in test results, its consequences and the process by which it occurs will probably be most evident in students' discourse, spoken (Barnes 1976) and written (Britton 1970). Following the leads provided by theory and research in language processes and development, classroom research needs to focus more carefully on such factors as the nature and frequency of students' language uses, student-initiated questions and talk about their reading, students' attempts to understand and comply with assigned tasks, and the cognitive activity reflected in their talk and writing.

A related problem for classroom research is that measures of learning outcomes, especially in language, are themselves controversial. In most studies relating teacher behaviors to student achievement in reading, for example, achievement is defined as scores on standardized tests. These tests have been challenged increasingly as failing to reflect students' actual reading competence in nontest situations. The rich database used in language-development and language-process research to assess and describe growth contrasts sharply with the stark data of test scores used to measure achievement in most classroom research. These differences in data, and in the meaning given to "achievement," may help to explain the frequent disparity between the teaching practices advocated by the two lines of research.

This disparity is one of the more interesting problems in language education today. For example, despite the continuing flow of theory and nonclassroom research findings in support of "natural," student-centered, progressive methods of early reading and writing development (e.g., Bissex 1980; Emig 1983; Harste, Burke, and Woodward 1981; Smith 1983), a large body of classroom correlational and experimental research continues to support very different approaches, at least with lower SES students. Rosenshine (1976), summarizing research on primary-grade reading and mathematics for low-SES children, concludes that the optimal pattern for this instruction might be labeled "direct instruction": "In direct instruction a great deal of time is spent on academic activities, with predominance of seatwork using structured materials. Teacher and workbook questions are narrow and direct, usually with a single correct answer. . . . Students work in groups supervised by the teacher with little free time or unsupervised activity, resulting in less off-task student behavior" (pp. 63–64). In direct contradiction to language theorists' stress on the importance of student talk in learning (Barnes 1976) and of child-initiated interactions in language development (Wells 1981), Rosenshine notes, "With one exception all types of student-initiated talk, whether academic or non-academic, yielded negative or low correlations [with achievement]. . . . [R]esearchers concluded that student-initiated talk does not appear to be as important for this type of achievement as once thought" (1976, p. 63).

Recent interest in the relationships among reading, writing, speaking, thinking, and learning has begun to stimulate classroom research focused on those relationships, but most research to date has stressed either reading or writing, separate from each other and from their significant uses in learning. Given the expense and complexity of such undertakings, it is not surprising that few classroom studies have investigated the interrelationship of teaching behaviors, learning behaviors, student background, and language-related outcomes. Perhaps the closest we have to such research have been several large-scale studies conducted in England involving extensive observation, description, and interpretation of school practices—from students' and teachers' perspectives—and the learning outcomes associated with them.

Rutter et al. (1979) conducted an intensive study of twelve inner-city London secondary schools, attempting to account for marked differences among the schools in students' attendance, school behavior, examination performance, and delinquency. The study provides strong evidence that school and teaching factors do have a significant influence on students' behavior and academic performance—over and above the effects of home background and prior schooling—and that many of the influential factors were "open to modification by the staff." Positive outcomes were associated with "the degree of academic emphasis, teacher actions in lessons, the availability of incentives and rewards, good conditions for pupils, and the extent to which children were able to take responsibility" (p. 178). It should also be noted in behalf of such multiple-variable studies that "the *cumulative* effect of these various social factors was greater than the effects of any of the individual factors on their own" (p. 179).

In *Extending Beginning Reading* (1981), Southgate, Arnold, and Johnson report on a four-year study of reading development in U.K. junior schools, with children aged seven to nine-plus, concluding with an intensive one-year study of reading instruction and pupil achievement in twelve schools, with over 1100 pupils, focusing primarily on 104 children with "average reading proficiency." Two main conclusions with clear implications for practice were as follows:

> The classes which made most reading progress were those in which the teachers placed the *least* emphasis on listening to children's oral reading. Furthermore, in these same most successful classes, a greater proportion of time was devoted to children's uninterrupted personal reading and to discussions about the books the children had read. (p. 319)

One problem associated with the practice of hearing children read aloud was that children outside the reading group were often not working productively and independently at assigned tasks, so that "the actual time devoted by a proportion of the children to the set reading and writing [was] extremely small" (p. 317). Other issues related to this practice are discussed by Dore and McDermott (1982) and Allington (1983), as noted above.

In *The Effective Use of Reading* (1979), Lunzer and Gardner and their associates report a three-year U.K. investigation of "how average and above-average readers [aged ten to fifteen] actually use reading in school, and what may be done to improve an existing competence" (p. xi). The study examined the uses of reading across the curriculum rather than the teaching of reading in English or special reading classes, and included extensive classroom observations and surveys of current practice, including the use of reading in homework. The project also included an experimental study on improving reading through group discussion activities. Two general findings were (1) that "the reading ability of average and above-average pupils in the 10–15 year age range can be improved" (p. 312), and (2) that classroom work which promotes students' "willingness to reflect," and provides opportunity and encouragement to increase the quality of their reflection is a key consideration in developing students' reading comprehension and their proficiency in using reading to learn (pp. 300–301).

The conclusions emerging from such large-scale multiple-variable studies as Southgate and Lunzer and Gardner often seem to conflict with the findings of limited-variable observation studies conducted in this country, which tend to support more structured, teacher-directed approaches. Several explanations suggest themselves. It may be, as Harste, Woodward, and Burke (1984) have argued, that teaching and learning behaviors look very different when studied together as interactive variables than when they are studied in isolation. Another explanation may be that England provides researchers with a greater number of competently run nontraditional classrooms in which to observe (though Lunzer and Gardner in fact had to create a situation in which to test their hypothesis that reading discussions could improve comprehension and learning). A third explanation is that the British classroom researchers, unlike many researchers of teaching in the U.S., were themselves experts in reading and language education. They began their studies with extensive investigations of the nature of reading, teachers' views about reading, and the range of classroom practices available for observation. When attempting to examine the nature of classroom learning and how it is influenced, it is useful to have a theoretical understanding of the learning to be investigated.

Toward an Explicit Theory of Language Pedagogy

A critical problem for language education generally, and especially for classroom research, is our need for a clear, explicit theory of language learning and pedagogy. We believe, with Harste, Woodward, and Burke (1984), that "researchers and teachers must proceed from theory, and, further, that this theory must constantly be subject to reflection and change" (p. 86). What theory of language learning and teaching guides us in the collection and interpretation of classroom data?

At least since the Dartmouth Seminar in 1966 there has been a mainstream theoretical stance in language instruction that has dominated much of the professional literature in English education. The architects of that theory include such figures as Barnes, Britton, Dixon, and Martin, from the U.K.; Cazden, the Goodmans, Graves, Moffett, Purves, Rosenblatt, and Squire, from the U.S.; and Frank Smith, from Canada. Based largely on propositions—some of them matters of deep controversy—about how language develops and is influenced, the pedagogical aspects of the theory are most clearly and explicitly stated in three publications: Dixon's report on the Dartmouth Seminar, *Growth through English* (1967); Moffett's *Teaching the Universe of Discourse* (1968); and the British state-of-the-art "Bullock Report" on language education, *A Language for Life* (1975).

This mainstream theory in language education has resulted in little classroom research into the teaching of literature. Applebee (1984a) notes that such research "has stagnated while the profession has turned its attention to composition and, more recently, 'reasoning' or 'higher order thinking' " (p. 229). One reason for this neglect, aside from the priority accorded to reading and writing in the past two decades, may be the lack of a compelling theory of literature learning and use to stimulate research (Fillion 1981). Whatever the reasons, it is certainly true that we know very little from research about how literature teaching is manifested in classrooms and how such teaching influences learning (literary or otherwise), or about the role of literary texts in language education. Given English education's continuing commitment to the teaching of literature, and the claims made for the influence of literature on students' linguistic, cognitive, and personal development, we must insist, with Applebee, that an adequate agenda for classroom research in language education include the teaching and learning of literature.

Although there is much greater consensus about language development than about the way schools can and should influence that development, one mainstream theory of language pedagogy has wide currency among researchers and teacher educators, even if it has yet to result in an integrated view of language teaching. It contains several related beliefs, the most basic of which is that virtually all children have a natural facility with language learning that we have failed to recognize or exploit in our schools and classrooms. In a culture where written language is prominent and readily available, basic literacy is a natural extension of an individual's linguistic development, given adequate environmental conditions. Language facility, written as well as oral, develops primarily through personally meaningful, active uses of language in the service of genuine human intentions, including the intention to learn, i.e., to build an adequate cognitive representation of the world. Teachers and schools can best influence students' language development by facilitating their intentional use of language, oral and written, for a wide range of personal, social, and academic purposes, rather than by drilling students in predetermined sequences of discrete skills apart from their significant use, or by teaching information about language. Students' language—vocalized, written, or as inner speech—plays, or should play, a significant part in virtually all mental activity and school learning, and these language uses not only promote better learning but linguistic and cognitive development as well. Following from these beliefs is the contention that the language environment in many existing classrooms is "unnatural," and detrimentally so, in that students are diverted from participation in meaningful language acts and events in which they would otherwise normally engage, and are made to participate instead in a narrow range of structured activities and situations distinct from purposeful, significant language uses and learning.

This theory of language development has continued to be supported and elaborated by language theorists (e.g., Emig 1983, Y. Goodman 1980, Smith 1978), by research (e.g., Graves 1982; Harste, Burke, and Woodward 1981; Wells 1981), by testimonial evidence from teachers (e.g., Martin et al. 1976, Medway 1980, Torbe and Medway 1981), and by occasional correlational studies (e.g., Southgate, Arnold, and Johnson 1981). However, there is still little classroom research evidence to support its efficacy. Various studies suggest that current classroom practice is patently out of line with the theory (Applebee 1981, Fillion 1979, Graves 1978, Lunzer and Gardner 1979), but there are few studies demonstrating that the theory can be translated into general practice on a large scale within present patterns of schooling, or that such practice will in fact produce the linguistic and cognitive results claimed for it.

It may well be that comprehensive theories can never be fully or usefully tested in classrooms, and that the ongoing tensions between theory and practice are the only real means to the long-range improvement of established institutions. Although there are a few defenders of the status quo, there are great differences of opinion among theorists, researchers, and teachers about the extent to which present knowledge warrants changes in established patterns of schooling. Can improvement best be achieved through changes at the level of lessons, materials, and methods, or does it require change at more profound levels that would significantly alter teacher-student relationships and classroom environments? Bereiter and Scardamalia (1982), addressing the issue of instruction versus natural development in writing pedagogy, express doubts about depending on profound changes in environmental conditions:

> Since we are dealing with a developmental process (i.e., writing) . . . the question naturally arises why it should be necessary to intervene instructionally at all. If proper conditions for developmental experience were provided, wouldn't things take care of themselves? . . .
>
> Let us agree that in a society where a high premium was placed on written composition skills and where everyone was expected to display competence in them, natural learning would probably take care of the problems [in composing skill] we have been wrestling with. . . . *But if such situations could be created freely, there would be no writing problem, at least not as we know it. It is precisely because conditions for learning to write are generally so unfavorable that natural development stands in need of considerable assistance* [emphasis added]. . . .
>
> Feedback to complex processes is usually inadequate and the level of mastery that the social environment supports is quite a bit short of what the culture actually seems to need. That is, development does go on in comprehension, analytical, and compositional skills, but in the end most citizens don't reach anything like the level that a liberal democratic philosophy deems desirable. (pp. 58–59)

Perhaps one of the central issues facing classroom research in this decade is the extent to which we believe that established and very persistent patterns of schools can or should be changed in order to improve language development and learning. To what extent should our research agendas accept present instructional patterns as "given," rather than as potentially variable at very profound levels? The issue will become increasingly acute as we consider the role of computers in classrooms: whether they should be used primarily to structure and program instruction ever more efficiently, or to provide expanded opportunities for students to use written language creatively and for a wider range of purposes. It now appears possible that in the next few decades technology will accomplish basic changes in schooling that generations of reformers were unable to achieve. But the nature and outcomes of those changes may be quite different from the ones envisioned by the reformers or warranted by the nature of language development and learning.

Most classroom observational research in the 1960s and 1970s appeared based on the assumption that any improvements would have to be made within the constraints of present patterns of schooling. As Rosenshine (1977) observes,

> If direct instruction is pervasive, then the research strategy becomes one of identifying effective and ineffective direct instruction. These steps would include developing a tentative list of major implementation variables, identifying discrepancies between the implementation ideal and actual practice, and most important, identifying which implementation variables are critical for student achievement and which can be dropped. Perhaps the important part of future research on direct instruction is that we would be looking for patterns rather than single variables. (pp. 119–20)

Research in language education has obviously followed quite a different agenda, especially in the last decade: first attempting to characterize the nature of and influences on language development, and then proposing instructional approaches and environments consistent with those findings. In primary education, for instance, there has been the frequent contention that schools should be more like home environments shown to be conducive to language development. Although there may be a strong case for and possibility of such a change in the primary grades, there is less research support for and perhaps less possibility of comparably profound changes in the upper grades.

Home and school research in early language learning has added an important dimension to primary-school classroom research by providing credible alternative images of educational settings, even though eventual school success is often the criterion used to assess homes as learning environments. Similarly, the Squire and Applebee study of English teaching in the United Kingdom (1969) provided American teachers with plausible images of practice very different from their own, and often more consistent with the theory of language education emerging from the Dartmouth Seminar. If one benefit of classroom research is to provide teachers with alternatives that prompt them to reflect on and change their own practice, then sound alternatives need to be created and tested, and this will involve observational research in a variety of settings and very likely a program of staff development as well. It is instructive that Donald Graves's research into early writing development could not have been conducted in a great many elementary schools because so little writing was being done, and that Lunzer and Gardner had to develop a secondary-school setting in which to examine the effects of discussion on students' reading comprehension. In order to provide perspectives for classroom observation and analysis, we need not only a theory of language development, but evidence of how such development may proceed in different circumstances, such as in on-the-job training, nonschool learning situations, and nontraditional school settings that may have to be created before they can be investigated.

The insights provided by multiple studies focusing on similar issues suggest the beneficial effects of research projects in which large issues are addressed through related studies. Such collaborative projects would be consistent with the NIE's proposed model for research centers, in which teachers, basic researchers from diverse disciplines, and students collaborate in the investigation and dissemination of findings influencing educational decisions.

Classroom research in language education can best be conducted in concert with research into language processes and development, and the work of teachers-as-researchers, to the mutual benefit of all the research. In language education, an adequate pedagogical model must reflect the insights derived from research into language development and processes, since, as Bruner (1966) says, "a theory of instruction . . . is in effect a theory of how growth and development are assisted by diverse means" (p. 1). Nonschool "basic" research into processes and development should also consider how the findings may have been determined by school contextual factors that have influenced virtually all school-age subjects used in such research. A working model of such interactive basic and applied research was developed by the Toronto Pedagogy of Writing Project at the Ontario Institute for Studies in Education, in which findings from basic research into writing processes were translated into classroom practice, and instructional research and field testing of these practices provided additional insights to inform the basic research (for an overview of the basic research, see Bereiter and Scardamalia 1982; for an example of the project's instructional output, see Scardamalia, Bereiter, and Fillion 1981). The potential benefits of including a network of teachers engaged in classroom research have been demonstrated in various Schools Council studies in the U.K., which typically begin with extensive discussions among project researchers and school practitioners (see, for example, the approaches used in Martin et al. 1976 and Southgate, Arnold, and Johnson 1981). Another useful component of such a research team might be historians, to provide historical perspectives on the problems and practices to be investigated, and perhaps some needed assurance that progress is, in fact, possible (examples of such perspectives are found in Pearson 1984.)

In our view the highest priority for classroom research in language education is to determine how our increasing knowledge of language processes, development, and use can be translated into practice for the purpose of improving our students' language development and use. If, as appears likely, this involves basic changes in the way most classrooms and teachers operate, then part of this agenda must consider the ways that such changes can be brought about. An agenda for classroom research must involve more than documenting the inadequacies of the status quo, comparing the effects of clearly specified techniques to ill-defined "traditional" methods used as "controls," or testing individual variables without regard to their interaction with a complex environment. Rather, it will involve an ongoing examination of the way that student language-learning behaviors are manifested and interact with complex classroom variables to produce qualitative and quantitative improvements in the way students learn to use language and the way they use language to learn.

References

Adams, R. S., and B. J. Biddle (1970). *Realities of teaching: Explorations with video tape.* New York: Holt, Rinehart & Winston.

Albritton, T. W. (1986). Summary of research on class size and English. In *Class size and English in the secondary school,* by W. L. Smith, chair, and the NCTE Task Force on Class Size and Workload in Secondary English Instruction. Urbana, Ill.: National Council of Teachers of English. ED 248 517.

Allington, R. L. (1983). The reading instruction provided readers of differing reading abilities. *The Elementary School Journal* 83: 548–59.

Applebee, A. N. (1981). *Writing in the secondary school.* Research report no. 21. Urbana, Ill.: National Council of Teachers of English. ED 197 347.

——— (1984a). Musings. *Research in the Teaching of English* 18: 229–31.

——— (1984b). Presentation at the Assembly on Research. Annual convention of the National Council of Teachers of English.

Bakhtin, M. M. (1981). Discourse in the novel. In *The dialogic imagination: Four essays,* edited by M. Holquist, trans. by C. Emerson and M. Holquist. Austin, Tex.: University of Texas Press.

Barnes, D. (1976). *From communication to curriculum.* New York: Penguin Education Books.

Barnes, D., J. Britton, and H. Rosen (1969). *Language, the learner and the school.* Harmondsworth, England: Penguin Education Books.

Bereiter, C., and M. Scardamalia (1982). From conversation to composition: The role of instruction in a developmental process. In *Advances in instructional psychology,* Vol. 2, edited by R. Glaser. Hillsdale, N.J.: Erlbaum.

Berliner, D. C. (1984). The half-full glass: A review of research on teaching. In *Using what we know about teaching,* edited by P. L. Hosford. Alexandria, Va.: Association for Supervision and Curriculum Development.

Berliner, D. C., and W. Tikunoff (1977). Ethnography in the classroom. In *The appraisal of teaching: Concepts and processes,* edited by G. D. Borich, 280–91. Reading, Mass.: Addison-Wesley.

Bissex, G. L. (1980). *Gnys at wrk: A child learns to write and read.* Cambridge, Mass.: Harvard University Press.

Bolster, A. S., Jr. (1983). Toward a more effective model of research on teaching. *Harvard Educational Review* 53: 294–308.

Borich, G. D., ed. (1977). *The appraisal of teaching: Concepts and processes.* Reading, Mass.: Addison-Wesley.

Brause, R. S. (1985). Classroom contexts for learning. *Contexts of reading,* edited by C. Hedley and A. N. Baratta. Norwood, N.J.: Ablex.

———— (Forthcoming). Two types of research. *Search and research,* edited by J. S. Mayher. Urbana, Ill.: National Council of Teachers of English.

Brause, R. S., and J. S. Mayher (1984). Teacher directed lessons: Organization and implications. Paper presented at the annual meeting of the American Educational Research Association.

Britton, J. (1970). *Language and learning.* Coral Gables, Fla.: University of Miami Press.

Bruner, J. S. (1966). *Toward a theory of instruction.* Cambridge, Mass.: Belknap Press of Harvard University.

———— (1978). The role of dialogue in language acquisition. In *The child's conception of language,* edited by A. Sinclair, R. J. Jarvella, and W. J. M. Levelt, 241–56. New York: Springer-Verlag.

———— (1984). Notes on the cognitive revolution. (OISE's Centre for Applied Cognitive Science.) *Interchange* 15, no. 3: 1–8.

Buike, S. (1981). The shaping of classroom practices: Teacher decisions. Research report no. 97. East Lansing, Mich.: Institute for Research on Teaching, Michigan State University. ED 206 622.

Bullock, A. L. C. (1975). *A language for life.* London: Her Majesty's Stationery Office.

Cahir, S. R., and C. Kovac (1981). *Exploring functional language.* Washington, D.C.: Center for Applied Linguistics.

Cazden, C. B. (1986). Classroom discourse. In *Handbook of research on teaching,* 3d. ed., edited by M. C. Wittrock, 432–63. New York: Macmillan.

Chanan, G., and S. Delamont, eds. (1975). *Frontiers of classroom research.* Windsor, Berks, England: National Foundation for Educational Research.

Cuban, L. (1984). *How teachers taught: Constancy and change in American classrooms,* 1890–1980. New York: Longman.

Delamont, S. (1976). *Interaction in the classroom.* London: Methuen.

Dennison, G. (1969). *The lives of children: The story of the first street school.* New York: Vintage Books.

Dillon, J. T. (1983). Cognitive complexity and duration of classroom speech. *Instructional Science* 12: 59–66.

Dixon, J., ed. (1967). *Growth through English: A report based on the Dartmouth Seminar.* Reading, England: National Association for the Teaching of English.

Dore, J., and R. P. McDermott (1982). Linguistic indeterminancy and social context in utterance interpretation. *Language* 58: 374–97.

Durkin, D. (1979). What classroom observations reveal about reading comprehension instruction. *Reading Research Quarterly* 14: 481–533.

Dyson, A. H. (1984). Learning to write/learning to do school: Emergent writers' interpretations of school literacy tasks. *Research in the Teaching of English* 18: 233–64.

Emig, J. (1983). Non-magical thinking: Presenting writing developmentally in schools. In *The web of meaning: Essays on writing, teaching, learning, and thinking,* 135–44. Upper Montclair, N.J.: Boynton/Cook.

Erickson, F. (1979). On standards of descriptive validity in studies of classroom activity. Occasional paper no. 16. East Lansing, Mich.: Institute for Research on Teaching, Michigan State University.

Fillion, B. (1979). Language across the curriculum: Examining the place of language in our schools. *McGill Journal of Education* 14: 47–60.

——— (1981). Reading as inquiry: An approach to literature learning. *English Journal* 70, no. 1: 39–45.

——— (1983). Let me see you learn. *Language Arts* 60: 702–10.

Flanders, N. (1964). Some relationships among teacher influence, pupil attitudes and achievement. In *Contemporary research on teacher effectiveness,* edited by B. Biddle and W. Ellena, 196–231. New York: Holt, Rinehart & Winston.

——— (1965). *Interaction analysis in the classroom—a manual for observers.* Ann Arbor, Mich.: University of Michigan.

——— (1970). *Analyzing teacher behavior.* Reading, Mass.: Addison-Wesley.

Gage, N. L. (1978). The yield of research on teaching. *Phi Delta Kappan* 60: 229–35.

Galton, M., and B. Simon, eds. (1981). *Progress and performance in the primary classroom.* London: Routledge & Kegan Paul.

Glass, G. V., and M. L. Smith (1978). *Meta-analysis of research on the relationship of class size and achievement.* Boulder, Col.: University of Colorado Laboratory of Educational Research.

Goetz, J. P., and M. D. LeCompte (1984). *Ethnography and qualitative design in educational research.* New York: Academic Press.

Good, T. L., and J. E. Brophy (1978). *Looking in classrooms.* 2d ed. New York: Harper & Row.

Goodlad, J. (1984). *A place called school: Prospects for the future.* New York: McGraw-Hill.

Goodman, K. S. (1970). Reading: A psycholinguistic guessing game. In *Theoretical models and processes of reading,* edited by H. Singer and R. Ruddell, 497–508. Newark, Del.: International Reading Association.

Goodman, K. S., ed. (1968). *The psycholinguistic nature of the reading process.* Detroit: Wayne State University Press.

Goodman, Y. M. (1980). The roots of literacy. In *Claremont reading conference forty-fourth yearbook,* edited by M. P. Douglas. Claremont, Calif.

Graves, D. H. (1978). *Balance the basics: Let them write.* New York: Ford Foundation.

——— (1982). *A case study observing the development of primary school children's composing, spelling, and motor behaviors during the writing process.* Final report NIE G-78-01741. Durham, N.H.: University of New Hampshire. ED 218 653.

Green, J. L. (1983). Research on teaching as a linguistic process: A state of the art. In *Review of research in education,* Vol. 10, edited by E. W. Gordon. Washington, D.C.: American Educational Research Association.

Harste, J. C., C. L. Burke, and V. A. Woodward (1981). *Children, their language and world: Initial encounters with print. Final report.* NIE-G-79-0132. Bloomington, Ind.: Language Education Department, Indiana University. ED 213 041.

Harste, J. C., V. A. Woodward, and C. L. Burke (1984). Examining our assumptions: A transactional view of literacy and learning. *Research in the Teaching of English* 18: 84–108.

Heap, J. L. (1982). Understanding classroom events: A critique of Durkin, with an alternative. *Journal of Reading Behavior* 14: 391–411.

Herndon, J. (1968). *The way it spozed to be.* New York: Simon & Schuster.

Holt, J. (1964). *How children fail.* New York: Pitman Publishing.

——— (1967). *How children learn.* New York: Pitman Publishing.

Johnston, P. H. (1984). Assessment in reading. In *Handbook of reading research,* edited by P. D. Pearson, 147–82. New York: Longman.

Kaufman, B. (1966). *Up the down staircase.* New York: Avon.

Kohl, H. (1967). *Thirty-six children.* New York: New American Library.

Kozol, J. (1967). *Death at an early age: The destruction of the hearts and minds of Negro children in the Boston public schools.* Boston: Houghton Mifflin.

Lopate, P. (1975). *Being with children.* New York: Doubleday.

Lunzer, E., and K. Gardner, eds. (1979). *The effective use of reading.* London: Heinemann Educational Books for the Schools Council.

Macmillan, C. J. B., and J. W. Garrison (1984). Using the "new philosophy of science" in criticizing current research traditions in education. *Educational Researcher* 13, no. 10: 15–21.

McDermott, R. P. (1978). Reading and learning: An analysis of two classroom reading groups. In *Linguistics and reading,* edited by R. Shuy, Rowley, Mass.: Newbury House.

McDermott, R. P., K. Gospodinoff, and J. Aron (1978). Criteria for an ethnographically adequate description of concerted activities and their contexts. *Semiotics* 24: 245–75.

Martin, N., P. D'Arcy, B. Newton, and R. Parker (1976). *Writing and learning across the curriculum, 11–16.* London: Ward Lock Educational.

Mayher, J. S., and R. S. Brause (1985). Learning through teaching: A structure for inquiry and change. *Language Arts* 62: 277–81.

Medley, D. M., and H. E. Mitzel (1963). Measuring classroom behavior by systematic observation. In *Handbook of research on teaching,* edited by N. L. Gage, 247–328. Chicago: Rand McNally.

Medway, P. (1980). *Finding a language: Autonomy and learning in school.* London: Writers and Readers in association with Chameleon.

Mehan, H. (1979). *Learning lessons.* Cambridge, Mass.: Harvard University Press.

Michaels, S., and J. Collins (1984). Oral discourse styles: Classroom interaction and the acquisition of literacy. In *Coherence in spoken and written discourse,* edited by D. Tannen, 219–44. Norwood, N.J.: Ablex.

Moffett, J. W. (1968). *Teaching the universe of discourse.* Boston: Houghton Mifflin.

Morine-Dershimer, G., and M. Tenenberg (1981). *Participant perspectives of classroom discourse.* Final report to the National Institute of Education. ED 210 105.

Pearson, P. D., ed. (1984). *Handbook of reading research.* New York: Longman.

Philips, S. (1982). *The invisible culture: Communication in classroom and community on the Warm Springs Indian Reservation.* New York: Longman.

Purves, A. C., with V. Rippere (1968). *Elements of writing about a literary work: A study of response to literature.* Research report no. 9. Urbana, Ill.: National Council of Teachers of English. ED 018 431.

Rist, R. C. (1973). *The urban school: A factory for failure.* Cambridge, Mass.: MIT Press.

Rosenblatt, L. M. (1976). *Literature as exploration.* 3d ed. New York: Noble and Noble.

——— (1978). *The reader, the text, the poem: The transactional theory of the literary work.* Carbondale, Ill.: Southern Illinois University Press.

Rosenshine, B. (1976). Recent research on teaching behaviors and student achievement. *Journal of Teacher Education* 27: 61–64.

——— (1977). Review of teaching variables and student achievement. In *The appraisal of teaching: Concepts and process,* edited by G. D. Borich, 114–20. Reading, Mass.: Addison-Wesley.

Rosenshine, B., and N. Furst (1973). The use of direct observation to study teaching. In *Second handbook of research on teaching,* edited by R. Travers, 122–83. Chicago: Rand McNally.

Rutter, M., B. Maughan, P. Mortimore, and J. Ouston (1979). *Fifteen thousand hours: Secondary schools and their effects on children.* Cambridge, Mass.: Harvard University Press.

Scardamalia, M., C. Bereiter, and B. Fillion (1981). *Writing for results: A sourcebook of consequential composing activities.* Toronto: OISE Press.

Silberman, C. E. (1970). *Crisis in the classroom: The remaking of American education.* New York: Random House.

Sinclair, J. M., and R. M. Coulthard (1975). *Towards an analysis of discourse: The English used by teachers and pupils.* London: Oxford University Press.

Singleton, C. M., P. B. Diederich, and W. Hill (1961). The classroom teacher as a researcher. In *Research methods in the language arts,* prepared by a committee of NCRE chaired by C. M. Singleton, 33–37. Champaign, Ill.: National Council of Teachers of English.

Smith, F. (1978). *Understanding reading: A psycholinguistic analysis of reading and learning to read.* 2d ed. New York: Holt, Rinehart & Winston.

——— (1983). *Essays into literacy: Selected papers and some afterthoughts.* Exeter, N.H.: Heinemann.

Southgate, V., H. Arnold, and S. Johnson (1981). *Extending beginning reading.* London: Heinemann.

Squire, J. R., and R. K. Applebee (1968). *High school English instruction today: The national study of high school English programs.* New York: Appleton-Century-Croft.

——— (1969). *Teaching English in the United Kingdom.* Urbana, Ill.: National Council of Teachers of English.

Stubbs, M. (1983). *Language, schools and classrooms.* 2d ed. New York: Methuen.

Stubbs, M., and S. Delamont, eds. (1976). *Explorations in classroom observation.* New York: John Wiley & Sons.

Tikunoff, W. J., and B. A. Ward (1983). Collaborative research on teaching. *The Elementary School Journal* 83: 453–68.

Torbe, M., and P. Medway (1981). *The climate for learning.* London: Ward Lock Educational.

Travers, D. M. M. (1984). The poetry teacher: behavior and attitudes. *Research in the teaching of English* 18: 367–84.

Travers, R. M.W. (1983). *How research has changed American schools: A history from 1840 to the present.* Kalamazoo, Mich.: Mythos Press.

Vygotsky, L. S. (1978). *Mind in society: The development of higher psychological processes.* Cambridge, Mass.: Harvard University Press.

Walberg, H. J., D. Schiller, and G. D. Haertel (1979). The quiet revolution in educational research. *Phi Delta Kappan* 61: 179–83.

Wasserman, M. (1971). *The school fix, NYC, USA.* New York: Simon & Schuster.

Wells, C. G. (1981). *Learning through interaction: The study of language development.* Cambridge: Cambridge University Press.

Classroom Practices and Classroom Interaction during Reading Instruction: What's Going On?

M. Trika Smith-Burke
New York University

Research on classroom practices and interactions resembles the story of the blind men and the elephant. Each researcher perceives the elephant based on the part that he touches. Due to their topics, paradigms, measures, and analyses, researchers of teacher-effectiveness management, reading researchers, and researchers of classroom interaction focus on different aspects of teaching and learning reading in the classroom.

Reviewing exemplary studies in reading, this paper is divided into three sections: (1) classroom management and teacher effectiveness, (2) comprehension instruction and classroom realities, and (3) classroom interaction during reading instruction. The first section concentrates on teaching and management characteristics which promote achievement in reading. The second section describes research on the relation of teachers' knowledge to instruction, on techniques for teaching comprehension, and on observed realities of reading instruction during classroom lessons. The third section reviews the research on interaction in traditional classrooms, interaction in nontraditional classrooms, and home/school and cultural differences in interaction.

In the final discussion four suggestions are made for future research and development in the areas of language, learning, research methodology, and curriculum.

Classroom Management and Teacher Effectiveness

The first research done on classroom practices and interaction was that on classroom management and teacher effectiveness (see Wittrock 1986). The purpose of this research was to identify critical process variables that are part of effective teaching by correlating them with achievement. Experimental studies were to be the final test. Only a few of these studies were conducted, however, before federal funding was reduced.

The primary focus of this research was on the teacher and teaching in relation to achievement. The decisions concerning which classrooms to study were made based on instructional factors, teacher characteristics, or the nature of the funding (e.g., the Follow Through evaluation grants). Students' cognitive processes during learning and the interaction between teaching and learning processes were not stressed. Nor were specific content-area methodologies the object of study. When and if reading was the topic of instruction in these classrooms, usually a structured reading program (e.g., basal programs, DISTAR, etc.) or a skills-management program was used. At the time there were few classrooms with integrated reading and writing programs available for study, since research on writing was in its infancy.

Usually at least ten classrooms were selected for each study. Several of the larger projects concentrated on particular segments of the population, namely teachers of low-SES students in Follow Through programs and beginning teachers (e.g., in the Beginning Teacher Evaluation Study). Predetermined observational schedules were used for a set amount of time to record behavior across grades. Standardized tests were the primary outcome measures. Thus success was often achieved by targeting instruction to focus on low-level, tested skills.

Findings from the Research on Management

What results have emanated from this research? One major part of being an effective teacher is maintaining order in the classroom, or classroom management. Echoing the story of the mule and the farmer, any teacher can tell you that you've got to maintain the students' attention or little learning will occur.

In several studies teachers who were effective classroom managers negotiated order, developed effective routines, and orchestrated activities so that disruptive behavior was prevented or at least kept to a minimum (Good 1979, Medley 1979). Activities such as redirecting student behavior and managing disruptions (e.g., telling students to stop talking and to look at their books) negatively correlated with achievement (Anderson, Evertson, and Brophy 1979).

Doyle (1983) describes one situation in which students were confronted with the ambiguity of difficult, higher-level cognitive demands (e.g., open-ended why and how questions) made by a teacher. As the students became less secure about what was expected, they pushed for specificity and became less manageable. To maintain order in this situation, the teacher became so specific that the difficulty level of the task was significantly lowered. For example, instead of asking a why or how question requiring a complex causal response, the teacher might ask a string of factual questions and then end up drawing the conclusion for the students.

Reading researchers (Allington 1983, Duffy and McIntyre 1982) have also documented that when teachers are overly concerned about management, they usually sacrifice content. However, Barr (1987) described a counter-example which showed that this need not be the case. In this situation, an English teacher modeled the higher-level thinking process involved in answering questions. By doing this, she avoided task ambiguity, management problems, and the resulting student need to lower the level of thinking required by the task.

Doyle (1985) characterizes management as the coordination of the social and academic/instructional aspects of the classroom to maintain order. This view replaces the concept of management as simply identifying and punishing misbehavior, or quelling behavioral disorders. He argues for five distinct properties which affect teaching: simultaneity, multidimensionality, publicness and history, immediacy or momentum of class life, and unpredictability. He has also identified and summarized six major themes from the current management research (pp. 424–25):

1. Classroom management focuses on solving the problem of creating and maintaining order in the classroom, not just responding to behavioral problems.

2. Order depends on how well teachers specify and orchestrate activities and routines which they must accomplish with their students.

3. Since programs must be jointly enacted by teachers and students, a struggle is likely to arise in maintaining order if students lack either the motivation or ability to carry out the teacher's intended goals.

4. Rules for social participation interact with the academic demands to define the basis of classroom activities.

5. Many different context-specific forces and processes affect order in the classroom. Consequently, routines, recitation, and seatwork appear more reasonable as means to offset potential problems in classroom life.

6. Teachers' success seems to depend on their ability to monitor and "read" what's going on in the classroom and then guide activities according to this information.

Findings from the Research on Teacher Effectiveness

Using slightly different terminology, researchers of teacher effectiveness have found that engaged time-on-task, academic emphasis in teaching, the pacing of the lesson, the content covered, the activeness of instruction, the detection of problems, and such items as grouping, monitoring, and helping during seatwork are important aspects of both management and effective teaching (Brophy and Evertson 1974, 1976; Evertson, Anderson, and Brophy 1978; Fisher et al. 1978; McDonald and Elias 1976; Rosenshine 1979; Tikunoff, Berliner, and Rist 1975).

The subset of these studies conducted during reading lessons suggests that students who were academically engaged under teacher direction and supervision scored higher on reading measures (Anderson, Evertson, and Brophy 1979; Fisher et al. 1978; Rosenshine 1979; Stallings et al. 1977, 1978). Achievement scores also tended to be higher when teachers used diagnostic information to place students in reading groups and to plan lessons (Rupley 1977; Tikunoff, Berliner, and Rist 1975). Data from the Beginning Teacher Evaluation Study (Fisher et al. 1978) indicate that time spent practicing skills is facilitative in the early grades but not as much in the later grades. In the fifth grade, application of skills in reading-comprehension exercises was positively correlated with achievement.

Patterns of individual differences were also evident. Rate of success, responses, use of patterned turns (i.e., round robin reading), and use of praise were differentially related to achievement for low- versus high-SES students (Brophy and Evertson 1974, 1976).

In these studies certain teacher characteristics were correlated with success in reading. Several studies (e.g., Brophy and Evertson 1976; Soar 1977; Stallings et al. 1977, 1978; Stallings and Kaskowitz 1974, Solomon and Kendall 1979) showed that successful teachers were strong, business-like leaders who had an academic emphasis and high expectations in their teaching. When they organized daily tasks, minimized "housekeeping" time, and used routines, their classes ran smoothly.

Less successful teachers seemed more child-centered in their approach and allowed students to select activities and working arrangements (Good and Beckerman 1978; Soar 1977; Solomon and Kendall 1979; Stallings and Kaskowitz 1974; Stallings, Needels, and Stayrook 1979). It is difficult to ascertain the exact nature of the social and academic contexts or the educational intent behind self-selection procedures in these studies. This obscurity contrasts with the clear descriptions of the purpose behind self-selection and the nature of tasks in successful classrooms in which reading and writing were integrated across the curriculum (Edelsky, Draper, and Smith 1983; Graves 1983; Hansen, this volume; Platt 1984).

Based on their findings that students who participated in teacher-directed instruction tended to be more engaged in academic tasks, Fisher et al. (1978) recommended whole-class instruction to provide direct contact with teachers. Others found that teacher-led instruction in small groups also was effective, more so than independent seatwork or individualized instruction (California State Department of Education 1977, Soar 1977, Stallings and Kaskowitz 1974, Tikunoff et al. 1975).

In 1974 Duncan and Biddle concluded that teacher-centered instruction was the most effective instruction. After ten more years of research, Brophy and Good (1986) drew exactly the same conclusion. It is important to remember that most of these studies were conducted in classes which contained structured reading programs.

Various components of teacher-directed instruction have also been examined for their effectiveness. Anderson, Evertson, and Brophy (1979) found that beginning a lesson with an interview and a demonstration of the assigned task was highly successful. In contrast, reading researchers stress the metacognitive aspects of instruction. They (Baker and Brown 1984, Roehler and Duffy 1984) argue that strategy lessons should begin with an "explanation" of *what* strategy students are to learn, *when* and *how* they are to use this strategy, and *why* it is important. The discrepancy between these approaches needs to be resolved.

In their reviews Brophy and Good (1986) and Rosenshine and Stevens (1984) conclude that breaking lessons into small sequenced steps, guided practice, clear directions for tasks, and teacher-monitored seatwork are additional instructional techniques related to achievement. The parallels between this research and the work of Madeleine Hunter developed many years ago are striking. It is important to remember that there are successful alternatives which do not follow these patterns (Edelsky, Draper, and Smith 1983).

Teachers' use of higher-order questions has been another topic of investigation. However, there is only mixed evidence from this research to support the use of such questions (Stallings and Kaskowitz 1974; see also Brophy and Good 1986 and Rosenshine and Stevens 1984 for discussion of this important issue). Most of these studies define the level of the questions without relating them to available oral or written discourse or to the types of responses produced by the students.

These findings raise serious research issues. What is meant by "difficulty level," "higher-order level," or "cognitive level" of questions? How is the function or intent of the questions related to this "level"? Can the difficulty or cognitive level of a question be assessed without examining the oral or written discourse on which it was based and in relation to the student responses? (See Pearson and Johnson 1978 for an alternative approach.)

By developing a different framework which addresses some of these questions, reading researchers (reported in a later section) have produced more support for the use of questions which promote inferential thinking. Their emphasis on comprehension processes raises an additional question:

is the success rate of students' responses adequate as the measure of their achievement?

Researchers in teacher effectiveness have also examined pacing and content covered. Barr and Dreben (1983) state that pacing was an excellent predictor of achievement in their studies. However, others found that it interacts with variables (Brophy and Good 1986, Fisher et al. 1978). Low-ability and low-SES students needed to move more slowly through material, while high-ability students required a brisk pace. Usually if content was more difficult or at a higher cognitive level, the pace had to be slower, the wait time was longer, and less content was covered (Brophy and Good 1986).

Clearly related to pacing, content covered is measured in a variety of ways, such as number of words teachers tried to teach (Barr 1973–74), amount of time allocated to reading, number of basal books completed (Anderson, Evertson, and Brophy 1979), or number of words read per unit of time (Allington 1984, Gambrell 1984). For example, the pace of instruction for lower-ability children was slower and the number of words read per week was much lower than the number for high-ability children. At the same ability levels, there was a high variability in content covered and pace across classrooms (Allington 1984).

Although positive relationships exist among pacing, content covered, and achievement, this work raises important questions: how is content defined at different grade levels, and which measurement instruments truly assess *relevant* aspects of achievement? It is also important not to infer causality prematurely.

Teacher criticism and praise also have been studied in the instructional context. Research shows that criticism during academic interactions is rare (Anderson, Evertson, and Brophy 1979; Stallings et al. 1977, 1978). Praise seems more effective for low-ability and low-SES students (Evertson, Anderson, and Brophy 1978). After reviewing the literature on praise, Brophy (1981) concludes that it is the quality of the praise which can make a difference. This is also true of criticism (Brophy and Good 1986).

Effective teaching also involves selection and use of materials, the choice of which is often influenced, if not determined, by the school or district. In Anderson, Evertson, and Brophy (1979) and Marliave (1978), materials which were relatively easy to read and therefore promoted a higher rate of success seemed to lead to higher achievement scores. However, in another study, in which rate of success interacted with SES, Brophy and Evertson (1974) discovered that low-SES children needed a higher rate of success than high-SES children. A high success rate was also related to positive student attitudes (Fisher et al. 1978).

These results seem inconsistent with the research on child language development and on reading as a psycholinguistic process. In both fields making errors and self-correction are considered natural and important (in language learning, Lindfors 1980; in early reading, Clay 1972). Goodman (1970) argues that making errors and self-corrections when meaning is disrupted is a normal facet of proficient reading.

The inconsistencies between the research model of effective teaching and that of language learning raise numerous questions. On what type of materials and under what conditions does success rate vary? What types of errors are generated? Do these patterns change with different types of discourse of varying levels of difficulty? Which types of errors are most facilitative of learning? What rate of success will promote the development of students' self-monitoring as well as a good sense of accomplishment, particularly for minority students?

Researchers of teacher effectiveness have realized that their work must become more differentiated and fine-tuned. Certainly the results suggest questions that future investigators need to ask: Time on which tasks for which purposes? Which teacher behaviors? Which group of students (i.e., which age, SES, and ability levels)? Given the dramatic contrasts between the characteristics of the classrooms in teacher-effectiveness research and those in which the language arts are integrated across the curriculum (see "Classroom Interaction during Reading Instruction" in this paper), we need to ask which type of classroom structure and curriculum is preferable under which conditions and for whom? Which most appropriately stimulates higher-order thinking? Also, which type of language curriculum produces students who enjoy reading and writing and learn to function as autonomous reader/writers?

Criticism of the observation schedules and standardized outcome measures in teacher effectiveness studies abound (see Johnston 1983; Otto, Wolf, and Eldridge 1984). The observational instruments are based on frequency counts of distinct behaviors, marked in time segments. The criteria used to select reading and writing behaviors for them are not entirely clear, but seem to be based on a discrete-skills approach to reading. There are many other literacy behaviors which bear watching, particularly in beginning reading, comprehension, and writing (Commission on Reading 1985; Graves 1983; Harste, Burke, and Woodward 1982; Mason 1984). In addition, sequences of verbal behaviors and the interrelation between verbal and nonverbal behavior need to be analyzed. Heap (1982) also gives an important rationale for analyzing the multifunctional nature of utterances in interpreting classroom behavior.

Outcome measures also need to be rethought and revised. Standardized tests are not sensitive over short periods of time and only test a limited domain of skills. As the Commission on Reading (1985) recommends, the ultimate goals of literacy, such as reading a variety of longer texts and writing about them, should be included.

Other nonacademic variables such as enjoyment of reading, quantity of reading in and out of school, social functioning and independent problem solving in the classroom, and autonomous student functioning as readers/writers need to be assessed. Care in making generalizations about current results must also be taken since Soar and Soar (1979) discovered that curvilinear relationships exist for certain teacher-effectiveness variables such as management behaviors. For example, at a certain point more teacher direction, or drill and practice, had little payoff. Similar nonlinear relationships have been found for other variables (Brophy and Good 1986).

Some ethnographic techniques are being added to the preplanned, observational frameworks and new outcome measures continue to be developed. However, much more work is needed in this area. The interrelationships of some contextual and individual variables are beginning to be examined. It has become clear that the curriculum content (e.g., reading or math curricula) and the social context also interact with other variables and therefore must be examined.

Comprehension Instruction and Classroom Realities

The second area of research on classroom practices and interaction involves the teaching of comprehension and the realities of classroom reading instruction. Taking a slightly different orientation, reading researchers focus primarily on the cognitive processes underlying comprehension and how these can be fostered through instruction. This research can be divided into two groups of studies. One group concentrates on teachers' mental models of the reading process and the development of techniques for teaching comprehension. The second group documents the realities of classroom reading instruction.

The methodologies vary significantly. Studies on teachers' models of reading have tended to rely on self-report techniques or inferences from observed behaviors. Quasi-experimental designs have frequently been used in tests of comprehension. These studies usually lasted from one to six weeks and infrequently tested long-term gains. Conducted primarily in reading but also in some content-area classes, observational researchers recorded reading behaviors through the uses of predetermined frameworks. In most of these studies, teachers and students were almost exclusively from middle-class homes.

Comprehension Instruction

The following findings from basic research on reading comprehension (see Pearson 1984 for reviews of this work) provided the foundation for comprehension instruction research: (1) prior knowledge is an important component of comprehension and planning instruction, (2) the ability to make inferences is developmental and related to prior knowledge, (3) text structure is related to comprehension and recall, and (4) active use of comprehension and monitoring strategies is a characteristic of good readers.

Prior Knowledge and Comprehension Instruction

Applied work on prior knowledge focuses on two different aspects: (1) how teachers' knowledge of the reading process relates to their teaching, and (2) the importance of eliciting or building concepts before reading to facilitate comprehension.

In order to plan and carry out reading instruction successfully, teachers must have knowledge about reading. Consequently the relation of teachers' knowledge of reading to instruction has been explored. For example, Harste and Burke (1977) and DeFord (1981, 1985) conclude that teachers' instructional practices reflect their models of the reading process. Extending this work, other researchers (Barr 1975, 1980; Bawden, Buike, and Duffy 1979; Borko 1982; Borko, Shavelson, and Stern 1981; Duffy and Metheny 1979; Metheny 1980a, 1980b; Shannon 1982) report that the model of reading is just one aspect of teacher knowledge that influences instruction. Still other researchers include as factors student characteristics, teachers' perceptions of administrative policies, materials, pacing, time allotted to reading, and other aspects of classroom management. In the work on general teacher planning, teachers have been seen to operate more like problem solvers (Clark and Yinger 1977) who consider many types of information: student data (e.g., sex, age, ability, cultural background), instructional tasks (e.g., materials, goals, procedures), the classroom environment (e.g., sense of community, the physical layout), and the school environment (e.g., mandated objectives, materials, scheduling, or the testing program).

In "limiting their problem space" (Newell and Simon 1972), teachers also conducted different types of planning—yearly, term, unit, weekly or daily—and tended to focus on different aspects of the curriculum and classroom life at different times in the school year (e.g., social rules and diagnosing reading ability for reading-group placement in the first weeks of school or yearly curriculum planning in the summer; see Clark and Yinger 1978 and Clark and Elmore 1979). There is some evidence that teachers at elementary levels versus high school levels order priorities differently (Clark 1984).

Clearly the issue of what prior knowledge teachers know and use to plan and carry out instruction is a highly complex issue which must be pursued. The use of self-report techniques needs to be cross-validated with classroom observations, as do the results of studies using hypothetical situations. Also, ethnographic techniques can add rich information.

Picturing the teacher as thoughtful and rational, the results from teacher-planning research conflict with those from the research on teacher decision making. Brophy states (1984) that "most studies of teachers' interactive decision making portray it as more reactive than reflective, more intuitive than rational, and more routinized than conscious" (p. 72). Again, research which coordinates examination of teacher planning with the teacher's actual decision making in the classroom should begin to resolve this discrepancy.

An example of the second type of applied research on prior knowledge is that on vocabulary. One way to elicit and/or build background knowledge before reading is to teach relevant vocabulary. Earlier research (e.g., Tuinman and Brady 1974; Jenkins, Pany, and Schreck 1978) did not support the teaching of vocabulary in relation to comprehension. More recently, studies which included elaborative activities stressing relationships among sets of words from the text (Beck, Perfetti, and McKeown 1982; Beck and McKeown 1983) have reported increases in both word knowledge and comprehension.

The research on prior knowledge seems to have neglected some major questions: How does knowledge develop? How much and what kind of knowledge is necessary for fully comprehending a text? How can prior knowledge be assessed (both in students and in terms of knowledge prerequisite for understanding a text)? Answers to these questions are essential for teachers who confront them daily.

Inferences and Questions

Many studies have concentrated on the development of inferencing ability through the use of questions. This research addresses the issue of higher-order thinking and the difficulty level of questions from a different framework than does the research on teacher effectiveness. For example, in a series of studies (Hansen 1981, Hansen and Pearson 1983, Raphael and Pearson 1982, Raphael 1982), researchers found that children learned to make inferences through being exposed to a rich diet of inferential questions and strategies for answering them at all levels of difficulty. Poor comprehenders benefited the most from this type of instruction.

In these studies, "level" of questioning was not determined by looking at the question alone. Instead, the question, the available discourse, and the student response were examined in relation to each other. Also, emphasis was placed on the process of constructing an interpretation, not just on the correctness of the answer itself. The one aspect of questioning which still remains to be included is the function(s) of questions during interaction.

Text Structure and Comprehension

Many studies have documented how text structure facilitates recall for good readers and the fact that poor readers often fail to use the structure as an aid to retention (see Meyer and Rice 1984 for an excellent summary of this research). In applied studies, students have been taught elements of narrative and expository structures in an attempt to improve recall. For example, Whaley (1981) and Fitzgerald and Speigel (1983) taught students parts of a story in order to help them predict and comprehend. Bartlett (1978) helped poor comprehenders use different expository structures, such as problem and solution or description, in order to comprehend. Barnett (1984) has successfully used a similar technique with college students. In all cases this instruction produced increased recall of text elements.

Based on the research on story structure, Beck, Omanson, and McKeown (1982) modified lessons for teaching comprehension of a basal story. They developed (1) prereading activities based on critical story concepts, (2) comprehension questions about the critical elements of the story structure in sequence, and (3) clearly related follow-up activities for teachers to use. Significant improvement in student comprehension was the result.

Active Comprehension and Monitoring

Basic research has shown that good readers actively plan purposeful reading based on their goals. They also predict, monitor, and "fix up" comprehension problems while reading (see Baker and Brown 1984 for an excellent summary of this work). Applied research in this area has focused on teaching students several strategies and monitoring techniques to improve comprehension.

In a series of studies, Palinscar and Brown (Palinscar 1984, Palinscar and Brown 1984) developed a routine to teach summarizing, question generating, clarifying, and predicting strategies to poor comprehenders. The students benefited and maintained gains over time in all studies. There even were transfer effects to reading tasks in content-area classrooms.

Brown and her colleagues stress that students must not only know how to carry out a strategy but also why and when the strategy should be used. They add that having students monitor the effectiveness of what they are doing must be an integral part of strategy instruction (Brown et al. 1983).

Classroom Realities

Another group of studies was produced by researchers who wanted to ascertain what really was being taught during reading and social studies lessons. The realities of classroom life were disappointing. For example, Durkin (1979), in a frequently cited study, describes middle-grade teachers as "mentioners, assignment givers and checkers, and interrogators" (p. 523). Teacher guides were used primarily to look up new vocabulary and comprehension questions for basal stories. Prereading exercises were brief; comprehension instruction and application exercises were rare. Students spent most of their time being given assignments (i.e., *what* to do, not *how* to do it) in workbooks or on ditto sheets and completing them. Neilsen, Rennie, and Connell's results (1982) essentially confirm Durkin's findings.

In analyzing workbook exercises, Osborn (1984) discovered that many of them contained confusing directions, did not correlate with the assigned story, and did not provide adequate or relevant skill practice.

In a follow-up study to assess the match between classroom realities and what was recommended in the teacher manuals, Durkin (1983) found that in using the manuals teachers ignored the suggestions for prereading activities, used the questions for story comprehension, and relied heavily on the written-practice assignments in workbooks and ditto sets. As in the first study, she found that teachers across grades did little to prepare students for reading, asked a myriad of questions, and were more concerned about correctness of responses than their diagnostic value.

Mason and Osborn (1982) observed third- and fourth-grade teachers to determine whether a shift from learning to read to reading to learn occurs between third and fourth grade. Unfortunately their answer was no! Third-grade teachers carried out more group instruction stressing oral reading. In contrast, fourth-grade teachers worked individually with students, while other fourth-graders read trade books or did nonreading activities. As students moved from third to fourth grade, a decrease in word recognition and oral reading was evident. There also was more emphasis on reading trade books and skill exercises on word- and sentence-level meaning. However, there was no increased emphasis on text-level comprehension.

L. Anderson (1984) examined what eight classes actually did during independent seatwork tasks based on commercially prepared basal materials. Explanations of what to do were inconsistently given, and in six of the classes students all did the same assignment, no matter what their level. The goal was to get the work done, one way or the other. As they juggled teaching reading groups and monitoring seatwork, teachers were more concerned with neatness, correctness, and class order than teaching or learning. They rarely retaught or helped students substantively on seatwork.

Low achievers expected that seatwork would be too difficult and that it would be a "meaningless" activity. Consequently they developed strategies for "getting through" and "looking busy." Dyson's results (1984a) found similar behaviors. This is all the more disheartening because Anderson and her colleagues found that from 40 percent to 60 percent of first graders' time during reading was spent on seatwork.

In social studies lessons, Pearson and Gallagher (1983) discovered that teachers wanted to make sure students learned the concepts. Consequently the teaching of comprehension strategies was abandoned. The most common instructional strategy, used by twenty-six of the forty teachers, was oral reading of text segments followed by factual questions from the teacher. Only two teachers taught any comprehension or study strategies which could be used independently by students.

Relatively little observational research has taken place in classrooms in which alternatives to basal reading programs are in use. Durkin's research has been a major contribution but has many of the same problems as the observational research from teacher-effectiveness studies. One major consideration which needs to be addressed is the function of utterances during interaction (for critiques of Durkin's work, see Hodges 1980 and Heap 1982).

All of the classroom studies provide a rather negative picture of classroom realities. A gap exists between the development and testing of successful instructional strategies and routines and the incorporation of these strategies in classrooms.

Three major constraints may be preventing the implementation of what is known from comprehension research. First, perhaps reading researchers do not spend enough time figuring out how specific reading routines can be successfully integrated into the total curriculum. They also need to consider how to constructively create and manage meaningful seatwork tasks for other students in order to free the teacher for small-group instruction.

Second, little of the research on comprehension is reflected in some of the basal reader manuals. Until this is so, there may not be much progress, since supervisors use these guides as the basis for training and evaluation. The fact that teachers use the manuals inconsistently may still prevent incorporation of these techniques, even if they were to be improved.

A final constraint is that this type of comprehension instruction requires teachers to cope with unfamiliar situations. It takes long-term inservice training and a great deal of support to help teachers begin to revise their teaching to accept multiple interpretations of a text, to help students develop the thinking involved in the construction of an interpretation, and to facilitate—not dominate—discussion (Smith-Burke and Ringler 1985).

This research also raises some questions for future research. How is background knowledge appropriately assessed in the classroom? When should a teacher attempt to build concepts for reading a text? When should a specific text be abandoned due to lack of concepts? As the research on writing has shown (Elley et al. 1979), direct teaching of grammar and text structure has not improved student composing. How much comprehension-strategy instruction is really necessary and for whom? How can strategy instruction be integrated into the teaching of subject matter? How are multiple interpretations of text managed by the teacher? How can seatwork be made more effective? What management strategies would help free the teacher to work with small groups?

More studies of classrooms in which comprehension strategies are being taught successfully are needed, particularly when rich descriptions of events are included to help generate hypotheses. Also, thanks to the research on writing, there are classrooms in which reading and writing are integrated across the curriculum. The research on these classrooms, which is still in its infancy, may provide important insights on the interrelation between reading and writing and on how this affects instruction.

Classroom Interaction during Reading Instruction

The third area of research centers on classroom interactions during reading instruction (for a more general review of classroom research, see Cazden 1986). This research provides rich descriptions about interaction during specific reading events and the roles that students and teachers play. Primarily ethnography or ethnographic techniques have guided the ways in which data were collected. Consequently only a few events and/ or classrooms are usually included in each study. Outcome measures such as standardized tests are rarely included.

Underlying this research is a model of language based on function. Dell Hymes (1972) extended the notion of linguistic competence to a new view of communicative competence as part of the ethnography of communication. The main purpose of research based on this view is to document the communicative competence of different speech communities. Thus, this research describes the range of linguistic variability and the social norms of different cultural groups. Such variability and norms can only be ascertained through observation in real contexts, since it is assumed that each communicative event is constructed in interaction (Cook-Gumperz and Gumperz 1982).

Judith Green (1983) extracted six constructs which have guided the research on classroom interaction so far. These are in stark contrast to the constructs guiding the teacher-effectiveness research:

1. Face-to-face interaction is a rule-governed process.
2. Contexts are constructed by participants in interaction, verbally and nonverbally.
3. Meaning is context-specific.
4. Comprehension of conversation involves inferencing.
5. Classrooms are considered communicative environments.
6. The teacher plays multiple roles in the classroom.

Cook-Gumperz and Gumperz (1982) stress the need to also consider the social transmission of knowledge through the curriculum when researchers examine communicative competence in school settings:

> The process of transmission of knowledge, the form that knowledge takes, and access to it, is both socially defined and socially constrained. We cannot assume therefore that the problem of cultural variability in the classroom can be solved by changes in language codes or discourse style or even teaching strategies, IF THESE ARE TAKEN AS SINGLE FACTORS TO BE MANIPULATED OUT OF CONTEXT. The task of exploring the cultural transmission of knowledge as communicative competence requires us to see the face-to-face relationships of teacher to student as embedded interactively within a context of the procedures of classroom practices within schools, which themselves are part of an institutional system of educational policies and ideology. (pp. 19–20)

Erickson (1982a, 1982b) also calls for examining the academic-task structures in classrooms, not just the social-participation structures. He specifies four aspects of the academic-task environment to study:

> a) the logic of the subject matter sequencing;
> b) the information context of various sequential steps;
> c) the "meta-content" cues toward steps and strategies for completing the task; and
> d) the physical materials through which tasks and task components are manifested and with which tasks are accomplished. (1982a, p. 154)

Comparable aspects of the social-participation structures also need to be investigated (Erickson 1982a):

> a) the social gatekeeping of access to people and other information sources during the lesson;
> b) the allocation of communicative rights and obligations among the various interactional partners in the event;
> c) the sequencing and timing of successive functional "slots" in the interaction; [and]
> d) the simultaneous actions of all those engaged in interaction during the lesson. (p. 155)

Barnes (1976) describes these structures as comprising a "hidden curriculum" which interacts with the curriculum of the class. He argues strongly for a student-oriented curriculum.

Ethnographers interested in schooling (Bloome 1981, 1984; Gilmore 1983; Heath 1983; Taylor 1983) indicate that attention should be focused on literacy as a social event, both in and out of school.

The studies in the following sections reflect the trends mentioned above. These studies fall into three major categories: interaction in traditional classrooms, interaction in nontraditional settings, and cultural and home/school differences in interaction.

Interaction in Traditional Classrooms

Teacher-directed instruction in the whole class or in small groups, based on a basal reading program, characterizes traditional classrooms. Ethnographic researchers have examined the structure and interactional patterns during reading events and how these patterns influence students' perceptions of reading. The differences between high- and low-reading groups and the use of nonverbal cues to signal interaction patterns are also described. A few studies relate interaction to outcome measures.

Building on the tradition of Bellack et al. (1966) and Sinclair and Coulthard (1975), Mehan (1979a, 1979b) proposed a discourse model based on his data from nine reading lessons. He found that each school day was divided into events: procedural/social time or circles and lessons (i.e., whole-class instruction, small-group instruction, and work time).

Each lesson was usually comprised of an opening phase, an instructional phase, and a closing phase. Phases consisted of interactional sequences—initiation-response-evaluation—which were often topically related in sets, particularly during the instructional phase. Specific behaviors, topics, and discourse forms (e.g., getting and holding the floor) were appropriate for different events and phases. Mehan comments that to successfully engage in classroom interaction which is mutually constructed but under control of the teacher, students must know *what* is appropriate to say and *when* and *how* to say it.

The pervasiveness of teacher control of classroom talk has been thoroughly documented (Barnes 1976, Bellack et al. 1966, Mehan 1979a, Sinclair and Coulthard 1975, Wells 1981). Comparing interactions at home and in school, Wells and Wells (1984) report,

> In contrast with their parents, these children's teachers dominated conversation, initiating the majority of interactions, predominantly through requests, questions, and requests for display. They were also more than twice as likely to develop their own meanings as they were to extend those contributed by the children, this ratio being almost the exact opposite of that found in the speech of parents. (p. 194)

Mehan (1979b) reports that most of the teacher questions in his study were known-information questions to evaluate student learning, not true information-seeking questions. When teachers did not get the expected response, they simplified and rephrased the questions. French and MacLure (1983) list five types of simplifying strategies to formulate *wh* questions: (1) a more specific question, e.g., "What are they planting?" as opposed to "What are they doing?"; (2) a yes/no question with an inappropriate option; (3) a yes/no question with the correct option; (4) a choice of two options, with one a preferred answer; and (5) a correct statement with a tag question, which only requires confirmation.

French and MacLure (1983) make an important point for American educators and researchers who separate questions from answers (e.g., Bloom's taxonomy) and interactional context (e.g., Bloom's taxonomy and Pearson and Johnson's taxonomy):

> What is important is that there is no single possible answer to a question, and that what counts as an acceptable answer or appropriate answer is determined not by abstract "knowledge," but by on-the-spot assessments by the answerer of what sort of person the questioner is, what sort of information he is likely to be seeking, how explicit he wants the answer to be. (p. 196)

In future research on classroom questions, this work shows that the interactional context must be considered along with the question, the content and form of the available oral and written discourse, and the student responses. The functional aspect of discourse may also add to our understanding of classroom interaction.

Categorizing types of teacher talk, Stubbs (1976) discovered that teachers spent a lot of time talking about language or metacommunicative comments. He inferred eight categories from his field notes: (1) attracting attention, (2) controlling the amount of speech, (3) checking or confirming understanding, (4) summarizing, (5) defining, (6) editing, (7) correcting, and (8) specifying topic. It would be interesting to ascertain whether teachers' modeling of these metacognitive behaviors influences students' acquisition of them.

Since teacher control is quite obvious in traditional classrooms, students often adopt definitions, discourse, and behavioral patterns deemed important by the teacher. For example, Griffin (1977) found that children defined reading as phonics and round-robin oral reading. Comprehension and reading for real purposes were not included in their definition because of the patterns established in their reading groups. Interviews also revealed that these children were more concerned about nonreading factors such as whose turn it was or how seating affected turn-taking during lessons or in comprehending a story.

In some situations students learn to present the form of the lesson without content. For example, Bloome (1981, 1983) discovered that the isolated, individual experiences of reading in junior high school contrasted with the social functions of reading in the peer group and at home. The students were able to use the behavioral patterns and discourse associated with school reading—what Bloome calls "procedural display"—to avoid certain interactions or tasks in class. Findings from Mehan (1979b) and DeStefano, Pepinsky, and Sanders (1982) provide additional data to confirm the concept of procedural display.

Another group of studies describes the interaction patterns which took place in low- and high-reading groups and how they related to students' perceptions of reading. Several researchers (Allington 1980, 1983; Collins and Michaels 1980; Hiebert 1983; McDermott 1978; also see Cazden 1986 for a review and comments on these studies) show that instruction in low-reading groups concentrated on skill activities (usually word recognition) and on reading. Students also did more oral reading. Instruction in high-reading groups focused on comprehension and meaning. Low groups were interrupted, and often turn-taking was less predictable for them. While teachers ignored the errors of a high-group reader, the same errors made by a low-group reader were corrected. Consequently, less able children received not only less "time on task," but also experienced different reading tasks and more disruption. Therefore, these children defined reading as decoding and isolated skills, not as a meaning-making activity. Slower children may not, in fact, benefit from grouping as much as the more able children do. Another disturbing finding was that group membership is rarely adjusted (Hiebert 1983).

Eder (1982) found that high-group members made more bids and were more successful at gaining the floor, but were reprimanded when their comments were not topically relevant. Low-group members were less assertive and needed encouragement. Therefore teachers often built on whatever they said or ignored inappropriate comments, but rarely reprimanded them for not being on target. Consequently high-group members perceived reading lesson discussions as topically relevant, whereas low-group members did not. In addition Collins (1982) discovered that the quality of teacher interaction with low-group students provided less comprehension practice and less average time in the reading group.

Several studies note that students and teachers use nonverbal cues as a critical part of signaling participation and meaning in reading groups (see Bremme and Erickson 1977 and Shultz and Florio 1979 for nonreading situations). For example, McDermott and Gospodinoff (1979) report that one student, Angelo, intentionally violated the nonverbal rules of his teacher in order to get the teacher to discipline another student. McDermott's well-known study of another student, Rosa, meticulously shows how nonverbal cues interact with verbal cues to negate them (McDermott 1978). Transitions from one activity to another are often signaled both verbally and nonverbally, and if they are changed, confusion results (Bremme and Erickson 1977).

A few researchers correlate certain interactional patterns with reading measures. For example, the students of teachers who integrated discussion during the story reading scored higher on retellings than those of teachers who waited until the end of the story (Green 1977). Mosenthal and Na (1980a, 1980b) learned that the registers of student response in class (i.e., imitative, contingent, or noncontingent to teacher initiatives) were reflected in their recall strategies.

Interaction in Nontraditional Classrooms

"Whole-language" or language-across-the-curriculum programs are commonly used in nontraditional classrooms. In this type of approach planning, writing, editing, and revising in peer conferences are used in writing activities with real purposes and audiences in mind. Reading activities include daily reading of trade books, magazines, newspapers, and child-written books. Facilitating student selection of topics for writing and books for reading, teachers monitor student activities and hold conferences and small-group instruction when needed. They prepare a rich literate environment which promotes language and learning. No two classrooms are exactly alike (see Graves 1983 and Florio and Clark 1982 for examples).

Because research on this type of classroom is in its infancy, the focus has been on the writing development of children (Calkins 1983; Dyson 1984a, 1984b; Edelsky 1981, 1983; Graves 1983), the different functions of writing (Dyson 1984a, Edelsky 1983, Florio and Clark 1982, Greene 1985, Staton et al. 1982), and the teacher as collaborator in research (Clark and Florio 1982; Edelsky, Draper, and Smith 1983; Florio and Clark 1982; Perl 1983).

Only recently have researchers begun to explore classroom activities and interactions in whole-language classrooms. The descriptions of these classrooms and the teachers' roles differ significantly from those emanating from the research on teacher effectiveness and management. The major differences are (1) the delegation of responsibility for learning to the students, with clear expectations; (2) curriculum stemming from students' interests; and (3) the use of teacher-directed instruction only when needed. More emphasis is also placed on learning through peer interaction.

For example, Platt (1984) describes a first/second grade which stressed literacy integrated across subjects, purposeful learning, a sense of community, student decision making, and functional communication to different audiences in different modes.

Looking at three multi-age elementary classrooms in which children's literature was used as a teaching tool, Hickman (1981) found seven "response events" which promoted reading, writing, discussion, and the enjoyment of literature: (1) selecting quality books, (2) assuring and promoting access to these books, (3) reading aloud and introducing literature every day, (4) discussing books using appropriate terminology, (5) assuring time for extension activities, (6) allowing for sharing and displaying of work, and (7) planning cumulative experiences to consider literature in a variety of ways over time.

Graves and his colleagues (Graves 1983, Graves and Hansen 1984, Calkins 1983) richly portray students' and teachers' experiences with literacy development. Underlying this model of literacy instruction are four assumptions: (1) the goal of the curriculum is individual creation of meaning (i.e., learning), communicated in different ways; (2) the content of the curriculum is based on children's interests and what they know; (3) language learning is integrated in terms of reading, writing, and discussion across subject areas; and (4) language is a functional tool to accomplish real purposes.

The support system in Graves's studies included many different types of written materials, writing and art paraphernalia, real audiences (in and out of school), and teachers who functioned in multiple roles—as promoter, supporter, questioner, advocate, recorder, and model. Flexibly shifting roles, teachers helped students stretch, learn with support, and eventually function independently.

The initial studies in this area provide a rich description of *what* happens. However, it is difficult to uncover exactly *how* the context is constructed (Erickson and Shultz 1981): how and when teacher goals, values, social rules and cues—whether implicit or explicit, verbal or nonverbal—are related to selections of materials and activities, classroom social structures, and students' roles and learning.

A few studies have attempted to document this. For example, how a teacher organized and orchestrated a whole-language program in a low-

SES urban sixth grade was the motivating question for Edelsky and her colleagues (1983). In contrast to the results of the teacher-effectiveness research, they found that the teacher (1) gave minimal directions, only when needed; (2) did not break down the lesson into small steps; (3) often suggested complex and confusing tasks for students to work on; and (4) allowed longer transitions to provide time for relationships to strengthen among students and between students and herself. She could articulate her instructional model, which was based on her own model of language and literacy learning.

Other studies focused on peer interaction during seatwork and peer tutoring, which is often prevalent in these types of classrooms. Researchers found that children used a wide variety of social strategies. Students used much richer language in all student situations than in exchanges with the teacher (Barnes 1976; Cooper, Marquis, and Ayers-Lopez 1982). For example, students understood the pragmatic constraints of requests and employed strategies such as directness, sincerity, specific address, persistence, and politeness to successfully make requests (Wilkinson and Calculator 1982). During seatwork, students also seemed to know whom to approach for assistance as well as when it was appropriate to seek help from a peer or the teacher. Developmental patterns of communicative competence were also evident (Cooper, Marquis, and Ayers-Lopez 1982).

Cazden (1980) lists three models of peer interaction in tutoring situations: (1) peer tutoring in which one student is clearly more knowledgeable; (2) equal-status collaboration; and (3) coteaching, in which resource and learner roles shift back and forth. Peer-tutoring research (Carrasco, Vera, and Cazden 1981; Steinberg and Cazden 1979) shows that child tutors use a variety of communicative strategies to accomplish their tasks, some better than others. The tutoring role permits children to communicate in ways quite different from typical, whole-class exchanges. Teachers also see students' abilities in a different light.

Since some children are better able to maintain interaction (Barnes 1976) or are more knowledgeable than others (Cooper, Marquis, and Ayers-Lopez 1982), the question of access to fluent interaction and/or the "teacher role" has been raised. Cultural differences may also have an effect on communication. Future research should address how these differences affect peer interaction and learning.

Home/School and Cultural-Interaction Differences

Differences between language development at home and at school are treated next, followed by differences in discourse structures for various cultures.

Home/School Differences

Research on child language development (see Lindfors 1980 for an excellent summary) shows that children are active, persistent seekers of meaning. In their quest for meaning, children learn language, learn through language, and learn about language (Halliday 1980). They also absorb social conventions surrounding language use in different social settings (Halliday 1980, King 1985).

Gordon Wells and his colleagues (Wells 1981, Wells and Wells 1984) have contrasted language development at home and in school in one of the few longitudinal studies from preschool into the elementary school years. They picture the interaction between parents and children as a collaboration in which participants negotiate meaning and intention. Based on their children's needs, the parents in Wells' study simplified statements, sustained and extended children's interests, provided resources, listened to children, and fielded questions. The children were active, loquacious partners in this context. Bruner (1978; also Ninio and Bruner 1978) proposes that parents build a "scaffold" for learning, upping the ante as the child shows readiness for increased difficulty.

Several studies (Harste, Woodward, and Burke 1984; Snow 1983) have found that literacy learning at home parallels oral-language learning. For example, parents used semantic contingency, scaffolding, accountability procedures, and routines to help children understand what a book is, the communicative and perceptual conventions of print, and the decontextualized nature of literate discourse. Reading-like behavior or reenactment and appreciation of stories emerged through repeated readings of favorite books in the company of a trusted adult (Holdaway 1979, Sulzby 1983, Doake 1985). Awareness of environmental print also developed children's learning about print, naturally mediated by others (Goodman and Goodman 1979; Harste, Burke, and Woodward 1982; Mason 1984; Haussler 1985).

Understandings of the functions and conventions of writing began to develop concurrently as children were given the opportunity to put crayon or pencil to paper to represent messages (Bissex 1980; Ferreiro 1980; Ferreiro and Teberosky 1982; Harste, Woodward, and Burke 1984). With the support of others, children moved back and forth between oral and written modes, between writing and reading, as literacy emerged at home.

This picture of children's language learning at home contrasts greatly with what happens at school. Wells and Wells (1984) report that in school children initiated fewer interactions and questions and took many fewer conversational turns. Semantically their utterances were constrained and syntactically they were simple—most often fragments. Rarely were children's interests extended by the teacher, who dominated and controlled interactions. Most of the day children were required to be silent.

There are major differences between the quantity and quality of oral interaction and the model of language teaching/learning at home and at school. Mason (1984) suggests that assumptions by school personnel about reading instruction, learning, and assessment may create mismatches between what young children already know about written language and what they encounter in beginning reading and writing programs.

For example, it is often assumed that children cannot read at all, yet they enjoy reenacting stories with their parents and know some sound-symbol correspondences (evident in their invented spellings). Existing reading programs need to be reviewed to see to what extent they are consistent with children's understandings about literacy. Another question is how much flexibility is provided for children who come to school with different literacy experiences as background.

Most beginning reading programs are structured so that students have limited opportunities to write. They are told when and what to write, since it is often assumed that students must learn to read before learning to write. These practices are quite unlike the self-regulated writing done at home and are not consistent with the research indicating that many children can "write" before coming to school.

Future research should develop ways to assess young children's knowledge of oral and written language. In addition, existing models of language learning used in schools and publishing must be reexamined in light of the new research on oral and written language development. We need to build on what children know. We also need to know if cultural or socioeconomic differences affect children's perceptions of literacy and literacy learning.

Cultural-Interaction Differences

Some research has been conducted on the different discourse and participation structures of minority groups. Boggs (1972, 1985) learned that native Hawaiian adults used direct questions primarily when admonishing children. Unlike white middle-class Americans they rarely asked questions for information. When telling a story Hawaiians cooperatively took turns to construct the story with voices overlapping, an activity called "talk story" (Boggs 1985). In addition, Hawaiians delegated household chores to the oldest child, who, in turn, made sure the work was accomplished. If children were to learn a new skill, apprenticeship and close observation were used, not explanation or discussion of the matter.

Two other cultural groups have similar participation structures for tasks and narratives. Philips (1982, 1985) discovered that Warm Springs Indians also taught through apprenticeship. Cooperation, not competition, was the norm among peers. This was also true for Athabaskan Indians, who performed collaborative narratives in groups. Individuals "resonated" in their own interpretations of the narrative (Scollon and Scollon 1981, Van Ness 1981). These cultures used participant structures and discourse forms which are quite different from typical American classroom practices.

Heath (1983) also documents uses of language by a minority group in the Piedmont community of "Trackton" which differed from the forms and functions of language used in school. In Trackton, reading was a social activity during which adults negotiated the meaning of, for example, a newspaper article or a tax form. The only example, of reading as a solitary activity was reading for church or school. Children had a good functional sense of environmental print for distinguishing, for example, products in stores.

In Trackton, stories were oral events; audiences participated. Common characteristics included no routine opening, mutual construction of context, evaluation of people and their actions, dialogues, an interplay between verbal and nonverbal cues, and no marked endings. This is in marked contrast to the prototypical story expected in school (Michaels 1981). Trackton adult questioning of children included analogies and connections—not school-related skills such as labeling, description of features, or isolated retelling of events in sequence.

Michaels' work on sharing time (1981; also Michaels and Cazden 1986, Michaels and Collins 1984; Michaels and Foster 1985) shows that some black children bring different discourse structures to school. White children generally select a limited topic and organize the discourse temporally and spatially; black children usually link personal experiences in an associative style.

Even excellent teachers have difficulty questioning, commenting on, and reacting to discourse styles different from their own. Quite unintentional, these problems may have limited black children's access to the kinds of focusing, structuring, and elaborating experiences which might have helped them produce language closer to the teachers' implicit ideas of literate discourse (Michaels and Cazden 1986).

Asking why some minority students were placed in advanced literacy classes and not others, Gilmore (1983) found that "attitude" was more important than literacy ability as a criterion. Also, informal literacy activities of minority children did not "count" as literacy in the formal school system.

In two of the above settings, Trackton and Hawaii, instructional programs to teach reading were developed using the cultural research information as a base. In Hawaii talk story structure and child-run work groups during reading were added to the basal curriculum. A focus on comprehension was also added based on current research (Au 1980, Au and Jordan 1981, Calfee et al. 1981). Reading scores increased (Tharp 1982). In Trackton a new school program was designed with the assistance of teachers and parents to help children learn about the discourse structures of school. Their progress in school improved. Teachers also gained insight into language diversity (Heath 1983).

The controversial, politically loaded question concerning intervention is: Who or what must change—the curriculum, the teacher, or the children from minority cultures?

Future Research

All fields suffer from a certain kind of myopia, and ours is no exception. The danger is that we focus on preserving our own research paradigms and institutions (e.g., higher education, public schools, or publishing) rather than constructively solving problems together.

In this final discussion I present four broad suggestions for future research and development in the areas of language, learning, research methodology, and curriculum.

The first suggestion involves language. A quiet revolution occurred when Chomsky wrote *Aspects of a Theory of Syntax,* which changed the way linguists and eventually educators viewed language form and meaning. Halliday, Hymes, and Gumperz started another revolution, the effects of which are just beginning to influence language arts research.

A functional model of oral language and, more recently, written language developed. Form follows function in social contexts. As different cultural groups use language in context, they learn language, learn through language, and learn about language (Halliday 1980). The experiential differences in context lead to differential development of language functions, forms, and meanings (Heath 1982).

In many of the studies reviewed in this paper, there is an underlying de facto model of language, one based on form alone. For example, instruction using published reading materials has been based on a sequence designated by the different forms of language, such as sound-symbol correspondences, words, sentences, and, now, the structure of narrative and exposition. Little attention has been paid to the functions of oral language use, writing, or reading, particularly for "real-world" purposes

(Mikulecky 1982, Kirsch and Guthrie 1984). Implicitly, certain functions are valued more than others in the school curriculum.

This lack of attention to function has occurred in spite of the fact that research has shown that purpose is clearly related to different types of materials and strategy selection in reading. Even more important, it is also related to criterion tasks which are represented by the outcome measures of the reading in research (Brown 1982). Little creativity in developing measures of reading for different purposes has been evident. Function has also been ignored in most of the frameworks in observational research (Heap 1982).

The first suggestion for future research, then, is to adopt a communicative-competence model of language to drive decisions about research, instruction, and curriculum development. Perhaps with this as a base, we would not isolate reading, writing, and discussion from "real-world" language functions and a search for meaning.

The second suggestion concerns the definition of instruction. In the fifties, behaviorism dominated. Consequently researchers placed the accent on the role of the teacher, who controlled and organized instruction. The research on teacher effectiveness and management still reflects this orientation.

When Chomsky critiqued Skinner in 1957, a change began to occur in learning theory. Not only was a different theory of language explicated, but a cognitive theory of learning was implied. As attention shifted to the learner as actively constructing meaning, the view of the learning became more social and interactive—a linguistic exchange between teacher and student. We returned to our roots in blending Vygotsky and Piaget to find a new definition of instruction as interaction and as construction on the part of the learner.

On one hand, teaching and learning researchers have had a difficult time expanding their notion of instruction to include social interaction through language. Just because a teacher performs certain tasks or says certain things does not mean that these cause learning to occur. On the other hand, researchers viewing teaching and learning as a sociolinguistic process have reacted against the behaviorism implied in the model of direct instruction and have failed to relate sociolinguistic and cultural phenomena to the outcomes of learning.

The second suggestion, then, is that future researchers focus on the students, on what is to be learned, and on the kinds of interactions in varied contexts that facilitate learning, not on one type of instruction versus another. Sometimes, lecturing may be useful. Elicitation teaching, a form of teacher-directed instruction, allows teachers to monitor students' progress. Other options include open discussion in small all-student groups, on-the-job apprenticeship, interacting with materials, and engaging in processes such as reading or writing with the students initiating bids for assistance.

We need to know which students, which goals, which tasks, which materials, and which teachers under which conditions fit most harmoniously to promote autonomous functioning and learning by students. We also need to know how the teaching/learning interactions are constructed to accomplish this, particularly in classrooms where there are many minority students who are having the most difficulty learning literacy skills.

Now for the third suggestion: In preparing for this paper, I read articles from seven distinct research "camps." What became apparent was the relative isolation of each camp. Each is defined by a limited set of topics, specific terminology, and a primary paradigm. There is only minimal overlap in references between camps. In some ways this is to be expected, since as problem solvers, researchers must limit their problem space to make it manageable. The danger lies in myopic overgeneralization and the inability to see the relevance of other research.

I think that the solution is to create multidisciplinary teams, not unlike the research group in the Kamehameha Project (Au 1980, Boggs 1985). If research is to be relevant to the real world, the teams must involve parents, teachers, administrators, and even publishers (Clark and Florio 1982, Florio and Walsh 1981, Wallat et al. 1981), as well as researchers from different disciplines. Team members, coming from different training and experiences, will approach problems differently. In an atmosphere of cooperation and trust, the resulting dynamic tension will foster multiple interpretations of data and generate further research questions.

Evertson and Green (1986) suggest that research methods can be viewed on a continuum, with each one more relevant for certain types of research questions than others. However, by using more than one method of data collection researchers can look for convergences among the data, generate new hypotheses, and gain greater insight.

For example, researchers on teacher effectiveness and management and on comprehension and classroom realities have just begun to incorporate more open-ended observational techniques from ethnography. Peterson et al. (1984) have combined process/product and sociolinguistic paradigms successfully. The ethnographic work of McDermott (1978) and Cook-Gumperz, Gumperz, and Simons (1981) on low- and high-reading group behavior was in turn confirmed by Allington (1983) in many classrooms using a more traditional observational schedule.

In another study Green, Harker, and Golden (in press) performed three different analyses on the same data: a sociolinguistic analysis, a propositional analysis on theme and content, and a response/literary analysis (i.e., relating the original text to student response and teacher-mediated response). Each analysis yielded part of the instructional picture.

Perhaps working collaboratively with a multidisciplinary team using multiple paradigms and multiple measures and methods of analysis would help us focus on truly solving the problem of fostering the development of literacy, particularly among minority children.

The fourth and final suggestion is a much more philosophical one, which we must answer as members of a society, not just as researchers. The question rings out from this research: What do we want children to learn?

The research points to the importance of prior knowledge for reading, writing, and future learning, yet there seems to be no systematic thinking about *what* content (function, form, and content in context) to teach and *how* to provide access to *all* students. With the knowledge explosion promoted by technology, this concern is even more important so that we do not end up with a bimodal society of an educated elite and uneducated masses (Burke 1978). Therefore, my closing suggestion is that we try to define what we want students to learn, both socially and academically, in order to develop into literate, well-informed citizens who can function actively as members of a democratic society in the twenty-first century.

References

Allington, R. L. (1980). Teacher interruption behaviors during primary-grade oral reading. *Journal of Educational Psychology* 72: 371–77.

——— (1983). The reading instruction provided readers of differing reading abilities. *The Elementary School Journal* 83: 548–59.

——— (1984). Content coverage and contextual reading in reading groups. *Journal of Reading Behavior* 16: 85–96.

Anderson, L. (1984). The environment of instruction: The function of seatwork in effective commercially developed curriculum. In *Comprehension instruction: Perspectives and suggestions*, G. G. Duffy, L. R. Roehler, and J. Mason, eds. New York: Longman.

Anderson, L., C. Evertson, and J. Brophy (1979). An experimental study of effective teaching in first-grade reading groups. *The Elementary School Journal* 79: 193–223.

Au, K. H. (1980). Participation structures in a reading lesson with Hawaiian children: Analysis of a culturally appropriate instructional event. *Anthropology and Education Quarterly* 11: 91–115.

Au, K. H., and C. Jordan (1981). Teaching reading to Hawaiian children: Finding a culturally appropriate solution. In *Culture and the bilingual classroom,* edited by H. T. Trueba, K. P. Guthrie, and K. H. Au. Rowley, Mass.: Newbury House.

Baker, L., and A. Brown (1984). Metacognitive skills and reading. In *Handbook of reading research,* edited by P. D. Pearson, 353–94. New York: Longman.

Barnes, D. (1976). *From communication to curriculum.* Harmondsworth, England: Penguin Education Books.

Barnett, J. E. (1984). Facilitating retention through instruction about text structure. *Journal of Reading Behavior* 26, no. 1: 1–14.

Barr, R. (1973–74). Instructional pace differences and their effect on reading acquisition. *Reading Research Quarterly* 9: 526–54.

——— (1975). How children are taught to read: Grouping and pacing. *School Review* 83: 479–98.

——— (1980). *School, class, group and pace effects on learning.* Paper presented at the annual meeting of the American Educational Research Association.

——— (1987). Classroom interaction and curricular content. In *Literacy and schooling,* edited by D. Bloome. Norwood, N.J.: Ablex.

Barr, R., and R. Dreeben (1983). *How schools work.* Chicago: University of Chicago Press.

Bartlett, B. (1978). Top-level structure as an organizational strategy for recall of classroom text. *Dissertation Abstracts International* 39: 6641–A.

Bawden, R., S. Buike, and G. G. Duffy (1979). *Teacher conceptions of reading and their influence on instruction.* Research series no. 47. East Lansing, Mich.: Institute for Research on Teaching, Michigan State University.

Beck, I., and M. G. McKeown (1983). Learning words well—A program to enhance vocabulary and comprehension. *Reading Teacher* 36: 622–25.

Beck, I., R. C. Omanson, and M. G. McKeown (1982). An instructional redesign of reading lessons: Effects on comprehension. *Reading Research Quarterly* 17: 462–81.

Beck, I., C. Perfetti, and M. G. McKeown (1982). Effects of long-term vocabulary instruction on lexical access and reading comprehension. *Journal of Educational Psychology* 74: 506–21.

Bellack, A., H. Kliebard, R. Hyman, and F. Smith (1966). *The language of the classroom.* New York: Teachers College Press.

Bissex, G. (1980). *Gyns at wrk: A child learns to read and write.* Cambridge, Mass.: Harvard University Press.

Bloome, D. (1981). An ethnographic approach to the study of reading activities among black junior high school students: A sociolinguistic ethnography. *Dissertation Abstracts International* 42: 2993–A.

——— (1983). Classroom reading instruction: A socio-communicative analysis of time on task. In *Searches for meaning in reading/language processing and instruction,* 32nd yearbook, edited by J. A. Niles and L. A. Harris. Rochester, N.Y.: National Reading Conference.

——— (1984). Reading: A social process. In *Advances in reading/language research,* Vol. 2, edited by B. Hutson. Greenwich, Conn.: JAI Press.

Boggs, S. T. (1972). The meaning of questions and narratives to Hawaiian children. In *Functions of language in the classroom,* edited by C. B. Cazden, V. John, and D. Hymes. New York: Teachers College Press.

———— (1985). *Speaking, relating and learning: A study of Hawaiian children at home and at school.* Norwood, N.J.: Ablex.

Borko, H. (1982). Teachers' decision policies about grouping students for reading instruction. In *New inquiries in reading research and instruction,* 31st yearbook, edited by J. A. Niles and L. A. Harris. Rochester, N.Y.: National Reading Conference.

Borko, H., R. Shavelson, and P. Stern (1981). Teachers' decisions in the planning of reading instruction. *Reading Research Quarterly* 16: 449–66.

Bremme, D. W., and F. Erickson (1977). Relationships among verbal and nonverbal classroom behaviors. *Theory into Practice* 16: 153–61.

Brophy, J. (1981). Teacher praise: A functional analysis. *Review of Educational Research* 51: 5–32.

———— (1984). The teacher as thinker: Implementing instruction. In *Comprehension instruction: Perspectives and suggestions,* edited by G. Duffy, L. Roehler, and J. Mason. New York: Longman.

Brophy, J., and C. Evertson (1974). *Process-product correlations in the Texas Teacher Effectiveness Study: Final report.* Research report no. 74-4. Austin, Tex.: Research and Development Center for Teacher Education, University of Texas at Austin. ED 099 345.

———— (1976). *Learning from teaching: A developmental perspective.* Boston: Allyn and Bacon.

Brophy, J., and T. L. Good (1986). Teacher behavior and student achievement. In *Handbook of research on teaching,* 3d ed., edited by M. C. Wittrock, 328–75. New York: Macmillan.

Brown, A. L. (1982). Learning how to learn from reading. In *Reader meets author bridging the gap,* edited by J. A. Langer and M. T. Smith-Burke. Newark, Del.: International Reading Association.

Brown, A. L., J. D. Bransford, R. A. Ferrara, and J. C. Campione (1983). Learning, remembering, and understanding. In *Handbook of child psychology,* Vol. 3, 4th ed., edited by J. H. Flavell and E. M. Markman. New York: John Wiley & Sons.

Bruner, J. S. (1978). The role of dialogue in language acquisition. In *The child's conception of language,* edited by A. Sinclair, R. J. Jarvella, and W. J. M. Levelt, 241–56. New York: Springer-Verlag.

Burke, J. (1978). *Connections.* New York: Little, Brown.

Calfee, R. C., C. B. Cazden, R. P. Duran, M. P. Griffin, M. Martus, and H. D. Willis (1981). *Designing reading instruction for cultural minorities: The case of the Kamehameha early education program.* Report funded by the Ford Foundation and the Bernice P. Bishop Estate.

California State Department of Education (1977). *California school effectiveness study: The first year, 1974–75.* Sacramento: California State Department of Education.

Calkins, L. (1983). *Lessons from a child: On the teaching and learning of writing.* Exeter, N.H.: Heinemann.

Carrasco, R. C., A. Vera, and C. B. Cazden (1981). Aspects of a bilingual student's communicative competence: A case study. In *Latino language and communicative behavior,* edited by R. Duran. Norwood, N.J.: Ablex.

256 *Classroom Practice, Classroom Interaction, and Instructional Materials*

Cazden, C. B. (1980). Peer dialogues across the curriculum. In *Oral and written language development research: Impact on the schools,* edited by Y. M. Goodman, M. M. Haussler, and D. S. Strickland. Urbana, Ill.: National Council of Teachers of English. ED 214 184.

———— (1986). Classroom discourse. In *Handbook of research on teaching,* 3d ed., edited by M. C. Wittrock. New York: Macmillan.

Cazden, C. B., S. Michaels, and P. Tabors (1985). Spontaneous repairs in Sharing Time narratives: The intersection of metalinguistic awareness, speech event, and narrative style. In *The acquisition of writing: Response and revision,* edited by S. W. Freedman. Norwood, N.J.: Ablex.

Clark, C. (1984). Teacher planning and reading comprehension. In *Comprehension instruction: Perspectives and suggestions,* edited by G. G. Duffy, L. R. Roehler, and J. Mason, 58–70. New York: Longman.

Clark, C., and J. L. Elmore (1979). *Teacher planning in the first weeks of school.* Research series no. 55. East Lansing, Mich.: Institute for Research on Teaching, Michigan State University.

Clark, C., and S. Floria (with J. Elmore, S. Martin, J. Maxwell, and W. Metheny) (1982). *Understanding writing in schools: A descriptive study of writing and its instruction in two classrooms.* Research series no. 104. East Lansing, Mich.: Institute for Research on Teaching, Michigan State University.

Clark, C. M., and R. J. Yinger (1977). Research on teacher thinking. *Curriculum Inquiry* 7: 279–304.

———— (1978). *Research on teacher thinking.* Research series no. 12. East Lansing, Mich.: Institute for Research on Teaching, Michigan State University.

Clay, M. (1972). *Reading: The patterning of complex behaviour.* London: Heinemann.

Collins, J. (1982). Discourse style, classroom interaction and differential treatment. *Journal of reading behavior* 14: 429–37.

Collins, J., and S. Michaels (1980). The importance of conversational discourse strategies for the acquisition of literacy. In *Proceedings of the Sixth Annual Symposium of the Berkeley Linguistics Society,* edited by C. Chiarello et al. Berkeley, Calif.: Berkeley Linguistics Society.

Commission on Reading (1985). *Becoming a nation of readers: The report of the Commission on Reading.* Washington, D.C.: Center for the Study of Reading, National Academy of Education, National Institute of Education.

Cook-Gumperz, J., and J. Gumperz (1982). Communicative competence in educational perspective. In *Communicating in the classroom,* edited by L. C. Wilkinson. New York: Academic Press.

Cook-Gumperz, J., J. Gumperz, and H. Simons (1981). *School-home ethnography project. Final report.* NIE-G-78-0082.

Cooper, C. R., A. Marquis, and S. Ayers-Lopez (1982). Peer learning in the classroom: Tracing developmental patterns and consequences of children's spontaneous interactions. In *Communicating in the classroom,* edited by L. C. Wilkinson. New York: Academic Press.

DeFord, D. (1981). Literacy: Reading, writing, and other essentials. *Language Arts* 58: 652–58.

———— (1985). Validating the construct of theoretical orientation in reading instruction. *Reading Research Quarterly* 20, no. 3: 351–67.

DeStefano, J., H. Pepinsky, and T. Sanders (1982). Discourse rules for literacy learning in a classroom. In *Communication in the classroom,* edited by L. C. Wilkinson. New York: Academic Press.

Doake, D. (1985). Reading-like behavior: Its role in learning to read. In *Observing the language learner,* edited by A. Jaggar and M. T. Smith-Burke, 82–98. Newark, Del.: International Reading Association and National Council of Teachers of English.

Doyle, W. (1983). Academic work. *Review of Educational Research* 53: 159–99.

——— (1985). Classroom organization and management. In *Handbook of research on teaching,* 3d ed., edited by M. C. Wittrock. New York: Macmillan.

Duffy, G. G., and L. D. McIntyre (1982). A naturalistic study of instructional assistance in primary-grade reading. *The Elementary School Journal* 83: 14–23.

Duffy, G. G., and W. Metheny (1979). The development of an instrument to measure teacher beliefs about reading. In *Reading research: Studies and applications,* 28th Yearbook, edited by M. L. Kamil and A. J. Moe. Clemson, S.C.: National Reading Conference.

Duncan, M. J., and B. J. Biddle (1974). *The study of teaching.* New York: Holt, Rinehart & Winston.

Durkin, D. (1979). What classroom observations reveal about reading comprehension instruction. *Reading Research Quarterly* 14: 481–533.

——— (1981). Reading comprehension instruction in five basal reader series. *Reading Research Quarterly* 16: 515–44.

——— (1983). *Is there a match between what elementary teachers do and what basal reader manuals recommend?* Reading education report no. 44, Champaign, Ill.: Center for the Study of Reading, University of Illinois at Urbana-Champaign. ED 235 470.

Dyson, A. H. (1984a). Learning to write/Learning to do school: Emergent writers' interpretations of school literacy tasks. *Research in the Teaching of English* 18: 233–64.

——— (1984b). Emerging alphabetic literacy in school contexts: Toward defining the gap between school curriculum and child mind. *Written communication* 1: 5–55.

Edelsky, C. (1981). From "Jimosalcsco" to "7 naranges se calleron y el arbol-est triste en largrymas": Writing development in a bilingual program. In *The writing needs of linguistically different students,* edited by B. Cronnell. Los Alamitos, Calif.: Southwest Regional Laboratory for Educational Research and Development. ED 210 932.

——— (1983). Segmentation and punctuation: Developmental data from young writers in a bilingual program. *Research in the Teaching of English* 17: 135–56.

Edelsky, C., K. Draper, and K. Smith (1983). Hookin' 'em in at the start of school in a "Whole Language" classroom. *Anthropology and Education Quarterly* 14, no. 4: 257–81.

Eder, D. (1982). Differences in communicative styles across ability groups. In *Communicating in the classroom,* edited by L. C. Wilkinson. New York: Academic Press.

Elley, W. B., I. H. Barham, H. Lamb, and M. Wyllie (1979). *The role of grammar in a secondary school curriculum.* Educational research series no. 60. Wellington, New Zealand: New Zealand Council for Educational Research.

Erickson, F. (1982a). Classroom discourse as improvisation: Relationships between academic task structure and social participation structures in lessons. In *Communicating in the classroom,* edited by L. C. Wilkinson. New York: Academic Press.

—— (1982b). Taught cognitive learning in its immediate environments: A neglected topic in the anthropology of education. *Anthropology and Education Quarterly* 13: 149–80.

Erickson, F., and J. Shultz (1981). When is a context? Some issues and methods in the analysis of social competence. In *Ethnography and language in educational settings,* edited by J. Green and C. Wallat, 147–60. Norwood, N.J.: Ablex.

Evertson, C., L. Anderson, and J. Brophy (1978). *Texas junior high school study: Final report of process-outcome relationships.* Report no. 4061. Austin, Tex.: Research and Development Center for Teacher Education, University of Texas.

Evertson, C., and J. L. Green (1986). Observation as inquiry and method. In *Handbook of research on teaching,* 3d ed., edited by M. C. Wittrock. New York: Macmillan.

Ferreiro, E. (1980). The relationship between oral and written language: The children's viewpoints. In *Oral and written language development research: Impact on the schools,* edited by Y. M. Goodman, M. M. Haussler, and D. S. Strickland. Urbana, Ill.: National Council of Teachers of English.

Ferreiro, E., and A. Teberosky (1982). *Literacy before schooling.* Exeter, N.H.: Heinemann.

Fisher, C. F., R. N. Marliave, L. Cahen, M. Dishaw, J. Moore, and D. Berliner (1978). *Teaching behaviors, academic learning time and student achievement: Final report of phase III-B, beginning teacher evaluation study.* San Francisco: Far West Laboratory for Educational Research.

Fitzgerald, J., and D. L. Speigel (1983). Enhancing children's reading comprehension through instruction in narrative structure. *Journal of Reading Behavior* 15, no. 2: 1–17.

Florio, S. (1979). The problem of dead letters: Social perspectives on the teaching of writing. *The Elementary School Journal* 80: 1–7.

Florio, S., and C. M. Clark (1982). The functions of writing in an elementary classroom. *Research in the Teaching of English* 16: 115–30.

Florio, S., and M. Walsh (1981). The teacher as colleague in educational research. In *Culture and the bilingual classroom,* edited by H. T. Trueba, G. P. Guthrie, and K. H. Au. Rowley, Mass.: Newbury House.

Florio-Ruane, S., and J. Dohanich (1984). Research currents: Communicating findings by teacher/researcher deliberation. *Language Arts* 61: 724–30.

French, P., and M. MacLure (1983). Teachers' questions, pupils' answers: An investigation of questions and answers in the infant classroom. In *Readings on language, schools and classrooms,* edited by M. Stubbs and H. Hillier. New York: Methuen.

Gambrell, L. B. (1984). How much time do children spend reading during teacher directed reading instruction? In *Changing perspectives on research in reading/ language processing and instruction,* edited by J. A. Niles and L. A. Harris. Rochester, N.Y.: National Reading Conference.

Gilmore, P. S. (1983). Spelling "Mississippi": Recontextualizing a literacy-related speech event. *Anthropology and Education* 14, no. 4: 235–56.

———— (1984). *Acquisition of access: The other side of literacy.* Paper presented at the annual meeting of the National Reading Conference.

Good, T. (1979). Teacher effectiveness in the elementary school. *Journal of Teacher Education* 30, no. 2: 52–64.

Good, T., and T. M. Beckerman (1978). Time on task: A naturalistic study in sixth-grade classrooms. *The Elementary School Journal* 78: 192–201.

Goodman, K. S. (1970). Reading: A psycholinguistic guessing game. In *Theoretical models and processes of reading,* edited by H. Singer and R. Ruddell, 497–508. Newark, Del.: International Reading Association.

Goodman, K. S., and Y. M. Goodman (1979). Learning to read is natural. In *Theory and practice of early reading,* Vol. 1, edited by L. B. Resnick and P. A. Weaver, 137–54. Hillsdale, N.J.: Erlbaum.

Graves, D. (1983). *Writing: Teachers and children at work.* Exeter, N.H.: Heinemann.

———— (1978). *Balance the basics: Let them write.* New York: Ford Foundation.

Graves, D., and J. Hansen (1984). The author's chair. In *Composing and comprehending,* edited by J. M. Jensen, 69–76. Urbana, Ill.: ERIC Clearinghouse on Reading and Communication Skills and NCRE. ED 243 139.

Green, J. (1977). Pedagogical style differences as related to comprehension performance: Grades one through three. *Dissertation Abstracts International* 39: 833-A.

———— (1983). Research on teaching as a linguistic process: A state of the art. In *Review of research in education,* Vol. 10, edited by E. W. Gordon. Washington, D.C.: American Educational Research Association.

Green, J., J. Harker, and J. Golden (In press). Lesson construction: Differing views. In *Understanding education: Qualitative studies of the occupation and organization,* edited by G. Noblit and W. Pink. Norwood, N.J.: Albex.

Greene, J. E. (1985). Children's writing in an elementary school postal system. In *Advances in writing research, Vol. 1: Children's early writing development,* edited by M. Farr. Norwood, N.J.: Ablex.

Griffin, P. (1977). How and when does reading occur in the classroom? *Theory into Practice* 16: 376–83.

Halliday, M. A. K. (1980). Three aspects of children's language development: Learning language, learning through language, learning about language. In *Oral and written language development research: Impact on the schools,* edited by Y. M. Goodman, M. M. Haussler, and D. S. Strickland. Urbana, Ill.: National Council of Teachers of English.

Hansen, J. (1981). The effects of inference training and practice on young children's reading comprehension. *Reading Research Quarterly* 16: 391–417.

———— (1983). Authors respond to authors. *Language Arts* 60: 970–76.

Hansen, J., and P. D. Pearson (1983). An instructional study: Improving the inferential comprehension of good and poor fourth-grade readers. *Journal of Educational Psychology* 75: 821–29.

Harste, J. C., and C. L. Burke (1977). A new hypothesis for reading teacher research: Both the teaching and learning of reading are theoretically based. In

Reading: Theory, research and practice, 26th Yearbook, edited by P. D. Pearson. Clemson, S.C.: National Reading Conference.

Harste, J. C., C. L. Burke, and V. A. Woodward (1982). Children's language and world: Initial encounters with print. In *Reader meets author bridging the gap,* edited by J. A. Langer and M. T. Smith-Burke. Newark, Del.: International Reading Association.

Harste, J. C., V. A. Woodward, and C.L. Burke (1984). *Language stories and literacy lessons.* Portsmouth, N.H.: Heinemann.

Haussler, M. M. (1985). A young child's developing concepts of print. In *Observing the language learner,* edited by A. Jaggar and M. T. Smith-Burke, 73–81. Newark, Del.: International Reading Association and National Council of Teachers of English.

Heap, J. (1982). Understanding classroom events: A critique of Durkin, with an alternative. *Journal of Reading Behavior* 14: 391–411.

Heath, S. B. (1982). Protean shapes in literacy events: Ever-shifting oral and literate traditions. In *Spoken and written language: Exploring orality and literacy,* edited by D. Tannen, 91–117. Norwood, N.J.: Ablex.

——— (1983). *Ways with words: Language, life, and work in communities and classrooms.* New York: Cambridge University Press.

Hickman, J. (1981). A new perspective on response to literature: Research in an elementary school setting. *Research in the Teaching of English* 15: 343–54.

Hiebert, E. H. (1983). An examination of ability grouping for reading instruction. *Reading Research Quarterly* 18: 231–55.

Hodges, C. A. (1980). Toward a broader definition of comprehension instruction (Commentary). *Reading Research Quarterly* 15: 299–306.

Holdaway, D. (1979). *The foundations of literacy.* Sydney: Ashton Scholastic (distributed by Heinemann).

Hymes, D. (1972). Models of the interaction of language and social life. In *Directions in sociolinguistics,* edited by J. J. Gumperz and D. Hymes. New York: Holt, Rinehart & Winston.

Jenkins, J. R., D. Pany, and J. Schreck (1978). *Vocabulary and reading comprehension: Instructional effects.* Technical report no. 100. Champaign, Ill.: Center for the Study of Reading, University of Illinois at Urbana-Champaign. ED 160 999.

Johnston, P. H. (1983). *Reading comprehension assessment: A cognitive basis.* Newark, Del.: International Reading Association.

King, M. (1985). Language and language learning for child watchers. In *Observing the language learner,* edited by A. Jaggar and M. T. Smith-Burke, 19–38. Newark, Del.: International Reading Association and National Council of Teachers of English.

Kirsch, I. S., and J. T. Guthrie (1984). Prose comprehension and text search as a function of reading volume. *Reading Research Quarterly* 19: 331–42.

Lindfors, J. (1980). *Children's language and learning.* Englewood Cliffs, N.J.: Prentice-Hall.

Marliave, R. S. (1978). Academic learning time and engagement: The validation of a measure of ongoing student engagement and task difficulty. In *Selected findings from phase III-B,* edited by C. W. Fischer, R. S. Cahen, N. N. Filby,

R. S. Marliave, and D. C. Berliner. San Francisco: Far West Laboratory for Educational Research and Development.

Mason, J. (1984). *Acquisition of knowledge about reading in the preschool period: An update and extension.* Technical report no. 318. Champaign, Ill.: Center for the Study of Reading, University of Illinois at Urbana-Champaign.

Mason, J., and J. Osborn (1982). *When do children begin "reading to learn": A survey of classroom reading instruction practices in grades two through five.* Technical report no. 261. Champaign, Ill.: Center for the Study of Reading, University of Illinois at Urbana-Champaign.

McDermott, R. (1978). Relating and learning: An analysis of two classroom reading groups. In *Linguistics and reading,* edited by R. Shuy. Rowley, Mass.: Newbury House.

McDermott, R., and K. Gospodinoff (1979). Social contexts for ethnic borders and school failure. In *Nonverbal behavior: Applications and cultural implications,* edited by A. Wolfgang, 175–95. New York: Academic Press.

McDonald, F., and P. Elias (1976). *The effects of teaching performance on pupil learning. Final report (5 vols.). Beginning teacher evaluation study, phase II, 1974–1976.* Princeton, N.J.: Educational Testing Service.

Medley, D. M. (1979). The effectiveness of teachers. In *Research on teaching: Concepts, findings and implications,* edited by P. L. Peterson and H. J. Walberg. Berkeley, Calif.: McCutchan.

Mehan, H. (1979a). *Learning lessons.* Cambridge, Mass.: Harvard University Press.

——— (1979b). "What time is it, Denise?" Asking known information questions in classroom discourse. *Theory into Practice* 18: 285–94.

Metheny, W. (1980a). *The influences of grade and pupil ability levels on teachers' conceptions of reading.* Research series no. 69. East Lansing, Mich.: Institute for Research on Teaching, Michigan State University.

——— (1980b). The influence of grade and pupil ability levels on teachers' conceptions of reading. In *Perspectives on reading research and instruction,* 29th Yearbook, edited by M. L. Kamil and A. L. Moe. Washington, D.C.: National Reading Conference.

Meyer, B. J. F., and G. E. Rice (1984). The structure of text. In *Handbook of reading research,* edited by P. D. Pearson et al., 319–51. New York: Longman.

Michaels, S. (1981). Sharing time: Children's narrative style and differential access to literacy. *Language in Society* 10: 423–42.

Michaels, S., and C. B. Cazden (1986). Teacher-child collaboration as oral preparation for literacy. In *Acquisition of literacy: Ethnographic perspectives,* edited by B. B. Schieffelin and P. Gilmore. Norwood, N.J.: Ablex.

Michaels, S., and J. Collins (1984). Oral discourse styles: Classroom interaction and the acquisition of literacy. In *Coherence in spoken and written discourse,* edited by D. Tannen, 219–44. Norwood, N.J.: Ablex.

Michaels, S., and M. Foster (1985). Peer-peer learning: Evidence from a student-run sharing time. In *Observing the language learner,* edited by A. Jaggar and M. T. Smith-Burke, 143–58. Newark, Del.: International Reading Association and National Council of Teachers of English.

Mikulecky, L. (1982). Job literacy: The relationship between school preparation and workplace actuality. *Reading Research Quarterly* 17: 400–19.

Mosenthal, P., and T. J. Na (1980a). Quality of children's recall as a function of children's classroom competence. *Journal of Experimental Child Psychology* 30: 1–21.

——— (1980b). Quality of children's recall under two classroom testing tasks: Towards a socio-psycholinguistic model of reading comprehension. *Reading Research Quarterly* 15: 504–28.

Neilsen, A., B. Rennie, and A. Connell (1982). Allocation of instructional time to reading comprehension and study skills in intermediate grade social studies classrooms. In *New inquiries in reading research and instruction,* 31st Yearbook, edited by J. A. Niles and L. A. Harris. Rochester, N.Y.: National Reading Conference.

Newell, A., and H. A. Simon (1972). *Human problem solving.* Englewood Cliffs, N.J.: Prentice-Hall.

Ninio, A., and J. Bruner (1978). The achievement and antecedents of labeling. *Journal of Child Language* 5: 5–15.

Osborn, J. (1984). Workbooks that accompany basal reading programs. In *Comprehension instruction: Perspectives and suggestions,* edited by G. G. Duffy, L. R. Roehler, and J. Mason. New York: Longman.

Otto, W., A. Wolf, and R. Eldridge (1984). Managing instruction. In *Handbook of reading research,* edited by P. D. Pearson. New York: Longman.

Paley, V. (1981). *Wally's stories.* Cambridge, Mass.: Harvard University Press.

Palinscar, A. S. (1984). The question for meaning from expository text: A teacher-guided journey. In *Comprehension instruction: Perspectives and suggestions,* edited by G. G. Duffy, L. R. Roehler, and J. Mason. New York: Longman.

Palinscar, A. S., and A. L. Brown (1984). Reciprocal teaching of comprehension-fostering and comprehension-monitoring activities. *Cognition and Instruction* 1: 117–75.

Pearson, P. D., ed. (1984). *Handbook of reading research.* New York: Longman.

Pearson, P. D., and M. C. Gallagher (1983). *The instruction of reading comprehension,* Technical report no. 297. Champaign, Ill.: Center for the Study of Reading, University of Illinois at Urbana-Champaign.

Pearson, P. D., and D. Johnson (1978). *Teaching reading comprehension.* New York: Holt, Rinehart & Winston.

Perl, S. (1983). How teachers teach the writing process: Overview of an ethnographic research project. *The Elementary School Journal* 84: 45–51.

Peterson, P., L. C. Wilkinson, F. Spinelli, and S. Swing (1984). Merging the process-product and the sociolinguistic paradigms: Research on small-group processes. In *The social context of instruction: Group organization and group processes,* edited by P. Peterson, L. C. Wilkinson, and M. Hallinan, 125–52. New York: Academic Press.

Philips, S. U. (1982). *The invisible culture: Communication in classroom and community on the Warm Springs Indian Reservation.* New York: Longman.

——— (1985). Participant structures and communicative competence: Warm Springs children in community and classroom. In *Functions of language in the classroom,* edited by C. B. Cazden, V. P. John, and D. Hymes. Prospect Heights, Ill.: Waveland Press.

Platt, N. G. (1984). How one classroom gives access to meaning. *Theory into Practice* 23: 239–45.

Raphael, T. E. (1982). Question-answering strategies for children. *Reading Teacher* 36: 186–91.

Raphael, T., and P. D. Pearson (1982). *The effect of metacognitive training on children's question-answering behavior.* Technical report no. 238. Champaign, Ill.: Center for the Study of Reading, University of Illinois at Urbana-Champaign. ED 215 315.

Roehler, L. R., and G. G. Duffy (1984). Direct explanation of comprehension processes. In *Comprehension instruction: Perspectives and suggestions,* edited by G. G. Duffy, L. R. Roehler, and J. Mason. New York: Longman.

Rosenshine, B. (1979). Content, time and direction instruction. In *Research on teaching: Concepts, findings, and implications,* edited by P. Peterson, and H. Walberg. Berkeley, Calif.: McCutchan.

Rosenshine, B., and R. Stevens (1984). Classroom instruction in reading. In *Handbook of reading research,* edited by P. D. Pearson. New York: Longman.

Rupley, W. H. (1977). Stability of teacher effects on pupils' reading achievement over a two year period and its relation to instructional emphasis. In *Reading: Theory, research and practice,* 26th Yearbook, edited by P. D. Pearson. Clemson, S.C.: National Reading Conference.

Scollon, R., and S. Scollon (1981). *Narrative, literacy and face in interethnic communication.* Norwood, N.J.: Ablex.

Shannon, P. (1982). Teachers' self-perceptions and reification of instruction within reading instruction. In *New inquiries in reading research and instruction,* 31st Yearbook, edited by J. A. Niles and L. A. Harris. Rochester, N.Y.: National Reading Conference.

Shavelson, R. J., and P. Stern (1981). Research on teachers' pedagogical thoughts, judgments, decisions, and behavior. *Review of Educational Research* 51: 455–98.

Shultz, J., and S. Florio (1979). Stop and freeze: The negotiation of social and physical space in a kindergarten/first grade classroom. *Anthropology and Education Quarterly* 10: 166–81.

Sinclair, J. M., and R. M. Coulthard (1975). *Toward an analysis of discourse.* New York: Oxford University Press.

Smith-Burke, M. T., and L. H. Ringler (1985). STAR: Teaching reading and writing. In *A decade of reading research: From theory to practice,* edited by J. Orasau. Hillsdale, N.J.: Erlbaum.

Snow, C. E. (1983). Literacy and language: Relationships during the preschool years. *Harvard Educational Review* 53: 165–89.

Soar, R. S. (1977). An integration of findings from four studies of teacher effectiveness. In *The appraisal of teaching: Concepts and processes,* edited by G. Borich. Reading, Mass.: Addison-Wesley.

Soar, R. S., and R. M. Soar (1979). Emotional climate and management. In *Research on teaching: Concepts, findings, and implications,* edited by P. Peterson, and H. Walberg. Berkeley, Calif.: McCutchan.

Solomon, D., and A. Kendall (1979). *Children in classrooms: An investigation of person-environment interaction.* New York: Praeger.

Stallings, J., R. Cory, J. Fairweather, and M. Needels (1977). *Early childhood education classroom evaluation.* Menlo Park, Calif.: SRI International.

——— (1978). *A study of basic reading skills taught in secondary schools.* Menlo Park, Calif.: SRI International.

Stallings, J., and D. Kaskowitz (1974). *Follow-through classroom observation evaluation 1972–1973.* SRI project URU-7370. Stanford, Calif.: Stanford Research Institute.

Stallings, J., M. Needels, and N. Stayrook (1979). *The teaching of basic reading skills in secondary schools, Phase II and Phase III.* Menlo Park, Calif.: SRI International.

Staton, J., R. W. Shuy, J. Kreeft, and L. Reed (1982). *The analysis of dialogue journal writing as a communicative event.* Final report to the National Institute of Education (NIE-G-80-0122). Washington, D.C.: Center for Applied Linguistics.

Steinberg, Z., and C. B. Cazden (1979). Children as teachers—of peers and ourselves. *Theory into Practice* 18: 258–66.

Stubbs, M. (1976). Keep in touch: Some functions of teacher-talk. In *Explorations in classroom observation,* edited by M. Stubbs, and S. Delamont. New York: John Wiley & Sons.

Sulzby, E. (1983). *Beginning readers' developing knowledges about written language.* Final report to the National Institute of Education (NIE-G-80-0176). Evanston, Ill.: Northwestern University.

Taylor, D. (1983). *Family literacy: Young children learning to read and write.* Exeter, N.H.: Heinemann.

Tharp, R. G. (1982). The effective instruction of comprehension: Results and description of the Kamehameha Early Education Program. *Reading Research Quarterly* 17: 503–27.

Tikunoff, W., D. Berliner, and R. Rist (1975). *An ethnographic study of the forty classrooms of the Beginning Teacher Evaluation Study known sample.* Technical report no. 75-10-5. San Francisco: Far West Laboratory for Educational Research and Development.

Tuinman, J., and M. Brady (1974). How does vocabulary account for variance on reading comprehension tests? A preliminary instructional analysis. In *Interaction: Research and practice for college-adult reading,* edited by P. Nacke. Clemson, S.C.: National Reading Conference.

Van Ness, H. (1981). Social control and social organization in an Alaskan Athabaskan classroom: A microethnography of "Getting Ready" for reading. In *Culture and the bilingual classroom,* edited by H. T. Trueba, G. P. Guthrie, and K. H. Au. Rowley, Mass.: Newbury House.

Wallat, C., J. Green, S. Conlin, and M. Haramis (1981). Issues related to action research in the classroom—The teacher and researcher as a team. In *Ethnography and language in educational settings,* edited by J. Green and C. Wallat, 87–111. Norwood, N.J.: Ablex.

Watson-Gegeo, K., and S. Boggs (1977). From verbal play to talk story: The role of routines in speech events among Hawaiian children. In *Child discourse,* edited by C. Mitchell-Kernan and S. Ervin-Tripp, 67–90. New York: Academic Press.

Wells, G., et al. (1981). *Learning through interaction: The study of language development.* New York: Cambridge University Press.

Wells, G., and J. Wells (1984). Learning to talk and talking to learn. *Theory Into Practice* 23, no. 3: 190–97.

Whaley, J. (1981). Story grammar and reading instruction. *Reading Teacher* 34: 762–71.

Wilkinson, L. C., and S. Calculator (1982). Effective speakers: Students' use of language to request and obtain information and action in the classroom. In *Communicating in the classroom,* edited by L. C. Wilkinson. New York: Academic Press.

Wittrock, M., ed. (1986). *Handbook of research on teaching.* 3d ed. New York: Macmillan.

Yinger, R. (1980). A study of teacher planning. *The Elementary School Journal* 80: 107–27.

Commentary

Arthur N. Applebee
Stanford University

These two papers provide a complementary set. Trika Smith-Burke provides a state-of-the-art summary of what we know about factors in effective classroom practice (e.g., teacher effectiveness, planning and decision making, management, comprehension instruction), as well as what we know about classroom interaction in a variety of settings (including influences of cultural variation). Bryant Fillion and Rita Brause, on the other hand, have given a thorough overview of our guiding philosophies: the current-traditional paradigm of teaching and learning in English language arts. Within that paradigm, they suggest a variety of emerging and critical issues. Their argument is convincing, primarily because I am in sympathy with its initial premises.

Nonetheless, I think Smith-Burke's final section may be the most important and helpful part of both papers. Here, she begins to push beyond our current assumptions toward new perspectives. As she notes, "All fields suffer from a certain kind of myopia, and ours is no exception."

I want to elaborate this last point in my remarks, raising three issues that will shape our research in the next decade.

Issue One: We lack a theory of language pedagogy.

We do have a well-elaborated theory of language learning, presented clearly by Fillion and Brause. They trace their intellectual forbearers to Moffett, Britton, Dixon, the Goodmans (and reaching out more broadly to Brown, Bruner, Piaget, Vygotsky)—and so do I. From these scholars, we have good theories of what is learned, and of the direction of growth. These theories lead to such conclusions as these from Fillion and Brause:

"All children have a natural facility with language learning."

"Basic literacy is a natural extension of an individual's linguistic development."

266

"Language facility . . . develops primarily through personally mean-ingful, active uses of language in the service of human intentions."

We also have increasingly better (if more recent) theories of classrooms as social environments. Both papers summarize important aspects of this understanding, including the following:

1. Interaction within classrooms is rule-governed.
2. The meanings that emerge are context-specific.
3. Teachers play multiple roles in classrooms.
4. Participants negotiate the roles they will play in interaction with the other participants.
5. Classrooms are systematic and sensible places.

Yet, as Smith-Burke points out, we have failed to bring these perspectives together in a productive way. They exist side by side, without providing us with a theory of teaching. We have no principled understanding of the teacher's role as a source or mediator of instruction and learning. There are exceptions, and this work will help clarify what I mean when I say we need a theory of language pedagogy. I am thinking of the instructional theories stemming from the work of Vygotsky, Luria, and their students; the studies of Michael Cole and his colleagues in San Diego; Ann Brown's recent work on reciprocal teaching; Merlin Wittrock's studies of instruction driven by his theories of comprehension; and Judith Langer's and my own studies of instructional scaffolding.

Perhaps it is helpful, too, to provide some examples of important studies that, at the same time, operate in a different realm and do not contribute to a theory of instruction of the sort I am thinking of. These would include metaphors of learning (such as John Dixon's personal-growth model), studies of the teaching of particular content or skills (such as Pearson's and Langer's studies of the effects of activating or providing relevant background knowledge), and studies of effective teaching (such as Graves's New Hampshire studies). Important in their own right, such studies do not contribute to a theory of language teaching.

Issue Two: We lack a full understanding of alternative research methodologies.

Both papers reflect the conflict in the field between experimental and ethnographic approaches, and tend to set the two approaches in conflict with one another. They note, for example, the differing results from the teacher-effectiveness research and from ethnographic studies and attribute them, at least in part, to methodological artifacts.

The field as a whole shows some confusion about these alternatives. There is a tendency to equate ethnographic studies with case-study or descriptive research—forgetting that both case-study and descriptive research have a long and honorable history within positivistic traditions. (Treatment of my own work provides a case in point. It has been cited, even in print, as part of the recent ethnographic emphasis—even though it is in fact deeply rooted in positivistic, experimental traditions.) If case studies are being adopted unthinkingly into an alternative tradition, ethnographic work is equally being adopted as "hypothesis-generating" within a broader view of the research enterprise. Yet my colleagues who are ethnographers would certainly reject a description of their work as limited to spinning hypotheses to be studied in more systematic samples later.

Here again, I want to return to one of Trika's points, and to urge that our field needs to be fully and honestly multidisciplinary, learning from each of the research traditions available to us. If we truly accept this view, we will take conflicting results (such as those from the teaching-effectiveness and case-study literatures) as interesting situations to examine more carefully, rather than seeking to dismiss them as methodological artifacts. In this case, we may find that the real conflict in the research may be between what *can* happen in unusual classrooms with unusual teachers receiving unusual support, and what *typically* happens given the complex institutional and contextual constraints on instruction. Perhaps there are lessons here about what we should be trying to change when we seek to reform teaching.

The current concern with teacher-as-researcher can be handled within this general framework. Teachers bring to this endeavor their own legitimate and extensive knowledge of teaching and children—knowledge which we too often have ignored. But, like the various disciplines and research traditions that have focused on language learning and language teaching, this is best seen as one kind of knowledge that contributes to our total understanding. Little is gained, and much is lost, by blurring the differences in what each discipline or realm of knowledge and experience has to contribute.

Issue Three: We are overly simplistic in our understanding of the relationship between research and practice.

It is easy to be too hasty in drawing implications from practice. Extending our understanding of what and how we teach is slow and difficult. We reach incomplete answers and develop partial theories—neither of which *should* reform teaching.

Much of what we do is best thought of as giving teachers (as well as researchers) ways of thinking about their subject and their teaching. In turn, they will make best use of those ideas in their own particular contexts. The ideas will provide frameworks that help them make principled use of the one-thousand-and-one things in their teaching repertoires. I believe there are many different ways to solve particular teaching problems, and the complexities of classrooms will lead different teachers to choose different solutions in different classrooms on different days.

This relates, too, to suggestions about how to share new ideas with teachers. There is much emphasis on models and examples, particularly with videotapes. In providing these models, however, the *whys* are more important than the *whats* of what the models provide for teachers as well as for children. And again, we are only beginning to address the why questions in language teaching, and until we do the effect of research on practice may continue to be trivial.

Commentary

Dolores Durkin
University of Illinois at Urbana-Champaign

Recollections of the years when I was a doctoral student bring to mind one outstanding feature of some of the research that was discussed in various courses: its tendency to be superficial. Often—at least in research on reading—a researcher would give a group of students a test at the beginning of a school year, return at the end of the year to administer another test, and then report correlations that presumably revealed something important enough to warrant an article. Even as a naive graduate student, I could not help but think that something of significance must surely have occurred in the classroom during the long interval between the two tests. Evidently I was in the minority, for at the time few researchers seemed to think that examining life in classrooms merited their attention. Or, as Fillion and Brause state in their paper, at that time "the world of educational research and the world of the classroom operated independently."

Given the nature of my initial contact with research, it may have been natural that my very first study involved classroom observations of the behavior of six boys in the process of acquiring reading ability during first grade (Durkin 1960). Since that research was done some time ago, I guess it is also natural for me to respond to the relatively recent interest in classroom studies with feelings like "It's about time!"

Another response is one that I always have to suddenly popular topics, namely, that it is all too easy for a type of research or for some particular topic to become "dangerously popular" in the sense that the interest spawns a large number of small, noncumulative studies carried out and reported in a climate characterized by far-too-little healthy skepticism. As a result, too much is accepted too quickly.

To cite one small example of this consequence for reading, just about every report or article concerned with student practice will claim—as the literature is being reviewed—that elementary school children spend as much as 70 percent of their time during the reading period doing written exercises. While such a finding may in fact be an accurate description of a very large number of students, it happens to be information that derives from a single study (Fisher et al. 1978). In addition, it is a description of merely one end of a continuum. While it *is* tempting to spice up a research report with such a finding, it may also be misleading to do so—at least until additional studies reach similar conclusions.

So is my first reaction. Basically it is the hope that interest in classroom studies persists, but also that the enthusiasm will be disciplined by the realization that, as with any kind of research on any topic, meaningful data do not emerge from brief, isolated, one-shot studies, of which we now have a generous number.

My second reaction relates to what I have learned from some of my own studies, including the very first effort, which, as I mentioned, was a case study of six boys in the process of learning to read in first grade. It was fortunate that home interviews as well as numerous classroom observations were included in that study, for, as things turned out, what accounted for the highest achiever's success as well as the dismal failure of two of the other subjects had to do with variables in their families, not factors in the classroom. And it was hardly unexpected to learn that family factors enjoyed special importance in the next research that I undertook, two longitudinal studies of children who could read before they entered school (Durkin 1966). Family factors came out on top once again in a more recent study, this one of poor black fifth graders who were very competent readers (Durkin 1984). In this case, preschool help with reading from grandmothers, which sent the children to school already reading, was a crucially important factor. Failure to discover this factor would have allowed for unwarranted conclusions about what contributed to the subjects' success. All of this is to say that, while observations in classrooms are rich sources of information, even at their best they can only supply one piece of a complex puzzle.

My third and final reaction is not confined to classroom or reading research but, rather, encompasses the reporting of research in general. In this instance, the reaction is the wish that an enforceable law or rule existed that prohibited authors from referring to research reports that they have not read. Based on the many years that I have been reading journals, and on the innumerable times that my own research data and conclusions have been so badly mangled that I no longer recognize them as being mine, I am now convinced that a fairly large number of quoted passages, interpretations, and misinterpretations are passed on from one article to another when no more than a single author ever took the time to read the report supposedly being reviewed. Such a practice—if it is as widespread as I believe it to be—promotes myth making and propaganda, not scholarship.

But this practice is hardly new. Again, I first became acquainted with it when I was a graduate student listening to professors and reading authors of textbooks, each stating with great certainty that children are not ready to learn to read until they have a mental age of about 6.5 years. Inevitably, this highly simplistic conclusion was documented with a reference to research done by Mabel Morphett and Carleton Washburne (Morphett and Washburne 1931). Curious and skeptical about both the conclusion and the research that promoted it, I actually read the report even though it was never assigned reading. Anyone here who has read it must have shared the shock that I experienced when I examined what, for decades, influenced the timing of beginning reading instruction. In truth, an article on flaws in the Morphett-Washburne research would be longer than their description of it. It is difficult to believe that the professors and the authors who constantly referred to this study had ever read it. Still, they quoted it.

I think the moral of the story is that those of us who review and refer to research almost on a daily basis have an obligation to make certain that we really know studies before we discuss them. Taking such an obligation seriously would help to ensure that only good research is honored by being influential.

References

Durkin, D. (1960). A case-study approach toward an identification of factors associated with success and failure in learning to read. *California Journal of Educational Research* 11: 26–33.

———— (1966). Children who read early. New York: Teachers College Press.

———— (1984). Poor black children who are successful readers: An investigation. *Urban Education* 19: 53–76.

Fisher, C., D. Berliner, N. Filby, R. Marliave, L. Cohen, M. Dishaw, and J. Moore (1978). Teaching and learning in elementary schools: A summary of the beginning teacher evaluation study. San Francisco: Far West Laboratory for Educational Research and Development.

Morphett, M. V., and C. Washburne (1931). When should children begin to read? *The Elementary School Journal* 31: 496–503.

V Developments in Technology: Implications for Language and Literature Education

Introduction

Given the possibilities of word-processing and text-editing systems for improving instruction in the language arts, concentration on these aspects of technology in the two papers presented here seems understandable. The researchers do not see as issues of major consequence such matters as the impact of computer-assisted or computer-managed instruction on the language arts. Rather they write out of their own research and development experience, describing how Project Quill on the one hand—developed at the independent research center of Bolt, Beranek and Newman—and Writer's Workbench℠ on the other—created and tested at Bell Laboratories—contribute new dimensions to the teaching and learning of language. What these articles gain in immediacy from the concreteness of the two projects may result in a loss in their failure to dwell on all aspects of current research in technology. Still, the vividness of these two projects, which have changed the arsenal of weapons teachers have at their disposal, clearly stimulates a vision of where technology may be leading curriculum and instruction—a vision so unsettling to some seminar participants that it elicited sharply divergent fears and disturbing imaginings, as well as confident assumptions.

An Examination of the Role of Computers in Teaching Language and Literature

Bertram C. Bruce
Bolt, Beranek and Newman Laboratories

What place should the computer have in the language arts classroom?[1] Many people would say, "None at all." If they see any connection between computers and language learning, it is that the study of language, with its attendant emphasis on culture and history, especially the study of literature, should serve as an antidote to a society that seems increasingly centered on technology.

Of all the new technologies, the one which appears to threaten humanistic learning and values the most is the computer. Thus, it seems appropriate to focus this discussion of technology in education on computers. But there is a deeper reason, or set of reasons, for focusing in this way which relates to the fundamental nature of computers. First, the computer is a tool for representing knowledge through symbols; as such, the essence of computer use is identical to what we do when we use language. Second, the computer is a device for interpreting symbolic structures, for making sense of linguistic representations. Third, the computer is a communication device. It can store representations of information, but more importantly, can transmit these representations to other people and other communication devices. Finally, the computer is an object in the process of becoming. Like other tools, the computer can be used in a variety of ways; unlike the others, its *very nature is to be redefinable.*

These aspects of the computer are not assumed in many of the discussions of computers in their relation to language arts—discussions on issues such as video games versus reading, the elevation of science and technology over the humanities, and methods of or appropriateness of computer-assisted instruction. By not addressing the deeper aspects of computers, we foster an either/or atmosphere in which the language arts

---

1. I use the term *language arts* in a broad sense to encompass classrooms at any grade level in which the focus is on learning how to use, understand, and appreciate language.

are often denigrated. Worse still, we fail to assert control over the direction of a tool which has an unquestionably powerful potential for teaching about language.

In the next section, I discuss the four aspects of the computer's relation to language outlined above. These aspects derive not just from consideration of computer applications but rather from an analysis of the computer's essential functions. Following that I describe a classroom of the future, one which is only a slightly extended composite of today's classrooms. For each aspect of the future classroom, I have tried to identify some current activities that capture at least some of its potential. One purpose of this excursion into the future is to demonstrate that "speaking computer" is not so inappropriate for the study of language and literature. The case becomes, then, not that computers are good or bad for teaching language, but rather that they inherently belong in that province, and should be shaped by the people who live there. The last section of this essay raises some questions for research based on this thesis.

Computers as Language Machines

We tend to think of the computer, quite naturally, as a device that computes—in particular, as one that essentially adds numbers very fast. In every field in which computers have been used—including the military, industry, business, mathematics, medicine, science, social science, the humanities, and education—the computer was perceived first as a device for counting and carrying out simple mathematical operations. Thus, the military used the ENIAC for calculating ballistics trajectories; businesses used early office machines for keeping accounts; medical researchers collected statistical data on correlations of symptoms and diseases; humanists used computer word counts for authorship studies; and educators put computers in schools to teach arithmetic.

Today, people in each of these fields are beginning to use computers in quite different ways; specifically, they are using them for help in writing and reading, for carrying out symbolic transformations, and for communicating with other people. These new uses are not merely additions to the computer's repertoire but rather precursors of the computer's fundamental role as the general language machine—or to use Steven Job's phrase, "wheels for the mind."

Why do we continue the pattern of using computers for numbers first and words second? Perhaps we have failed to understand some of the subtle relations between computers and language. There are four of these relations I would like to discuss here: the computer as (1) a means for representing knowledge, (2) a device for interpreting symbols, (3) a communication device, and (4) a redefinable tool.

Computers as Tools for Representing Knowledge

A computer is, at its core, not just a collection of flip-flops or integrated circuits. Nor is it simply a big numerical calculator. At the deepest level, a computer is a device for encoding and storing symbols. Symbols thus encoded can be associated with other symbols; in that way, symbolic structures of arbitrary complexity can be constructed and maintained. Thus, the computer is a tool for representing any knowledge that can be symbolized.

Computers as Tools for Interpreting Symbols

Other technologies (for example, the book) are also convenient for recording symbols. But computers differ from books and other technologies in a way which has a special significance for the teaching of language. Computers are physical realizations of the concept of a totally general symbol manipulator, a device which can not only store, but also create, transform, or interpret essentially any symbolic representation. Thus, when we talk of what computers are, or should be, we must operate in the realm of Kant, Frege, or Levi-Strauss, not that of the BASIC programming manual.

Computers as Communication Devices

Computers are also communication devices: they can store and interpret symbols, but they can transmit them as well. The use of computers in transforming every other communication device, from telephone to video discs—in fact, the entire communications industry, whether its physical medium be books, magnetic tapes, or cathode-ray tubes—is increasingly dependent upon computers because only computers make possible the control flexible and precise enough to transmit just what is needed, or to record the right data. To a large extent the computer and the communications industry have already become one. The consequences of this fact for language use are significant.

Computers as Redefinable Tools

There is a fourth reason why computers are intimately tied to language: they are redefinable. Unlike typewriters, tape recorders, ditto machines, telephones, televisions, and other technological devices that might be used in education, the computer is a tool whose very nature is a process.

Many tools undergo rapid development, but the computer is itself a tool for making tools. For example, a computer when unpacked from its box might appear to be a LOGO (Feurzeig and Papert 1969; Feurzeig et al. 1969) machine. That is, one could use it to carry out the basic LOGO functions, such as moving a "turtle" about the screen. But one could also use LOGO, or any general-purpose computer language, to define new features—for instance, a program to find rhymes in a dictionary. The added functions would mean that one's machine would no longer be simply a LOGO machine, but rather, a LOGO-PLUS machine. One could also turn the LOGO machine into a BASIC machine by writing the proper function (an "interpreter" program). In fact, there is no known theoretical limit to what sort of machine the computer could become.[2]

The protean nature of the computer implies that we always need to look beyond current uses in order to assess whether and how these machines might best be used. In particular, we need to consider functions other than the usual ones of classroom management, multiple-choice testing, drill-and-practice, and frame-based computer-assisted instruction. Most importantly, we need to explore computers as general symbol manipulators. The next section is designed to encourage some speculation regarding desirable functions for computers.

The Language Classroom of 2010

This section presents some sketches of how computers have been and might be used in teaching reading and writing. The first sketch focuses on the computer as a tool for knowledge representation. The second emphasizes the computer's role as interpreter of symbols. The third looks at the computer as a communication device—for reading and sharing ideas, for collaborative writing, and for networking. The last sketch looks at the computer's redefinability and the implications for creativity. For each sketch we will look in on Hannah Lerner and her classroom in the year 2010, then look backward to the late 1980s to find precursors of what we see in her class.

Knowledge Representation

When students in Hannah Lerner's class in the year 2010 work at the computer, they engage in what they call "idea processing." Idea processing

---

2. Church (1932) proposed a thesis, now generally accepted, which said, in effect, that the general-purpose digital computer could execute any function that could be precisely defined. There are, of course, practical limits to available memory and time (also perhaps to our imaginations).

means working at the level of concepts and higher-level text structures, such as "counter-argument" and "elaboration." When students process ideas with the computer, they think of what they do as building structures, testing, and debugging. Thus, idea processing goes far beyond the word processing familiar in the 1980s. Similarly, the students might be said to be programming, but again, the activity bears only a slight resemblance to the old, rigid procedural paradigms. The focus is on the project they are doing, not on the syntactic details of either a programming language or a word processor. What has happened in 2010 is a merging of two earlier modes of computational interaction. Computer programming per se has begun to resemble natural language use, and writing with the aid of a machine has come to resemble very high-level programming.

The reason for this is that defining a procedure for a computer to carry out or creating a text both require the person to formulate and organize ideas. Writers of programs and writers of texts are concerned with planning and revisions; they both need to be aware of their audience (Newkirk 1985). *With programming sufficiently removed from the bits-and-bytes level and text processing from the letter-by-letter level, these two once-disparate activities become essentially one. As a result, Hannah's students often find themselves working with ideas in similar ways, regardless of the end product—a text, a computer program, a graphical display, or simply a deeper understanding of a domain of study.*

Precursors of the above scenario could have been seen in the seventies and eighties. For example, programming languages such as SMALLTALK (Goldberg and Robson 1983) allowed a programmer to define an object and a set of rules for how that object should behave (e.g., how to display itself on a CRT screen, how to provide information about its current status, how to change as a result of changes in its environment, etc.) This tended to free the programmer from concern about the precise sequence of actions the computer should take. Similarly, *rule-based systems* such as MYCIN (Davis, Buchanan, and Shortliffe 1977) allowed the programmer to define hundreds of rules of the form IF X THEN Y without concern for which rule should be checked first.[3]

While object-oriented languages and rule-based systems were being developed, artificial-intelligence programmers were also developing higher-level functions in their programming languages. For example, transition networks (Woods 1970) were developed as a language for describing in computational terms the set of grammatical rules for a language. Each such language enhancement moved programmers further

---

3. In the case of MYCIN the set of rules could be activated by a patient's history to help a physician diagnose a bacterial infection.

from the machine qua machine and closer to the problems they were addressing.

At the same time, word processors were giving way to idea processors (see Olds 1985). The early signs of this change could be seen in the emergence of programs to help with planning a text (Planner in Quill, Bruce and Rubin 1984a), organizing ideas (Thinktank, Owens 1984), examining texts in a nonlinear fashion (Org in Writer's Workbench, MacDonald 1983), managing text annotations (Annoland in Authoring-land, Brown 1983), and exploring and modifying data bases. As this class of programs matured, it enabled a form of interaction between a person and an emerging text in which the linking of ideas, the examination of an argument, or the search for related concepts was as easy as the correction of a spelling error with a word processor.

For example, in 1984 Linda Juliano, a sixth-grade teacher in Cambridge, Massachusetts, wanted to push the limits of how a computer might facilitate language use. One of her students had written a story about a trip to the circus which was extremely long and unfocused. The student didn't know how to cope with revising the text, to some extent because of the volume of material. The text had been written using a text editor known as Writer's Assistant (Levin, Boruta, and Vasconcellos 1982), which had a special feature called Mix that allowed a writer to start every every sentence at the left margin. Ordinarily, this feature was used to check for syntactic errors—first-letter capitalization, end punctuation, repetitious first words, and so on. Juliano saw that it could also be used to facilitate examining and manipulating a long text. She suggested that the student format his text in the separated-sentence fashion, print it out, and cut the sentences apart with scissors (a pre-2010 device used by writers to help in revising). With the sentences apart, it was easy to experiment with various deletions and rearrangements. Once the student had formed his revised text as a pile of sentences, he used the text editor again to recreate the final text. The computer thus became a tool for thinking of his text in a new way.

Interpretation of Symbols

Although Hannah continues to be the essential teacher of her class, the computer plays an important role as assistant tutor. This is possible because the computer can interpret, not just represent, symbols. For example, the computer can analyze stylistic features of the text—everything from spelling to paragraph forms—and provide information for the writer to use in revising.

The computer can also model processes of revision by showing successive alterations of a text, together with audio or textual annotations giving the reasons the author had for changes. This modeling can be run in slow mode, showing letter-by-letter changes, or fast-forward, showing higher-level revisions. Since the computer has stored examples from Hannah's own writing and the writing of experts, as well as that of students in the class, the study of various revision strategies often leads to valuable discussion of writing and writing styles.

Back in 1985 a program which took advantage of the computer as a symbol manipulator was Iliad (Bates et al. 1981). Iliad had a large amount of knowledge about transformational grammar (Chomsky 1965) that enabled it to generate many different possible transformations of any given sentence (if it knew the parts of speech). For example, the sentence "Bill ate the cake" could be transformed into the following: "Did Bill eat the cake?" "Bill should eat the cake," "Didn't he eat it?" "It might have been eaten." With this capability, a variety of activities could be designed to help children develop the ability to express their ideas in different ways.

Sharples (1980) developed several programs along this line, together with a set of activities that he used to teach writing in a fifth-grade classroom. One of these programs was Gram, which generated text on the basis of a set of rewrite rules. These rules were expanded until a string of words was generated. For example, Sharples developed a poetry generator by specifying that a poem could be rewritten as a title and a body. The title could be any noun phrase. The body could be any number of lines. He provided several different possible definitions for a line (e.g., noun phrase plus intransitive verb phrase plus preposition plus noun phrase). A noun phrase in turn could be a plural noun, and a plural noun might be *lillies* or *frogs*. The poetry generator made each of these choices randomly, thus producing a poem within the constraints of the grammar. By manipulating the grammar, students came to see how different constraints produced different kinds of poems.

Another program, Tran, allowed students to write their own transformations, like those in Iliad. These were written as pattern-action rules: if a piece of text matches the pattern to the left side of the rule, that part of the text is replaced by the right-hand side of the rule. For example, the rule "noun1 1 noun2—noun2 1 noun1" swaps the first two nouns in a sentence (the 1 between noun1 and noun2 allows for a string of any length). Sharples worked out a set of activities based on Tran to teach children sentence combining and other manipulations of sentences. In one activity children wrote descriptions and the computer replaced all the adjectives it knew by a star. The object for the children was to try to produce as many adjectives as they could that the computer did not know. These activities allowed children to explore language by manipulating the language systematically.

Another symbol-manipulating program was Writer's Workbench (Frase 1983, Gingrich 1983, MacDonald 1983), an automated Strunk and White. It analyzed a text and made comments that the writer could choose to use or ignore. For example, it could point out frequent use of words like *seem* or the conjunction *and* between clauses. It was originally designed for adults doing technical writing, but was later used as a tool for learning to write.

Communication via Computer

Hannah entered her classroom well before her students were expected to arrive. She had found that in the minutes before they appeared she could check her mail on the computer and review her plans for the day. On this particular day, one group of students would be completing a botany project they had begun earlier in the spring. Its purpose was to compare bean plant growth rates at various altitudes and under various climatic conditions.

"Good morning, Ms. Lerner."

The untimely end of the quiet period was signaled by the early arrival of two of Hannah's students, Kit and Adam. Kit immediately went to his computer to see if there had been any additions to the plant data base. Luckily, there was a message from São Paulo presenting some data from their greenhouse project. These data would be incorporated with other data from Rome, Tokyo, Mexico City, and Hannah's classroom in producing the science group's botany report.

Meanwhile, Adam sat down at another computer to see what changes his coauthors had made in their collaborative novel project. Using a multicolored screen with holographic projections, he could examine both the original text and any author's additions or alterations. New portions of text could be alternately highlighted or blended into the original. Comments by one author on another's passage could also be examined, or not, as Adam chose. The three-dimensional quality of the display conveyed a sense of what texts and comments were available in addition to those immediately visible. Adam was eager to read what his coauthors had done; perhaps one had sent in more text last night. It would be interesting to see if their semantic network for text, also presentable graphically, had changed because of any text changes.

Hannah's class in the year 2010 is in a sense a group of people who get together in one place and time for learning. But in a larger sense, the boundaries of the class are not easy to define. Students who are away from school because of illness, family business, bad weather, or whatever reason often check in via a network that links their homes, the school, other schools, and the outside world. This network allows transmission of text, pictures, graphics, audio—voice, music, other sounds—and video. One problem that arises is remembering where someone really is. Since it is as easy to share information with someone at a computer five thousand miles away as with someone five feet away, students have to learn to observe carefully the dateline that comes with each message. Networking also diminishes the distance created by time. Lisa can read a story that was finished on another continent six hours ago while she was sleeping. She can search a data base containing the entire Library of Congress to read texts written at any time and place. The process of searching this data base is similar to the one she goes through in looking for writings of her classmates, since most of the students' writing is stored in a network-accessible data base, too. (Lisa also keeps a journal in a traditional blank book, believing that no single form of technology is appropriate for all types of writing.)

Back in 1982, Jim Aldridge's sixth-grade class in Hartford was also using the computer for learning through reading and writing.[4] Jim described a special time in the morning before class when he turned on the "electronic classroom." There was a television, used for news and educational programs, a microcomputer, and a tabletop greenhouse project with vegetables in pots and fluorescent lights. During that time, Jim, like Hannah, would often do his own writing, or reading of children's works.

Each of Jim's students had a plant growing in the greenhouse. They would periodically take the plant over to the computer to record data on its growth. Another task was to compare diagrams in their science texts with the actual plant structures, using the computer as a mediator. Programmed with questions written by Jim, the computer mediated between the words of the text and the biological world of the plant. After collecting data over an extended time, the students could write lab reports detailing their observations.

Meanwhile, five girls in Jim's class were using the computer for the fourth chapter of their romantic novel about Menudo, the Puerto Rican rock group. The novel was inspired by another project in the class, writing a prospectus for a to-be-produced class play. But the Menudo story took a separate course, becoming a secret saga shared among only its authors and a few select friends. The girls would, at every possible moment, add pieces to their collaborative text. Sometimes they would write literally side-by-side, in groups of two or three at the computer. At

---

4. In this classroom example and in several others to follow, the students were using Quill, a system of writing tools and communication environments (Bruce and Rubin 1984a, Rubin and Bruce 1984). I've chosen to deemphasize the particular technology used since the function served is a more central issue.

other times they would add a portion to be read and perhaps modified their collaborations later.

Unfortunately, these girls had only a text editor for their writing. Text editors facilitate writing because they enable easy editing and help in the production of clear copy. But they facilitate neither collaborative writing nor thinking of ideas and text in larger units. Authoringland (Brown 1983, Watt 1983), in contrast, was a system—partly realized and partly envisioned in the '80s—which did just that. In the Authoringland computer environment a writer could modify a text but leave an "audit trail" which showed other authors (or the original author) what was changed, when, and why. A writer could also make comments: passing thoughts, identification of problems in the text, concepts to be elaborated later, or comments on other comments. The information in the computer was then no longer a single piece of connected text, but a network of text parts, ideas, reasons for changes, and notes to think about. The computer allowed a simple and clear graphic representation of relevant portions of this network, so that the writer could explore it, modify it, or draw from it a writing product.

Early in 1984, students in Shungnak Elementary School in Alaska used a satellite to talk with students in the nearby village of Kiana and the city of Fairbanks. They then used a computer to write, edit, and publish an article in *Educational Technology/Alaska* (Douglas et al. 1984) about their audio conference:

> We talked to Kiana and Fairbanks to learn more about different communities. To get ready for the conference we wrote letters and took pictures of ourselves, then we sent them to Kiana and Fairbanks. . . .
> We learned a few things from Kiana and Fairbanks. Kiana told us how to make an igloo. . . . We found out that Kiana eats the same Eskimo food we do. Some of these foods are frozen fish (quaq), Eskimo ice cream (akutuq) and dried fish (paniqtuq). When one girl in Fairbanks told us her father had a plane and she might come and visit us, we were very excited.
> Towards the end of the conference we sang a song to the other schools. The song was Pearly Shells. First we sang it in English and then we sang it in Inupiaq. . . . We enjoyed talking to the kids in the other communities. We discovered we have many things in common, but also some of us do things differently. (p. 8)

While these students were learning about others through audio conferencing, reading, and writing, students in other towns were also using networking to communicate. Some of these students used CCNN, the Computer Chronicles News Network (Riel 1983), a UPI or AP for kids. Members of the network wrote stories, poems, editorials, and other articles appropriate for a newspaper and sent them via a computer network to a large computer in Virginia. When a class wanted to produce a newspaper or magazine, they could then supplement their own articles with selected articles from CCNN. Naturally, in order to make a selection, they had to read a large number of articles others had written; in writing they had to think of their audience, taking into account the fact that their readers had different cultural experiences and background knowledge.

The computer was doing several things to facilitate the sharing of writing seen with CCNN. First, an article was transmitted almost immediately to anyone who wanted to read it. Second, there was essentially no limit to the number of possible readers. Moreover, the author did not have to make multiple hard copies and address envelopes to all the readers. Third, if a reader wished to incorporate a CCNN article into his or her newspaper, the text was already in a machine-readable form so it could be formatted, edited, and merged with other newspaper articles. Some examples of CCNN articles are included in the appendix to this paper.

Computer Redefinability

The fact that a computer is a tool for arbitrary symbol manipulation is the reason that it is the only general communication device. It is also the basis for computers being redefinable. In Hannah's class, students think of their computers as devices for creating. They create ideas, texts, pictures, graphs, charts, numbers, but also devices for enhancing their own creativity. In other words, the computer is not only a tool but a medium which is used for symbolic expression. Hannah's students create with the computer as an aid; they also re-create the computer to express their own ideas in a dynamic form.

Back in 1984, Nancy Sopp's junior high students in Fairbanks, Alaska, wanted to write a story in the form of a computer Adventure game (Sopp 1984, Addams 1985). This would be an interactive text in which the next passage a reader sees depends upon his or her actions. They realized that to accomplish this it would help to have a program to handle the details of connecting reader actions to text passages so that readers would focus on the texts per se. Moreover, this program should be suitable for any set of texts, not just the first draft they would write. What the students did was to write an Adventure game-maker using the language LOGO. The result was a new language, both more powerful and more specialized. Their project had already blurred the traditional boundaries between learning about computers and learning about language.

A generalization of the Adventure game-maker was a computer language called ITI (Interactive Text Interpreter, Levin 1982). ITI was a "high-level" language that redefined what the computer could do. Using it, students or teachers could create poetry generators, Storymaker-like programs (Rubin 1980) or Adventure games. The sports editor for a student newspaper, for example, could create a tool to use in writing sports stories that would remind the writer to include the final score or to conform to stylistic conventions. Levin and his colleagues used ITI to create tools such as the Expository Writing Tool; Letter Writer, which helped students learn various formats for letters; the Narrative Writing Tool; a Poetry Prompter; and Computer Chronicles, a tool for newspaper writing. These tools showed how the computer could be successively redefined, first as a PASCAL machine, then as an ITI machine, and finally as (for instance) an Expository Writing Tool.

Future Research

If the computer is a general language machine, then those interested in language learning might reasonably be expected to engage in studies of the computer vis-à-vis language. But the possible connections are many. What are the areas that need the most emphasis?

One area concerns the computer in its knowledge-representation function. Today we typically use a computer as a means for representing linear texts. Thus, we can change the spelling of a word, insert a sentence, or delete a paragraph. More complex manipulations of the text tend to detract from a focus on language use. Yet software can be designed to facilitate all sorts of nonlinear representations: outlines, associative networks, multiple connections, annotations, and so on. How to design and how to make good use of such possibilities are questions that need much attention.

A second area revolves around the computer as an interpreter of symbolic structures. Here, more work needs to be done on the computer as tutor.[5] All too often, ideas for the computer as tutor degenerate into constricted and boring activities that diminish rather than enhance students' excitement about language. Nevertheless, the computer has a strong potential as an intelligent tutor for language learning (see Collins 1985). The computer can present problems, act as a coach, or model the

---

5. Taylor (1980) suggests that we think of the computer as *tutor, tool, or tutee*. In the tutor role, the computer teaches directly; in the tool role it assists in doing something, for instance, reading and writing; and in the tutee role it is used as a device that can be "taught" (or redefined) to become something new.

revision process. These approaches need to be explored, especially in conjunction with new uses of the computer as a tool.

The third area of needed research is in the further extension of the computer as a tool for communication. For example, the Alaska Quill project (Barnhardt 1984, Bruce and Rubin 1984b) has begun to look at networking among teachers, which is potentially more significant than networking among students (as with CCNN). Also, there needs to be more work on integrating language software with software and activities in other domains, for example, in science and social science.

A fourth area in which research is needed is on the redefinable nature of computers. Redefinability is a powerful concept that may alter our understanding of what language is, or can be. Smith (1982) has argued that the core problems of computer science are not merely analogous to, but identical with, those in the philosophy of language. It is no accident that terms such as *self reference, interpretation, syntax, semantics, model,* or *reflection* appear in discussions of computer languages and architecture. The notion of redefinability, or definability from within, is central to both computer science and language. Moreover, at the level of use, the very act of programming, or redefining, is not unlike the act of writing, with similar ideas of hierarchy, problem solving, and elegance (see Newkirk 1985). These relations need to be better understood, as well as applied in developing useful computers.

Finally, this paper has said little about the larger context of the use of computers, or of the problems that come with such use. There needs to be more work on equity of access in terms of hardware, software, and the way computers are being used (Michaels, Cazden, and Bruce 1985; Sanders 1985). We also need to question both the reasons that schools choose to use computers and the alternatives they forego in doing so. The resources necessary to supply schools with hardware, software, and training cannot be ignored. But the dollars spent on computers become insignificant against either the rosiest or gloomiest views of how using computers may alter our relationship to language and the world. Will children no longer distinguish the model from reality, as Weizenbaum (1976) asks? Or will the use of models deepen their understanding? Will our sense of what language is diminish or expand as we adopt computer metaphors for our own thinking and communicating (Young 1984)? Does the ease of revision mean that written texts lose the sense of permanence they once held? What are the consequences of that for society in general? (I am reminded of Kundera's [1980] concern about the "forgetting" of truth in history.) What are the consequences for language learning? Questions such as these need to be investigated thoroughly.

Conclusion

Computers are fundamentally devices for carrying out essential language functions such as creating, interpreting, and communicating symbolic structures. Furthermore, their capabilities are redefinable, or open-ended, in much the same way that language itself is open-ended. Thus, on a theoretical basis, as well as a practical basis, computers are intimately linked to language.

There are dangers inherent in the use of computers for education; there are also great potential benefits from their use. But assessing the likely effect of computers in education is not a simple matter of comparing lists of pros and cons. One reason is that we simply don't yet know what computers are or could be. What seems clear, though, is that we have underestimated the deep relations between computation and language both at the theoretical and the practical levels. If we are to make the best use of computers for language and literature education, we need to ensure that those already involved in that area begin to think more about what computers can and should be.

Appendix

This appendix contains some articles from the Computer Chronicles News Network. All of the articles were written by students using computers and were sent via electronic mail through the Source (PARTI: CCNN), a commercial information utility.

> (Lincoln Vista, California, October 22, 1984)
> Article for section on Fashions
> The clothing in Vista is probably very different than the kinds of clothing you wear in your country. In Vista the girls like to wear floresant colors. Personaly I don't think they are that exciting but I am not the one wearing them. Mini-skirts are also popular but I have noticed that they are slowly dieing out.
> The guys wear Levis (501's) and they usualy roll the legs up so that they are known as high waters. Hightops are also very popular for guys. They are shoes which come above the ankle.
> This concludes my article on Fashions I hope you like it.
> By Marcie Teuber

> (Harbor View, Juneau, Alaska, April 24, 1984)
> New Store Opens
> They are putting up a Fred Meyer shopping center in Juneau. There are only two other shopping centers that can be driven to in Juneau. We either need a boat, or a plane to go enywere else. A lot of people

are excited about this, becouse things like this hardly ever happen in Juneau.

By Pete Ellis, Grade 6

(Kamehameha, Honolulu, Hawaii, March 13, 1984)

Sashimi

Sashimi is a Japanese type of food. Anybody can get it. It contains raw fish. The best kind of raw fish is AHi (Tuna). You could also make it out of Maguro (Sword Fish) or AKu (another type of Tuna). Sashimi is a red colored fish. It is made by cutting the raw fish into small and thin slices. You do not have to cook it. You eat it as an appetizer. In Hawaii we call it pupus. There is a sauce you eat it with. The sauce is made of hot mustard and shoyu (soy sauce). Most people like to eat it at New Year's Eve. That is the most expensive time to get it. You pay about $20.00 a pound, but people still buy it. Sashimi is my favorite appetizer. If you ever come to Hawaii and you go to a nice restaurant ask for Sashimi as an appetizer.

By Ana Vidinha, age 10

(Our Lady of Mercy College, Parramatta, New South Wales, Australia, October 19, 1984)

A Special Birthday

Today is our principal's birthday, whose name is Sister Janet. Yesterday we collected 20 cents from each pupil to buy her a present. We hope that she will let us out early today as her present to us.

She will be leaving us next year in August to study in the United States. It will be an exciting experience for her, and we will miss her very much.

By Gabrielle and Nicky

References

Addams, S. (1985). Interactive fiction. *Popular Computing,* March, 97–99, 180–82.

Barnhardt, C. (1984). The Quill microcomputer writing project in Alaska. In *Alaska's challenge: Computers in education—strategies and solutions,* edited by R. V. Dusseldorp. Anchorage: Alaska Association for Computers in Education (P.O. Box 4-652, Anchorage, AK 99502).

Bates, M., J. Beinashourtz, R. Ingria, and K. Wilson (1981). Generative tutorial systems. Paper presented at the annual meeting of the Association for the Development of Computer-based Instructional Systems. ED 222 196.

Brown, J. S. (1983). Process versus product: A perspective on tools for communal and informal electronic learning. In *Education in the electronic age,* edited by S. Newman and E. Poor. New York: Learning Lab, WNET/Thirteen Educational Division.

Bruce, B., and A. Rubin (1984a). *The utilization of technology in the development of basic skills instruction: Written communications.* Report no. 5766. Cambridge, Mass.: Bolt, Beranek and Newman.

———— (1984b). *The Quill writing project for Alaska, final report.* Report no. 5789. Cambridge, Mass.: Bolt, Beranek and Newman.

Chomsky, N. (1965). *Aspects of the theory of syntax.* Cambridge, Mass.: MIT Press.

Church, A. (1932). A set of postulates for the foundation of logic. *Annals of Mathematics* 33: 346–66.

Collins, A. (1985). Teaching reading and writing with personal computers. In *A decade of reading research: Implications for practice,* edited by J. Orasanu. Hillsdale, N.J.: Erlbaum.

Davis, R., B. Buchanan, and E. Shortliffe (1977). Production rules as a representation for a knowledge-based consultation program. *Artificial Intelligence* 8: 15–45.

Douglas, E., et al. (1984). Audio links to words show new but familiar world. *Educational Technology/Alaska,* 8.

Feurzeig, W., and S. Papert (1969). Programming-languages as a conceptual framework for teaching mathematics. *Proceedings of the colloquium: Programmed Learning Research: Major Trends.* Paris: Dunod.

Feurzeig, W., S. Papert, M. Bloom, R. Grant, and C. Solomon (1969). *Programming language as a conceptual framework for teaching mathematics.* Report no. 1889. Cambridge, Mass.: Bolt, Beranek and Newman.

Flower, L., and J. R. Hayes (1981). Plans that guide the composing process. In *Writing: The nature, development, and teaching of written communication,* Volume 2, edited by C. H. Frederiksen and J. F. Dominic, 39–58. Hillsdale, N.J.: Erlbaum.

Frase, L. T. (1983). The UNIX Writer's Workbench software: Philosophy. *The Bell System Technical Journal* 62: 1883–90.

Goldberg, A., and D. Robson (1983). *SMALLTALK-80: The language and its implementation.* Reading, Mass.: Addison-Wesley.

Gingrich, P. S. (1983). The UNIX Writer's Workbench software: Results of a field study. *The Bell System Technical Journal* 62: 1909–21.

Kundera, M. (1980). *The book of laughter and forgetting,* trans. by M. Heim. New York: Penguin Education Books.

Levin, J. A. (1982). Microcomputers as interactive communication media: An interactive text interpreter. *The Quarterly Newsletter of the Laboratory of Comparative Human Cognition* 4: 34–36.

Levin, J. A., M. J. Boruta, and M. T. Vasconcellos (1982). Microcomputer-based environments for writing: A Writer's Assistant. In *Classroom computers and cognitive science,* edited by A. C. Wilkinson. New York: Academic Press.

Levin, J. A., and Y. Kareev (1980). Personal computers and education: The challenge to schools. CHIP report no. 98. La Jolla, Calif.: Center for Human Information Processing, University of California, San Diego.

MacDonald, N. H. (1983). The UNIX Writer's Workbench software: Rationale and design. *The Bell System Technical Journal* 62: 1891–908.

Michaels, S., C. B. Cazden, and B. Bruce (1985). Whose computer is it anyway? *Science for the People* 17: 36, 43–44.

Newkirk, T. (1985). Writing and programming: Two modes of composing. *Computers, Reading and Language Arts* 2, no. 2: 40–43.

Olds, H. F. (1985). A new generation of word processors. *Classroom Computer Learning,* March, 22–25.

Olds, H. F., J. L. Schwartz, and N. A. Willie (1980). *People and computers: Who teaches whom?* Newton, Mass.: Education Development Center.

Owens, P. (1984). Thinktank and Promptdoc. *Popular Computing,* April, 186–88.

Riel, M. (1983). Education and ecstasy: Computer chronicles of students writing together. *The Quarterly Newsletter of the Laboratory of Comparative Human Cognition* 5: 59–67.

Rosegrant, T., and R. Cooper (1963). *Talking screen textwriting program manual: A word processing program for children using a microcomputer and a speech synthesizer.* Glendale, Ariz.: Computer Adventures, Ltd.

Rubin, A., B. Bruce, and the QUILL Project (1984). *QUILL: Reading and writing with a microcomputer.* Reading education report no. 48. Champaign, Ill.: Center for the Study of Reading, University of Illinois at Urbana-Champaign. ED 240 516.

Rubin, A. (1980). Making stories, making sense. *Language Arts* 57: 285–98.

Sanders, J. S. (1985). Making the computer neuter. *The Computing Teacher,* April, 23–27.

Sharples, M. (1980). A computer written language lab. DAI working paper no. 134. Edinburgh, Scotland: Artificial Intelligence Department, University of Edinburgh.

Smith, B. (1982). Reflection and semantics in a procedural language. MIT Laboratory for Computer Science report MIT-TR-272. Cambridge, Mass.: MIT.

Sopp, N. P. (1984). Advanced language arts applications. In *Alaska's challenge: Computers in education—strategies and solutions,* edited by R. V. Dusseldorp. Anchorage: Alaska Association for Computers in Education (P.O. Box 4-652, Anchorage, AK 99502).

Taylor, R. P., ed. (1980). *The computer in the school: Tutor, tool, tutee.* New York: Teachers College Press.

Watt, D. (1983). Mind-mirroring software. *Popular Computing,* October, 65–66, 68.

Weizenbaum, J. (1976). *Computer power and human reason: From judgment to calculation.* San Francisco: W. H. Freeman.

Woods, W. A. (1970). Transition network grammars for natural language analysis. *Communications of the Association for Computing Machinery* 13: 591–606.

Young, M. (1984). Information technology and the sociology of education: Some preliminary thoughts. *British Journal of Sociology of Education* 5: 205–10.

Technology, Reading, and Writing

Lawrence T. Frase
AT&T Bell Laboratories

In recent years my work has moved increasingly toward computing, although my professional interests remain in the study of reading and writing. This newfound computer enthusiasm results, in part, from participation in the development of the UNIX Writer's Workbench™ software, a set of text-editing programs. No doubt working in an environment rich in technology has also drawn me to computing. But even more important is the wide public use of computers and the problems and potentials that this use creates for society. When society changes, it is difficult not to be interested.

In this paper, I explore the potential of computers to help or hinder work in the humanities. I hope this perspective will be useful to people who have not been involved professionally in software or hardware development. First, I summarize general conclusions about research and computer applications; after that, I discuss development and research that ought to be pursued; finally, I discuss general resources we need to do the job right. Discussion of those resources stresses that computer applications will progress faster if we build development environments (not just computer programs), create mechanisms for exchanging computer tools, train computer-knowledgeable people explicitly for educational applications, and ensure that research and theories address the concrete tasks that challenge our reading and writing skills.

Research in Instruction, Psychology, and Composition

Instruction

There are many ways to teach. Brown (1983) and Lesgold (1983), for instance, advocate carefully developed coaching systems, or "intelligent tutors." These systems are based on a theory of errors derived from

294

analysis of a student's mistakes, or on other features of the student's current state of performance. Tutorials based on calculations of current performance may have no predetermined sequence. Brown and Lesgold strive for elegance and completeness in instruction. But in reality, tutorial systems most often consist of canned frames of information to which the student must respond. This "drill-and-practice" teaching is viewed by many as a misuse of computer resources (Arons 1984); however, drill-and-practice has legitimate uses, especially for young students or for instruction where mastery of specific concepts or skills is critical.

Teaching is expensive. The Open University (United Kingdom), for instance, spends about one million dollars to develop each college course (Bjork 1984). Computer instruction, even drill-and-practice, is also expensive. An hour of instruction requires about one thousand hours of course development time. Clearly, less expensive alternatives are needed, and the intelligent tutor, adapting so readily to different students, might seem to be one. However, it is expensive to develop a model of student or teacher performance, and since not many intelligent tutors exist we can only guess at development costs for these systems. It is clear that development of expert systems in education will be labor-intensive, so we must continue to look for other alternatives.

Recently (Frase 1984) I argued that we have the capacity to develop a new class of computer tools, educational advisory systems, that supplement and go beyond traditional computer-assisted instruction. These advisory systems could provide information resources for students, with feedback contingent on student response, without strong management of student activities. A modest level of tutoring would be done in an advisory system; the major aim would be to encourage and support independent problem solving while reducing the need for detailed courseware development. The Writer's Workbench programs (Frase et al. 1985) are an example of an advisory system. They provide an expert assistant that can identify and comment on specific aspects of a student's writing; however, detailed solutions to problems are not given, only the resources to solve them. Advisory systems seem relevant for domains in which detailed control of student behavior is undesirable or difficult. Complex domains for which methods of teaching are not precise, like the teaching of composition, seem especially well suited to advisory systems, and there is evidence (Kulick 1985) that adults prefer and profit most from advisory systems rather than tutorial systems.

Another trend in applications of computers in the schools is toward their use as adjuncts to existing instruction (Chambers and Sprecher 1980). The aim is to increase the freedom of computer uses, helping teachers who have to fit technology into ongoing course activities.

In the extreme, we might transfer all written knowledge into electronic form and place it at students' disposal. Today, one can access automated dictionaries, thesauruses, and encyclopedias through computer networks. The use of such resources might be controlled, for different purposes, by overlays of teacher-guided activities. This "computer-managed instruction" is feasible to the extent that all appropriate resources for learning are available on-line. What students do today by running to libraries and taking field trips might well be done at a terminal. If a computer provides students one rich experience after another, who can criticize such page turning?

Psychology

Studies of expert and novice problem solving (see Larkin 1983 for a concise summary) have led to research methods for studying the skills of any domain. The methods developed for these studies seem as important as their specific findings: they create possibilities for exploring human performance in domains other than those studied. Advances have also been made in the study of reading, especially in regard to the important role of subject-matter knowledge (Glaser 1984) and higher-level strategies for the learning of new material (Kintsch and van Dijk 1978). In addition, much has been learned about the effects of adjunct aids on learning (Anderson and Biddle 1975) that can contribute to the development of effective ways to control student interactions with computers. The possibilities for controlled but flexible human-computer interactions should be explored using research from cognitive psychology as a basis.

Cognitive psychology has taught us to think of reading as a form of problem-solving activity supported by a set of procedures for processing information and a base of knowledge for relating the ideas that emerge from that processing. This problem-solving approach has recently been extended to the study of written composition, as described below.

Composition

Scardamalia and Bereiter (1986) reviewed areas in which research on writing has progressed significantly within the past decade. These areas of progress include the following:

1. The structure of subject matter (discourse analysis and story grammar)
2. Instructional techniques (student response techniques, such as the student-teacher conference and journal writing)
3. The composition process

To these areas I would add "written products"—the study of the products of composition (for instance, stylistics).

Several books have appeared that summarize major issues and the state of the art of computer applications in composition. A book by Wresch (1984) is among the best of them; it shows clearly how diverse today's computer developments are, and it shows the rich intellectual problems that technology poses for a particular domain of teaching. (See also Bridwell, Nancarrow, and Ross 1984.) The really interesting questions begin to appear only when one tries to apply technology to a specific task.

Much research has been devoted to the process of composition. Models of how documentation is written (Frase, Keenan, and Dever 1980) suggest broad areas for the application of computer aids. In addition, cognitive models of the writing process (Hayes and Flower 1980) specify detailed activities of writing that might profit from computer support. Models like these can help build instructional procedures (Flower 1981). Along with work on the structure of texts, representation of knowledge (Beaugrande 1980, Kintsch and van Dijk 1978), and discourse theory (Cooper 1983, Kinneavy 1971), the work on cognitive processes in writing circumscribes the areas of knowledge we need to make the best use of computers. The problem is how to coordinate this knowledge with new technology, which I explore in the next section.

Issues in Computing

This section focuses on the creation of new computer tools, especially how those tools should be implemented in the classroom. Today's educational spirit recognizes a new set of imperatives. Perhaps for the better, we are trying to break the chains of drill-and-practice as a primary method of instruction. And we have new theories of learning to complement our desire to go beyond those old methods of instruction. Through technology we have the capability to educate, not just train; to encourage creativity and discovery, not just memorization; to teach communication, not just mimicry. Many people believe that we have the technology to teach almost anything in any way we want. They may be right.

In an excellent paper, Reddy (1983) summarized the memory, micro-processor, and output technologies that exist or will be developed in the next ten years. Whereas today's schools are tied primarily to small 8-bit machines, he conjectures that by 1990 the state of the art will include a 100-mips (millions of instructions per second) processor, a megabyte of memory, and four megabytes of read-only memory, all in a package of less than 10 cubic inches—at an affordable price. Reddy's review of future output and input devices is equally optimistic. If anything, the pace of development seems to be running ahead of his projections. The question is not whether we will have adequate technology but how we should use it.

If we have the technology, do we have the understanding needed to apply that technology? Certainly not enough of it. We have only a dim understanding of what to use computers for, how best to use them, and the consequences of their use. For instance, detailed analyses of the everyday reading and writing tasks to which computers might be applied are just now beginning. So we only weakly perceive what human skills and activities technology might best aid. Furthermore, we are only beginning to think about domain-specific languages that will help us transfer human knowledge and skill into computer programs: for example, to put rhetorical knowledge into algorithms and heuristic procedures that can assist teachers and student writers in finding errors in a composition.

Our attempts to program computers will force on us a clearer understanding of subject matter, but for the present our computer use seems driven more by immediate needs, and a good deal of media hype, than by reasoned debate. We have no educational equivalent of the Japanese Ministry of International Trade and Industry's Fifth Generation project, i.e., a concrete plan to exploit technology to the fullest. Yet, in spite of weaknesses in our understanding, programmers continue to invent a variety of computer aids even for such complex activities as medical diagnosis and writing.

The joy of invention, in this early stage of electronic technology, may be a dangerous seduction for education. The educational community lacks prerequisites necessary for producing, deploying, and assimilating inventions in an orderly and efficient way. A laissez-faire attitude in commercial educational software development has led to uncoordinated efforts and poor-quality products. For instance, in mathematics only 30 percent of commercially available software meets minimal standards of acceptability (Komoski 1985). In short, we are creating pieces of a technological puzzle that tomorrow will fit together poorly, if at all. We need a rational foundation for future educational tool development. We can build such a foundation even though we cannot foresee tomorrow's educational problems. One aim of the rest of this paper is to provide a guideline for this foundation.

Concepts to Clarify Computer Use

A recent conference on computers and writing, held at the Bank Street College of Education in New York City (Pea and Kurland 1984), showed how far we have come in our thinking from the simple conception of a student alone with a computer. A major theme emerging from that conference was that computer applications are really events within an organizational and social context; consequently, systems thinking is likely to produce the most effective, educationally useful, and durable innovations. What emerged in that conference was not a focus on specific applications but rather a set of concepts to deal with the relations among elements in various technological scenarios. One of these concepts was "symbiosis."

Symbiosis

"Symbiosis" summarizes the notion that computers are more useful if a thinking person uses them, and thinking people are more useful if a computer supports them. The idea is that we get more mileage out of simple computer tools if we use them to do only some things that humans do (not that they could do everything humans can), namely, components of everyday tasks that are tedious for humans. Symbiosis suggests that one might have an interactive program that completes much of a task, then asks for human input, which then allows the computer to resume completion of the task. In turn, a human would work on a complex task, like writing, and request computer help only when needed. In this way, humans might assume responsibility for some tasks, computers for others. Close coupling of human and computer, with each providing data or analysis where appropriate, produces a closer working of human and machine than we often see today. This scenario suggests an intimate future between humans and machines.

Thinking through the components of reading or writing tasks in which symbiotic relations would be especially useful will help us define requirements for new programs and in turn lead away from naive attempts to make the computer a complete and flawless tutor. The symbiotic relation between people and computers will change the way people work and also increase productivity.

Compatibility

Another concept that emerged in the Bank Street conference was "compatibility." Compatibility is an important concept relating primarily to computer software and hardware. There are two kinds of compatibility: horizontal and vertical. Both are desirable.

Horizontal compatibility. Horizontal compatibility refers to the transferability of resources across people and places at a particular time. For instance, development of a new word-processing program might be done in such a way that the program can run on several different machines, or software developments in one school might be done so that they are consistent and easily transferred (electronically) to other schools in a school district. Horizontal compatibility thus involves various instances of compatibility that are concentrated at one point in time. The main point is the potential for resource sharing, for instance, across equipment, schools, states, or other boundaries.

Vertical compatibility. In contrast to horizontal compatibility, vertical compatibility reaches across time. For instance, hardware designed today should fit with hardware to be designed tomorrow, or a word-processing program developed today should be seen as only one part of a larger text-managing system for tomorrow. The person who slowly acquires the separate parts of a complex system over a period of time can, if the parts are vertically compatible, integrate the new parts with the old easily when new parts become available. Vertical compatibility is recognized as an important consideration in the design of hardware and software, especially by administrators who need to keep their systems current. It is also an argument for standards in the development of educational technology.

Adaptability

"Adaptability" was another concept to emerge from the Bank Street conference. Adaptability reflects the capacity of a system to assume a form appropriate to a particular person or environment. For instance, a program might analyze data and produce words for one audience; for another audience it might produce a graphic summary of the same data. Thus, the system would deliver alternate representations of information for different user populations. For example, one form of adaptability, used in the Writer's Workbench editing programs, allows the user to alter the form or content of program outputs by adding qualifiers to the program command. For example, when a user types a command to get editorial advice about a text, the program normally gives detailed explanations. However, if the user follows the command with an "-s," only the most relevant summary advice is given. The short output is enough for seasoned program users.

The concept of adaptability suggests that computer tools should be modifiable by the user, or should modify themselves to adapt to different uses. Adaptability has useful implications for research and development. For instance, if we believe that programs should be suitable for different audiences, then we should do research on how to define those audiences. Having solved that problem, we then face the problem of changing local program features to correspond to those audience characteristics. General human characteristics seem a poor bet for an adaptive focus; for instance, there are serious doubts about the usefulness of work on aptitude-treatment interactions. Suppes (1979) concluded that we have not yet shown that we can systematically produce aptitude-treatment effects, and the extensive treatment of aptitude-treatment interactions by Cronbach and Snow (1977) supports his conclusion. If this conclusion is correct, we should look elsewhere for a rationale for computer-aided instruction.

The rest of this section emphasizes that computers must be congenial, unobtrusive companions in the classroom or home. My comments are based on what seemed to me a consensus in several meetings in which I have participated, including a recent conference held at Harvard University (Schwartz 1985) and two earlier ones (Lesgold and Reif 1983, Pea and Kurland 1984).

Contextual Appropriateness

One simple, but sometimes ignored, implementation concept, "contextual appropriateness," asserts that computer tools only belong where they are wanted or needed. In other words, some thought should go into the places computers are sent and to the tasks to which they are applied. One-dimensional thinking is not appropriate here—the aim is to anticipate the effects of technology on many classroom components.

Contextual appropriateness includes how computers fit within the school, home, and community. A wide range of issues concerning teacher and parent training, appropriate age or grade for introducing computers, community resources, and so forth emerge from pursuing questions of context. Contextual appropriateness is thus a rich and useful criterion for educational computer applications.

Usability

Usability has two dimensions. The first is friendliness, which simply means that a computer system should be easy to use for whatever purpose people use it. Friendliness is especially important, since technology is reaching out to new populations, for instance, young children and older adults.

The second dimension of usability is self-explanation: we can demand that a computer carry with it the resources to explain itself at whatever level the user needs information. This implies an interactive information system that can explain commands on demand or that can guide the novice to specific actions using menus or whatever representation is most appropriate.

These two dimensions of usability—friendliness and self-explanation— are important for classroom implementations because they keep the effort of introducing new technology to a minimum for administrators, teachers, and students.

Flexibility

Flexibility concerns how computers might best be used in the classroom. At one extreme, a computer might be used for one purpose, for instance, to run complex problems in mathematics classes. At the other extreme, a computer might be an enigma to be understood, an example of technology to be studied as an oddity of culture or a way of teaching computer literacy.

The rational alternative is to treat technology flexibly, making it available for different uses at different times, so that it tends to be seen as a pervasive tool, one that can be used for mathematics, for writing, for graphic arts, for planning activities, and so on. In addition, however, there should be no coercion to use this technology—there are times when it is inappropriate.

If we apply the concepts above as a test of the current state of the art, we see that education has a long way to go before it becomes comfortable with technology. Our best course is to treat the computer as a powerful, but not dominant, addition to our bag of educational tools. To make the most of this new tool we need to develop supporting resources, which I discuss in the next section.

Development and Research Needs

Computing technology offers many research opportunities. Lepper (1985) has made an eloquent appeal for psychologists to study computing before it has passed them by. But research proposals often just rephrase old questions. An entirely new development and research effort is needed to support the exchange of information across the boundaries of the humanities, science, and engineering.

It is time that we let practice stimulate the development of theory, rather than expecting theory to influence practice. Technology will no doubt introduce constraints that shape the questions we ask. A major contribution of computing technology could be to make the consequences of our conjectures and theories concrete and so challenge us with its bald empiricism. Already we see a move away from abstract general theories of cognitive performance to those that embody elements of performance in everyday tasks (expert systems, in particular).

Below I list development and research activities needed to advance the practical applications of computers to reading and writing tasks.

Tools

Many people have discussed the potential of computers for reading and writing. A review of current tools can be found in Collins (1983), along with suggestions for how computers might be used to shape student learning. A review of work done on the Writer's Workbench system is in Frase et al. (1985). A fascinating paper by Weyer (1982) describes in detail how a "responsive book" might interact with human search behaviors. In addition, Milic (1981, 1982) has discussed how text-analysis programs can be used to study various qualities of literature, while a study by Pollard-Gott and Frase (1985) shows that stylistic analysis can be used to discriminate between students with different writing experience. Burton (1981) has reviewed work on automated concordances and indexes.

We seem well on the road to moving the humanities, and education, into computing. To do that most effectively we need information and resources that we do not now have. Chief among these I would include the need for systematic record keeping—tracking the consequences of computer use through automated course memories and perhaps personal records that students keep throughout their lives. Without this information we cannot know whether our tools succeed or fail.

Tasks

We need more detailed and practical descriptions of the tasks that people perform. Task descriptions are necessary for designing new products for educational or other markets. Certainly we need theory, but if theory is not translated into practice it has no consequence. Hence, we need to develop concepts and tools that are relevant to the tasks that we want to support, and this requires detailed analysis of performance in various domains of human activity. I have in mind here the level of detail involved in developing an expert-knowledge–based system (Hayes-Roth, Waterman, and Lenat 1983). Detailed cognitive-task description might be the most important contribution that psychology could make today.

Concepts

Computer technology forces us to recognize a new imperative: to be clear, precise, and accurate. Many ideas that once seemed so complex as to escape empirical testing are now testable using computers. A general test of whether an idea is workable is whether it can be realized as a computer program; if it can't be expressed in a rigorous form (i.e., a program that runs on a computer), then there is something unclear about the idea that probably will not communicate with humans, either. Although this is an extreme form of the imperative, it is not extreme to suggest that the computer has opened new possibilities for communication among different disciplines. The computer can be a common playground, encouraging the meeting of different disciplines so that each begins to understand and appreciate the others' concepts. As work on expert systems shows, subject-matter experts become the focus for development of computer problem-solving systems. It couldn't be otherwise, since it is their knowledge that it is to be described and incorporated into programs. If the use of computers is to advance in the humanities, members of the profession will necessarily become the hub around which development occurs.

Social Contexts

We should not study just what it is that people like or do not like about interactions with computers, or whether computer use improves performance, because computers might facilitate a wide range of behaviors, for instance, social interaction. It is well known that people act differently in the presence of others than when they are alone. This social effect can work to improve or deteriorate human performance, depending on the task and person. There is some evidence (Frase et al. 1985) that using a computer helps overcome embarrassment at making mistakes (the computer, after all, is not a person). In any case, these social effects should be researched.

Another type of social facilitation occurs when people communicate with each other over networks. Opportunities to communicate with children in other countries, for instance, stimulate a student's writing, as shown by Levin's (1982) exemplary work with message systems at the grade-school level, in which students in California exchanged messages with students in Alaska.

Styles of communication, and their effects on people's accomplishments, should be studied. Computer mail, for instance, might increase our ability to contact people, but the level of contact may be brief and certainly less personal than face-to-face contact. Peer tutoring, often an effective method of instruction, could be done easily and on a large scale over computer networks.

Other Resource Needs

More effort should be put into the careful planning of educational technology. Industry has developed many tools and techniques for planning computer systems. Educators should explore links with business and industry to make use of this computer expertise.

Training

Colleges and universities should begin to give in-depth computer training to students in all disciplines, not only to teach computer literacy but to make students effective users and even inventors of computer tools.

Shared Environments

Charp (1978) lists the following qualities of computer-assisted instruction as fundamental concerns of educators: reliability, accessibility, economy, ease of use, compatibility of systems, and available software. One way of achieving these qualities is to establish shared-development environments from which inventions can propagate to other similar environments. A start has been made in this direction with the wide use of the UNIX operating system (Kernighan and Mashey 1979) by educational institutions. Efforts to standardize environments in our schools should be supported by a broad coordination of educational resources.

Data Bases

We have a critical need to move information from paper to electronic form. Many resources in the humanities—literary classics and so forth—are not now on-line. Much high-quality research, including studies of changes in literacy demands across the ages, has resulted from the availability of a corpus of literary works in electronic form.

A new range of jobs, with associated training needs, is likely to arise as we begin to recognize the need to enter, code, and classify information that is not now stored electronically.

Software

We need good educational software, but premature concentration on highly structured tutorial packages will create software shackles that will be difficult to discard later. A more reasonable approach is to develop tools, such as course-authoring systems or educational advisory systems, which can be used in many different ways for many different ends.

Disciplines

Software can be written by individuals, but proper planning and execution of software projects requires the cooperation of people from several disciplines. Development of popular word-processing and text-editing software invariably has involved a variety of individuals. Products such as the Bank Street Writer have originated not within the engineering community but within the teaching community, where the need for such software was first expressed. We need to encourage team development efforts focused on solving priority educational problems.

Conclusions

Computing in the humanities has a bright future. Many resources exist; others must be developed and nurtured. I have tried to cover these resources and needs in this paper.

Let me summarize by reviewing the major concerns of our professions and how technology has addressed them. In these concerns I see a major shift in the perception of researchers and teachers:

1. Dissatisfaction with empirical research as a guide for the improvement of practice

2. A shift away from general behavior and learning theory toward domain-specific and task-specific performance

3. Concern that educational resources be shared effectively

4. Concern for the ability of different disciplines to understand, appreciate, and communicate with each other

5. Concern for nonverbal modes of representing and transmitting information

6. Concern that academic work have functional consequences

Careful use and study of computers in the humanities would address most of the above concerns. Serious computer use, as defined by the issues that this paper recommends be addressed, would have the following effects: shared resources, such as programs and data; common languages for transmitting knowledge across domains (imposed by the languages and operating systems of the computers used); and common mechanisms for educational sharing and innovation (such as networks and electronic mail facilities). Furthermore, we would be forced to be explicit about what we know in order to program it, and this would have favorable effects on our ability to test and communicate our knowledge to others. Finally, our work would become undeniably functional if coupled with good applications software. To do this, we don't need a research agenda as much as a development agenda. We need to step back from haphazard computer acquisitions and do systematic systems planning.

All that I have said entails an important social imperative. People in the humanities have an obligation to understand, use, and create new applications for computers. Only in this way will computers evolve to satisfy more than limited industrial and business needs.

References

Anderson, R. C., and W. B. Biddle (1975). On asking people questions about what they are reading. In *The psychology of learning and motivation*, Vol. 9, edited by G. H. Bower. New York: Academic Press.

Arons, A. B. (1984). Computer-based instructional dialogs in science courses. *Science* 224: 1051–56.

Beaugrande, R. de (1980). *Text, discourse, and process.* Norwood, N.J.: Ablex.

Bjork, A. (1984). Computer futures for education. *Creative Computing* 10 (November): 178–80.

Bridwell, L. S., P. R. Nancarrow, and D. Ross (1984). The writing process and the writing machine: Current research on word processors relevant to the teaching of composition. In *New directions in composition research,* edited by R. Beach and L. S. Bridwell. New York: Guilford.

Brown, J. S. (1983). Learning by doing revisited for electronic learning environments. In *The future of electronic learning,* edited by M. A. White. Hillsdale, N.J.: Erlbaum.

Burton, D. M. (1981). Automated concordances and work indexes: The process, the programs, and the products. *Computers and the Humanities* 15: 139–54.

Chambers, J. A., and J. W. Sprecher (1980). Computer assisted instruction: Current trends and critical issues. *Communications of the ACM* 23: 332–42.

Charp, S. (1978). Futures: Where will computer-assisted instruction (CAI) be in 1990? *Educational Technology* 18: 62.

Collins, A. (1983). Learning to read and write with personal computers. (Unpublished paper.) Cambridge, Mass.: Bolt, Beranek and Newman.

Cooper, C. R. (1983). Procedures for describing written texts. In *Research on writing: Principles and methods,* edited by P. Mosenthal, L. Tamor, and S. A. Walmsley. New York: Longman.

Cronbach, L. J., and R. E. Snow (1977). *Aptitudes and instructional methods: A handbook for research on interactions.* New York: Irvington Publishers.

Flower, L. (1981). *Problem-solving strategies for writing.* New York: Harcourt Brace Jovanovich.

Frase, L. T. (1984). Knowledge, information, and action: Requirements for automated writing instruction. *Journal of Computer-Based Instruction* 11: 55–59.

Frase, L. T., S. A. Keenan, and J. J. Dever (1980). Human performance in computer-aided writing and documentation. In *Processing of visual language,* Vol. 2, edited by P. A. Kolser, M. E. Wrolstad, and H. Bouma. New York: Plenum.

Frase, L. T., K. E. Kiefer, C. R. Smith, and M. L. Fox (1985). Theory and practice in computer aided composition. In *The acquisition of written language: Revision and response,* edited by S. W. Freedman. Norwood, N.J.: Ablex.

Glaser, R. (1984). Education and thinking: The role of knowledge. *American Psychologist* 39: 93–104.

Hayes, J., and L. Flower (1980). Identifying the organization of writing processes. In *Cognitive processes in writing,* edited by L. W. Gregg and E. R. Steinberg. Hillsdale, N.J.: Erlbaum.

Hayes-Roth, F., D. A. Waterman, and D. B. Lenat, eds. (1983). *Building expert systems.* Reading, Mass.: Addison-Wesley.

Kernighan, B. W., and J. R. Mashey (1979). The UNIX programming environment. *Software—Practice and Experience* 9: 1–15.

Kinneavy, J. L. (1971). *A theory of discourse: The aims of discourse.* New York: W. W. Norton & Co.

Kintsch, W., and T. A. van Dijk (1978). Toward a model of text comprehension and production. *Psychological Review* 85: 363–94.

Komoski, P. K. (1985). An analysis of elementary mathematics software produced between 1981 and 1984. Has it improved? A symposium presentation at the annual meeting of the American Educational Research Association.

Kulick, J. A. (1985). Consistencies in findings on computer-based education. A symposium presentation at the annual meeting of the American Educational Research Association.

Larkin, J. H. (1983). The new science education. In *Computers in education: Realizing the potential,* edited by A. M. Lesgold and F. Reif. Washington, D. C.: U.S. Government Printing Office.

Lepper, M. R. (1985). Microcomputers in education: Motivational and social issues. *American Psychologist* 40: 1–18.

Lesgold, A. M. (1983). Paradigms for computer-based education. In *Computers in education: Realizing the potential,* edited by A. M. Lesgold and F. Reif. Washington, D.C.: U.S. Government Printing Office.

Lesgold, A. M., and F. Reif, chairs (1983). *Computers in education: Report of a research conference held November 20–24, 1982, Pittsburgh, PA.* Washington, D.C.: U.S. Government Printing Office.

Levin, J. A. (1982). Microcomputer communication networks for education. *The Quarterly Newsletter of the Laboratory of Comparative Human Cognition* 4, no. 2. La Jolla, Calif.: University of California, San Diego.

Milic, L. T. (1981). Stylistics + computers = pattern stylistics. *Perspectives in Computing* 1: 4–11.

——— (1982). The annals of computing: Stylistics. *Computers and the Humanities* 16: 19–24.

Pea, R. D., and E. M. Kurland (1984). *Toward cognitive technologies for writing.* (Final report of the workshop "Applying Cognitive Science to Cognitive Technologies for Writing Development.") New York: Bank Street College of Education.

Pollard-Gott, L., and L. T. Frase (1985). Flexibility in writing style: A new discourse-level cloze test. *Written Communication* 2: 107–27.

Reddy, R. (1983). Technologies for learning. In *Computers in education: Realizing the potential,* edited by A. M. Lesgold and F. Reif. Washington, D.C.: U.S. Government Printing Office.

Scardamalia, M., and C. Bereiter (1986). Research on written composition. In *Handbook of research on teaching,* 3d ed., edited by M. C. Wittrock, 778–803.

Schwartz, J. L., chair (1985). Microprocessors and expert systems: Can it be either or should it be both? Paper presented at the Conference of the Educational Technology Center. Harvard University, January 11–12.

Suppes, P. (1979). Current trends in computer-assisted instruction. In *Advances in computers,* Vol. 18, edited by M. C. Yovits. New York: Academic Press.

Weyer, S. A. (1982). The design of a dynamic book for information search. *International Journal of Man-Machine Studies* 17: 87–107.

Wresch, W., ed. (1984). *The computer in composition instruction.* Urbana, Ill.: National Council of Teachers of English. ED 247 602.

Commentary

Johanna DeStefano
Ohio State University

Let me begin my discussion of these two papers by paraphrasing Joshua Fishman's justly famous question characterizing the field of sociolinguistics as being the study of "What do we say to whom when and how?" To frame research questions, I ask, "What do we need or want to know about whom and how?" And I could add, "All to what end?" My rather generalized answer to that question is I think it crucial to learn how to enhance students' communicative competence. That competence includes, in this society, both oral and written language abilities, with a strong emphasis on literacy.

Within this framework of communicative competence is placed the question "What do we need to know about whom?" What do we need to know in order to help students become more competent? And how can we go about doing that? I offer as a major area of research concern those students who persistently and pervasively don't do well in our schools in achieving some of these competencies. They are the children who will hit a dead end in school and possibly in life, children who will be marginally literate at best and illiterate at worst. And these students are often members of groups who are linguistically and culturally different. They seem to be the ones at most risk in learning to control the forms of communication demanded by the society. They tend to be, in disproportionate numbers, inner-city children, whether black or Appalachian or other minority group—children whose culture may be based more on spoken words than on written words. And the children of the poor.

Whether we live low-tech lives or high-tech lives, these children have been with us and will continue to be with us. I can't foresee any sure end to the problems we face as researchers in helping educators increase the communicative competence of these children. It is in this spirit of inquiry, of feeling impelled by a pervasive problem, that I approached these two papers and looked for potential applications of the technology to the improvement of these students' educational possibilities. I am suggesting

309

a problem-driven approach to the use of the technology, but one which counts on what Frase calls the symbiotic nature of new computers.

Perhaps one of the most important characteristics of the computer in this sense—as an educational tool to help disadvantaged students achieve a level of communicative competence they rarely had before—is its symbol-manipulation ability, as Bruce puts it. It seems to me that the computer as a language device—one which can interact even now—must be used in some way to engage these students in language-use situations ultimately leading toward the competence deemed necessary by society.

For example, research into language use by children with their peers often shows them to be much more competent than is demonstrated during their interactions with teachers. Thus, in some way the teacher or the interactional situation involving the adult authority figure inhibits the use of a wide range of communicative abilities. It may also preclude the development of other types of competence. Could the computer serve as an interactive partner for these children, a patient yet challenging language manipulator which could be programmed to better match their discourse styles?

Here I mean not the drill-and-practice that both Bruce and Frase simply state we must get beyond. What I am talking about is what Frase calls the educational advisory system, in which there is not strong management of the tasks but rather information and feedback to the student using the system. Bruce also envisions the computer as tutor, tool, and tutee all rolled into one, playing whichever interactive role is needed at the moment. Could such a system duplicate in a sense an adult who would not use language largely for control and regulation (i.e., management) but, as Wells (1981) describes the needed interaction, "behave" in such a manner as to engage in conversation with children, simultaneously engaging their communicative competence by being slightly ahead of their understanding? In other words, could a computer, partially through the use of synthetic speech, help provide the communicative experiences that children from at-risk groups may need for better school success?

I feel strongly that such use of computers could be an extremely promising research direction, since the students who often fail to learn to read, or who don't gain control over a set of registers which includes forms of so-called standard English, are people who use language in intense face-to-face interaction and to manipulate, establish, and maintain control over others. It could be that they would well appreciate the computer system's ability to manipulate symbols and language, and would react positively to interaction with a machine. We need to find this out, and I think we have at least begun, based on some of the detail presented in the two papers.

However, it has been suggested by researchers such as Mitchell-Kernan and Kernan (1977) that children in high-risk groups use language often as a vehicle for social meaning, and use the negotiation of relationships as the "content" of the message. When will computer systems in education have the qualities that allow for personal, contextualized uses of language (i.e., symbiotic capability, compatibility with and adaptability to the culturally different—along with appropriateness, usability, flexibility, and alternative-presentation abilities) and then expand beyond that into the less personal, decontextualized uses which are part of communicative competence? It doesn't seem computer systems have those qualities now, since they have been characterized as forcing us to be clear, precise, and accurate. This means that currently we have to essentially conform to their logic, and that we "give" much more in our interaction with them.

It seems that both Bruce and Frase give at least some indication of the possibilities for applying computers to the persistent educational problem of children who fail. But it also seems we have our work cut out for us in the sense that not only will computer systems have to grow in sophisticated interactional abilities and become more user-friendly, but we researchers will also have to work with computer scientists in devising the systems which could achieve the symbiotic effects we may need; combine the roles of the computer as tutor, tool, and tutee all into one; and help us conduct the research we need to do to determine a rational use of the tool. In a sense, to quote Pogo, "We are faced with overwhelming opportunities," thanks largely to the capabilities of the "extender of knowledge," as Wilson Dizard refers to the computer.

References

Dizard, W. P. (1985). *The coming information age: An overview of technology, economics, and politics.* 2d ed. New York: Longman.

Mitchell-Kernan, C., and K. Kernan (1977). Pragmatics of directive choice among children. In *Child discourse,* edited by S. Ervin-Tripp and C. Mitchell-Kernan, 189–208. New York: Academic Press.

Wells, G. (1981). *Learning through interaction: The study of language development.* New York: Cambridge University Press.

Commentary

Edmund J. Farrell
University of Texas at Austin

My comments will be a bit polemical, purposefully so, but they should not be interpreted as being adversely critical of the Bruce or Frase papers. Both of these papers strike me as being very even-handed, very temperate in their descriptions of what computers and computing systems or information systems are capable of at present and what they may be capable of in the near future.

Further, both papers are cautionary in tone about our not knowing as yet what the long-range effects of computers and word processors will be on language learning, including the acts of reading and writing. Finally, both papers call for the participation of persons outside the computer industry—users and humanists—in determining the direction that computers will take in the future.

Much of what I have to say argues for research to substantiate the computer's merit or lack of merit. In the absence of that research, I am willing to allow my remarks to stand as opinion—opinion that I would like to believe is somewhat informed. Nevertheless, not for a moment do I wish to imply that I am a computer expert. I am not. I am rather a person increasingly troubled by the effects that the computer is having on him as a scholar and as a citizen.

In preparation for this conference and for my part in it, over a year ago I began gathering materials on the current uses of the computer in American society, including the computer's present and potential uses in education. The more information I gathered and read carefully, the more concerned—if not convinced—I became that the computer is having at present a detrimental effect on writing, on reading, and on scholarship; further, I infer from my reading that the computer's deleterious effects will increase rather than wane unless scholars soon take strong steps to counteract those effects.

Before I proceed, permit me to insist that I am not a neo-Luddite desirous of smashing mainframes and microcomputers and/or replacing them with manual labor. Just as I would render unto Caesar that which is Caesar's, I am willing to render unto the computer that which is the computer's. I am pleased that the computer is helping kindergarten and first-grade students to read and write (ETS 1984); that it has made revision a next-to-painless process; that it can be programmed to make congenitally poor spellers appear to be in command of *sought, rot,* and *accommodate;* that it can be employed for international networking among students, an activity which could with time appreciably lessen the possibility of nuclear war. I am grateful to the computer for programming within seconds my airplane ticket to Chicago, for monitoring the flight and, with it, helping assure the safety of the aircraft which transported me here. I share Bruce's and Frase's visions of the computer as being central to innovate curricula, producing curricula in which sophisticated symbolic systems replace isolated drill exercises or tutorial systems.

But just as I am unwilling to render unto Caesar that which is not Caesar's, I am unwilling to concede to the computer responsibilities which it should not possess. At present the computer is, I believe, impeding scholarship as much as it is abetting it. I work with graduate students who increasingly are finding it impossible to review the literature for doctoral dissertations. With neither the time nor the money to review original source documents, they are being driven to do abstracts of abstracts. I need not tell those in this audience that an abstract distorts data. My doctoral dissertation was 395 pages; my abstract of that document was 3-1/2 pages. Something obviously gave, and what gave were data that had furnished flesh and texture and individuality to the frail skeleton left by the abstract. Most professors in even the least of the lesser colleges and universities are being told nowadays to publish or perish. To the detriment of scholarship, most are electing to do the former, with the consequence that both shoddy and sound work is being transmitted via computer, with discrimination between the two being left to the judgment of the reader, who, if he or she is like me, feels crushed by what seems to be a continuing onslaught of information, little of it being very important, even less of it truly wise.

Because I am deluged with periodical print about the status of English in its myriad linguistic forms, I seem to have little time to read works of the imagination, works that initially attracted me to the profession. Moreover, I spend far too much time each week sorting through fourth-class computer-generated mail, mail that attempts to be personable, even chummy (one rule of thumb: any letter that begins "Dear Edmund" is cast away immediately; even my mother didn't call me *Edmund*). If I find it difficult to wade through junk mail, Congress-people find it even more difficult:

The development in the 1970s of computerized direct mail, for example, may have given congressmen a powerful new tool with which to raise money, but it also gave interest groups a powerful new tool with which to bury Congress in trivia. In 1972 members of the House received 14.6 million pieces of mail; last year the figure was 161 million, and this year mail is running at a rate of 200 million pieces. That comes to 459,770 pieces of mail for each representative. On a single day this fall Tip O'Neill, the speaker of the House, received *five million* pieces. One staff aide, who worked for Hubert Humphrey in the 1960s and now works for one of the Senate's lesser-known members, recalls, "During the height of the debate on the Civil Rights Act of 1964, Humphrey got 3,000 letters. This was considered astonishing. Now we can get 3,000 letters a day even when there's nothing going on."

Most of the letters are sparked by mass-mailing campaigns made possible by computers and targeted address lists. . . . (Easterbrook 1984, p. 65)

In an article in *The Atlantic,* Jacques Barzun argued that scholarship was coming between citizens and their direct apprehension and appreciation of culture—art, music, dance, literature. Barzun expressed his belief that most individuals are highly intimidated by scholarship: they seem to believe that they must first do considerable scholarly background reading before they are justified in enjoying a painting, a novel, a sonata, or a ballet. The consequence of this belief is that fewer people are willing to risk, sans homework, enjoyment of works of art. Because of the ever-mounting glut of secondary-source materials, Barzun predicts that the present scholarly systems of the humanities and of the social sciences will inevitably collapse of their own weight. These systems, which modeled themselves after those of the sciences, lack the latter's empirical methodology, with the result that one can find no final word on any cultural phenomenon (Barzun 1984). In my own library, I have more works about Faulkner than works by Faulkner, more critical commentaries on Hemingway than novels by that gentleman, more varied perceptions on *The Scarlet Letter* than Hawthorne ever dreamed possible. And the computer only heightens the torrential flow of secondary-source information.

Clearly, I sympathize with Barzun: I do not believe the rush of scholarly information can continue unabated without readers eventually throwing up their hands and refusing to indulge the systems further. Without clear controls being employed to govern the quantity and quality of information being transmitted by the computer, scholarship in both the humanities and the social sciences will perforce bog down within a few years. Determination of who will exert that control and in what ways is a matter for careful deliberation within each branch of knowledge outside the sciences.

Let me exert one final caution about the computer, or rather about the word processor. An increasing number of writers are expressing concern about the harmful effects on substance and style that the word processor may be having. Anthony Burgess (1985) has warned that the word processor separates writers from their ears:

> Writers write well only when they listen to what they are writing— either on magnetic tape or in the auditorium set silently in their skulls. But more and more writers—not only of pseudoliterature but of political speeches—ignore the claims of the voice and ear.
>
> I think that, with the increasing use of the word processor, the separation of the word as sound from the word as visual symbol is likely to grow. The magical reality has become a set of signs glowing on a screen: this takes precedence over any possible auditory significance. The speed with which words can be set down with such an apparatus (as also with the electric typewriter), the total lack of muscular effort involved—these turn writing into a curiously non-physical activity, in which there is no manual analogue to the process of breathing out, using the tongue, lips, and teeth, and accepting language as a bodily exercise that expends energy.
>
> What is wrong with most writing today is its flaccidity, its lack of pleasure in the manipulation of sounds and pauses. The written word is becoming inert. One dreads to think what it will be like in 2020. (p. 28)

Edsger W. Dijkstra, one of the world's foremost computer programmers, shares Mr. Burgess's distrust of the word processor as an instrument at which to compose. In a keynote address delivered last November to fellow computer experts, Dijkstra, who himself writes longhand, made the following observations:

> As a referee I have to judge many manuscripts, and the ones prepared on word-processors are invariably the worst, qua printing quality, or qua layout, or qua style, notation, and contents. The proposed style of composing—write first, improve later—rarely leads to a text from which all ill-considered turns have been weeded out. Finally, the suggestions that the proposed style of composing itera-tively would save time is an obvious and blatant lie. And yet the equipment is sold by the millions.

I repeat: There is much about the computer for which I am thankful; much about the computer which I find pedagogically promising; and much about the computer and its handmaiden, the word processor, which I find deeply troublesome. At this point, rather than offer huzzahs to our newest vehicle for orchestrating human communication, I offer only the sound of one hand clapping.

References

Barzun, J. (1984). Scholarship versus culture. *The Atlantic,* November, 93–104.

Burgess, A. (1985). The future of the language. *Harper's Magazine,* January, 270:28.

Dijkstra, E. W. (1984). The threats to computing science. Unpublished keynote address at the Association for Computing Machinery South Regional Conference, November 16–18, Austin, Texas.

Easterbrook, G. (1984). What's wrong with congress? *The Atlantic,* December, 57–84.

Educational Testing Service (1984). *The ETS evaluation of writing to read.* Executive summary. Princeton, N.J.: Educational Testing Service.

VI Combining Process and Product Orientations in English and Reading

Introduction

Do we stress process or product in teaching the language arts? For all of our recent dialogue on the process of composing, the process of comprehending, and the process of thinking, teachers continue to be held accountable for developing specific skills.

Jane Hansen describes how with colleagues at the University of New Hampshire she developed ways of studying how pupils grow in the processes and skills of reading and writing. Significantly, in light of discussion at this seminar on enlisting teachers in defining and interpreting studies, her inquiry led her into shared classroom experiences.

Peter Johnston then argues cogently that a balance between process and content in the language arts classroom cannot be achieved as long as we use product measures to asses process teaching.

Jerome Harste and David Pearson extend the discussion of collaborative teaching and collaborative researching and offer a mandate for change, an appropriate finale to the consideration of discrete issues in research.

Organizing Student Learning: Teachers Teach What and How

Jane Hansen
University of New Hampshire

Organization. Management. Control. The writing-process approach to composition scares many university professors, principals, and teachers, because we fear we will lose our authority. Classrooms organized around learners rather than teachers can appear unorganized, but they have an internal structure analogous to the roles of an endoskeleton. The writers support each other, protect each other against nonproductive forces, and encourage each other's goals.

The interactive classroom is most easily organized by structured teachers. These teachers deliver information as they did in their product-oriented classrooms, but they spend less time telling the students what to do and more time helping them realize options for decisions about their work. They want their students to learn as much as possible without relying on the teacher. The independence they foster in their students reflects a major difference between a product classroom and a process classroom—a change in the balance of control.

In a process classroom the learners have considerable control over their learning as they make many decisions on topic, form, audience, and final product. Teachers' roles change as they allow their students to teach them. They may know more than their students, but they have much to learn about their students' topics and writing strategies. The teacher becomes one of the learners and shares the operation of the classroom workshop with the other learners. He or she establishes an environment in which the students come to understand their learning process (Papert 1980) as they work toward final products. This role requires a careful look at what students do when they learn.

Language development gives us a model of learning upon which to build a process/product classroom because both child and adult combine a process and product orientation during the years the child learns to talk. Everyone assumes children's talk will evolve from their own language into adult language (Dale 1976). Adults expect mistakes, but the child

321

wants to produce a clear product and the adults do all they can to find something clear in the message. The adults' role maximizes the children's chances of learning to talk.

In this analysis I will draw parallels between the ways we teach children to talk and the methods we can use to teach them to write and read. In the first of the three sections I show how *adults set the stage* for children's language development by nurturing them in language-rich environments and by letting the children talk, write, and read about the world as it interests them. Next I explain how *people respond to language*. Parents, other adults, and children themselves respond to the meaning of messages rather than to the surface structure of language. This is their behavior in oral communication, and they maintain this emphasis in writing and reading interactions. Finally, *language is a mode of learning*. We often understand something better after we have talked about it, and writing about something can also clarify our thoughts. Reading is another way of learning, especially for readers who insist on making language coherent. The persistence we see in young children as they learn to talk is a force we want to capitalize on as we teach them to write and read.

Adults Set the Stage[1]

Children Use Language Frequently

Young children exist in the midst of language from their date of birth onward. They unravel the notion of communication as they assess the talk around them. They want something, so they cry, and gradually they refine these bursts until the glorious day when Sally casually comments, "May I please have the keys to the car?" They have many opportunities to learn about language in real contexts (Donaldson 1979, Nelson et al. 1978).

Similarly, writers need to be immersed in writing. When print is used in their classroom to convey messages, they discover the basic aspect of

---

1. All references in this paper to children, classrooms, and teachers are taken from data I've collected since 1981 in two research projects in which I studied relationships between reading and writing.

I conducted the first project with Donald Graves from 1981 to 1983 in the first-grade classroom of Ellen Blackburn in Somerworth, New Hampshire. We learned about the reading and writing processes of three case-studied children each year.

We began the second project at Mast Way Elementary School in Lee, New Hampshire, and continued until May 1985. Graves and I conducted this project with Ruth Hubbard, Lorri Neilsen, Ann Marie Stebbins, and Tom Romano, all researchers at the University of New Hampshire. We worked with many staff members at Mast Way, but we particularly collected case-study data with Phyllis Kinzie, Janice Roberts, Leslie Funkhouser, Patricia McLure, John Lowy, and Marcia Taft. We learned about the environment in a school where teachers explored ways to teach both reading and writing from the theoretical perspective underlying Graves's early research on the writing process.

print: it deals with something that someone has to tell. Just as children learn to talk in real, meaningful, language-rich environments, they become writers when they have something at stake in the notes, letters, and messages they circulate among themselves (Newkirk 1984, Matthews 1985).

Paper and pencils surround the young students, and their teacher, as a demonstrator, writes notes and messages to the class and individual children. They want to respond, and they do. The teacher occasionally writes stories and reads them to the children when he or she shares literature with them. The children know that their teacher values writing and that he or she provides time for them to write every day.

Traditionally, writing teachers have not given children time to write. For example, Florio and Clark (1984) found that students used their pencils for isolated skillwork on worksheets and exercises in texts, but writing as a composing process happened only once in ten days. This is still a common scene (Bridge, Hiebert, and Chesky 1983; Applebee 1981). However, recent researchers (Graves 1983, Wolf 1984) say writing teachers must organize their schedules so their students will have time to compose messages.

In the process classroom, writers spend their time reading as well as writing. They are drawn to the work of other writers, and writing teachers feel the need to immerse their students in reading. The teachers organize the school day so the children read as part of their regular activities. To read a book is to pursue honorable work. It's not just something to do if your work is done. Reading books is important enough to set aside time for it in the busy schedule.

Teachers with a process orientation immerse their students in the entire reading process so they can sort it out and see how the pieces work. This is a change from the product-oriented classroom, in which little reading is done (Mason 1984). Eddie, a new student at Mast Way School, commented after one week, "In my old school we only read a story a week. In this room we read and write all the time." Second graders like Eddie can read at least a book a day. Maybe reading researchers and teachers need to muster the courage to let students read.

Children Decide What They Want to Say

Sally's parents did not tell her to ask for the car and no one told her to scream at the age of nine months when she wanted some juice. Sally decides what she will say. Language is goal-directed, organized by the plans of the speaker (Wells 1981).

When researchers study language development, they analyze utterances children make on their own volition because children don't say much when they are told to talk on a researcher-assigned topic. And when children are asked to reproduce adult talk, they can't if the speech patterns are more complicated than those they use. To find out what children can do with language, we listen to them talk in natural situations where they make their own decisions about what they want to talk about.

One of the hardest changes for teachers to make when they decide to let their writing instruction reflect the writing process is to let children choose their own topics. Traditionally, teachers assign topics, thus putting students in a position to write about something they may not know very much about. However, writers can write more clearly when they write about things they know (Murray 1982). A child who doesn't know anything about dinosaurs may write a sparse paper, but if, on the same day, his dog just had puppies, he can write a detailed account. When research began on the writing process, topic choice emerged as the place where writers begin; therefore, writing teachers with a process orientation organize their class time so students will learn how to choose their own topics.

Some children make lists of possible topics and add to the list whenever they think of something they might write about in the future. Others think of topics when they listen to classmates share their writing. Some students start to look at their world as an arena of writing topics and come to school with their writing topics on the tips of their pencils, such as on the day Daniel marched in and said, "I know what I'm writing about today. Our cat got stuck in the dryer last night."

Other children have topic-choosing conferences when they want input, as Matt did when he said to Todd, "I have three ideas but I don't know which one to use."

"What's the first one?"

"I could write about my dad's football."

Todd didn't think that sounded too exciting: "Sounds boring. What's your second one?"

"I could write about the snake I caught. I noticed it had a thorn in its tail so my sister held it while I tried to pull out the thorn . . . "

Their conference continued through the third idea and Matt left with his writing choice ready to go. These children write every day and they know they have to generate their own topics. They can't rely on the teacher to get them started. They have to learn to recognize what they know or what they would like to learn about, and pursue this information further when they write about it.

When teachers begin to teach writing they find out that their students think they have nothing to write about because they don't think they know anything. But children who write frequently and choose their own topics come to realize they are storehouses of knowledge. They look forward to writing class.

In the area of reading, the matter of choice is virtually ignored; I can't find a major piece of research based on what readers do when they read information that they have selected. The word *process* has dominated reading research for several years, but that research hasn't started at what can often be the beginning of the process. No one has studied the process Johnny uses to choose a book. Nor has anyone studied the reading process Johnny uses when he reads something he chooses to read, wants to read, and insists on figuring out. We have studied the reading process of students doing assigned reading, but it may be time to study some independent readers so we can determine what they do when they read.

When I taught elementary school I would have been afraid to let students choose their own books, and when I give workshops many teachers express this fear. They think that their students will choose books that are too easy or too hard. In Somersworth (Blackburn 1984), we observed children's book choices and learned that they chose books at all levels: easy books, hard books, and books of moderate difficulty. Books from all categories give them a complete "diet."

The teachers at Mast Way have started to help their students learn how to choose books. The children reread easy favorites; they return again and again to a challenge book to monitor their own progress until the day comes when they can read it; and they spend the majority of their time with books we would label at their "instructional level." The teachers sanction all levels of reading, and when you ask students about the level of books they're reading, they can tell you if a book is easy, hard, or "the one I'm working on now."

Reading class for these children begins with choice. The students ask, "What do I want to read today? Is there something I want to learn about? Do I want to sit back and relax? Do I want to enjoy the cadence of language? What do I want to read today?" The students get most of their ideas for books from each other, and they know what they want to read next, next, and next. Similar to adult readers who have a stack of books on the nightstand, these students plan ahead.

They know what to do when reading class begins. The label "independent readers" appears to fit students who start to read without the teacher telling them what to read. Students who have time to read and want to read are ready to learn (Parkerson et al. 1984).

People Respond to Language

Adults Are Interested in What Children Have to Say

Young children must get feedback from others in order to know whether their talk is clear. When children realize that a message didn't come through and it's something important, they often choose to try again. Sometimes children repeat themselves for days, weeks, months, or years before they can say something as clearly as an adult. But this is not adult-directed repetition; this is child-chosen, purposeful repetition. Such hypothesis-testing behavior is a hallmark of the way children learn language (Galda 1984). When adults respond to these hypotheses, they respond to the content and meaning, rather than the structure, of the child's utterance (Menyuk 1980).

In writing classrooms, teachers are interested in what their students have to say and write; the teachers are listeners. Their students write about topics that the teacher knows less about than the students, and that the teachers want to learn about. When Jon read his piece of writing about archery bows, his teacher sat with the class and was one of the responders. She had a puzzled look on her face as she raised her hand, "You said your bow is backstrung and your brother has a compound bow. What's the difference?" As when children talk, the adult must be interested in the message (Galda 1984) because the information, not the structure, is more important to the writer.

A student in one of my teacher-preparation classes learned this for himself recently after hearing me say it several times. His young son wrote about a weekend the two of them had spent together. The father could hardly read the account because the son's emerging writing skills were minimal, but he said, "It was the most moving piece of writing I've ever read. Now I know what you mean when you say information is the essence of writing."

This fall in one of the first-grade classrooms at Mast Way, Roger read his piece of writing, *The Big Fed* (the big field), to his class. He knew he had written a winner because as soon as he finished several hands shot up: "Which field do you mean? How long is the grass? Did you go alone? What did you do there?" His classmates and his teacher (who sat on the carpet with the class) were interested in what Roger wrote. Because of this interest, he wanted to continue experimenting with writing the next day.

Roger didn't add information to his piece of writing, but more advanced writers may choose to elaborate on their information when they realize that their readers want to know more. Sometimes, however, revision can be problematic. In second grade Seth wanted to insert information in his piece of writing but couldn't figure out how, so his teacher suggested he make a star to mark the place and then write the information at the bottom. Seth shared his new process knowledge with the class that day when they met for a session on "What I Learned Today in Writing or Reading." In such classrooms, the children not only learn about bows and big fields from each other, but their teacher structures the day so that they teach each other how to assemble their information into clear messages.

Writing teachers who think meaning is the most important element in a piece of writing organize their time so they can listen to their students. In the fourth-grade classroom where I collected much of my data, the teacher carried a chair around during writing, stopping beside one child after another throughout much of the time they wrote because she realized her children knew more than they wrote, and she wanted to learn as much as possible about what they knew. She asked them the same kinds of questions I hear in the whole-class sharing sessions. Traditionally, elementary teachers either have their students write while the teacher is busy with a group of students, or the teachers spend their time providing spelling words while the children write. However, teachers who emphasize the process of learning not only spend their time as writing teachers with their students, but they view a piece of writing as a point of departure to learn from a student. They respond to the information in the writing.

Response is a new term for reading teachers. Traditionally, reading teachers haven't responded to what children glean from a book. Instead, we determine what children should understand—which may inhibit children's thinking (Clark 1984, Doyle and Carter 1984). However, if the determining factor in a person's comprehension is his or her prior knowledge of a topic (Anderson 1984), then researchers need to think about the ramifications of this for instruction. If comprehension is the interpretation of a message in terms of the knowledge a reader already has (Anderson 1984), then we may need to base instruction on our response to what students know. The responsibility of producing a coherent message rests with the reader (Rosenblatt 1978, Galda 1984), the student. It is our responsibility in reading, as in writing or speaking, to learn about the student's message.

If the reading process begins with book choice, then the books students choose to read can provide the basis of instruction and the instruction can take the form of response. Many teachers have started to inch toward a belief in book choice, but they may need to take bolder steps. They set aside a period of time each day when everyone reads silently from whatever book they choose, but response to the books is not included in the twenty minutes. These teachers use real reading as a supplement rather than the basis for their instruction.

In order to respond, the Mast Way teachers first set aside time to listen, to learn what their students have to say about what they read. Initially, teachers tend to think book conferences won't work because they may not have read the books a student chooses. However, reading teachers who also teach writing discover a parallel between writing conferences and reading conferences. For example, a teacher didn't know about Johnny's camping trip, but she learned about it when he talked about his writing. If he could write about it clearly enough for someone who wasn't there to understand it, then he understands the nature of writing. Similarly, a teacher may not have read *The Indian in the Cupboard,* but if the teacher honors the child's reading process and considers herself a learner, she finds out about the book when the child talks about it. The teacher considers the child the informant (see Harste, Woodward, and Burke 1984 for an extension of this concept).

When the teacher responds to a reader, he or she first listens to the child read or we researchers tell the teacher about the book, such as on the day Derek told me about the turtle book he was reading: "Look! This is just like my turtle. When he's on his back and wants to stand up, he uses his head to turn over. He first does this, then this, just like these pictures." I didn't know this about turtles, so I asked questions and Derek continued to teach me. I didn't know if that was the most important part of Derek's book, but he was interested, and with the response system in his room based on what *he* chooses as a focus, I sanctioned his reading process and he looked forward to choosing another book the next day.

Derek's teacher scheduled her time so that each day she moved about the classroom for a while to find out what a few of the students were reading. She didn't need to listen to each one every day, but she listened often enough to know what they were learning, and they knew that when she stopped she wanted to know about their book. Information in this classroom moved not only from teacher to students; it also moved from students to teacher (Berliner 1985, Lunenburg 1983). Derek and his classmates liked to teach the adults in their classroom.

Children Interact with Many People

Children talk to, and receive response from, many people when they learn to talk. Children talk differently to adults than to younger children; they talk differently to the next-door neighbor than to either their mother or their teacher. Their language grows in richness as they talk to various people (Halliday 1978) because outsiders cannot understand them as well as close acquaintances, so they have to polish their communication skills. They have to try harder to get their meaning understood. This interactive aspect of language development provides teachers with their greatest opportunities to contribute to children's growth (Lindfors 1980).

The writing teacher teaches students to respond to each other's information so that, over time, they learn to adjust their messages. Students follow the teacher's model when they tell the writer what they learned and ask questions. The writer feels the urgency of the questions when his or her classmates really want to know more. The interest of classmates has more effect on writers than the teacher's interest because the students care more about writing something their friends find interesting than writing something to please the teacher. Writing teachers realize this and organize their classrooms so that children seek and get response from each other.

Students share their writing with individuals, small groups, and/or the entire class. They share when the writing is in progress and/or when it is finished. The children at Mast Way School also share their writing in other classrooms, and the librarian schedules two times each week when students from any grade may come to share with each other. One day recently a child shared his book about his coin collection and the librarian knew a child in another class had also written about coins, so she arranged for the boys to discuss coins. This interaction helps students get to know each other (Pratzner 1984) and enriches their writing.

In typical reading programs, teachers do not organize their instruction to capitalize on student interaction (e.g., Mason 1984). The purpose of reading groups is usually not for students to learn from each other. Rather, teachers want to find out if the students got meaning from the story. However, reading is a constructive process. A text does not "have" a meaning; rather, a text is an abbreviated recipe from which the student elaborates a meaning (Duffy, Roehler, and Mason 1984). In process classrooms, teachers help students create these meanings and help them value each other's construction (Smith-Burke 1985).

In many of the classrooms at Mast Way School, the teachers have created formats for reading discussions which encourage students to realize that the control of their reading process rests in their own hands. For example, the students may come to a discussion with a comment and a question about the selection they have all read. The format for comments and questions is similar to the format the students use when they respond to each other's writing: the comment is something they appreciated in the writing, while the question is something they didn't understand. Again, as in writing response, the question is an honest question asked by someone who wants to know more. In this session the students know they will understand the story better if they bring questions about what they didn't understand and discuss those concerns with other readers.

Students in the Mast Way classrooms also come together in small groups or as a class to learn about a book a student wants to share. Or a few students may meet, with each bringing the book he or she is currently reading. The reader tells the others what the book is about and/or reads part of it to the group. The others tell the reader what they understood and ask more about the book. And, if the book reminds them of other writing or personal experiences, they talk about these "reminders." The focus of the group is on the importance of response from others as a way to increase the reader's understanding.

These various response sessions lead to a classroom climate that strengthens students' support for each other (Chavez 1984). They realize what each other knows and use each other's expertise when they need help. The teachers build their classroom organization on this knowledge. They establish a workshop environment in which everyone must be productive and, therefore, must be able to get help when they need it. The children ask each other for help frequently: "I can't figure out this page. Will you read it with me?" This atmosphere of ready assistance permits movement during work time and increases opportunities for learning to occur.

Teachers worry about control when students seek interaction with their peers, but this needn't be a fear. A second-year, seventh-grade English and social studies teacher who teaches reading and writing with an emphasis on process as well as product says, "I have no discipline problems in my English class. Someday I'll figure out how to teach social studies this way." Students don't need to perform antics to get attention, because the routine response pattern for their work is the acceptance of what they know. An emphasis by everyone on what each other knows raises respect both for self and for each other.

Language Is a Mode of Learning

Children who lead busy, active lives have more to talk about than other children, and they learn about their experiences when they explain them to someone who wasn't there—an interested person who asks questions. Then, if they have a similar experience in the future, they will understand this new situation better because of their increased knowledge of the earlier activity. The more children talk about what they do, the better they understand their world and themselves. Talking is a way of learning about what you know (DeVilliers and DeVilliers 1979, Galda 1984).

Similarly, in writing, children write about what they know. They write about personal experiences, and these may evolve into nonfiction accounts about squirrels, chickens, and snakes. Or their narratives may become fictional accounts about weekends with Grandfather and unicorns at birthday parties. The personal narrative plays an important role because through it writers come to realize they know something, and someone who knows something can write. Writers write best when they know their topic, so if they know what they know, they will be better able to choose profitable topics.

Writers of all ages come to appreciate what they can learn when they write personal narratives. Kathleen Meyer, a professional author of children's books, was one of my students in the New Hampshire Summer Writing Program. I wondered what she could ever gain from me, but at the end of the first week she explained, "I've learned so much because we write personal narratives. I've never written about myself before and I didn't think I could. I didn't think I'd ever done anything interesting, but now I know I'm not a dull person. I already know I have lots of things to write about."

A similar awareness happens in Chapter I reading classrooms. In New Hampshire the state guidelines ask Chapter I reading teachers to teach writing, and these teachers say that the first payoff from the writing is an improvement in their students' self-concepts. These students, who often have depressed opinions of themselves, take on new life when they realize that they know interesting things. Writing is a way of learning about yourself.

Writers also learn about their topic when they write, especially during revision. However, they don't revise everything, and sometimes they publish a piece of writing they didn't revise at all because when they wrote, the words flowed. But even young writers make major revisions as they work with a topic. A narrative about yucky, rainy days turned out to be a poem about all the things six-year-old Daniel likes to do in the rain. Josh, a fourth-grade writer, wrote a story about frogs, revised it to science-fiction about frogs in a time warp, and revised it again so that it was about people in a time warp. When Eric started a personal narrative about his border collie, he decided he wanted to learn more about this breed, so writing class became a time for him to research his new interest. I myself have written five articles or book chapters about our current research project even though this study isn't finished because writing about what I am learning helps me sort it all out.

However, writing teachers usually don't view writing as a mode of learning (Fulwiler 1983). Instead, writing is primarily used as an assessment of what students have already learned (Eblen 1983). Most composition in schools is for essay answers to test questions, but researchers and teachers who write regularly (Emig 1982, Kantor 1984) and share their writing know what it means to say, "Writing is a mode of learning." When they teach writing, they may view it as a time when their students can make discoveries.

Reading is also a mode of learning: one way to increase our understanding of something is to read about it. Unfortunately, many of our students read without comprehension, which keeps them from discovering both the joys and content of print. However, reading teachers who teach writers find that their students use reading as a way to learn. This is evident in the fact that when students put strings of words on pages, they don't randomly choose those words. They know how print works.

For some time we have divided readers into early readers who are "learning to read" and older readers who "read to learn" (Mason 1984), but young writers demand meaning from what they read even when they have stilted, preprimer texts in front of them. A first-grade boy at Mast Way wondered why the man had a mop and a top in the sand. This child questioned writing every day and expected quality writing from his texts as well as from his friends and himself. He wanted the information in his preprimer books to make sense (Hansen 1983). His purpose in reading was to learn what other authors know.

A focus on information keeps children interested when they are learning to talk and write, and this focus can improve their interest in reading. The librarian at Mast Way has noticed an increase in the number of books checked out of the library since the project began, "especially nonfiction books." When the process of learning receives emphasis, children seek books from which to learn.

These students often interact with each other when they try to read their selections. In their classrooms I hear them conduct their own small learning groups and whole-class discussions. I can watch first-grade students lead a twenty-minute discussion among themselves with the teacher not saying a word. They talk about the books and topics they have chosen to learn about, and they talk about how they will continue to learn about their choices.

The students usually decide what they will learn because this increases the chances that they will learn for themselves rather than for the teacher. They decide their goals and they decide when they have achieved those goals. If they need help they have a classroom of learners from whom to receive support. Their activities along the way are real—not contrived, not isolated from their chosen purpose. When I ask them why they are doing something, they know. They can tell me what preceded what they're doing now and what they intend to do next.

These children become independent learners—learners who need other learners and whom other learners need.

References

Anderson, R. C. (1984). Some reflections on the acquisition of knowledge. *Educational Researcher* 13, no. 9: 5–10.

Applebee, A. N. (1981). *Writing in the secondary school.* Research report no. 21. Urbana, Ill.: National Council of Teachers of English. ED 197 347.

Berliner, D. C. (1985). The executive functions of teaching. In *Reading education: Foundations for a literate America,* edited by J. Osborn, P. T. Wilson, and R. C. Anderson, 87–107. Lexington, Mass.: Lexington Books.

Birnbaum, J., and J. Emig (1983). Creating minds, created texts: Writing and reading. In *Developing literacy: Young children's use of language,* edited by R. P. Parker and F. A. Davis, 87–104. Newark, Del.: International Reading Association.

Blackburn, E. (1984). Common ground: Developing relationships between reading and writing. *Language Arts* 61: 367–75.

Bridge, C., E. Hiebert, and J. Chesky (1983). Classroom writing practices. In *Searches for meaning in reading: Language processing and instruction,* edited by J. Niles. Rochester, N.Y.: National Reading Conference.

Chavez, R. (1984). The use of high-inference measures to study classroom climates: A review. *Review of Educational Research* 54: 237–61.

Clark, C. M. (1984). Teacher planning and reading comprehension. In *Comprehension instruction,* edited by G. G. Duffy, L. R. Roehler, and J. Mason. New York: Longman.

Dale, P. S. (1976). *Language development: Structure and function.* 2d ed. New York: Holt, Rinehart & Winston.

De Villiers, P. A., and J. G. De Villiers (1979). *Early language.* Cambridge, Mass.: Harvard University Press.

Donaldson, M. (1979). *Children's minds.* New York: W. W. Norton & Co.

Doyle, W., and K. Carter (1984). Academic tasks in classrooms. *Curriculum Inquiry* 14: 129–49.

Duffy, G. G., L. R. Roehler, and J. Mason (1984). The reality and potential of comprehension instruction. In *Comprehension instruction,* edited by G. G. Duffy, L. R. Roehler, and J. Mason. New York: Longman.

Eblen, C. (1983). Writing across-the-curriculum: A survey of a university faculty's views and classroom practices. *Research in the Teaching of English* 17: 343–48.

Emig, J. (1982). Non-magical thinking: Presenting writing developmentally in schools. In *Writing: The nature, development and teaching of written communication,* Vol. 2. Hillsdale, N.J.: Erlbaum.

Florio, S., and C. M. Clark (1984). The environment of instruction: The forms and functions of writing in a teacher-developed curriculum. In *Comprehension Instruction,* edited by G. G. Duffy, L. R. Roehler, and J. Mason. New York: Longman.

Fulwiler, T. (1983). Why we teach writing in the first place. In *Fforum: Essays on theory and practice in the teaching of writing,* edited by P. L. Stock, 273–86. Upper Montclair, N.J.: Boynton/Cook.

Galda, L. (1984). The relations between reading and writing in young children. In *New directions in composition research,* edited by R. Beach and L. S. Bridwell. New York: Guilford Press.

Graves, D. H. (1983). *Writing: Teachers and children at work.* Exeter, N.H.: Heinemann.

Halliday, M. A. K. (1978). *Language as a social semiotic: The social interpretation of language and meaning.* Baltimore: University Park Press.

Hansen, J. (1983). Authors respond to authors. *Language Arts* 60: 970–76.

Harste, J. C., V. A. Woodward, and C. L. Burke (1984). *Language stories and literacy lessons.* Portsmouth, N.H.: Heinemann.

Kantor, K. (1984). Classroom contexts and the development of writing intuitions: An ethnographic case study. In *New directions in composition research,* edited by R. Beach and L. S. Bridwell. New York: Guilford Press.

Lindfors, J. W. (1980). *Children's language and learning.* Englewood Cliffs, N.J.: Prentice-Hall.

Lunenburg, F. C. (1983). Pupil control ideology and self-concept as a learner. *Educational Research Quarterly* 8, no. 3: 33–39.

Mason, J. (1984). A question about reading comprehension instruction. In *Comprehension instruction,* edited by G. G. Duffy, L. R. Roehler, and J. Mason. New York: Longman.

Matthews, K. (1985). Beyond the writing table. In *Breaking ground: Teachers relate reading and writing in the elementary school,* edited by J. Hansen, T. Newkirk, and D. H. Graves. Portsmouth, N.H.: Heinemann.

Menyuk, P. (1980). What young children know about language. In *Discovering language with children,* edited by G. S. Pinnell, 5–8. Urbana, Ill.: National Council of Teachers of English.

Murray, D. (1982). *Learning by teaching: Selected articles on writing and teaching.* Montclair, N.J.: Boynton/Cook.

Nelson, K., L. Rescorla, J. Gruendel, and H. Benedict (1978). Early lexicons: What do they mean? *Child Development* 49: 960–68.

Newkirk, T. (1984). Archimedes' dream. *Language Arts* 61: 341–50.

Papert, S. (1980). *Mindstorms: Children, computers, and powerful ideas.* New York: Basic Books.

Parkerson, J. A., R. G. Lomax, D. P. Schiller, and H. J. Walberg (1984). Exploring causal models of educational achievement. *Journal of Educational Psychology* 76: 638–46.

Pratzner, F. C. (1984). Quality of school life: Foundations for improvement. *Educational Researcher* 13, no. 3: 20–25.

Rosenblatt, L. (1978). *The reader, the text, the poem: The transactional theory of the literary work.* Carbondale, Ill.: Southern Illinois University Press.

Smith-Burke, M. T. (1985). Reading and talking: Learning through interaction. In *Observing the language learner,* edited by A. Jaggar and M. T. Smith-Burke, 199–211. Newark, Del.: International Reading Association and National Council of Teachers of English.

Wells, G. (1981). *Learning through interaction: The study of language development.* Cambridge: Cambridge University Press.

Wilson, P. T., and R. C. Anderson (1985). Reading comprehension and school learning. In *Reading education: Foundations for a literate America,* edited by J. Osborn, P. T. Wilson, and R. C. Anderson, 319–28. Lexington, Mass.: Lexington Books.

Wolf, D. (1984). Learning about language skills from narratives. *Language Arts* 61: 844–50.

Assessing the Process, and the Process of Assessment, in the Language Arts

Peter Johnston
State University of New York at Albany

Being asked to address the problem of assessment in the language arts, particularly within relatively strict page limits, is hazardous. The topic encourages one to perpetuate the serious error, inherent in current assessment practice, of separating assessment from teaching and learning. This separation has been responsible for many of our woes in language arts education. To avoid this problem, I will address the issue of how assessment fits into language arts education. I shall argue that there are serious problems with our current approach to assessment which cannot be solved within the present measurement framework. The major problem with the current approach is that it does not focus on processes but products. The assessment of processes is necessarily less formal (though not less rigorous) and not externally accountable. I will argue for reducing the emphasis on formal methods of assessment and transferring control of assessment into the hands of the teacher and the learner. Viewing language arts learning as a process which includes assessment by learners themselves, I will argue for a reintegration of teaching, learning, assessment, and the language arts.

Goals, Assessment, and Education in the Language Arts

Before discussing methodological issues of assessment in the language arts, I find it crucial to consider the reasons for assessment in the first place. After all is said and done, whatever we choose as the goal for assessment has serious implications for the nature of our assessment procedures.

The major goal of assessment is optimal learning for all. This is the bottom line. While the reasons given by various writers are often numerous, (e.g., Baker 1979, Mehrens and Lehmann 1984), most of them should be thought of as subgoals. Three major subgoals are generally represented: individual instructional tailoring, selection for special programs, and accountability. In our attempts to serve these subgoals, we have elevated them to goal status, out of the context of the original motive. Accountability assessment, for example, is only one of a number of potential ways of helping to achieve optimal learning for all. But the pursuit of the accountability subgoal has not furthered our progress toward our ultimate goal. Indeed, the reverse is true. Accountability assessment has forced teachers to adopt as their goal good performance on tests. However, many important goals cannot be evaluated within the framework of the current group-oriented model of assessment. Consequently, many highly relevant goals will not be addressed adequately, if at all, in the classroom (Frederiksen 1984). Similarly, the selection subgoal is only relevant if one believes that separating some children from the others for a different program (tracking and pull-out programs) is an appropriate part of achieving optimal instruction. This belief is far from unanimous.

The picture is complicated further by the existence of certain hidden agendas. These unstated goals are problematic because they cannot be confronted directly. Some of these second-order goals have to do with power and money. The current approach centralizes power, taking it away from students and teachers. Furthermore, conservative estimates of annual expenditures in school testing programs range from 25 to 40 million dollars (Anderson and Lesser 1978, Baker 1979). This represents a vast industrial commitment to the status quo. A more process-oriented approach to assessment, if adopted, would reduce this expenditure substantially while returning control to the teachers and students. Thus it is not likely to be accepted gladly by the assessment industry or those holding the power.

Language processes and learning processes also have goals. Why do children engage in the various language activities, and why should they bother to improve their performance in them? These are important considerations, especially when frequently the answers relate more to a method of assessment than to any personal communicative or aesthetic goal. There have been many attempts to describe the goals of linguistic activities. For example, Halliday (1977) proposes the following set of goals: to fulfill needs, to control, to relate to others, to define self, to find things out, to imagine, and to communicate intent. While these attempts differ in their descriptions, it is rare that any of the goals described have anything at all to do with those invoked in current assessment situations. Such goal conflicts distort assessments and any instruction and learning which might be directed by the assessment. We note, for example, that children's substitutions of nonsense words for real words while reading reflect a misunderstanding of the goal of reading. Their misreading of nonsense words on tests as real words (a common error, as reported by Walmsley 1979) reflects a misunderstanding of the assessment task as a reading task. Similarly the perception of an accurate, neat written product as the goal of writing has consequences for children's development of the writing process, particularly their motivation and the communicative and expressive aspects of the process. Assessment practice has the power not only to influence what a child perceives to be the goal of a language task, but also to modify the teacher's goals and, hence, instruction (Frederiksen 1984).

For the remainder of this paper, I will assume that both language-learning activities and assessment are goal-directed processes. In this regard, I shall go "back to basics" and assume that the ultimate goal of assessment is optimal learning for every student, and that the goals of language arts processes are of the type described by Halliday (1977) and others. Also, since instruction must be oriented toward language and learning processes, it follows that our assessment should similarly focus on these language and learning processes.

The Context of Language Arts Assessment

Context is an important factor with respect to processes (Leontiev 1979; Vygotsky 1962, 1978; Wertsch 1979). Processes are organized around goals, but there is usually more than one way to attain a goal. Consequently, the actual organization and implementation of a process are influenced by the context within which the process occurs.

If we are to examine the language arts and their learning as processes, then, we must take into account the context within which they take place, particularly in relation to the context created by our assessment. The effects of context on oral language have been recognized for some time now, especially in assessment situations (e.g., Labov 1973). There has been some impact of this realization on the assessment of oral language in that, in general, researchers recognize that there is no substitute for a natural language sample (Danwitz 1981). Recent work by Clay (1975, 1979b) and Ferreiro (1978) in the field of reading, and Graves (1983) and Calkins (1983) in the field of writing, has also stressed the need for natural samples of behavior. However, if such assessment practice is suggested within a curriculum which does not allow children time to independently exercise their own reading, writing, and oral language, there are bound to be problems. Thus, the instructional context of the assessment process is important in terms of the assessment options which it allows.

Similarly, if we are to examine assessment as a process, we must look at the context within which it takes place. The societal context of education has had an important impact on how we assess. The teaching profession generally has a poor public image, especially with regard to the teaching of literacy (e.g., Broadfoot 1979, *Time* 1980). Accountability evaluation is a consequence of this basic lack of trust. Because of its lack of faith in teachers and students, the public sees force (accountability) as its only option for attaining optimal learning for all children. However, it should be noted that this view does not extend to all of the language arts. Traditionally, children go to school to learn to "read 'n write." Oral language is learned at home and has generally not been seen as the responsibility of the schools. Thus, oral language assessment has been spared many of the indignities imposed by accountability assessment. Educational assessment of oral language has tended to be limited to diagnostic assessment of abnormal development. Of course, this exclusion has been aided by the fact that spoken language is so much more difficult to measure, particularly in a group test. Individual listening tests, on the other hand, have been used at least since the thirties (e.g., Durrell and Sullivan 1937) as indicators of reading capacity, in much the same manner as IQ tests, and this practice continues (e.g., Spache 1981).

I noted earlier that the public shares with educators a concern for the insurance of a quality education, particularly in literacy. However, the concern of both groups is often ill-informed. For example, while the public is prepared to accept a normal distribution of intellectual capacity, and even linguistic skill, neither of which is considered to be the province of the school, it has a different notion about reading and writing achievement. In these areas, there is concern if any child is reading below grade level. By definition, this notion ensures massive amounts of "failure." Rather than a reasonable concern for development, the concern is inappropriately normatively based. To have one's child "reading below grade level" is a source of considerable anxiety. This guarantees, even under optimal instruction, many anxious parents and children. Educators, too, have had some misconceptions. We have not had even a semblance of a developmental theory of writing and/or reading in our possession for very long. This lack has hampered instruction in that instruction has been based on an adult view of language rather than on a child-oriented view. However, the public and some educators have not noted that this theoretical void also has affected the assessment of literacy development. It is unfortunate that the public is less critical of the assessment devices and the industry responsible for them than it is of teachers.

The present somewhat atheoretical approach to assessment is flawed, even damaging, and it would help if the public recognized the flaws so that we might replace the approach with less formal and more individual efforts. Given the present social context, however, it seems unlikely that the public would accept such a replacement. An attempt to do so would simply be viewed as a ploy to avoid being held responsible. We have two potential ways of dealing with such inclement contexts: we can accept them and try to modify practice within their constraints, or we can attempt to modify the contexts. Since the approach to assessment which I shall discuss is virtually prohibited by the present context, and the current approach so inadequate, I will argue that we *must* attempt to change the context. In particular, we must make substantial efforts to educate the public and to win its trust.

Problems with the Current Approach to Assessment

The bulk of current assessment in the language arts, particularly in reading, is based on tests which are group-administered, standardized, comparative (norm-referenced), and product-oriented. While all tests do not have all of these characteristics, virtually all have most. Even individually administered tests have most of the same characteristics as the group tests. I shall call the model of assessment which this represents the *measurement model*. The following characteristics and assumptions of the measurement model are problematic:

1. Group assessment is more efficient than individual assessment.

The decision to use group assessment rather than individual assessment is based on the idea that the trade-off between time requirements and information quality is a reasonable one. There are several reasons for doubting this assumption:

1. Most of the important aspects of language processes cannot be assessed with group tests. For example, the critical concepts about print (Clay 1979b), phonemic segmentation, prediction, monitoring, and self-correction cannot be assessed. The aesthetic component of reading (Rosenblatt 1978) simply goes away when current assessment procedures are introduced, since they enforce efferent reading. Even critics of current assessment practice, while noting the failure to assess important areas, believe that part of the solution is to test them. For example, Frederiksen (1984) comments on the importance of:

   > how one adopts playful attitudes by deliberately relaxing rules in order to explore the possibilities of alternative rules. . . . [Such attitudes] also should be taught and tested. (p. 199)

I hope that it will become clear that the mere suggestion that one "test" playfulness is counter-intuitive, given the measurement model.

2. When people compare individual and group assessment in terms of efficiency, the notion of individual assessment used in the comparison is simply the same standardized test format, only administered one-to-one. Although this procedure might sometimes be desirable, usually it is not. Such tests contain many unnecessary items which are too hard or too easy for each student, and the format prevents the gathering of some of the more important information.

3. Furthermore, when individual and group assessment are compared, it is assumed that instruction and assessment cannot take place at the same time. I will show later in this paper that while this is necessarily true with current assessment methods, it is not necessarily true of assessment in general. Indeed, optimal assessment often does double-duty as instruction.

4. Even if current assessment data were highly informative, research suggests that teachers do not use the information (Boyd et al. 1975, Dorr-Bremme 1982). Thus, *any* time spent on such assessment is not well spent.

2. Individual, informal assessment by teachers is subjective and of little value. Assessment must be objective.

There are several misconceptions underlying this assumption. First, there is the confusion over the meaning of the term *subjective*. In the qualitative sense, it means *unreliable* and *biased*. In the quantitative sense, it refers to that fact that only one person's observations are involved (Scriven 1972). For example, the observations made by Piaget and by Vygotsky would be subjective in the latter sense, but not in the former.

Our current approach to assessment is referred to as "educational measurement." "Measurement" is generally considered to be a detached, amoral activity, as scientific research in the field has focused on accuracy of measurement rather than, and quite separate from, the improvement of learning. Society in general has been indoctrinated well with the notion that "scientific" tests, constructed by experts, provide veridical, objective, nonreactive measures. As Baker and Herman (1980) note,

> The scientist remains outside of the action of instruction and passive with respect to creating "better" performance. . . . [A]mong the most serious errors a scientist can make is to perpetrate reactivity, where inadvertent effects are produced by the process of measurement itself. (p. 150)

This idea of detached, accurate objectivity is clearly in error. For example, measurement requires comparability of data (Wolf 1984), which implies standardization of contexts. The more the assessment procedure is standardized, the more the context produced differs from the context in which the process normally occurs, and the more it distorts the very nature of the process being assessed. The act of measuring changes the object of the measurement.

A second way in which current assessment is reactive stems from the comparative, ego-involving (Nicholls 1983) nature of measurement practice. The essence of measurement is comparing outcomes and ranking individuals with respect to greater and lesser ability. Comparative situations represent threats to individuals' egos. When people's egos are threatened, they tend to alter their goals from being task-related to being ego-defense–related. Thus, by virtue of their comparative nature, most current assessment practices are extremely reactive. Furthermore, this reactivity is increased if the assessment has an accountability function (e.g., Hill 1980).

That reactivity is not generally seen as a problem seems to be because methods of assessment have become the ends for researchers in the field of measurement. This is attested to by the fact that the bulk of studies in the field of measurement involve procedural concerns (Broadfoot 1979). Method, then, has largely been divorced from motive and consequence. The consequence of this divorce is that teachers have little, if any, use for the information derived from standardized tests (Dorr-Bremme 1982). While the notion of "usability" is cited as being one of the three criteria for evaluating tests (e.g., Gronlund 1976), we have tended to use the term to refer to factors such as cost and the ease of administration and scoring of the test rather than the ease and likelihood of use of the information obtained. Some test manuals are even quite blatant about this. For example, consider the following quote from the manual for a popular test:

> [T]est results . . . should be viewed as tentative until substantiated by additional information. . . . Accept the test results as a challenge to your ingenuity in finding out why the class or individual pupils obtained certain scores. . . . (Nurss and McGauvrin 1976, p. 16)

3. Success or failure on a test item is useful information.

Recent research in reading and writing has stressed the importance of teaching students the processes involved in effective performance. This implies that we should also be concerned about how to assess these processes in order to tailor our instruction. Current approaches to assessment are incapable of being adapted to serve this function. I base this claim on the definition of the term *process*. According to Webster's dictionary (1979) there are two definitions, each of which is applicable. The first definition notes that "a process involves how something was accomplished." The measurement model focuses on outcomes. The definition of an "item" is anything for which there is a success/failure outcome, and test scores are simply accumulations of these outcomes. One cannot determine how the outcomes were arrived at.

The second dictionary definition of process, "a continuing development involving many changes," suggests a time course. It implies observing something in motion rather than as a static entity—a shift from the snapshot metaphor to the cinematic metaphor. In this regard I refer not only to the processes of reading/writing/speaking/listening but also to the process of learning to read/write/speak/listen. A consequence of this view should be a concern for continuous assessment, and *progress* rather than *success*. In a process approach, definitions of student difficulty would revolve around failure to show progress (self-referenced assessment) rather than failure to accurately complete a given task as well as other students (norm-referenced), which is the focus of the measurement approach.

4. *Elements of a process can be taken out of the context of the process without distortion.*

Human mental activity is goal-directed (Leontiev 1979, Vygotsky 1978, Wertsch 1979). This goal-directedness implies that understanding a mental process requires that we understand its goal. It is important to distinguish the goals of language processes from the goal of success on a test, since these are somewhat unrelated. However, that the process is goal-directed also implies that there is an internal unity and coherence within a process conferred by the goal-direction. Current assessment practice frequently addresses isolated elements of language processes, and by focusing attention on these isolated elements, encourages teaching and learning to follow suit. Thus, instruction is focused on the teaching of isolated subskills. This approach to assessment is probably responsible for current reading instruction, in which children actually read (i.e., exercise the integrated process) approximately 3 minutes a day (Gambrell 1984).

5. *Standardizing the assessor-assessee relationship and context produces more interpretable information.*

As I noted earlier, the context within which assessment takes place has a substantial impact on the nature of the procedure. Thus, a process-oriented approach to assessment or instruction must be context-sensitive.

Current measurement efforts deal with context by attempting to eliminate it as a variable by standardizing the context of performances. The incorrect assumption is that the resulting highly unusual context does not affect the performance, and that the standard context will be interpreted similarly by all those experiencing it.

As I noted earlier, assessment of oral language has generally tended to be more sensitive to this issue except in an educational context (Launer and Lahey 1981), and some writers in the fields of reading and writing (Clay 1979b, Graves 1983) have begun to suggest methods which deal more adequately with this problem. However, in each case the solutions focus on samples of the language activity taken in a context which is nonthreatening, and as natural as possible. This will be discussed more fully later.

6. The same assessment can be used for both accountability purposes and accurate instructional feedback to teachers and students.

The act of using a test to hold someone publicly accountable makes the test-taking an ego-involving task. This is the most reactive situation possible (Maehr 1983, Nicholls 1983). It is likely that in such a situation an individual will do whatever is necessary to prevent the assessor from detecting his or her weaknesses. However, in order for assessment to be instructionally useful, it is essential that weaknesses be personally confronted—that the assessment become task-involving (Nicholls 1983). This fundamental conflict makes the current use of the same test for both instructional and accountability purposes quite unacceptable. If possible, assessment should be done when the learner is task-involved and thus is performing optimally and not concerned with ego-defense. Task involvement requires personally interesting tasks of appropriate difficulty under no external threat. This is most likely to occur when tasks are self-selected and individualized.

7. Holding individuals accountable for their teaching and learning will improve learning.

Accountability assessment is based on several untenable assumptions. It assumes that teachers are willing to alter their behavior based on student achievement, and that they are able to do so given that the only information available is that the last group of students they taught did or did not do as well as other students. These assumptions and the assumption of "all else being equal" seem to be somewhat unsound. However, possibly the most damaging is the assumption that teaching and learning are fundamentally unenjoyable activities. "Giving students something to work for" implies that the activities with which the children are provided in school are not engaging and are meaningless. Frequently, this means that the tasks are not matched well to the students, particularly the less able students (e.g., Jorgenson 1977). The whole approach is like a mechanic mismatching the threads on a nut and bolt and then forcing the fit with a hammer in the interests of haste, rather than taking the time to find a better matched thread.

Since intrinsic motivation is assumed to be unlikely, extrinsic motivation is seen as necessary. This position is taken in spite of work in the area of motivation which suggests that (*a*) extrinsic motivation often has the effect of eliminating existing intrinsic motivation, and (*b*) extrinsically motivated behavior tends to disappear when the extrinsic motivation goes away (deCharms 1983). Mental processes are motivated, and motivation implies emotion. Interestingly, emotion is an aspect of the language arts more often discussed by teachers than by measurement folk. Words such as *enjoy* are abhorrent to those involved with the assessment of learning— a situation which, through the constraining effects of assessment on instruction (Frederiksen 1984), poses a serious problem.

A Process Evaluation Approach

What characteristics seem most important for effective assessment? First, we would like to be sure that the information which is collected is useful and comes in such a form and with such timing that it is likely to be used. We want our assessments to be reactive in the sense that they change teaching and learning activities in a positive way. We should be sure, however, that any reactivity should have only positive side-effects on children's learning. Second, the procedure must be efficient. I have argued that the measurement model fails on each of these grounds. Third, as with any evaluation, we would like quality information. This information will need to be process-oriented and represent the processing which normally takes place. Let us take these concerns seriously and consider how research in the language arts and in evaluation might help us.

Gathering Information Which Will Be Used

What characteristics of assessment information would help to ensure that the information would be used? Another way to put this is to ask, "How can we put assessment, teaching, and learning back together?" Dorr-Bremme (1982) has provided some of the answers to this question. The features of assessments which are most used by teachers include the following: immediate accessibility, proximity between their intended purposes and teachers' practice activities, and consonance (from the teachers' perspectives) between the content the assessments cover and the content taught. I would add to this that the information should be personally "owned" by the teacher and that the information should be clearly identified in the teacher's mind with the appropriate student. Note that each of these characteristics is maximized in the less formal, one-to-one approaches to assessment.

As a simple contrastive example, consider a test component in a kindergarten/first-grade basal reader. Such a test is likely to have a multiple-choice word-identification section (some consist entirely of this). Such a test will have a high error component, particularly with the age group responding to it. It will also take some time to administer the text, then to score it, and then to transfer the scores to the class record sheet. However, more importantly, if the teacher were asked to describe a given child's performance, he or she would have difficulty doing so without consulting the records. Supposing, instead, that the teacher simply called each child up one at a time to read the list of words, and then entered the information directly into the class record sheet. First, the information gained would be of higher quality. Second, there is a good chance that the whole procedure would take less time. Third, after testing, the teacher would be more likely to remember a given child's performance and use the information without consulting the class chart at all. Fourth, the children not being assessed could simply read, perhaps even a book of their own choosing. Such a privilege is not generally extended to them in class time.

In the long run, we are not only going to be concerned about the teacher using the information, but the student must somehow be involved in its use too, unless we erroneously view language arts learning as a passive, externally directed activity. Thus, on order for an individual to confront and deal with weaknesses, he or she must also be in a supportive environment. This is one of many points at which assessment intersects with teaching and learning. I shall come back to this intersection often. We must also consider, then, how to get students to own the assessment information.

I believe there are several approaches to assessment in the language arts currently available which reflect these principles. However, they are not the ones in most common use, and they are certainly not the focus of the bulk of research in the assessment field. Current assessment practices involve rather awkward relationships between teacher and student which produce restricted language activity. Graves (1983) has described this relationship as adversarial. Adversaries sit opposite the child in a higher chair, ignoring eye contact, and take the child's work. The adversarial role conveys to the child that his or her perspective and and position are not valued and that it is unwise to show any weakness. While Graves's description is offered at the level of one-to-one interactions, it is equally applicable at the level of group assessment. The role which Graves prefers for the teacher is that of an advocate. An advocate sits beside the child, as close to equal height as possible, engages eye contact, and waits to be offered the child's work. The role of advocate conveys to children that they and their concerns are legitimate and deserving of serious attention by both parties. Holdaway (1979) refers to this relationship as a professional-client relationship. The implicit roles are similar to those described by Graves in that they accord respect and rights to both parties. Each has an element of recognizable control, and the client has a guarantee of confidentiality. The student clients must have confidence in the teacher to hold an expressed weakness in confidence and neither hold the weakness against them nor publicize it.

In the field of reading and writing there has been growing acceptance of the notion of "getting alongside children" (e.g., Clay 1979b, Graves 1983, Nicholson 1984). This expression can be taken both literally and figuratively. In the literal sense, it is represented by the work of Marie Clay (1979b) in her running records and Concepts About Print Test, in which, contrary to all other reading assessments, teacher and student sit next to each other and work toward the same end. In the figurative sense this getting alongside the children refers to the alignment of teacher's and children's goals and perspectives and the adoption of a collaborative relationship. The assessor's task is to understand the child's understanding of the reading or writing process, and to help the child understand what he or she is doing and how to extend it.

In the field of writing, this approach can be found in the recent work of, for example, Calkins (1983) and Graves (1983) in the "writing conference." Within this framework, children's self-reports are taken very seriously. Indeed, part of the function of the conference is to help the child to be sensitive to his or her own processes. Within the current measurement framework, self-reports are considered unscientific and generally of dubious value. (Indeed, they may be, within the context of current assessment and teaching practices.) These one-to-one conferences last perhaps five minutes, are highly focused, and deal with manageable chunks of information. Resulting assessments are likely to be responded to actively and accurately by both teachers and students.

Nicholson (1984) describes a similar technique of "interviewing" in working with secondary school students in content areas. Paris and his colleagues (Paris and Jacobs 1984; Paris and Myers 1981) have also used more structured interviews in examining children's knowledge of reading.

They found that the information gathered about children's knowledge of planning and regulating aspects of reading was strongly related to reading comprehension skill. A structured interview procedure has also been developed by Wixson et al. (1984) for diagnostic use in schools.

I think that the use of the terms *interview* and *conference* is also significant in that both imply trust, client status, and a valuing of the student's perspective. Current practice has little in common with this relationship. Indeed, since accountability and labeling are major functions of present assessment, learners are likely to act as if they have been read their rights: "You have the right to remain silent. Anything you say may be used against you. . . ." Most students choose silence. Failure to accord client status to students drastically limits the information the teacher is likely to be given. Since the information is not given, the teacher has to "take" it, but this information will not be the same as the information which would be given.

Making the Procedure Efficient

A major assumption underlying group assessment procedures is that they are more efficient than individualized assessments. I noted earlier the current separation of assessment, teaching, and learning activities. This separation is extremely inefficient. The reintegration of the assessment process with the instructional process has been a common thread in recent research on reading, writing, and cognitive assessment. The dynamic assessment procedures proposed by Feuerstein (1979) and Vygotsky (1962, 1978) have many similarities to the work of Graves (1983) in writing and Clay (1979b) in reading. The assessment is individualized and involves thoughtful, theory-generated prompting of the learning as part of the teaching-assessing interaction. This approach represents a radical departure from the mainstream of psychometrics for a variety of reasons. The interactive nature of the assessment technique makes each assessment unique. Controlling or standardizing the assessment is deemphasized in favor of gathering more valid information. This makes it difficult to compare the performances of different individuals—a characteristic which the measurement model assumes to be necessary.

Just as research has emphasized the reintegration of evaluation and teaching, it also strongly suggests a reintegration of evaluation and learning. Evaluation is the feedback element which guides the learning process. Without feedback a process cannot be controlled. In order to be responsible for one's own learning process, it is thus necessary to gather one's own continuous feedback. Thus, the central component of the evaluation/learning relationship is, of course, self-evaluation. Psychotherapists such as Rogers (1942) contend that no personal change occurs without an awareness of the need to change. This awareness arises through self-evaluation. Self-assessed difficulties are at the teachable point at which instructional effort pays the most handsome dividends.

The importance to learning of self-evaluation cannot be overstated. For example, in reading, probably the strongest indicator of unhealthy reading development is failure to self-correct. Self-evaluation is at the heart of the revision process in writing. Without self-correction, learning systems cannot become self-improving; and without self-monitoring, self-correction cannot occur. When learners do not self-evaluate they must learn to do so. Questions must be directed at causing "intelligent unrest." The child's reestablishment of control by finding answers to the questions constitutes real learning. Such questions are "questions that teach" (Graves 1983). They are reflective and focused. These questions also give responsibility for assessment back to the student. Graves takes this responsibility further by proposing, for example, that students be asked to choose the work which should be included in their cumulative folders. This practice alone would probably reduce the anxiety involved in student evaluation.

A critical aspect of current approaches to assessment in general is their externally dependent nature, which contrasts drastically with the less formal approach presently being described. An assumption underlying the latter approach is that students need to be thought of as intelligent decision-makers in need of information about their own performance. The same statements could easily be made about teachers and teacher evaluation. As previously noted, this type of respect has not been a characteristic of our approach to education.

Assessment can also contribute to children's learning strategies through the modeling of self-evaluation strategies. We often suggest to teachers that they model the reading and writing processes as part of instruction. It is this modeling which teaches children not only to value literacy but also how to become literate. Thus it is somewhat distressing that we rarely find suggestions that teachers model self-evaluation for children. This may have something to do with the fact that current assessment practices would generally be of very little help to children in developing self-evaluation. However, consider the possibility of a secondary school teacher grading a paper in collaboration with a student, thinking aloud while doing so. Marking papers usually takes extra time outside of school and contributes relatively little to student learning. Perhaps we are wasting a valuable resource.

It is similarly distressing that we never hear teachers being told to model the listening process. Along with Pearson and Fielding (1982), I think of listening as an active attempt to understand another individual through the auditory-oral mode. Thus, the type of questioning described by Graves (1983) in writing and Clay, Nicholson, and others in reading is part of listening. These questions are reflective, helping the child to clarify for him- or herself the problem to be dealt with. Easley and Zwoyer (1975), coming from the field of mathematics education, have coined the term "teaching by listening" to refer to the same idea. This notion of listening also involves helping children to be articulate. In order to listen to them, one has to get them to talk. Listening and speaking are not well-accepted aspects of schooling in this country.

Questions in current tests, unlike process-oriented questions, demand a response which is right or wrong by some external criterion. This approach to assessment has followed us into the classroom to informal assessment, at least in the fields of reading and writing, at considerable cost, particularly to the development of oracy and intrinsic motivation. Consider the grilling which children receive from the questions asked at the end of basal reader selections. These produce a threatening situation which will stifle discussion and hence not contribute to the development of the children's oral language. As an alternative, consider the type of questions proposed by Graves, Nicholson, and others as described above. These questions are far less likely to be threatening, especially within the advocate-teacher–pupil relationship. It is important to note that such questions generally focus on processes and foster discussion, the oral aspect of language. This means that children are more inclined to take risks—a crucial part of literacy learning (Clay 1979, Holdaway 1979).

It should be clear by now that I am advocating turning over as much of the evaluation responsibility as possible to teachers and learners. From a management standpoint, one could think of this as efficient delegation of responsibility. From the teaching standpoint it might be thought of as an apprenticeship model. From the perspective of learning, it can be viewed as returning independence and control to the learner.

Gathering High-Quality Information

I argued earlier in this paper that the most important information a teacher needs about a pupil's learning is process information, i.e., knowledge of how an activity was performed and the reasons that it was performed in that manner. In reading, for example, it is important to know whether a reader predicted, monitored, and verified at the word, sentence, and text levels. We also need to know the information sources the reader used for performing these activities, regardless of whether or not he or she could answer certain questions about the text. Some readers blunderbuss their way through passages, comprehending by brute force and sometimes ignoring even important words, even though they have the necessary strategies to figure out the words. The longer readers manage to use such strategies to successfully "pass" tests, the more difficult it is to change the strategies.

How do we find out about these strategies? The first method is by simple rigorous observation. Researchers in all areas of language have begun to depend on samples of behaviors which occur in more or less natural situations. This emphasis came first in the area of oral language, which is based on case studies of individual's language development. While such evaluation procedures have been accepted in oral language research for a long time, in the educational setting clinicians are still usually bound to standardized tests, despite knowledge of the limitations of those tests (e.g., Labov 1973). However, only recently have reading and writing been seriously approached as developmental tasks. They have generally not been thought of as behaviors which are learned, but rather as behaviors which are taught. Thus, the onus has been on educators to structure the learning in a "rational" and efficient manner and assess progress with respect to what was taught. It is unfortunate that children's reasoning and structuring of these tasks is not simply that of little adults but quite different, and each child differs in the manner in which he or she acquires this knowledge. Thus assessments have been insensitive to aspects of children's learning which have not been "taught" in the program, and basal-directed teaching has been less than sensitive to children's development.

The most important insensitivity, however, has been in teachers whose evaluations of the children's, and their own, progress has been tied to tests, particularly ones which cannot provide information on important aspects of language development. The concepts assessed with the Concepts About Print Test (Clay 1979b), for example, cannot be assessed other than on an individual basis. Furthermore, because researchers have until recently failed to come up with developmental models of literacy, it has been difficult to supply research-based help with informal observations to teachers. Frequently, unless one knows what one is looking for, one is unlikely to see it. For example, if a teacher does not know that prediction is important in reading, he or she is unlikely to be able to report on progress in that area. In writing, unless teachers understand the principles underlying children's writing development (e.g., as reported by Clay 1975), all they are likely to see is scribble. In this sense, when we talk about refining the assessment instruments, making them more valid and reliable, we should be talking about teacher education, since the teacher *is* the instrument.

This argument is particularly crucial when we face the complaint that observation takes so much time that it is inefficient. Because some aspects of behavior occur infrequently, it is often necessary to develop probes and prompts to see what a child can do. To do this efficiently requires knowledge of the process, and of how context influences the process. One must know, for example, not to draw a conclusion about the complexity of a child's language from a formal interview situation, and one must constantly strive to collect information in less formal contexts. This is what is being referred to by Clay (1979b) when she talks about sensitive observation and Graves (1983) when he talks about listening to children. One should certainly not think of informed observation as "soft" data. Yes, bias and other issues will arise within such a framework, but since these must be dealt with regardless of the data source, teacher education is still implicated. Instead of teaching teachers more about standard scores, grade-equivalents, and the like, perhaps we should spend more time helping them to learn more about teaching by listening, and about developing collaborative relationships with children.

I noted earlier that, from a process-oriented perspective, motivation is very important. Consider what this means in terms of our assessment practice: Generally, motivation is not assessed. The reason for this is not that it cannot be assessed, but that its assessment cannot be done within the measurement model. To evaluate motivational aspects, one must supply a situation in which children have choice and note the extent to which they engage in the activity of their own volition. For reading and writing, one might simply arrange a room with lots of enjoyable activities which include reading and writing, and count the collective amount of time which students spend engaging in literacy-oriented activities. This is the acid test of a literacy program. As a matter of interest, it is one of the only tests which, if used for accountability purposes, would have a positive impact on children's learning.

Tying this motivational issue back to the outcome focus of the measurement model I think that "success" is more associated with outcomes and the affects associated with winning and losing, whereas "progress" is more associated with processes and the affect that comes from the activity itself (cf. Csikszentmihalyi 1975). Consequently, if, through our assessment, we focus children's attention on outcomes, their affect is tied to the success or failure of the activity. They do not get the affective support for the activity until it is complete. It also sets up a comparative-competitive situation which is motivationally damaging (Maehr 1983, Nicholls 1983). Furthermore, since the activity itself is not self-reinforcing, we would not expect learners to indulge in it when the reinforcement is gone. The major deficiency of less able readers and writers is that they rarely engage in the activity. (And we worry about time on task in class.)

The same principle might be applied to teachers. If, through assessment, we tie their feelings of satisfaction to educational products, then it becomes more difficult for them to enjoy the teaching process. Continuous feedback about processes and progress not only helps focus the teaching, but provides continuous motivation which is intrinsically oriented, along with a noncompetitive, nonpunitive atmosphere.

The Notion of Process Evaluation

Some writers in the field of evaluation have specifically addressed the issue of process evaluation. For example, Hayman and Napier (1975) describe process evaluation as examining "the reasons why events occur in a particular manner at a particular time" (p. 62). They note that process evaluation is collaborative from beginning to end, with information being shared with those involved in the process as much as possible. They also state that it involves flexible formation of short- and long-term objectives and an action orientation. To complete the extreme contrast to the measurement approach, they note that,

> Both task and emotional or maintenance problems arise as a program develops. Task problems are issues that surround the structural and operational methods used in an effort to accomplish the program goals. Maintenance or emotional issues relate to how people feel about what is happening to them and others as the program evolves and how these attitudes and feelings influence program outcomes. (p. 63)

While measurement is seen as amoral, then, evaluation is clearly a moral activity. Beeby (1977) proposes that evaluation is "the systematic collection and interpretation of evidence, leading, as part of the process, to a judgement of value with a view to action" (cited in Wolf 1984, p. 3). He stresses that an important element in this definition is the action orientation. Furthermore, Wolf notes that whereas comparison is required in a measurement model, it is neither required nor often even desirable in an evaluation model. As defined, there is relatively little place for "measurement" in the educational process because (a) it is not action-oriented, and (b) most of the assessment involves areas in which "the major attributes studied are chosen because they represent educational values" (Wolf 1984). On these grounds alone, we are involved with evaluation rather than with measurement. I believe that the notions of process and evaluation fit quite naturally together, and fit rather well with some of the recent research in the teaching and learning of the language arts. Perhaps we should turn to the field of evaluation for our model of information collection and use in the language arts.

I have stressed this more informal, volitional approach to evaluation in the language arts as if it were related only to the classroom. There are, however, examples of the application of these principles to population-level evaluation. For example, a national assessment in Britain has used matrix sampling techniques with volunteer schools, in which different students are assessed on a variety of language tasks. Interviewers are trained to set up naturalistic tasks and contexts within which oral language samples can be obtained (Clearinghouse for Applied Performance Testing 1984).

Conclusion

In this paper I have suggested that we take a more radical approach to the improvement of assessment in the language arts than we have in the past. I have purposely downplayed formal assessment since virtually all of our efforts in the field of assessment have been focused on that area and I am suspicious that we are simply trying to hone a sledgehammer. I have tried to point out the costs of this focus, particularly in terms of the value and use of the information obtained and the consequent fragmentation of language arts education. It is not at all clear that our present methods advance our goal of optimal learning for all children.

While I have deemphasized product-oriented assessment, I do not wish to argue that we are not interested in educational outcomes. However, I do believe that many of the outcomes which we would like to see are in fact processes. Unless the processes are well-developed, independently motivated, and self-correcting, we are unlikely to see development taking place outside of school. In this regard, I have particularly stressed the importance of motivation. If through our assessment procedures we manage to kill children's motivation to participate in and experiment with the language arts—even though we might teach them *how* to participate—we will have failed.

There are some components of present assessment techniques that may be salvageable. I have not dwelt on these. Instead I have emphasized the need for a fresh approach. To date we have compared children's learning with other children's learning in order to evaluate it. A better standard for evaluation would be a solid developmental theory of literacy or oracy. If we shift to a greater emphasis on informal, nonaccountable assessment, then we will be less concerned about developing instruments which will accurately measure regardless of the teacher. Our greater concern will be with teacher development because the teacher will have become the assessment instrument. We will be concerned about teaching teachers to be sensitive observers, and about how to teach by listening. We will have put assessment back into its proper relationship with teaching and learning.

I have suggested that if we wish to have such a model of assessment, we must change some aspects of the context in which we operate. The most needed change is in society's attitude towards educators. The Scottish Council for Educational Research (Broadfoot 1979) has expressed this well:

> We stopped short of asking the parents bluntly: "Do you trust the teachers?" If they do not, then it is time we took steps to remedy our public relations. If we are not to be trusted, then the whole edifice of the school falls down, whatever the external supports. We have to show that we can be trusted, by accepting our full responsibilities instead of passing the buck. Perhaps if we prove that we know our pupils, this will challenge the community to value our work more highly. (p. 23)

Parents (and administrators) need to have less faith in numbers and be more impressed when a teacher can tell them, without preparation, about children's literacy development and pull out a file documenting specifically where growth has occurred. The length and quality of the description would seem to be a very effective measure of teacher quality. If such an approach were adopted, while doubtless initially we would have some skeptical parents (we have them already), we would also have some defenseless teachers. Some teachers depend on standardized test scores to provide them with information about the children's learning. The ability of teachers to provide accurate process information about specific children on request is a tough test of teacher quality. The only real excuse for failure is too high a teacher-pupil ratio, and that excuse is not a reflection on the teacher or the assessment model, but on social values.

Unless we know our students, we cannot presume to tailor our instruction to their needs, particularly in the language arts, which require a supportive, communicative context. In order to know our students, we must listen to them and interact with them on an individual basis. Further, unless we take the role of advocates, we will find that they will not let us know them. If they will not talk, we cannot listen. I believe that these principles hold equally well at levels of assessment above the teacher-student relationship. Unless trust is restored to the whole educational enterprise, we will be unable to enter into honest dialogue directed at improving the learning of our children.

References

Anderson, B. D., and P. Lesser (1978). The costs of legislated minimum competency requirements. *Phi Delta Kappan* 59: 606–8.

Baker, E. (1979). *Achievement tests in urban schools: New numbers.* St. Louis: CEMREL.

Baker, E. L., and J. L. Herman (1980). Task structure design: Beyond linkage. *Journal of Educational Measurement* 20: 149–64.

Beeby, C. E. (1977). The meaning of evaluation. *Current issues in education: No. 4 Evaluation*. Wellington, New Zealand: Department of Education.

Boyd, J., B. H. McKenna, R. H. Stake, and J. Yashinsky (1975). *A study of testing practices in the Royal Oak (Michigan) public schools*. Royal Oak, Mich.: Royal Oak City School District. ED 117 161.

Broadfoot, P. (1979). *Assessment, schools and society*. London: Methuen.

Calkins, L. M. (1983). *Lessons from a child: On the teaching and learning of writing*. Exeter, N.H.: Heinemann.

Catterall, J. (1982). *The cost of school testing programs*. CSE report no. 194. Los Angeles: Center for the Study of Evaluation.

Clay, M. M. (1975). *What did I write?* Auckland, New Zealand: Heinemann.

——— (1979a). *Reading: The patterning of complex behavior*. 2d ed. Exeter, N.H.: Heinemann.

——— (1979b). *The early detection of reading difficulties: A diagnostic survey with recovery procedures*. 2d. Exeter, N.H.: Heinemann.

Clearinghouse for Applied Performance Testing (1984). Spotlighting Great Britain: Practical assessment with the personal touch. *CAPTRENDS*, no. 2 (September).

Csikszentmihalyi, M. (1975). *Beyond boredom and anxiety*. San Francisco: Jossey-Bass.

Danwitz, M. W. (1981). Formal versus informal assessment: Fragmentation versus holism. *Topics in language disorders* 1: 95–106.

deCharms, R. (1983). Intrinsic motivation, peer tutoring, and cooperative learning: Practical maxims. In *Teacher and student perceptions: Implications for learning*, edited by J. M. Levine and M. C. Wang, 391–98. Hillsdale, N.J.: Erlbaum.

Dorr-Bremme, D. (1982). *Assessing students: Teachers' routine practices and reasoning*. CSE report no. 194. Los Angeles: Center for the Study of Evaluation.

Durrell, D. D., and H. B. Sullivan (1937). *Durrell-Sullivan reading capacity and achievement tests*. New York: Harcourt, Brace & World.

Easley, J., and R. Zwoyer (1975). Teaching by listening—toward a new day in math classes. *Contemporary Education* 47: 19–25.

Ferreiro, E. (1978). What is written in a written sentence? A developmental answer. *Journal of Education* 160, no. 4: 25–39.

Feuerstein, R. (1979). *The dynamic assessment of retarded performers: The learning potential assessment device, theory, instruments and techniques*. Baltimore: University Park Press.

Frederiksen, N. (1984). The real test bias: Influences of testing on teaching and learning. *American Psychologist* 39: 193–202.

Gambrell, L. B. (1984). How much time do children spend reading during teacher-directed reading instruction? In *Changing perspectives on research in reading/language processing and instruction*, 33rd Yearbook, edited by O. Niles, 193–98. Rochester, New York: National Reading Conference.

Graves, D. H. (1983). *Writing: Teachers and children at work*. Exeter, N.H.: Heinemann.

Gronlund, N. E. (1976). *Measurement and evaluation in teaching,* 3d ed. New York: Macmillan.

Halliday, M. A. K. (1977). *Explorations in the functions of language.* New York: Elsevier North-Holland.

Hayman, J. L., Jr., and R. N. Napier (1975). *Evaluation in the schools: A human process for renewal.* Monterey, Calif.: Brooks-Cole.

Hill, K. T. (1980). Motivation, evaluation and educational testing policy. In *Achievement motivation: Recent trends in theory and research,* edited by L. J. Fyans. New York: Plenum.

Holdaway, D. (1979). *The foundation of literacy.* New York: Ashton Scholastic.

Jorgenson, G. W. (1977). Relationship of classroom behavior to the accuracy of the match between material difficulty and student ability. *Journal of Educational Psychology* 69: 24–32.

Labov, W. (1973). *Sociolinguistic patterns.* Philadelphia: University of Pennsylvania Press.

Launer, P. B., and M. Lahey (1981). Passages: From the fifties to the eighties in language assessment. *Topics in Language Disorders* 11: 11–29.

Leontiev, A. (1979). The problem of activity in psychology. *The concept of activity in Soviet psychology,* edited by J. V. Wertsch, 37–71. Armonk, N.Y.: Sharpe.

Maehr, M. L. (1983). On doing well in science: Why Johnny no longer excels; why Sara never did. In *Learning and motivation in the classroom,* edited by S. G. Paris, G. M. Olson, and H. W. Stevenson, 179–210. Hillsdale, N.J.: Erlbaum.

Mehrens, W. A., and I. J. Lehmann (1984). *Measurement and evaluation in education and psychology.* 3d ed. New York: Holt, Rinehart & Winston.

Merwin, J. C. (1982). Standardized tests: One tool for decision making in the classroom. *Educational Measurement: Issues and Practice* 1: 14–16.

Nicholls, J. (1983). Conceptions of ability and achievement motivation: A theory and its implications for education. In *Learning and motivation in the classroom,* edited by S. G. Paris, G. Olson, and H. Stevenson, 211–37. Hillsdale, N.J.: Erlbaum.

Nicholson, T. (1984). Experts and novices: A study of reading in the high school classroom. *Reading Research Quarterly* 19: 436–51.

Nurss, J., and M. McGauvrin (1976). *Teacher's manual, Part two: Interpretation and use of test results.* New York: Harcourt Brace Jovanovich.

Paris, S. G., and J. Jacobs (1984). The benefits of informed instruction for children's reading awareness and comprehension skills. *Child Development* 55: 2083–93.

Paris, S. G., and M. Myers (1981). Comprehension monitoring, memory, and study strategies of good and poor readers. *Journal of Reading Behavior* 13: 5–22.

Pearson, P. D., and L. Fielding (1982). Research update: Listening comprehension. *Language Arts* 59: 617–29.

Rogers, C. R. (1942). *Counseling and psychotherapy.* Boston: Houghton Mifflin.

Rosenblatt, L. M. (1978). *The reader, the text, the poem: The transactional theory of the literary work.* Carbondale, Ill.: Southern Illinois University Press.

Scriven, M. (1972). Objectivity and subjectivity in educational research. In *Philosophical redirection of educational research*, edited by L. G. Thomas. 71st Yearbook of the National Society for the Study of Education, Part one. Chicago: University of Chicago Press.

Spache, G. (1981). *Diagnostic reading scales*. New York: McGraw-Hill.

Time (1980). Help, teacher can't teach. *Time*, 16 June, 56–63.

Vygotsky, L. S. (1962). *Thought and language*. Cambridge, Mass.: MIT Press.

—— (1978). *Mind in society: The development of higher psychological processes*. Cambridge, Mass.: Harvard University Press.

Walmsley, S. (1979). The criterion referenced measurement of an early reading behavior. *Reading Research Quarterly* 14: 574–604.

Webster's New Twentieth Century Dictionary. (1979). 2d ed. New York: Simon & Schuster.

Wertsch, J. (1979). The concept of activity in Soviet psychology: An introduction. In *The concept of activity in Soviet psychology*, edited by J. Wertsch, 3–36. Armonk, N.Y.: Sharpe.

Wixson, K. K., A. B. Bosky, M. N. Yochum, and D. E. Alvermann (1984). An interview for assessing students' perceptions of classroom reading tasks. *The Reading Teacher* 37: 346–52.

Wolf, R. M. (1984). *Evaluation in education: Foundations of competency assessment and program review*. 2d ed. New York: Praeger.

Commentary

Jerome C. Harste
Indiana University

The thing that both Hansen and Johnston are talking about is curriculum. Curriculum is that place where theory and practice transact. They call for "practical theory"—for the development of a theory of language in use. The keys to this advancement are collaboration (between researchers and teachers, teachers and children, evaluators and evaluatees) and reflexivity (for learners as teachers and teachers as learners).

These papers are, I think, extremely important. Curriculum is what all too often falls in the cracks in recent attempts to improve instruction.

The function of curriculum is to provide perspective. I read Hansen as arguing that in organizing a good language arts program three things must be considered. Children must have opportunities to engage in, see demonstrated, and come to value the strategies that we associate with successful written language use and learning.

Hansen's "engage-in" criterion means that teachers must provide children with multiple opportunities (invitations) to use reading and writing functionally as tools for learning each day. Reading and writing must be juxtaposed such that reasoning is highlighted.

Hansen's "see-demonstrated" criterion acknowledges the social nature of language and language learning and says that classrooms must be places for authors and authorship, where children see themselves and their teachers as authors and learn from each other and from the social-participant structures that such an environment provides. Teachers need to write, too. Their engagement in the invitations given to children provides strategic demonstrations of proficient written language use and learning in operation, as well as allowing the educator to experience, savor, and self-critique the curricular experience.

Hansen's "come-to-value" criterion says that lots and lots of opportunities to engage in reading and writing each day, and to be in an environment where children can learn the strategies of successful written language use and learning from adults and each other, are not enough. Children also need group sharing times where what they have learned from engagement and demonstration can be brought to the level of conscious awareness. In this process children come to value and revalue strategies that otherwise would be lost. By stressing this "coming-to-value," Hansen means that children must be given the opportunity to talk about what problems they encountered and what strategic moves they used to solve or circumvent problems. What worked for you can work for me. This criterion acknowledges the social nature of knowing and the fact that, if what we know is not confirmed by others, that knowing will atrophy.

Johnston wants to do lots of things. But when you are talking relationships (between teaching and learning, teachers and children, plans and accomplishments, evaluation and instruction), you are talking curricula. Educators have responsibility to plan. Their paper curricula are more than lesson plans; they are envisionments of what a literate learner is. They are envisionments of how learners strategically use reading and writing as tools for learning. That's what it really means to be literate. Reading and writing are processes of signification which permit the users to reflexively explore, expand, and critique their world, and also their formulations for exploring, expanding, and examining that world in the first place. While reading and writing are vehicles by which we preserve our heritage of literacy, they are also important ways by which we re-perceive ourselves and our world for purposes of growth. By tying the Johnston and Hansen papers together with this response, "paper curricula" are planes which explicate a series of language experiences designed to permit children to engage in, see demonstrated, and come to value the strategies we associate with successful written language use and learning.

But the paper curriculum isn't "curriculum." Curriculum is always a relationship. It's a relationship between our plans and the mental trip that the language user takes. In this regard, we let materials and tests be our curricular informants. But this is wrong. The child must be our curricular informant.

There are no inherently good or bad language activities. If the language environment we create does not get the child to take the mental journey that we think important, then we must revise our plan and attempt to set up an optimum environment. That is what the processes of evaluation and curriculum development are all about. And that is why curriculum evaluation and curriculum development are much too impor-tant to be left in the hands of those who rarely come in contact with teachers, children, and classrooms. I agree with Johnston: if it doesn't improve instruction, throw it out. If assessment is to be useful, it cannot be divorced from the specifics of practice.

Evaluation is a final frontier for those advocating a process approach to reading and writing instruction. This doesn't surprise me. Evaluation is such a sordid business that it should surprise no one that humanists would find the labeling of teaching, programs, and children the least consecrated ground to walk on.

But assessment must be addressed. We have been using product measures to judge the value of our process curriculum. In doing so, we have confused the public, children, and ourselves.

If access to literacy is defined as engagement in the process of signification for purposes of reflexivity, then collaboration—not convention—is paramount. We have to become, and help our children become, more interested in understanding the process by which convention and conventional thinking arise than in convention itself. That does not mean that the conventions that exist as a function of the strategies of positivism and reductionism are not worth knowing or doing. Rather, what it means is that history is alive, and that the heritage of literacy which is given to us is a potential for taking the mental journeys our parents took and reflexively going beyond those journeys. The products of literacy—what appear to be convention and control—are the dinosaur tracks of what earlier was a dynamic period of existence. Convention and control represent thought at rest and must be recognized for their potential as a new beginning, not as a paragon of truth or an admission ticket to watch the show. The function of evaluation is to help us and children maintain this curricular perspective. Both Johnston and Hansen are right: little and not-so-little things do make a difference.

I recently had the opportunity to observe instruction in a series of elementary school classrooms in an attempt to understand what the teaching of reading comprehension meant from the perspective of the participants involved. It was a fascinating experience. One of the conclusions I too have reached is that little things make a huge curricular difference. Some even make it unlikely that curriculum will ever be experienced or addressed by the participants involved.

A similar event occurred in a number of the classrooms I observed, when a class member would ask the teacher for help in spelling a word. Although this may seem like a rather insignificant event given the topics of organizing and evaluating instruction in the language arts, I wish to argue that what happened was of great organizational and evaluative significance.

While writing a story, Kammi, a kindergarten child, asked Mrs.

Mattson how to spell the word *bird*. Mrs. Mattson replied, "Isn't that a first draft you are working on? . . . Well then, do the very best you can. . . . We'll take care of it later, if and when you decide to take this piece to publication."

Later I examined Kammi's rough draft. Initially she had spelled *bird* B-R-D, quite phonetically. Her second attempt was spelled B-R-D-A, indicating that she had said it slowly out loud, listening to the sounds as she recorded them, i.e., "bir . . . da." Her third attempt, B-R-I-D, obviously was made because she didn't like the way B-R-D-A looked.

Kammi wrote her story to go along with a set of xeroxed pictures she had selected from a book that Mrs. Mattson introduced during Group Sharing Time. One of the pictures depicted a group of children burying a dead bird they had found. The epitaph on the tombstone in one of the pictures read "HERE LIES A BIRD THAT IS DEAD." When Kammi encountered this picture and its text, she was obviously ready for the spelling information that was provided, as her final three spellings of *bird* were penned B-I-R-D.

In another classroom, I observed a little girl also ask her teacher for the spelling of the word *bird* as she attempted to complete a worksheet on *r*-controlled words. The teacher, in this instance, gave the child the word. The child took this information back to her seat and used the teacher's spelling as a template for her own.

In a third classroom, Maura and Jennifer were writing in their science journals. Both were members of the Bird Club in Myriam Revel-Wood's classroom. At one point, Maura asked Jennifer how to spell the word *parrot* as she was making an entry about having gone to the zoo. Jennifer took a scrap of paper and wrote out several versions: P-A-R-O-T, P-A-R-E-T, P-A-R-A-T-E. Together they looked at the three and elected P-A-R-O-T as the best of the lot.

Later, but still writing in her science journal, Maura wanted to record her observations on an Australian emu she had also seen at the zoo. Instead of asking Jennifer this time, she simply moved to the top of her paper and wrote out several versions of the spelling of *emu*, electing E-M-U as her final choice.

These stories, for me, are the essence of what the Hansen and Johnston papers are all about. I agree with Hansen that it is through authoring— creating personal narratives—that we make sense of our world. Unlike Moffett, I think this is as true for adults as it is for children. James Moffett made the following point in *Teaching the Universe of Discourse* (1968) in relation to his theory of development:

> Whereas adults differentiate their thought into specialized kinds of discourse such as narrative, generalization and theory, children

> must for a long time make narrative do for all. They utter themselves almost entirely through stories—real or invented—and they apprehend what others say through story. (p. 49)

I do not believe only children do this; I believe it to be a cognitive universal. That is why my latest book is called *Language Stories and Literacy Lessons*.

But enough! Let me just say that it is these three classroom spelling stories that helped me make sense of Hansen's and Johnston's papers. Each of the three stories, curricularly, represent different mental journeys.

If Kammi's teacher had given her the spelling of *bird,* a quite different set of cognitive processing operations would have characterized Kammi's repeated penning of *bird* in her story. Similarly, if the participant structures that normally surround written language use were not permitted to occur in Myriam Revel-Wood's classroom, Maura would not have had such ready access to the successful spelling strategies which Jennifer had developed. In contrast, in the second classroom, time-on-task was the battle cry of the administration. In that classroom, written language use and learning were not permitted to occur, as they were seen as residing outside of learning and literacy. In fact, the lack of understanding or appreciation of the sociological as well as the psychological strategies of successful written language use and learning caused the language arts curriculum to be subverted. Talk during reading and writing was seen as off-task. Assertive discipline and direct instruction, rather than assertive and direct learning, became the dominant focus and the dominant activity masquerading as literacy.

What you believe makes a difference. It affects how you organize and evaluate instruction. I am very pleased with the Hansen and Johnston papers. Their message is clear and direct: think curriculum! For by thinking curriculum, we ensure that children experience reading and writing as tools for learning—that children think curriculum, too. Organizationally and evaluatively, the end result may not be conventional, but it will be collaborative. Who could ask for anything more, given what we know about the social nature of literacy and literacy learning?

References

Harste, J. C., V. A. Woodward, and C. L. Burke (1984). *Language stories and literacy lessons.* Portsmouth, N.H.: Heinemann.

Moffett, J. (1968). *Teaching the universe of discourse.* Boston: Houghton Mifflin.

Commentary

P. David Pearson
University of Illinois at Urbana-Champaign

As I looked at Jane Hansen's and Peter Johnston's papers, I worked for a theme to unite them. The theme, I think, is transparent: what Jane and Peter have given us is a mandate and a process for change. But in doing so, they have complicated our lives and the lives of teachers tremendously, for they have taken the "convenience" out of being educators.

Jane has told us, at least by example, that we cannot change education on a massive scale and has suggested that if we want to change we had better recognize that we may have to do it "one teacher at a time," leading, of course, to the conclusion that we should all stop teaching our methods courses and writing articles and see if we can convince a teacher or group of teachers to adopt us.

Peter has told us that information worth getting to help teachers and students decide where they are with respect to teaching and learning is going to be hard to get and, once we have it, hard to use because we have to evaluate those data rather than measure them.

First let me elaborate on Jane's and then Peter's key notions and then close by returning to the theme of change.

I haven't seen Mast Way School, but I know that what Jane is doing will work. In a more modest way, it has worked for Rob Tierney and me at Metcalf School in Bloomington, Illinois. But to make it work requires much energy, time, and patience. The energy and time requirements are obvious. Patience comes into the scene when one realizes that the adaptation—not the adoption—of new ideas is all you can hope for. And we, like the teacher of remedial readers who is thrilled with a student's decoding of the word *horse,* take our success in small doses. We are thrilled when we see that "prior knowledge" has crept into Mary Rozum's fifth-grade social studies unit on Canada in the form of wall charts that track the progress of kids' growing knowledge of the products, land forms, and climate of the prairie provinces. And we are thrilled when Mary Kay Fairfield puts the skills taught in the basal reading workbook pages to a reality test by seeing how they operate in other basal selections, in her writing, and in the kids' writing. And we know this exhilaration operates at Mast Way; Jane Hansen shared it with us earlier. Maybe one teacher at a time is our only real option.

Peter Johnston's paper reminds me of an historically relevant quote provided me by Miles Olson at the University of Colorado: "The examiner pipes and the teacher must dance—and the examiner sticks to the old tune. If the educational reformers really wish the dance altered they must turn their attention from the dancers to the musicians" (Wells 1892, p. 382).

I am also reminded of a college classmate of mine—a fellow debating team member at Berkeley. As we prepared to march on the San Francisco courthouse to protest the HUAC hearings, we were lamenting the lack of free speech in American society and I heard him say, "Well if we're going to have prior restraint of free speech, let's shut up all those lousy conservative witch-hunters."

We are in a similar bind in assessment. Do we say, "Well, we know assessment drives instruction and as long as that is true, let's replace those bad tests with better ones—or at least get our ideas rather than theirs into the tests"? Or do we side with Johnston and say that the system is so rotten to the core that we have to abandon it and start over? Do we use *infiltration* or *confrontation* to change our schools?

While I agree with Peter that standardized tests are evil indices of product rather than good indices of process, I am surprised that he did not come down harder on what I perceive to be an even greater assessment evil: criterion- and/or objective-referenced tests. I see all the mastery tests in all the basal series we use as even more dangerous to the health of children's literacy because they have a seductive veneer to them: they *look* like they assess what we teach and should therefore be more useful and valid in our attempts to improve individual literacy achievement. But these tests are worse than standardized tests because:

1. They focus on bits and pieces; at least standardized tests require you to read occasionally.
2. They take on a reality that exists only on tests and workbook pages: a workbook page–passage genre, if you will.
3. They can readily be used to make bad instructional decisions (this is what David Dickinson found).
4. The skills that are tested become the ends of instruction rather than the means. Hence we become accountable for things we ultimately don't care about.

I could echo Peter Johnston's hope for the future, but if I were not such an eternal and steadfast Pollyanna optimist, I would say, "Peter it won't work! We had better try infiltration. By the way, Peter, maybe Larry Frase and Chip Bruce can help us now. They have prototypes for interactive, dynamic computer-driven assessment that have the 'right feel' to run them. They are just hard to do and very expensive."

Now back to change. The schema-theory tradition has provided us with an alternative worldview about comprehension processes. But it has emphasized the effect of existing knowledge on comprehension. In the future, researchers will turn their attention to the more difficult question of schema acquisition, or, if you will, the effect of comprehension on knowledge. We will look more carefully at what Bransford, Nitsch, and Franks (1977) identified as the issue of "changing states of schema." And when we do, we will, of course, be returning to a recurrent theme in psychology usually labeled "learning." A vital component of this work on schema acquisition will focus on the issue of vocabulary (it has, in fact, begun—see Nagy and Anderson 1984; and Nagy, Herman, and Anderson 1985), for we will finally recognize that words are but the surface representations of our knowledge.

The text-analysis tradition will change its focus also. Now that we can do a decent job of parsing texts to characterize underlying relations among ideas, we will turn to an age-old issue: what makes a text readable? And our search will be guided by principles very different from long sentences and hard words. In their place, we will substitute principles that come under the label of considerateness (see Armbruster and Anderson 1981, 1982, 1984); these principles will emphasize whether authors provide frameworks for interrelating ideas, analogies that permit cross-topical comparisons, and examples that solidify concept acquisition.

Schema-theory and text-analysis traditions will merge so as to become indistinguishable from one another. This event will result from our discovery that the goal of every author is the same as the goal of every reader—to represent knowledge in as coherent a framework as possible.

We will learn much more about basic relationships between reading and writing (more specifically between comprehension strategies and composing strategies). The promise of an exciting integrated view of language processes, expressed so eloquently by many in recent years, will finally reach fruition.

Finally, we will develop the grace and good judgment necessary to overcome our tendency to debate whether reading is a word-based process or a meaning-based process so that we can come to understand the intrinsic relationship between growth in comprehension strategies and growth in word-identification abilities, particularly in beginning reading.

We will discover the precise ways in which writing activities benefit reading comprehension and vice versa. We will also develop and evaluate programs in which children are taught to read texts for different purposes and from different perspectives (see Wixson and Lipson, in press). For example, we will learn that even young children can be taught to read texts from the perspective of an editor or a critic, and that such instruction benefits both their own writing and their critical reading skills.

We will discover that the benefit of explicit instruction found in many of the existing pedagogical experiments and program-evaluation studies of the early 1980s derives not so much from the explicitness of the instruction as it does from the considerateness of that instruction and from the collaboration that is required when teachers and students learn that it is all right to share cognitive secrets publicly.

We will make even greater strides in learning how to help students develop those mysterious evaluation, monitoring, and repair strategies that come under the rubric of "metacognition." Our greatest progress will come in the area of repair strategies.

We will learn that we can get by without an entire compendium of comprehension skills in our scope-and-sequence charts. We will finally admit what we have known for thirty years: they all reduce to a few basic cognitive processes like summarizing, detecting relationships in an explicit message, filling in gaps, and detecting tricks authors use to try to con us.

What, then, will be going on in our schools in the year 1990 in the name of reading comprehension? Will any current or future research find its way into practice? The answer to these questions is quite complex, for it requires that we consider not only issues of reading-comprehension processes and instruction but also issues of dissemination and change. While I think that the gap between research and practice will always exist, I am optimistic about narrowing it. My optimism stems from two observations. First, the research of the last decade is more deserving of implementation than that of earlier decades. It is more central to what reading is all about, and it is more focused on issues that influence what teachers are responsible for in their classrooms. Second, practitioners are more receptive to research findings now than they have been at any other time during the last twenty years.

Let me close by outlining what I believe to be the requirements of an effective collaborative program for promoting educational change in our schools. There are several essential ingredients that have to be present in such efforts in order for them to work effectively:

1. Teachers have to *want* to try something new. There has to be some disequilibrium in their own minds as a motive for trying something

new. It takes a fair amount of courage to admit (even to ourselves) that what we are doing presently is not what we want to be doing.

2. Administrative support helps—the more the better. Teachers need someone up there saying that this is a good idea.

3. Teachers have to direct the planning for change. Others can try to legislate it, but change proceeds much more smoothly when teachers feel a sense of ownership of the project.

4. Services must be delivered at the level of the people doing the changing. It's not really enough to give a couple of lectures to a group of administrators and supervisors. Change occurs more rapidly when change agents work directly with teachers in their classrooms and schools.

5. Change agents have to establish a forum in which teachers can interact with one another on things that matter and in which teachers are rewarded for behaving professionally. In two efforts I have been involved with in the last year, I have come to the conclusion that my most important role as a change agent is to establish such a forum. Teaching can be a very lonely profession, even when you are in the constant company of your peers. A friend of mine says that the best index of the professional climate of a school is the topic of conversation in the teachers' lounge. She is probably right. Indeed, the teachers in our two projects have corroborated just such a phenomenon in their schools: they found themselves discussing different issues than they used to, and they found themselves using one another as resources.

6. Change efforts need time!

Now, how does all the stuff we have talked about at this seminar about comprehension research fit with what I have just outlined as a set of requirements for effective change? I do not want to conclude that disseminating knowledge about research is any better or any worse than working with teachers directly on change efforts. While direct collaboration is probably more powerful, we might not have any ideas worth implementing. Materials and tests will continue to have an impact on practice whether we like it or not; to avoid getting our hands dirty in this arena is to seal our fate as powerless bystanders. But neither the new knowledge nor the new material will do us any good unless we learn to work together on matters we care about. I see that cooperative potential all over the country: in Hickory Hills, Illinois, and at Metcalf School in Bloomington, Illinois; in Orange County, Florida, and in Kalispell,

Montana; in New York City and in Zion, Illinois; in Fairfax County, Virginia; in Montgomery County, Maryland; in Honolulu; in Wading River, New York; and in Media, Pennsylvania. There is hope in our discontent. Many teachers are tired of curricula and testing programs that drive them into corners and their students away from books. There is also hope, and high expectation, amidst the disillusionment espoused by the critics of education and the fear engendered by those who want to coerce us into change through legislation requiring new and tougher standards for skills we know are not at the heart of literacy. Working together is our only option; if we do not, we will lose the day to the more hostile forces of coercion. I'd rather we changed our school curricula because we realized that we had found more effective choices than because some quasi-official body told us we had to.

References

Armbruster, B., and T. Anderson (1981). *Content area textbooks.* Reading education report no. 23. Champaign, Ill.: Center for the Study of Reading, University of Illinois at Urbana-Champaign.

———— (1982). *Structures for explanations in history textbooks, or so what if Governor Stanford missed the spike and hit the rail?* Technical report no. 252. Champaign, Ill.: Center for the Study of Reading, University of Illinois at Urbana-Champaign.

———— (1984). *Producing considerate expository text: Or easy reading is damned hard writing.* Reading education report no. 46. Champaign, Ill.: Center for the Study of Reading, University of Illinois at Urbana-Champaign.

Bransford, J., K. Nitsch, and J. Franks (1977). Schooling and the facilitation of knowledge. In *Schooling and the acquisition of knowledge,* edited by R. C. Anderson, R. J. Spiro, and W. E. Montague. Hillsdale, N.J.: Erlbaum.

Nagy, W. E., and R. C. Anderson (1984). How many words are there in printed school English? *Reading Research Quarterly* 19: 304–30.

Nagy, W. E., P. Herman, and R. C. Anderson (1985). Learning words from context. *Reading Research Quarterly* 20: 233–53.

Wells, H. G. (1892). On the true lever of education. *Educational Review* 4: 380–85.

Wixson, K. K., and M. Lipson (1986). Reading disability: An interactionist perspective. In *The contexts of school-based literacy,* edited by T. E. Raphael, 131–48. New York: Random House.

Note: Many of the ideas expressed in this commentary are developed more fully in Pearson, P. D. (1986). Twenty years of research in reading comprehension. In *The contexts of school-based literacy,* ed. by T. Raphael, 43–62. New York: Random House.

VII Analysis and Observations

Constructing Useful Theories of Teaching English from Recent Research on the Cognitive Processes of Language

M. C. Wittrock
University of California at Los Angeles

My role at this conference is to stimulate thought about future productive lines and topics of research that will build upon the studies and theory presented. I begin with a discussion of our current state of knowledge in relation to its history. To understand where we are going and where we might go, we need to understand where we have been and where we are now.

Next, I will relate our past to our present and our future by discussing the perspective that unites the research and theory presented at this seminar. I will then focus on the central idea I derived from the conference, which is that research in cognition, English, and reading has recently developed a knowledge base that enhances understanding of the learning of language. That knowledge provides a theoretical and empirical basis for creating a useful theory of the teaching of language. These recent advances lead to a next step for us to take, which is the central implication of my comments for our future.

The main point about our future that I want to make is that we should now focus some of our energy on the important problems of developing a practical theory or theories of teaching language and literacy. Recent research summarized at this conference and models of language learning, curriculum design, instructional activities, teachers' thoughts and learners' cognition—all of which share a common perspective—need to be synthesized into useful conceptions of language teaching. The basis for their synthesis derives from the same paradigm or worldview that brings us together, which is that research on cognition in language enhances our understanding of the learning and teaching of English.

The Study of Cognition in Language

The study of cognition in language brings together in a productive way researchers in English and language arts, psychologists, linguists, and educational researchers. It is fitting that a language scholar, Noam Chomsky, revived in America the ancient cognitive approach to learning and memory that B. F. Skinner and John Watson had opposed. The revival of cognitive theory by people who study language seems especially appropriate because rhetoric, the ancient art of public speaking, fostered its early development. Aristotle, Cicero, Quintilian, and the anonymous authors of ancient rhetorics wrote about cognition and memory, and about teaching students, orators, teachers, and lawyers how to remember speeches and talks.

Aristotle believed that information was stored in images in memory. In the summary of a section on memory in his work entitled "On Memory and Recollection," he wrote, "Thus we have explained what memory or remembering is. It is a state induced by a mental image related as a likeness to that of which it is an image" (I.15). And later in the same work, he wrote what I think is the beginning of cognitive psychology: "Acts of recollection occur when one impulse naturally succeeds another. . . . When we recollect, then, we re-experience one of our former impulses until at last we experience that which customarily proceeds the one which we require. That is why we follow the trail in order, starting in thought from the present or some other concept and from something similar or contrary to or closely connected with what we seek" (II.10–20).

Cicero carried this theory a bit further and developed some of its teaching implications. He described a system for training the memory that was devised by a Greek poet, Simonides: "He inferred that persons desiring to train this faculty must select localities and form mental images of the facts they wish to remember and store those images in the localities, with the result that the arrangement of the localities will preserve the order of the facts, and the images of the facts will designate the facts themselves, and we shall employ the localities and images respectively as a wax writing tablet and letters written on it" (*De Oratore* II.lxxxvi.354).

The anonymous author of the *Rhetorica Ad Herennium* carries the pedagogical implications another step further and discusses how to teach this memory system: "We should, therefore, if we desire to memorize a large number of items, equip ourselves with a large number of backgrounds, so that in these we may set a large number of images. I likewise think it obligatory to have these backgrounds in a series, so that we may never by confusion in their order be prevented from following the images— proceeding from any background we wish, whatsoever its place in the series, and whether we go forwards or backwards—nor from delivering orally what has been committed to the backgrounds" (III.xvii.30).

On this same topic of teaching memory systems, Quintilian wrote, "The first thought is placed, as it were, in the forecourt; the second, let us say, in the living-room; the remainder are placed in due order all around the *impluvium* and entrusted not merely to bedrooms and parlours, but even to the care of statues and the like. This done, as soon as the memory of the facts requires to be revived, all these places are visited in turn and the various deposits are demanded from their custodians, as the sight of each recalls the respective details" (XI.II.20).

In these ancient writings on rhetoric lie the central ideas of cognitive approaches to language learning and teaching. These ideas have flourished for about two millennia. In the Middle Ages they provided a basis for designing cathedrals, statues, and paintings to make memorable some abstract religious concepts and some Bible stories and events. In the Renaissance the imagery and the verbal techniques became generative and were used, according to the British historian Frances Yates (1966), to stimulate the construction of new ideas.

In these ancient beginnings and in their newly revived model counterparts we see the fundamental principles of cognitive learning in the teaching of the art of public speaking. They are, first, that something to be learned must be associated with some prior knowledge. That's an ancient idea, even though we may think that it was conceived of only within the last century. Second, the learner must be active in the construction of relations between something new and something old. Learning is a constructive or generative process. Third, the teacher presents the learner with a strategy, or a system, and guides its use. But the learner develops the personally meaningful relations between experience and concepts to be presented in a speech, using the strategy.

With this background let us turn to the research presented at this conference, its central points, and its implications for future research. I find the research presented here highly encouraging, and I want to support the directions that it takes. The lines of work fall into three areas: (1) reading comprehension; (2) relations between oral and written language; and (3) the teaching of reading, writing, and literature. These three lines or areas of research have in common the study of the thought processes people use to convey meaning and understanding to one another through language using their prior knowledge, common experience, and literary abilities. These lines of research also show that it is once again scientifically respectable to study the cognitive complexities of reading, writing, composition, and comprehension.

Reading Comprehension

In this area of research, the idea I mentioned earlier—that comprehension is a constructive process involving the learner's building of relations between the text, on the one hand, and prior knowledge and experience, on the other hand—comes through clearly.

Comprehension also involves constructing a structure for the text: an understanding of the relations among the paragraphs and among the other parts of the text. And the construction of a text structure or grammar involves the reader or the listener as well as the author or the speaker.

From these lines of research on reading comprehension, one of the next things that we need to do, or that I would suggest we think about doing, is to study ways to teach the construction of these relations and structures. This presents a challenging teaching opportunity that we need now to pursue and see where it leads.

The first topic on reading comprehension that we considered was research on the relations between reading and writing, and our discussion led us toward the second and third major areas of this conference, research on the design and writing of comprehensible text and the relations between written and oral language. The papers presented showed that the thought processes involved in comprehension in reading and writing have important relations with each other that only recently have been discovered and articulated. We studied those relations because we employed a cognitive model. As a result of our worldview, we searched for cognitive processes that might be common across different language activities and behaviors. That is the primary reason we are now searching for relations across reading and writing.

The next topic that we talked about regarding reading comprehension was research on the design and writing of comprehensible text. Closely related ideas about the writing of text also emerged. These ideas acknowledged that comprehension is a search for a text design, and that text design involves themes, distinctive elements, and the constructing of links among the elements for different forms of discourse. This is a logical extension of the argument Calfee presented. It leads to the study of patterns among his themes, elements, and links.

From a cognitive perspective, effective writing is more than putting meaning on the pages, and reading with comprehension involves more than getting meaning off the pages. To pursue this direction further, I suggest we think about studying composition and reading as different sides of the same coin, as a few researchers are beginning to do. An important caveat to remember when we adopt that perspective is that there may well be differences in the teaching of reading and writing even though the cognitive processes are closely related or are the same.

Relations between Oral and Written Language

The second major topic was research on relations between oral and written language. Whether or not oral and written language provide different ways of thinking (a topic discussed extensively and well at this seminar), oral language does provide the foundation for reading, writing, and literature, as well as the source of prior knowledge about language and common sign systems. This point is one that we can build upon in future research. The study of cognition in language emphasizes commonalities and fundamental language abilities.

However, oral language and written language represent somewhat different types of problems and activities for speakers and writers, as was stated here several times. For example, writing or giving a talk is quite different from writing an article or a chapter, as presenters of talks at AERA meetings or similar conferences know. The usual and faulty assumption of the planners of those conferences is that you can write one talk, deliver it at the conference, and later publish it largely intact. However, the words we want to *say* to people are different from the words we want to *write* to people. Speaking and writing require different styles and different approaches to language. They are different kinds of activity, different art forms. Yet I believe there are fundamental cognitive processes that oral language shares with reading and writing.

One of the complexities of a cognitive model is that a commonality at one level might turn out to lead to a difference at another level. Commonalities among cognitive abilities in writing and speaking might produce different kinds of teaching activities for writing and speaking. Conversely, different kinds of teaching activities in writing and speaking might involve the same cognitive processes in learners. That is not an unbearable complexity. That is the nature of relations across different levels of language (cognition and behavior). We can learn to live with the complexity and to build on it.

Empirical evidence does show weak relations between reading and many language skills but strong relations between reading and writing skills. Reading also involves the same knowledge structures as oral language. That finding seems well substantiated. The recommendation I would make regarding these complex findings is that we study relations between cognitive abilities and teaching activities.

The Teaching of Reading, Writing, and Literature

The best way to comment on the third major topic of the conference— the teaching of reading, writing, and literature—is to discuss research that's needed. It is clear from points made at this conference that the teaching of reading and the teaching of writing have commonalities not understood well before. These commonalities involve knowledge structures. They involve learning how to use decontextualized language (if there is such a thing). Several participants, in fact, questioned this generalization. I do not pretend to know how to resolve that issue; but I am quite willing to be convinced on either side. The teaching of composition and the teaching of literature also have commonalities of cognitive processes not obvious earlier. Again, they too involve the same knowledge structures.

Some influential models of language learning also could provide the common substrata for teaching composition, reading, and literature. We need to test models of language learning that have utility for teaching. In other words, we have separate models of language learning and of language teaching. We need models of literature teaching, for example, that have been built upon models of language acquisition. We also need to study language development in close relation to language teaching. In addition, we need to study teachers' models of language teaching, as Trika Smith-Burke wrote, as well as cultural differences in language learning. In brief, we need to study the processes, models, and strategies students use to learn and understand language. Our teaching theories and classroom interventions will be enhanced by this research.

We then should try to teach strategies relevant to reading and writing that will refine students' and teachers' models and preconceptions. To accomplish this goal we need multidisciplinary research teams.

I support these points. However, there are some questions about their implementation. Should we teach reading and writing in the same way that we teach speaking? That is a profound problem. As we know, children learn to talk in quite a different way from the way they learn to read and write. It has been implied at this conference that if there are basic cognitive processes underlying language, then we could teach reading and writing in the same way we teach speaking. Although that logic is sound, I do not think that we should teach speaking, reading, and writing in the same way. It is better to teach reading and writing by the best and most efficient pedagogical activities and curriculum sequences we can design, even when they are unlike the protracted natural activities used in informal and natural settings to teach speaking.

Should we be studying the models of comprehension? Clearly we should. That is an important point that was discussed several times.

Should we be using the computer as a tool? People at the conference were ambiguous about the uses of the computer. It has possibilities for use as a tool in the teaching of reading, as I saw with the marginally literate soldiers that I have recently studied (Wittrock 1984). These men were afraid of the microcomputer at first. They sometimes did not want to work with a machine. They would much rather work with other students, who also could not read, and with a supportive teacher. But in our study they changed their minds after a few weeks, when they had learned some of the possibilities of the computer. The pedagogical use of the microcomputer is an area that is open for study.

Larry Frase asked, "Can we use the computer and do away with drill and practice?" There are good reasons to believe that we can. We ought to try. Frase also asked if theory should grow from practice, as well as practice grow from theory. There's no question about that. Theory and practice should be symbiotic and reciprocal, with each leading to advances in the other.

We also need to study the effects of student choices upon learning. Student choices exemplify the age-old idea that learners have to be mentally active in the construction of what they learn. However, they should be active not only by making choices (which usually means curricular decision making) but also active in constructing relations between what they know and the information in the text. We need research in all these areas, and it must be unified in its conception of language learning.

It seems that we need to implement a unifying cognitive approach to the study of the teaching of English. We have adopted such an approach in research on the basic processes of language, as I mentioned earlier. We now should apply that approach to the understanding of how language teachers change their methods.

I believe that change in teaching comes about not through individual research findings but through changes in the worldviews of teachers and learners. That perspective implies that we need to study teachers' and learners' theories and models of language learning *before* we intervene with new teaching strategies.

Sometimes we are too eager in the study of reading comprehension to develop teaching interventions without considering these models of language learning. It is time for us to back off a little and think the matter through before we tell people how they ought to teach language.

One of the most important topics we took up at this conference in the area of language teaching was evaluation and assessment. And one of the most important points about evaluation that I heard was the idea that we ought to be assessing learners' mediating thought processes. As some of you know, about twenty years ago, with the help of many others, I started the Center of the Study of Evaluation at UCLA. This center has done many good things. I would like to see it increase its study of students' and teachers' mediating thought processes, which are central to evaluating teaching and learning.

We can change education for the better if we can either get rid of evaluation as it now exists, as was said at this conference several times, or if we begin, at the very least, to study the ways people use prior knowledge, examples, images, analogies, metaphors, summaries, questions, grammars, and other ideas and structures to learn. Information about these thought processes is useful to teachers. In fact, one of my students, Helen Schultz, and I (1982) recently completed a survey of reading teachers in several schools in California. These teachers stated that process data were the kind of test information that they could definitely use in their teaching.

For these same reasons, cultural differences and expectations of teachers and learners also need to be studied very closely. In brief we need to devise methods to assess the cognitive and affective processes of learners and teachers.

Research Design and Methods

The main implication I draw about research design is that the cognitive, mediational paradigm of research on language learning and teaching leads to productive findings about teaching language because it includes the learners' prior knowledge and strategies in the study of writing, speaking, and reading. In this research, instruction influences the learners' thought processes, which in turn influence learning. In this paradigm teaching can no longer be directly related to learning. Teaching relates to learners' thought processes, which determine or influence achievement.

We also need ethnographic or observational research to identify the models, strategies, and prior knowledge of the learners which influence language learning. These studies should include theory-based naturalistic research on explicit teaching of the strategies of comprehension.

There is room within a cognitive approach for a variety of methods of research. We need to choose the research method appropriate for the substantive problems, rather than ally ourselves with one kind of research. We do not need to classify ourselves as experimentalists or as naturalists, or to feel that we do only observational research or only case studies. These narrow conceptions of ourselves put the horse before the cart. We ought to broaden our conception of ourselves as researchers and use the appropriate research methods for the problem. The problem should come first, not the method.

In the coming years, research studies will be much broader in the methods and forms of data they can accept, now that we are using cognitive models to shape our worldviews. Many people can play the research game now. You need not be a card-carrying experimentalist or a behaviorist. Even introspective data have utility in recent research.

Summary

One of the most important strengths of the study of cognition in language is that it brings together researchers from a variety of perspectives and disciplines, just as we saw here at this conference. It also brings together researchers and teachers who share a common or everyday vocabulary that enables them to communicate with each other better than they could in the days of behaviorism. Through recent research on the cognitive processes of language we now have a knowledge base relevant to the improvement of language teaching and to the development of useful models of teaching. We should now direct much of our energy to this development.

Although we have most of the building blocks of a useful theory of teaching, we are still missing several of them. We are, for example, not knowledgeable about the affective processes of learners—their motivations and self-concepts—as I discovered when I studied reading comprehension among marginally literate soldiers. Some of the most important problems we faced in the teaching of reading comprehension were the problems of motivation and self-concept. Many of these young men felt that they could not succeed in or out of school—that they could not get married, could not have a family, could not get a job in the Army, and could not get a job out of the Army—all because they could not read. These were pressing problems for them. The emotionally laden problems made learning stultifying. They destroyed the formal opportunities the soldiers had to learn.

We also need to study learners' models of comprehension and why learners persevere in these models. An inadequate model of comprehension is difficult to unlearn or to replace. People sometimes believe that if they just learn vocabulary they then can read with understanding. Even when you show them that their model is not adequate, they still do not give up the model. I do not understand why these models persevere, but they do persevere. We need to change learners' beliefs about reading comprehension and their roles in it. Many poor readers feel that comprehension is an automatic process that occurs if they just read the words on the page. That model has to change. How do we go about that change process?

In sum, we need to turn some of our energy toward using a cognitive paradigm to synthesize findings and knowledge about the cognitive processes of language learning, curriculum, instruction, learners, and teachers into testable and practical theories of teaching, as did the ancient teachers of rhetoric, who developed pedagogical procedures from models of the cognitive processes of memory. We have come full circle. The study of language and rhetoric continues today to be a primary source of ideas about cognition and teaching, as it was in ancient Greece and Rome. Our proud heritage brings us together today and provides us with useful ideas for synthesizing knowledge and improving on teaching.

References

Anonymous, *Rhetorica ad herennium,* trans. H. Caplan (1968). Cambridge: Harvard University Press.

Aristotle, *On the soul, Parva naturalia,* and *On breath*, trans. W. S. Hett (1935). Cambridge: Harvard University Press.

Cicero. *De oratore,* trans. E. W. Sutton (1942). Cambridge: Harvard University Press.

Quintilian. *Institutio oratoria*, trans. H. E. Butler (1953). Vol. 4. Cambridge: Harvard University Press.

Wittrock, M. C. (1984). *Teaching reading comprehension to adults in basic skills courses*. Final report, Basic Skills Resource Center Project, 3 vols. Los Angeles: University of California.

Wittrock, M. C., and H. J. Schultz (1982). School and classroom evaluation. In *Testing achievement in basic skills,* Vol. 1, edited by H. Singer, R. Ruddell, J. McNeil, and M. C. Wittrock, 151–200. Final report. University of California.

Yates, F. (1966). *The art of memory.* Chicago: University of Chicago Press.

Themes and Progressions in Research on English

John T. Guthrie
The University of Maryland

In this reflection I will first remark on the current of methodology for research in English and suggest three polarities that characterize the substantive trends. Then I will suggest three forms of progress that have occurred in the first half of the 1980s.

An appraisal of current progress, however, is remiss without the inclusion of an historical landmark. Since I am commenting on a review of research, my landmark will consist of another review of research. In 1941, William S. Gray published a synthesis of social and behavioral science research on reading. Originally appearing in the *Encyclopedia of Educational Research*, it was reprinted in 1984 by the International Reading Association under the title *Reading*.

According to Gray, there had been 1,951 "scientific studies relating to reading" published by 1941. He observed that in the first half-century of research,

> Only a limited number of studies [had] related specifically to the mental processes involved in the apprehension of the meaning of what is read. All investigators agree that these processes are numerous and complex. . . . Only in so far as the reader's experiences relate in some form or other to the concepts or situations to which the author refers can the reader comprehend what is read. . . .
>
> In the act of reading, however, one cannot always rely on the meanings which he has previously attached to specific words. This is due to the fact that they are often used by the writer in a new or different sense. As a result the reader must search, sometimes quite vigorously, for the specific meanings implied by the words read. The essence of this phase of the reading . . . is to select and combine relevant items of experience that are implied by the immediate context, by the author's mood, tone, or intention, and by everything the reader knows that makes clear the meaning of a passage. . . .
>
> . . . The reader may engage also in a number of supplementary steps or processes of which the following are examples: drawing inferences, seeing implications, and judging the validity of the ideas presented;

> making judgments concerning the quality, effectiveness, or complete-
> ness of the author's presentations; comparing the views of different
> authors concerning the same issue; applying the ideas gained to new
> situations; using the information secured in the solution of personal
> and social problems; and integrating the ideas gained through reading
> with previous experience to acquire improved patterns of thinking
> and of action. Whether an individual compares the ideas read with
> previous experience, judges their validity, or applies them in the
> solution of a personal problem depends on his motives, purposes,
> attitudes, and interests at the time. (pp. 26–29)

This was Gray's understanding of reading in 1941. Although I do not
know how widely shared this viewpoint was, the conceptual framework is
remarkably similar to the understanding of the reading process that is
conveyed in this mid-decade appraisal of progress. An important distinction between then and now is that reasonably controlled empirical studies
have been performed to verify the importance of most of the features of
this view of reading. Modern-day formations of literacy indeed entail all
of the complex dimensions that Gray expected. The following commentary
will address two questions. First, what themes describe these recent
findings from research? Then, what forms of progress can be observed?

Themes

There are three polarities that may be used to construe the trends
reported at this conference. The first polarity pertains to the research
findings, and consists of literacy processes on the one hand and instructional strategies on the other. Knowledge about literacy processes is
based on observations of readers and writers but rarely on interventions
with them. Although experiments may be conducted in which performance is compared on different tasks to draw inferences about reading
strategies, the experimental conditions are not serious instructional
developments. We seldom learn about students' basic processes from
engaging them in instruction that will be durable and consequential in
other educational activities. The conference participants reiterated that
while knowledge of process may inform people who construct teaching
models, it does not in itself have strict implications or prescriptions for
an instructional theory.

Instructional research, in the main, has been oriented to relatively
global literacy processes that may be measured by standardized reading-
comprehension tests or the primary-trait scoring of written essays. This
research has emphasized characteristics of teachers, students, texts, and
their connections as they may influence a composite literacy that is rarely
enlightened by literacy-process research. Instructional research, then,

has not shed light on the nature of the literacy processes. Although we know, for example, that the quality of writing depends on distinctions among purposes in writing, systematic instructional research has not taken the teaching of purpose in writing as worthy of separate attention and deliberate analysis. This is not to say that purpose should be disembodied from other aspects of writing but rather that we have too few empirically documented strategies for improving literacy processes.

A second polarity is methodological. There is a tension between our need for discovery and our need for verification. The papers in this conference incorporated a broad array of scholarly fields and the methods that are indigenous to those disciplines. A brief accounting shows that the authors drew from experimental psycholinguistics (Schallert), sociolinguistics (Harste), the philosophy of language (Myers), systematic classroom observation (Fillion and Brause), educational anthropology (Hansen), correlational research (Smith-Burke), system design (Frase), rhetorical text analysis (Calfee), applied measurement (Johnston), literary criticism (Schallert), computer science (Bruce), and semiotics (Tierney). Findings from all of these areas have been woven into the fabric of the presentations in this conference.

Despite the pluralism of sources for inquiry, the issue of methodology was conspicuous by its absence. The study of method, consisting of thinking about the nature of evidence and its limits, was not evident in the papers. Epistemological qualms may have occurred to the authors while they were composing them, but I suspect not. The tone of these papers is rather one of discovery. Their separate searches for good sense about literacy processes or teaching have led these authors to unearth a plethora of new concepts. These concepts have been adopted to the degree that they are novel, provocative, and reasonably capable of being related to the authors' perspectives. Discovery of relationships, trends, and future possibilities has been the tenor. By contrast, descriptions of verification, either within a disciplinary research method or across disciplines, did not appear. In the search for relatively broad, complex, and inspiring intellectual frameworks, the threshold of empirical and logical verification has been lowered. This process is overdue and healthy. I have no doubt that skepticism will return in a cycle and uproot the few perverse notions that inevitably sprout in periods such as this.

The third polarity relates to the recommendations for research that were made by the authors. This polarity can be referred to as contextualism versus isolationism. Several authors recommended research that will illustrate the fine detail in the pragmatics of literacy. How do the functions of reading elicit different strategies for accomplishing those functions? How do the purposes for writing lead learners to produce different forms? How does the social context of communication influence what is said, written, or learned?

Contextualism also pertains to instruction. Recommendations from the authors include the notion that to learn about teaching, we need more direct study of effective teachers and tutors. This study of instruction cannot take place in a detached setting but must occur in the classrooms and communities. Contextualized studies of instruction also need to be both global and analytical. They may be analytical by focusing on a particular process such as purpose, word use, revision, or rhetorical structure. This focus need not, however, eliminate the contextual background that gives literacy its essential properties.

Attempts to understand literacy processes apart from one another or to conduct research on independent instructional techniques have been discouraged. Because literacy processes are part of a communicative milieu, they must be studied in their natural habitats. Since instructional techniques are never used in isolation they must be examined in situ. The ecology of instruction for literacy processes must be understood. We need to learn about the laws of natural selection for activities in educational environments.

Progressions

The notion of progress in research is a substantial challenge for philosophers of science. Without attempting to fully meet that challenge in this limited space, I nevertheless submit that three forms of progress in research on English can be observed in this conference.

The first form may be termed improvements of theory. I presume that the basic aim or goal of science is understanding, and that this understanding is achieved through theoretical knowledge. Theoretical knowledge is distinct from conjecture or opinion since it is supported by empirical facts or observations. Theories improve in proportion to their increases in predictive accuracy, internal coherence, external consistency, unifying power, fertility, and simplicity. As theories improve they become more inclusive than previous theories and resolve apparent contradictions from previously conflicting perspectives. If new theories emerge with reasonable frequency within a community of scholars, progress may be considered to occur in that field (Mosenthal 1985).

One basic phenomenon in English that calls for a theoretical account is the processing of written language. Passages of narration or exposition are composed by writers and comprehended by readers. Gray (1941) was attempting to explain this phenomenon with his proposals, and the same phenomenon has drawn attention during the 1980s. Accounting for written-language processing has been improved by moving beyond the word and the sentence to the macro-structure of language. The understanding and active use of story constituents and information hierarchies in exposition have been documented. In addition, metaprocessing, consisting of plans for understanding language structure, has been found in both writers and readers. These advances fulfill the criteria of increasing predictive accuracy and enhancing external consistency with the theories and disciplines outside of English.

A second form of progress in research on English is a change in values. In scientific inquiry of any kind, value systems necessarily undergird the enterprise. Human consciousness gives rise to beliefs which are the ground from which both theories and observations spring. The physicist Fritjof Capra captured this notion when he said, "My conscious decision about how to observe, say, an electron will determine the electron's properties to some extent. If I ask a particle question, it will give me a particle answer; if I ask a wave question, it will give me a wave answer!" (1975). Different definitions of a phenomenon are often interpretations about its character.

A plurality of values, however, does not make us dependent on mere social consensus for establishing progress. The continued use of the criteria for improvements in theoretical explanations, that is, predictive accuracy and so on, will prevent the aimless wanderings of relativism. Changes in belief bring new concepts and conjectures. These are eventually entered into the competition for scholarly respectability. To the extent that these beliefs are verified by independent observations and critical analyses, they may lead to theoretical advances.

Several changes in value may be seen in the reviews of research presented at this conference. One of them is based on the theme of contextualism. The conference participants for the most part embrace the perspective of semiotics as necessary to defining the phenomenon of language comprehension. In this view, the text as a written language artifact cannot be processed by the reader or writer outside of a social and personal milieu. Such factors as the reasons people have for communicating and the assumptions they make about who they are communicating with are defined as part of the phenomenon of literacy. The belief is that reading should be understood as part of a personal and social endeavor. The social context does not account for reading or explain it in some sense; rather, the social context is the *ground* of literacy, its necessary condition.

Another belief stated in these reviews is that the facets of literacy should be considered in unison. Reading, writing, exposition, and narration are seen as interconnected. Value has been placed upon the similarities rather than the differences among these aspects of written language. The belief that we should emphasize and extend our understanding about the cognitive basics of all literacy stands in contrast to the attempt to fractionate the processes into parts and subparts that prevailed in the 1970s and is retained now in certain research communities.

A third aspect of progress is the practice of English. An endless stream of human actions are literate or enhance literacy in some way. One such action is the reading event. Another is the action of teaching literacy. Practices in English that might have been discussed in this conference and might have been thought to progress have regrettably suffered neglect from researchers. There is little value placed on determining, for example, how much people read, and little theory to account for the phenomenon of the quantity and quality of reading activity.

Substantial progress has been made in identifying teacher behaviors and cognitions that are correlated with or causally related to student acquisition of literacy. It is interesting to note, however, that research on teacher behavior has been related to literacy achievement and not to literacy behavior. No studies mentioned instructional conditions or teaching activities that are successful in meeting literacy goals, or the criterion for inducing students to achieve personal goals through literacy. It is probable, however, that the semiotic perspective, which has come to be valued, will draw attention to the act of literacy as a purposeful, social tactic. Since action for literacy has entered the definition of the phenomenon of literacy, it will beg for a theoretical account. As a theory of action evolves we are likely to learn to foster teaching that will engender high amounts of time engaged in literacy activities among learners of all ages.

References

Capra, F. (1975). *The Tao of physics.* Boston: Shambhala Publications.

Gray, W. S. (1984). Reading. In *A research retrospective, 1881–1941,* edited by J. Guthrie. Newark, N.J.: International Reading Association.

Mosenthal, P. B. (1985). Defining progress in educational research. *Educational Researcher* 14, no. 9: 3–10.

Retrospect and Prospect

James R. Squire

To assess the changes in research in the English language arts occurring during recent decades, one needs only to compare the discussions at the Mid-Decade Seminar with the proceedings of similar national conferences called earlier in this century. Julie Jensen did this in her commentary, pointing to the interest in British and Swedish studies in 1972. But more startling in contrast was the conference twenty-five years ago, Needed Research in English, convened at Carnegie Institute of Technology in 1962 during the last academic reform movement. Only one of the participants in NCRE's Mid-Decade Seminar participated in the Project English Conference, but most were affected by the recommendations arising from the conference, since they defined for years the priorities used by the Cooperative Research Branch of the U.S. Department of Health, Education, and Welfare in allocating research funds.

A summary of these deliberations by Erwin R. Steinberg (1963), the conference convener, reviewed the major concerns, most of which no longer guide thinking about research in English and reading.

Surprisingly, in retrospect, the topic which elicited the greatest reaction in papers and in discussion twenty-five years ago was whether grammar should be taught, and if so, which grammar: traditional, structural, generative, or some synthesis of the three. By 1985 these issues remained unmentioned by conferees, if indeed they had not been resolved.

A second high priority in 1962 concerned the structure and sequence of courses (referred to as "multilevel research")—an important issue always but not one for which today's professional leaders would seem likely to turn to research for answers.

A third problem—the relation of what is taught in school to the subculture from which the student comes—remains a major concern, but in 1985 concern focused more on basic literacy instruction than on content and subject.

In analyzing what happened at Chicago in 1985, Robert Dykstra, president of NCRE, also saw striking differences in attitudes toward reading today from those expressed in a 1962 research conference that considered what came to be regarded as the First Grade Studies. At that time, according to Dykstra, leaders of NCRE were primarily responsible for obtaining financial support from the U.S. Office of Education for a cooperative study of beginning reading instruction. Research proposals were solicited with the understanding that each study was to address the basic issue of how we could improve the teaching of reading. The principal investigators of the funded research projects then met as a group to work out ways in which they could cooperate in order to obtain the best possible data. Dykstra recalls that the overriding question addressed at the meeting of principal investigators was "What is the best way to teach children to read?" He reflects on how the conferees addressed that question:

1. I am sure that research to most of us in 1962 meant "horse-race" research of the A versus B and C variety. We were interested in comparing the relative effectiveness of conventional basal readers with newfangled instructional materials, such as the initial teaching alphabet, words in color, so-called linguistic programs, and the like. As I recall, there was little discussion about any research design other than that of the horse-race experimental model.
2. We tended to consider instructional method as being synonymous with published materials. We looked to published instructional programs to provide the answer to "What is the best way to teach children to read?" In fact the basic comparison that emerged was that between the conventional Dick and Jane or Alice and Jerry sight word–emphasis basal reading series and the "Dan can fan Nan," so-called linguistic readers or similar published phonics-emphasis basal series.
3. We tended to ask, "What is the best way to teach a child to read?" rather than asking, "How can we better assist children to learn to read?"
4. We tended to view the teacher's role as that of a technician whose responsibility was to administer the treatment, which meant that his or her responsibility was to follow explicitly the mandates of the publisher and basal series author as set down in the teacher's manual or teacher's guide. Any deviation from the teacher's manual was perceived as a threat to the study. In short, the instructional method resided in the materials.
5. Assessment of the relative effectiveness of the various published programs was carried out by means of standardized reading achievement tests. Emphasis was on the products of instruction: on children's ability to identify words and to answer questions about very short passages.

These questions led to a cooperative research endeavor which found that in general children who were taught to read using materials that emphasized a good deal of phonics scored better on standardized reading tests at the end of grades 1 and 2 than did children who were taught to read using the conventional basal readers of the day. This finding was in agreement with the conclusions reached by Jeanne Chall in her then-current best-selling book, *Learning to Read: The Great Debate*. Within a relatively short time, moreover (a matter of a year or two or three), primary-grade children were inundated with phonics drills and work sheets. Not only did a spate of supplementary phonics materials hit the market, but conventional basal readers were quickly revised to include earlier and more intensive phonics. How different the basic view of the process of reading and the researchable questions in 1962 from those expressed in Chicago in 1985! How different are our views of teachers, instruction, and the change process! "Horse-race" research is now not only largely ignored but is an approach vigorously rejected by several seminar participants because of the negative impact it has sometimes had on teaching.

Conferees in 1962 also worried about research methodology (albeit from a limited perspective), an issue also widely discussed at the San Francisco Research Conference in 1963 and the Minneapolis Conference of 1972, but not a major problem to those in Chicago in 1985. At all conferences, of course, the discussion addressed the usefulness of research, the kinds of answers it could and could not provide, and the research questions most likely to be productive. But unlike their forebears in 1962 and 1972, those who gathered at the Mid-Decade Seminar were less concerned with the profession's insistence on carefully controlled experimentation than with the negative impact that certain interpretations of experimental research could and often did have on practice.

What happened during the intervening twenty-five years to explain these changes in perception of researchers in English? One factor was the shift from research paradigms grounded in behavioral psychology to those informed by studies of cognitive and conceptual development. In 1960, Jerome Bruner's *The Process of Education* was only beginning to influence deeply our professional thinking, and Piaget and Vygotsky were just beginning to be read or understood. In addition, the rise of courses on the language development of children, the growing understanding of Norm Chomsky's work, and the concern with interactive process which came to influence our views of language acquisition were largely yet to come.

Judged from the deliberations at the Chicago Seminar, today's major concerns are legion and seem sharply identified in the papers, commentary, and discussion. Still, the seminar returned again and again to discussing six overriding issues:

1. Research in English and reading will become truly effective only as we are able to engage classroom teachers in defining and modifying the researchable questions and in drawing teaching implications.

Virtually all researchers at the seminar spoke to the need for valuing the expertise of teachers and their knowledge of teaching and learning. Researchers unable to enlist such expertise in interpreting findings clearly limit the value of their work. Indeed some discussants felt strongly that basic researchers may be almost incompetent when they draw teaching implications. The concept of the researcher as change agent was largely discredited. Thus, more significant than any specific recommendation of the seminar may be changes in the way we think about research. The assumption that research alone should drive teachers and teaching is questionable, at best. Direct participation of teachers with researchers in exploring researchable issues and in rethinking classroom practice can have more potent effect than isolated studies and lists of implications for teaching.

2. Basic research in literacy skills requires substantive redirection.

Seminar participants recognized that the acid test of literacy is found in the time a child engages in reading and related literacy activities. Yet too frequently the skills of reading are separated from the act of reading. Indeed a substantive number of seminar participants felt that literacy and literary instruction are inseparable. Disabled readers too easily disassociate literacy from reading and writing, and thus require much teacher help.

Further, research in literacy among members of lower socioeconomic groups must recognize the interplay of different attitudes, values, social rules—indeed a different knowledge base. Given recent research by William Labov suggesting an increasing divergence in the nature of the language used by blacks and whites in our society, the lack of involvement of researchers from minority groups in studying the requirements of literacy is a priority concern that must be addressed by the profession.

3. Critical differences and critical commonalities in discourse processing need to be studied more precisely, particularly at the activity level.

We need a much clearer perception of the specific events in speaking, reading, and writing that have real impact on learning. Seminar participants agreed that too little attention has been focused on oral language and that much of the work on interrelationships has tended to study reading or writing separately. Few researchers have concerned themselves with discourse processing in relation to teaching behavior, learning, student backgrounds, or even desired learning outcomes.

Conferees seemed to agree that speaking, reading, and writing may be similar aspects of basic cognitive processes, even though differences are apparent at the activity level. Some of these differences may be most visibly studied in the processing that occurs through speech events which seem to underlie development of both oral and written language. In any case, speech-event analysis, applied to writing as well, can help connect the taxonomy of writing with larger linguistic structures.

Conferees also observed that oral language may provide the foundation for literature as well as writing and reading, and for prior knowledge about language and our common sign system.

Relating research in oral language, reading, and writing in important new ways thus becomes a research priority.

4. *Studies of meaning making in reading comprehension and response to literature may help to identify crucial central tendencies which can be taught.*

Current research in meaning making in comprehension seems to suggest that readers in time learn to control the rhythm and nature of discourse processing. For decades studies of response to literature have indicated similar behavior. Readers skip around, refer to outside sources, and sharpen and level impressions as they relate perceptions to their own experience. Developmental studies may inform us as to which of these modes of response are desirable behaviors in mature readers and thus perhaps should be taught.

Further, more studies are needed to clarify the ways in which different kinds of relationships develop between the distinctive elements employed in the processes of languaging, the ways in which various learners employ mediating thought processes as they respond, the ways in which readers use prior knowledge, their understanding of story grammars, and their use of specific strategies in the complex interplay of forms and function in the various disciplines. These seem fruitful lines of inquiry.

5. *Research should play a major role in helping the profession reintegrate the processes of evaluation with the processes of instruction.*

Present assessment procedures used in America's schools are frequently counterproductive. We use product measures to assess process goals. We confuse internal and external tests. We have permitted most evaluation processes to become adversarial in nature. In fact, the long-range impact of criterion-referenced measures—with their emphasis on picky, discrete skills—can now be seen as having a disastrous impact on the teaching of reading and writing. The results are mirrored perhaps in the lack of progress in reading of most American children reported in the 1984 National Assessment of Educational Progress (NAEP 1987).

On no issue were seminar participants more vocal or more unified than on the issue of assessment, and researchers with strong backgrounds in experimental studies and research design were among the most critical. All agreed that many important aspects of language processes cannot be measured by the current group tests employed by schools throughout the country. Assessment which does not serve the needs of instruction should be thrown out. Critical steps must be taken to ensure that decision-makers in education understand the full significance of assessment requirements in relation to basic instructional needs.

6. Research in language learning and language development needs to be more concerned with WHAT and WHY, and much less with HOW.

We require a greater awareness of purpose and meaning in language use and language development, and we may achieve this only with more investigations of the philosophical and social aspects of language, and fewer studies of a strictly sociolinguistic nature.

Certainly we sorely need a broader perspective on language development, language learning, theory of language pedagogy, the impact of content on skills, and similar concerns.

Conferees differed on whether unifying theories best emerge from practice or whether such theories are needed initially to generate practice and research. But the group agreed that the current spate of language studies frequently seems overly descriptive and a bit mindless when viewed as a total cluster.

Models which relate teaching and learning seem to need both practice and research. Current interaction models are incapable of explaining instruction because they don't take into account the role of the teacher. Knowledge of process is useful for those constructing learning models, but not for developing prescriptions for instruction. The separate models for language teaching and language learning currently available offer insufficient guides for practice and research. Changes may come only as we develop unifying models that are coherent and understandable, whatever their source.

There were other issues, of course. The range is reflected in the papers and commentaries presented in this volume. But the concern of today's researchers with the above overriding issues reflects the tone of the seminar.

Many of those who participated at Chicago will direct the significant studies of the next decade. If the discussion and analysis succeeded in modifying the way in which they think about research in English and reading, we can look forward expectantly to the insights of the nineties.

References

Bruner, J. (1960). *The process of education.* Cambridge: Harvard University Press.

Chall, J. (1967). *Learning to read: The great debate.* New York: McGraw-Hill.

National Assessment of Educational Progress (1987). *The reading report card.* Princeton, N.J.: Educational Testing Service. ED 264 550.

Russell, D. H., E. J. Farrell, and M. J. Early, eds. (1964). *Research design and the teaching of English.* Urbana, Ill.: National Council of Teachers of English.

Steinberg, E. R. (1963). *Needed research in the teaching of English.* U.S. Office of Education, Cooperative research monograph no. 11. Washington D.C.: Office of Education, U.S. Department of Health, Education, and Welfare.

Author Index

395

Subject Index

Contributors

Arthur N. Applebee is an associate professor in the Stanford University School of Education. Applebee specializes in studies of language use and language learning, particularly as these occur in school settings. In addition to articles in the areas of writing, reading, psychology, and English, Applebee's major works include a developmental study of children's storytelling and story-comprehension skills (*The Child's Concept of Story: Ages Two to Seventeen*), a national study of the teaching of writing in the major secondary school subject areas (*Writing in the Secondary School: English and the Content Areas*; *Contexts for Learning to Write: Studies of Secondary School Instruction*), and a comprehensive history of the teaching of literature in American secondary schools (*Tradition and Reform in the Teaching of English*). He has also had experience in program evaluation, high school teaching (English and drama), and clinical assessment and treatment of children with severe reading problems. Applebee is coeditor of *Research in the Teaching of English* and president of the National Conference on Research in English.

Rita S. Brause, an associate professor in the Language, Literacy and Learning Program at Fordham University, has taught English and reading K–12. She conducted an ethnographic study of bilingual students' classroom communicative competence with John Mayher and Jo Bruno that was funded by NIE and published by the National Clearinghouse on Bilingual Education. In addition to presentations at NCTE and AERA, she has published in books (*Contexts of Reading* and *Measures for Research and Evaluation in the English Language Arts, Volume 2*) and in journals (*Anthropology and Education Quarterly, Research in the Teaching of English,* and *Language Arts*). Brause currently serves on the executive board of the Conference on English Education. Consistent with her focus on the teaching-learning process, she collaborates with school districts in implementing teacher-researcher staff development projects.

Bertram Bruce is manager of the Education Department at Bolt, Beranek and Newman Laboratories in Cambridge, Massachusetts. He has been a senior scientist there since 1974, doing research in the areas of artificial intelligence, language, and education. Since 1976 he has been associate director of the Center for the Study of Reading (based at the University of Illinois at Urbana-Champaign, with a branch at BBN). He is known for his theory of story understanding based on the interacting plans of characters, his comparative analyses of stories in basal readers and trade books, and his work on Quill, an integrated computer-based reading and writing program. Bruce has nearly one hundred publications in areas such as the teaching of reading and writing, discourse structures, artificial intelligence, computational models of language use, educational software design, and the consequences of computer use in classrooms.

Robert Calfee is an experimental cognitive psychologist. He earned his degrees at the University of California at Los Angeles, did postdoctoral work at Stanford University, and spent five years in the Psychology Department at the University of Wisconsin at Madison. He returned to Stanford as an associate professor in the School of Education, and at present is professor of education and psychology. His interests have evolved over the past decade from a focus on prereading and beginning reading skills to a concentration on methods of assessing reading, and to his current emphasis on improvement of instruction in reading and related literacy skills. His theoretical efforts are concerned with the broad question of how education influences human cognition, and how an understanding of thought processes can improve the practice of schooling. He is currently involved in research on school improvement through Project READ, the enhancement of school leadership in the Stanford/San Jose Administrator Training Project, and an examination of social studies and science textbooks through the federally sponsored Textbook Analysis Project.

Johanna S. DeStefano is a professor of education on the graduate faculty of language, literature and reading at Ohio State University, and is chair of the steering group of the Committee for International Tele-Education. She also directs the Project on Educational Development and Telecommunications Technology at the Mershon Center. Her publications and presentations in this area apply telecommunications technology to the teaching of English as a second language and to literacy learning. Recently she spoke on the use of this technology for educational development at a conference in the Caribbean, and at the fortieth anniversary of the Fulbright Scholarly Exchange Program commemorative conference in Washington, D.C.

David K. Dickinson, after graduating from Oberlin College in 1971, taught elementary school for five years, then continued his education at the Harvard Graduate School of Education. After receiving his doctorate in 1982, he worked at Boston University and currently is in the Eliot-Pearson Department of Child Study at Tufts University. His work has two major thrusts: study of the developing language-using abilities of young children, and examination of preschool and early elementary school settings that may affect acquisition of abilities related to literacy. Currently he is studying the effects of context on teacher-child talk in a day-care classroom, book-reading styles of preschool teachers, and the effects of the literacy environments in Head Start classrooms on children's linguistic and emergent literacy development.

David Dillon teaches language arts education at the University of Alberta. He also edits NCTE's Elementary Section journal, *Language Arts*.

Dolores Durkin is a professor in the Department of Elementary and Early Childhood Education at the University of Illinois at Urbana-Champaign. In addition to teaching and conducting research, she has written seven books. *Teaching Them to Read,* now in its fourth edition, is a reading methodology textbook that is used widely on campuses in the United States and Canada. Professor Durkin has also written a large number of articles, many of which report research findings. Specializing in classroom-observation studies of reading, she has described what teachers do with comprehension and, more recently, what is done to teach reading at the kindergarten level.

Robert Dykstra is a professor of language arts education at the University of Minnesota. He serves as head of the elementary teacher education program at that institution, following a ten-year stint as chair of the Department of Curriculum and Instruction. He is a past president of the National Conference on Research in English and a former chair of the Elementary Section Committee of the National Council of Teachers of English. Dykstra has been active in a number of other roles within these organizations as well as in the International Reading Association. His primary research interest is beginning reading and writing.

Edmund J. Farrell is a professor of English education at the University of Texas at Austin and the author of over sixty articles on the teaching of English. He has served as an associate executive director of NCTE, chair of the NCTE Commission on Literature, and chair of the trustees of the NCTE Research Foundation. A past president of both the California Association of Teachers of English and the Texas Joint Council of Teachers of English, he received in 1982 the NCTE Distinguished Service Award.

Bryant Fillion is a professor of education in Fordham University's Graduate School of Education. A former NCTE Research Committee member, he has taught junior high and high school English, and has spoken and written widely in the United States and Canada on language development, language across the curriculum, and the pedagogy of writing and literature. In addition to journal articles and book chapters, he has coauthored and edited several books: *Teaching English Today, Writing for Results,* the four-volume Canadian *Inquiry into Literature* series, and *Home and School: Early Language and Reading* (in press).

James Flood is a professor of reading and language development at San Diego State University. He has been an elementary and secondary school teacher, and he is currently working with the teacher-preparation program and the doctoral program at San Diego State. His research interests include reading-comprehension instruction, text analysis, and teacher preparation in the language arts.

Lawrence T. Frase is a member of the technical staff at Bell Laboratories. He has published about seventy papers on human learning, reasoning, instruction, writing, text design, and computer applications. His current work is on psychological processes in software development. Frase is a member of the Association for Computing Machinery, the Institute of Electrical and Electronics Engineers, AERA, and NCTE, and he is a fellow of APA. He is a recipient of the AT&T Bell Laboratories Distinguished Technical Staff Award for outstanding accomplishments.

John Guthrie is currently the director of the Center of Educational Research and Development and professor of curriculum and instruction at the University of Maryland at College Park. He was the research director of the International Reading Association from 1974 to 1984. Guthrie's research interests include the multidimensionality of literacy cognition and the practices of literacy in society. He has edited five books on cognition, comprehension, and reading instruction, and written one volume on measuring literacy activities.

Jane Hansen is an associate professor of reading at the University of New Hampshire and teaches in the New Hampshire Summer Writing Program. She has been an elementary classroom and Chapter I reading teacher. Since 1981 she has taken part in research projects in elementary classrooms to learn about ways to improve instruction in reading and writing. In addition to writing journal articles and book chapters, she has edited, with Thomas Newkirk and Donald Graves, *Breaking Ground: Teachers Relate Reading and Writing in the Elementary School.* She has also written a book titled *When Writers Read.* Hansen makes presentations at conferences and conducts workshops for teachers throughout the U.S. and Canada.

Jerome C. Harste is a professor of language education at Indiana University in Bloomington. Together with his colleagues, Carolyn Burke and Virginia Woodward, Harste has completed a seven-year study of what young children know about reading and writing before coming to school (*Language Stories and Literacy Lessons*). More recently, Harste and his colleagues have worked collaboratively with teachers in an attempt to build a theoretically based curriculum from what we currently know. This work has resulted in an eight-part preservice and inservice teacher-education videotape series (*The Authoring Cycle: Read Better, Write Better, Reason Better*). In addition to children's books (*It Didn't Frighten Me,* and others), Harste's writings range widely over theoretical and practical issues related to language use and learning.

Roselmina Indrisano is a professor of education and director of the Center for the Assessment and Design of Learning at Boston University. She is president of the International Reading Association and a fellow of the National Conference on Research in English. Dr. Indrisano was guest editor for the themed issue "The Reading-Writing Connection" of *The Reading Teacher,* and is currently an author of the Ginn Reading Program.

Julie M. Jensen is a professor of curriculum and instruction at the University of Texas at Austin and president-elect of the National Council of Teachers of English. She formerly taught fourth grade in the Minneapolis Public Schools, served as president of the Central Texas Council of Teachers of English, and was a member of many NCTE bodies, including the Editorial Board and the Standing Committee on Research. From 1976 to 1983 she edited *Language Arts.* Her other NCTE publications include *Composing and Comprehending* and, with William Fagan and Charles Cooper, volumes 1 and 2 of *Measures for Research and Evaluation in the English Language Arts.*

Peter Johnston was an elementary school teacher in his native New Zealand and is now an associate professor in the Reading Department of the State University of New York at Albany. He directs the reading clinic, teaches teachers, and does research on assessing literacy development and understanding and preventing literacy failure.

Stephen B. Kucer is an assistant professor of curriculum and instruction at the University of Southern California. As well as teaching courses in literacy and cognition, he serves as the program director for the Graduate Reading and Writing Specialization. Kucer's major research interests are in the relationships between the reading and writing processes and in applying current literacy theory and research to the process of schooling. Currently he is examining the effects which thematically based literacy curricula have on reading and writing development.

Judith A. Langer is an associate professor in the School of Education at Stanford University. Her research focuses on how people become skilled readers and writers, how they use reading and writing to learn, and what these processes mean for instruction. In addition to her academic experience, she has been both a teacher and a school district curriculum director. Langer has published in a wide range of educational journals and is coeditor of *Research in the Teaching of English*. Her books include *Reader Meets Author: Bridging the Gap; Understanding Reading and Writing Research;* and *Children Reading and Writing: Structures and Strategies*. Her fourth book, *Language, Literacy, and Culture: Issues of Society and Schooling* will be released in 1987. Also forthcoming is *Writing Across the Curriculum: Teaching and Learning in High School Classes*.

Diane Lapp is a professor of reading and language development at San Diego State University. She has been an elementary and secondary teacher, and is currently involved in the teacher-preparation program and doctoral program at San Diego State. Lapp teaches research and instruction in reading and writing. Her specialized areas of research include teacher preparation, reading, and writing instruction and learning theory.

Miles Myers has served as president of the California Federation of Teachers (AFT) for the past two years. He has been a secondary teacher of English in Bay Area schools; a supervisor of student teachers at the University of California, Berkeley; the director of an NIE study of English teaching in inner-city schools, also at UC, Berkeley; and from 1975 to 1985, administrative director of the Bay Area Writing Project and the National Writing Project. Myers received his degrees at UC, Berkeley. His most recent book is *The Teacher-Researcher: How to Study Writing in the Classroom,* published by NCTE. In 1986, Myers received the Distinguished Service Award of the California Association of Teachers of English.

P. David Pearson is a professor of education at the University of Illinois at Urbana-Champaign, where he splits his time between chairing the Department of Elementary and Early Childhood Education and conducting research at the

Center for the Study of Reading. He is the general editor of the *Handbook of Reading Research* and the coauthor of *Teaching Reading Vocabulary* and *Teaching Reading Comprehension*. His recent work focuses on the link between instruction and assessment.

Alan C. Purves is a professor of education and director of the Center for the Study of Literacy at the State University of New York at Albany. He is chair of the International Association for the Evaluation of Educational Achievement, a forty-nation organization concerned with studies of educational performance and their relation to curriculum, instruction, and educational policy. He is currently also editor of *Contrastive Rhetoric* (1987) and coeditor of the *International Encyclopedia of Research in Reading and Writing* (to be published in 1991).

Diane Lemonnier Schallert is an associate professor of educational psychology at the University of Texas at Austin, where she teaches courses in psycholinguistics, comprehension, learning, and writing. She is also currently an associate editor of the *Reading Research Quarterly*. Schallert spent three postdoctoral years at the Center for the Study of Reading, University of Illinois at Urbana-Champaign. Her research generally deals with how people understand and use language—specifically, how secondary students learn from textbooks, how textbook authors present concepts, how contextual variables influence students' interaction with textbooks, and how children and adults write and think about writing.

M. Trika Smith-Burke is an associate professor in the Department of Educational Psychology at New York University. She is president-elect of the National Reading Conference and a member of the Committee on Teacher Effectiveness for the International Reading Association. Recently she coedited two volumes: *Observing the Language Learner*, with Angela Jaggar, and *Reader Meets Author: Bridging the Gap*, with Judith Langer. Collaborating with teachers to institute curriculum change, Smith-Burke has worked in many districts to share information on oral and written language development, and on the factors involved in comprehension and writing, as a base for designing and implementing new programs in regular and special-education classrooms.

James R. Squire was president of the National Conference on Research in English when the Mid-Decade Seminar on the Teaching of Reading and English was proposed. He served as convener, director, and editor. Currently executive consultant for Silver Burdett & Ginn, Squire has been senior vice president and publisher of Ginn and Company, executive secretary of the National Council of Teachers of English, and professor of English at the University of Illinois at Urbana-Champaign. He has also been lecturer in education, supervisor of the teaching of English, and codirector of teacher education at the University of California, Berkeley.

Robert J. Tierney is a member of the faculty of education at Ohio State University, where he teaches graduate courses in comprehension and composition. For several years he was affiliated with the Center for the Study of Reading, and he has been a visiting professor at Harvard University; the University of California, Berkeley; and the University of Minnesota. His research, theoretical ideas, and practical concerns have been published in various journals and edited volumes. Currently his major interest relates to reading, writing, and the development of critical thinking.

Merlin Wittrock is professor and chair of educational psychology in the Graduate School of Education at the University of California, Los Angeles. He studies and publishes articles, books, and chapters on reading comprehension and cognition. His latest book is the *Handbook of Research on Teaching, Third Edition,* which he edited in 1986 for the American Educational Research Association. He recently received an award from AERA for outstanding contributions to educational research. Wittrock was also recently elected president for the Division of Educational Psychology in the American Psychological Association. In addition, he recently received the E. L. Thorndike Award from APA for outstanding contributions to research in educational psychology.